# GARDENER'S SUPPLY BOOKS

Eliot Coleman, *The New Organic Grower: A Master's Manual of Tools and Techniques for the Home and Market Gardener*

Leandre Poisson and Gretchen Vogel Poisson, *Solar Gardening: Growing Vegetables Year-Round the American Intensive Way*

Lynn Byczynski, *The Flower Farmer: An Organic Grower's Guide to Raising and Selling Cut Flowers*

Eliot Coleman, *Four-Season Harvest: How to Harvest Fresh Organic Vegetables from Your Home Garden All Year Long*

Katherine LaLiberte and Ben Watson, *Gardener's Supply Passport To Gardening: A Sourcebook for the 21st-Century Gardener*

GARDENER'S SUPPLY COMPANY was founded in 1983 in Burlington, Vermont, to make available innovative tools and equipment that would bring the joys and rewards of gardening to as many people as possible. Gardener's Supply serves gardeners of all interests and abilities with seasonal catalogs that offer earth-friendly methods for growing plants in all climate zones and seasons. Four seasonal and specialty catalogs, a retail store and the renowned community and demonstration gardens in Burlington's "Intervale," and a complete line of high-performance home greenhouses combine to make Gardener's Supply "America's Gardening Resource."

To further its mission as the leading source of new ideas and information for gardeners, Gardener's Supply has joined Chelsea Green Publishing Company to co-create and co-publish a series of gardening books. The books in this series are written by pioneering individuals who have firsthand experience in using innovative, ecological techniques to grow healthy food and flowers that enhance our lives — and the well-being of Earth.

Ian Baldwin, Jr.
*President, Chelsea Green*

Will Raap
*President, Gardener's Supply*

GARDENER'S SUPPLY COMPANY

# PASSPORT TO GARDENING

## A Sourcebook for the 21st-Century Gardener

by Katherine LaLiberté
and Ben Watson

CHELSEA GREEN PUBLISHING COMPANY
White River Junction, Vermont

*The authors and publisher wish to acknowledge the efforts of Alan Berolzheimer, who wrote or contributed to several chapters in this book, as well as providing overall editing and coordination for the project.*

Copyright information continued on page 308.

Designed by Jill Shaffer.

Printed in United States of America.

00  99  98  97  1  2  3  4  5

First printing, October 1997.

Library of Congress Cataloging-in-Publication Data

LaLiberte, Katherine, 1955-
Gardener's Supply Company Passport to Gardening: A Sourcebook for the 21st-Century Gardener / Katherine LaLiberte and Ben Watson.
    p.    cm.
    "Gardener's Supply books" — P.
    Includes index.
    ISBN 1-890132-00-4
    1. Gardening.   I. Watson, Ben, 1961-   .  II. Gardener's Supply
Company.
    SB453.L25    1997
    635—dc21

                                                        97-31662

Chelsea Green Publishing Company
P.O. Box 428
White River Junction, Vermont 05001
800-639-4099

# contents

# introduction

Welcome to the world of gardening! We've designed the *Gardener's Supply Passport to Gardening* to be just that — your passport to a world of information and resources on subjects ranging from native wildflowers to hydroponic tomatoes, from garden literature to saving your own seeds. In the 32 chapters we've assembled, we have tried to select topics that are either of "perennial" interest to gardeners (such as Roses) or ones that in recent years have "grown" in popularity (such as Backyard Biodiversity and Natural Lawn Care).

From its conception, we've seen the *Passport* as more than a typical sourcebook. Other books simply provide lists of addresses, and many of these contacts are out-of-date as soon as the book hits the shelves. Our intention was to write an overview of each subject, to put the important issues in context, and to give you, the reader, a reason to explore some new area of gardening that may be unfamiliar to you. After all, the world of gardening is so vast that almost everyone — even a seasoned grower — specializes in something, whether it be raising tea roses or growing in containers. The *Passport to Gardening* gives you a basic understanding of topics that may be less familiar to you, and provides the names of specialized resources that even experienced gardeners will find useful.

We are living, undeniably, in the Age of Information — a fact that becomes evident as soon as you scan the gardening section of a bookstore or look at all the magazines, newsletters, videos, television programs, and web sites that focus on the subject of gardening. The sheer amount of information out there is overwhelming and can quickly produce a kind of sensory overload. How can you tune out all the static and find what you're really interested in?

That was the other reason we decided to write the *Passport to Gardening*: to do a lot of the sifting and evaluating for you, and to lead you to what we think are some of the best sources of information available on any given subject. In each chapter we've included short book reviews, names of nurseries and suppliers, informative Web sites, and even some of the best tools and products that relate to the subject at hand. Our mission, in other words, was to take the overwhelming and to make it interesting and relevant.

Is this book the last word on the subject? Hardly. Have we missed anything in this book? Sure. Although it may be true that there is "nothing new under the sun," try telling that to garden writers and merchandizers. New books, new products, and new (or newly rediscovered) ideas are coming onto the scene every day. But that's why we are asking you, the reader, to help us make the *Passport* even more comprehensive and useful. Send in your comments, corrections, or suggestions, and we'll consider including *your* favorite books, magazines, Web sites, suppliers, and products in the next edition of the *Passport to Gardening*.

One word about how we've selected our favorite books and other resources. There is a lot of redundancy in the field of gardening, something that isn't obvious until you look through 50 books on, say, herbs, and find that maybe 45 of them are so similar that they represent "old wine in new bottles." In the *Passport* we have attempted to list the most unique, original, and useful resources as our "best bets" for gardeners. Often this meant that we passed over a beautiful, but relatively content-free, book or other resource in favor of one that really conveyed useful information for a practicing (not an armchair) gardener. For the same reason, we've included messages from Guest Experts in most of the chapters — passionate and experienced gardeners who will inspire you, challenge you, or simply offer up their wisdom on a particular question. In other words, we want to get you *out* of the armchair and into the garden, where the real rewards begin.

In 1811 Thomas Jefferson wrote that "No occupation is so delightful to me as the culture of the earth, and no culture comparable to that of the garden. . . . But though an old man, I am but a young gardener." Even in Jefferson's time, acquiring gardening knowledge was an ongoing, lifelong pursuit. No one knows everything about all aspects of gardening, a fact that we learned every day in writing this book, as we came across ideas that we had never encountered before, even after years of tending our own gardens (and poking around other people's gardens).

That's the beauty of gardening: it forms a common bond between people of every language, race, and culture (like music); it provides the most direct relationship most of us have to nature, offering us her joys and teaching us her lessons; it has been practiced for thousands of years and yet seems constantly changing, with new discoveries sprouting up every year. In a weary world, it never grows stale. Now, let's go to the garden!

Kathy LaLiberte
Ben Watson

PART I

the basics of ecological gardening

# building healthy soil

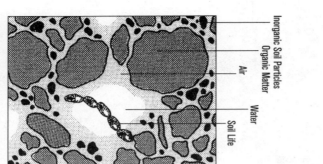

Inorganic Soil Particles
Organic Matter
Air
Water
Soil Life

*Healthy soil is composed of inorganic matter such as weathered rock, organic matter, water, air, and living organisms.*
—from "Simple Steps to Successful Soil" (Gardener's Supply Bulletin #5)

The quality of the soil in your yard and garden affects every aspect of your gardening and landscaping activities. Though some gardeners may be blessed with perfect soil, most of us garden in soil that is too heavy, too hard, too light, or too stony. Turning a poor soil into a plant-friendly one is not difficult to do, once you understand the components of a healthy soil. It is also one of the most rewarding pursuits a gardener can undertake.

## What's in the Soil?

Soil is composed of weathered rock and organic matter, water, and air. But the "hidden magic" in a healthy soil is the organisms — small animals, worms, insects, and microbes — that flourish when the other soil elements are in balance.

**MINERALS.** Roughly half of the soil in your garden consists of small bits of weathered rock that has been broken down by the forces of wind, rain, freezing and thawing, and other chemical and biological processes. Soil type is generally classified by the size of these inorganic soil particles: sand (large particles), silt (medium-sized particles), or clay (very small particles). The proportion of sand, silt, and clay particles determines the texture of your soil and affects drainage and nutrient availability, which in turn influence how well your plants will grow. Though it is not possible to change the mineral characteristics of your soil, there are many ways to improve its structure.

**ORGANIC MATTER.** Organic matter is the partially decomposed remains of soil organisms and decomposing plant life, including lichens and mosses, grasses and leaves, trees, and all other kinds of vegetative matter. Although it only makes up a small fraction of the soil (normally

5 to 10 percent), organic matter is absolutely essential for several reasons. First, it binds soil particles into porous crumbs or granules. This helps to create pore spaces, allowing air and water to move through the soil. Organic matter also retains moisture (humus holds up to 90 percent of its weight in water), and is able to absorb and store nutrients, making them available when needed. Most importantly, organic matter is food for microorganisms and other forms of soil life.

You can increase the amount of organic matter in your soil by adding compost, aged animal manures, green manures (cover crops), mulches, or peat moss. Because most soil life and plant roots are located

## Guest Expert

# Grace Gershuny

If there is any goal I have had in mind in writing and teaching about soil, it is to help gardeners and farmers gain the recognition that soil is a complex, living organism. While you can learn about soil's biological intricacy from books and workshops, seeing for yourself is the only way to truly understand what this means. That's why I encourage people to observe their soil closely and keep good records of those observations, especially when working on building soil in a new location. You can do purely visual inspections, such as using a hand lens to look for as many different life forms as you can find, or you can systematically count the number of earthworms in a given square foot of soil. After a few seasons of this you will see how using methods that stimulate soil life result in soil that is easier to work, has better drainage, and produces healthier crops. Beyond this scientific approach to understanding, I firmly believe that working with the soil in this way and carefully observing what happens there gives you a personal appreciation for it that cannot be conveyed secondhand. I know that my soil is alive not just because I have read scientific studies that say so, but because of my direct experience of working with it and feeling the joy of putting my hands in it, realizing that my own life depends on the life of the soil.

*Grace Gershuny, former editor of* Organic Farmer: The Digest of Sustainable Agriculture *and author of* Start with the Soil, *is on the staff of the USDA's National Organic Program.*

## Favorite Books

**Improving the Soil**
*by Erin Hynes* (Rodale Press, 1994).
Written for the beginning to intermediate gardener, this book combines engaging color photographs with meaty how-to text. It will take you from the basics of soil composition through building the soil and dealing with specific soil problems. Clear, practical, and inspiring. 106 pages, paperback, $14.95.

**Start with the Soil**
*by Grace Gershuny* (Rodale Press, 1997). The basics and beyond. More in-depth information about specific fertilizers, amendments, and organic matter, including analysis and recommended application rates. Good discussion of how to recognize soil deficiencies and how to correct them. Covers specific soil needs for vegetables, flowers, trees, and lawns. Highly readable, with line drawings and charts. 256 pages, paperback, $14.95.

**Fertile Soil**
*by Dr. Robert Parnes* (Ag Access, 1990).
A technical, yet quite accessible reference that is chock full of information for the budding soil scientist. It explains exactly how nutrients, organic matter, and microbes function in the soil and how they feed your plants; covers complex processes such as cation exchange, nitrification, and chelation; and includes lots of charts with very specific information about nutrient content and recommended application rates. 190 pages, paperback, $39.95.

in the top 6 inches of the soil layer, you will want to concentrate your additions of organic matter in this upper layer. Be cautious about incorporating large amounts of high-carbon materials (straw, leaves, wood chips, and sawdust). Soil microorganisms will consume a lot of nitrogen in their efforts to digest these materials, and they may deprive your plants of the nitrogen they need for healthy growth. Eventually, this nitrogen will become available again, but in the meantime you may need to supply extra nitrogen to cover your plants' short-term needs.

**SOIL LIFE.** Soil organisms include the bacteria and fungi, protozoa, nematodes, mites, springtails, earthworms, and other tiny creatures that are found in healthy soil. These organisms are essential for plant growth. Their task is to convert organic matter and soil minerals into the vitamins, hormones, disease-suppressing compounds, and available nutrients that plants need to grow. Their excretions also help to bind soil particles into the small aggregates that make a soil loose and crumbly. As a gardener, your job is to create the ideal conditions for these soil organisms to do their work. This means providing them with an abundant source of food (the carbohydrates in organic matter), oxygen (present in a well-aerated soil), and water (an adequate but not excessive amount).

**AIR.** A healthy soil is about 25 percent air. Insects, microbes, earthworms, and other soil life require this much air to live. The air in soil is also an important source of the atmospheric nitrogen that is utilized by plants. Well-aerated soil has plenty of pore space between the soil particles or crumbs. Fine soil particles (clay or silt) have very tiny spaces between them — in some cases, too small for air to penetrate. Soil composed of large particles, such as sand, has large pore spaces and contains plenty of air. But, too much air means your soil will be droughty, causing organic matter to "burn up" (decompose) too quickly. To ensure that there is a balanced supply of air in your soil, add plenty of organic matter, avoid stepping in the growing beds or compacting the soil with heavy equipment, and never work the soil when it is very wet.

**WATER.** A healthy soil will also contain about 25 percent water. Water, like air, is held in the pore spaces between soil particles. Large pore spaces allow rain and irrigation water to move down to the root zone and into the subsoil. Small pore spaces permit water to migrate back upwards through the process of capillary action. Ideally, your soil should have a combination of large and small pore spaces. Again, organic matter is the key, because it encourages the formation of aggregates, or crumbs of soil. Organic matter also absorbs water and retains it until it is needed by plant roots.

## Determining Your Soil's Texture

Every soil has unique physical characteristics, which are determined by how it was formed. The silty soil found in an old floodplain is inherently different from stony mountain soil; the clay soil that lay under a glacier for millions of years is unlike the sandy soil near an ocean. Some of these basic qualities can be improved with proper management — or made worse by abuse. Most important is to understand the texture of the soil in your garden and learn how to make the best of it.

Soil texture can range from very fine, mostly clay particles, to coarse and gravelly. You don't have to be a scientist to determine the texture of the soil in your garden. To get a rough idea, simply place a sample in the palm of your hand and wet it slightly, then rub the mixture between your fingers. If it feels gritty, your soil is sandy; if it feels smooth, like moist talcum powder, your soil is silty; if it feels harsh when dry, sticky or slippery when wet, or rubbery when moist, it is high in clay. You can also use the simple experiment (see "Identifying Your Soil Type," right) to get a better picture of your soil's physical characteristics.

**SANDY SOIL.** Sand particles are large, irregularly shaped bits of rock. In a sandy soil, large air spaces between the sand particles allow water to drain very quickly. Nutrients tend to drain away with the water, often before plants have a chance to absorb them. For this reason, sandy soils are usually

## Other Good Books

**Best of Fine Gardening: Healthy Soil** (Taunton Press, 1995). A collection of 25 in-depth how-to articles about everything from conducting a home soil test, to planting cover crops, the miracle of seaweed fertilizers, and how to drain a wet soil. 95 pages, paperback, $14.95.

**Rodale's Illustrated Encyclopedia of Gardening and Landscaping Techniques** ed. *Barbara W. Ellis* (Rodale Press, 1995). Though this book covers many other topics, it has an excellent section on soil and soil improvement techniques. 432 pages, paperback, $17.95.

## Identifying Your Soil Type

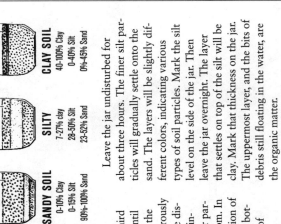

**SANDY SOIL**
0-10% Clay
0-15% Silt
90%-100% Sand

**SILTY**
7-27% clay
28-50% Silt
23-52% Sand

**CLAY SOIL**
40-100% Clay
0-40% Silt
0%-45% Sand

Soils are generally described by the predominant size of particle they contain: sand, silt, or clay. By conducting a simple soil test, you can easily see what kind of soil you are dealing with. Because your soil may differ from one part of your yard to another, you may want to do this test with several different soil samples.

Fill a quart jar about one-third full of topsoil and add water until the jar is almost full. Screw on the lid and shake the mixture vigorously until all the clumps of soil have dissolved. Now set the jar on a windowsill and watch as the larger particles begin to sink to the bottom. In a minute or two, the sand portion of the soil will have settled to the bottom of the jar. Mark the level of sand on the side of the jar.

Leave the jar undisturbed for about three hours. The finer silt particles will gradually settle onto the sand. The layers will be slightly different colors, indicating various types of soil particles. Mark the silt level on the side of the jar. Then leave the jar overnight. The layer that settles on top of the silt will be clay. Mark that thickness on the jar. The uppermost layer, and the bits of debris still floating in the water, are the organic matter.

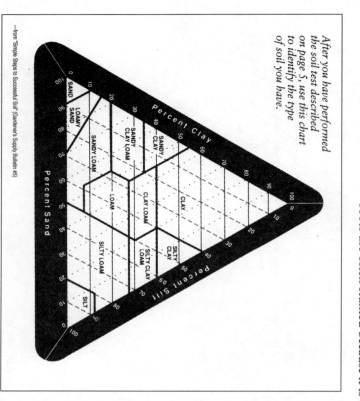

*After you have performed the soil test described on page 5, use this chart to identify the type of soil you have.*

—from "Simple Steps to Successful Soil" (Gardener's Supply Bulletin #5)

nutrient-poor. A sandy soil also has so much air in it that microbes consume organic matter very quickly (which means you must add twice the amount). Because sandy soils usually contain very little clay or organic matter, they don't have much of a crumb structure. The soil particles don't stick together, even when they're wet (which means that compaction is rarely a problem).

To improve a sandy soil, start by working in three to four inches of organic matter, such as well-rotted manure, finished compost, or composted leaves. Mulch around your plants with a generous layer of leaves, grass clippings, wood chips, bark, hay, or straw. Mulch will help to retain water in the soil, and will also keep it cooler, which slows microbial activity and the resulting breakdown of organic matter. Mulch also helps to slow the flow of water through the soil, providing plants with a steadier trickle that they can absorb. If your soil is sandy, you should strive to add at least two inches of organic matter each year, working it in deeply in the fall or winter. Green manures are another effective way to improve the structure of sandy soils (see "Frequently Asked Questions" on page 10).

**CLAYEY SOIL.** Clay particles are small and flat. They tend to pack together so tightly that there is hardly any pore space at all. When clay soils are wet, they are sticky and practically unworkable. They drain very slowly and can stay waterlogged well into the spring. Once they finally dry out, they often become hard and cloddy, and the surface cracks into flat plates. Lack of pore space means that clay soils are generally low in both organic matter and microbial activity. Plant roots are often stunted because it is too hard for them to push their way through the soil. Foot traffic and garden equipment can cause compaction problems. Fortunately, most clay soils are rich in minerals, which will become available to your plants once you improve the texture of your soil.

If you have clay soil, you need to incorporate a lot of organic matter to develop a crumbly structure that will promote good drainage and improve aeration. Start by working two to three inches of organic matter into the surface of the soil. Add at least one more inch of organic matter each year. For best results, add organic matter in the fall and leave the soil surface in a rough condition over the winter to allow frost action to break up large clods.

Permanent raised beds are a good solution for gardeners with heavy clay soils. They improve drainage and keep foot traffic out of the growing area. They also minimize the amount of tilling and spading that is required. Mix as much organic matter as possible into the soil before you construct the beds. After that point, you can concentrate future additions of organic matter right in the growing area.

**SILTY SOIL.** Silty soils contain very small irregularly shaped particles of weathered rock, which means they are usually quite dense and have relatively small pore spaces and poor drainage. They tend to be more fertile than either sandy or clayey soils. If your soil is silty, you should add organic matter to improve soil structure and increase permeability. Working one inch of organic matter into the soil each year should be sufficient for silty soils. Concentrate the organic matter in the top few inches of soil to help prevent surface crusting, a common problem in silty soils. Compaction can also be a problem, so avoid unnecessary tilling and walking on garden beds, or consider constructing raised beds.

## Improving Soil Structure

The texture of your soil, whether sandy, clayey, or silty, is an inherent characteristic that is difficult, if not impossible to change. But the *structure* of your soil can be altered dramatically. Good soil structure depends more on how the soil particles are held together than on the physical characteristics of the soil particles.

Soil with good structure has a crumbly, cake-like consistency. Between these ¼- to ½-inch crumbs are millions of tiny passageways that allow air, water, soluble nutrients, and life forms to move through the soil. Organic matter is the key to creating good soil structure. It helps loosen clay soils and knit together sandy or silty soils. Organic matter also feeds earthworms and other soil organisms, which release sticky gums that help bind soil particles together.

Good soil structure, whether inherited or created, needs to be carefully maintained. Add organic matter whenever you can, and disturb the soil as little as possible. This means avoiding excessive tilling, and keeping foot traffic and heavy equipment use to a minimum.

## Why Is Soil pH Important?

The pH level of your soil indicates its relative acidity or alkalinity. A pH test measures the ratio of hydrogen ions (positive ions) to hydroxyl ions (negative ions) in the soil water. When hydrogen ions and hydroxyl ions are present in equal amounts, the pH is said to be neutral (pH 7). When

> " Considering all of air's benefits to the soil, we might be tempted to add a bicycle pump to our array of garden tools, but in fact air is naturally present, flowing through the open space, or pore space, of the soil. We create this pore space by building up the soil's structure, encouraging the formation of aggregates that combine the primary particles of sand, silt, and clay with organic matter. This structure-building in turn increases the ability of air to circulate throughout the soil, making it possible for microorganisms to thrive and operate effectively."
>
> —from *Solar Gardening*, by Leandre Poisson and Gretchen Vogel Poisson (Chelsea Green, 1994)

## *Web Sites*

**Something To Grow On**
http://www.cals.cornell.edu/dept/flori/growon/index.html
*Several soil-related publications available. Produced by Cornell University, Long Island Nurserymen's Association, and New York State State Nurserymen's Foundation.*

**Get Set! To Garden!**
http://www.gardening.com
*Lots of good information about soil and soil improvement.*

**Illinois Cooperative Extension Service**
http://www.ag.uiuc.edu/~robson/solutions/horticul
*Good soil information is available in their Horticulture Solutions Series.*

# CORRECTING SOIL pH

To raise the pH of your soil by a factor of one, (i.e., 5.5 to 6.5), follow these recommendations:

In very sandy soil, add 3 to 4 pounds of ground limestone per 100 square feet.

In loam (good garden soil), add 7 to 8 pounds per 100 square feet.

In heavy clay, add 8 to 10 pounds per 100 square feet.

To lower soil pH by about 1 point follow these application rates:

In sandy soil, add 1 pound ground sulfur per 100 square feet.

In loam, add 1½ to 2 pounds per 100 square feet.

In heavy clay, add 2 pounds ground sulfur per 100 square feet.

---

the hydrogen ions prevail, the soil is acidic (pH 1 to pH 6.5), and when the hydroxyl ions tip the balance, the pH is alkaline (pH 6.8 to pH 14).

Most essential plant nutrients are soluble at pH levels of 6.5 to 6.8, which is why most plants grow best in this pH range. If the pH of your soil is much higher or much lower, soil nutrients start to become chemically bound to the soil particles, which makes them unavailable to your plants. Plant health suffers because the roots are unable to absorb the nutrients they require. Adding liquid or granular fertilizers may help for a short time, but these nutrients will soon become "tied up" as well.

To break the chemical bonds and improve the fertility of your soil, you need to get the pH of your soil within the 6.5 to 6.8 range. This can be achieved by applying agricultural lime to de-acidify the soil (raise the pH) or elemental sulfur to make it more acid (lower the pH). Remember that you can't, and shouldn't, try to change the pH of your soil overnight. But you can gradually alter it over one or two growing seasons and then maintain it every year thereafter. Liberal applications of organic matter are good insurance against pH problems, because it helps to moderate pH imbalances.

### CORRECTING SOILS THAT ARE TOO ACIDIC.

If the pH of your soil is less than 6.5, it may be too acidic for most garden plants (although some, such as blueberries and azaleas, actually require acidic soil). Soils in the eastern half of the U.S. are usually on the acidic side. The most common way to raise the pH of your soil (make it less acidic) is to add powdered limestone. Dolomitic limestone is usually recommended because it also corrects manganese deficiencies. It takes several months for limestone to alter the pH, so fall is the best time to apply it. Wood ash can also be used to raise the pH of your soil. It works much more quickly than limestone, and also adds potassium and trace elements. But if you apply too much wood ash, you can drastically alter the soil pH and cause nutrient imbalances. For best results, apply wood ash in the fall or winter, and apply no more than 2 pounds per 100 square feet, every two to three years.

---

“There is little doubt that the best soils produce the best vegetables. The advantages of building a good, humus-rich, nutritionally balanced soil are the obvious positive effects it will have in producing larger yields, earlier crops, and less work for you. But there are some additional benefits often hidden to the eye. Scientific research is beginning to confirm that plants grown in healthy organic soils have more nutritional value than their counterparts grown in chemically boosted mineral soils. Evidently the balance of trace minerals and the more even growth cycle are capable of producing crops with small, but measurable increased levels of vitamins and minerals necessary in the human diet.

“Additionally, recent attention to biological pest control methods has looked into the role that certain plant hormones have upon insect pests. It now appears that under stressful conditions of drought, nutrient deficiency, or poor soil texture, plants either fail to produce some insect-repelling hormones or instead produce excesses of other hormones that attract some pests. This may explain the observation of many organic gardeners that pests somehow seem to prefer the least healthy of plants, leaving the robust individuals alone or less ravaged. In the rich organic soils of the intensive garden, stressful conditions are largely eliminated by proper soil management. Our own experience confirms this notion. As our soil has improved over the years, our pest problems have become noticeably less severe, and some pests that rampage through the neighbors' gardens are endangered species in ours.”

—from *Intensive Gardening Round the Year* by Paul Doscher, Timothy Fisher, and Kathleen Kolb (reprinted as *Efficient Vegetable Gardening* by Globe Pequot, 1993).

**CORRECTING SOILS THAT ARE TOO**

**ALKALINE.** If your soil is too alkaline, which means the pH is higher than 6.8, you will need to acidify your soil. Soils in the western U.S., especially in arid regions, are typically alkaline. Alkaline soils are usually acidified by adding ground sulfur. You can also incorporate naturally acidic organic materials such as conifer needles, sawdust, peat moss, and oak leaves.

## Fertilizing the Soil and Feeding Your Plants

There is no substitute for long-term soil building with yearly applications of organic matter. A rich, organic soil is perfectly capable of supporting most garden plants. But fertilizers — whether natural or synthetic — do have their place. They are often necessary for "heavy feeder" crops such as corn, for soils that are imbalanced or lacking in specific nutrients, or for depleted soils that you are slowly restoring to their original fertility levels. Adding fertilizer helps to ensure that your plants can get the nutrients they need, when they need them.

The nutrients required by plants are usually grouped by their relative concentration in the plant. The "primary" elements are nitrogen, phosphorus, and potassium. The "secondary" elements are calcium, magnesium, and sulfur. The trace elements or micronutrients are boron, chlorine, cobalt, copper, iron, manganese, molybdenum, and zinc.

Before you start stocking up on fertilizers, it is a good idea to learn more about the nutrients that are already in your soil. A good soil test will identify significant nutrient deficiencies or pH problems, and can be a useful benchmark for a long-term soil improvement program. Plants can also be good indicators of nutrient deficiencies, though it can be difficult to tell if the nutrients are really lacking or if they are simply bound to the soil particles because of high or low pH levels.

**NITROGEN.** This is the least stable soil nutrient because it leaches out of the soil very quickly. Since it is a major nutrient required by all plants, it is the one you must be most attentive to. Symptoms of nitrogen deficiency are pale green or yellow leaves; spindly or stunted plants; or small

## Testing Your Soil

Your local Cooperative Extension Service office (usually located at state land grant colleges) may offer a professional soil testing service. The advantage is low cost and results that are specifically geared to your location. If this service is not available, you can also have your soil tested by an independent soil lab. If possible, choose one in your own region of the country. If you are in a hurry, a home soil test kit will give you quick results.

Soil test results usually rate the levels of soil pH, phosphorus, potassium, magnesium, calcium, and sometimes nitrogen. (Most labs do not test for nitrogen because it is so unstable in the soil.) Some labs also offer tests for micronutrients such as boron, zinc, manganese, and others. Unless you feel there may be a deficiency problem, you probably won't need micronutrient testing. As a preventative measure, you can apply organic fertilizers that include micronutrients (such as greensand and kelp meal).

To get the most accurate test results, take a soil sample from each

garden area: lawn, flower garden, and vegetable garden. Spring and fall are the best times to perform a soil test. The soil is more stable, and these are good times to incorporate any recommended fertilizers. Many labs will give recommendations for specific organic amendments upon request. If not, you will have to compare labels to find organic substitutes for the chemical fertilizers that may be suggested.

### SOIL TESTING LABS

**Woods End Soil Labs**
RFD 1, Box 4050
Old Rome Road
Mt. Vernon, ME 04352
207-293-2457

**A & L Agricultural Labs**
7621 White Pine Road
Richmond, VA 23237
804-743-9401

**Green Gems**
P.O. Box 6007
Healdsburg, CA 95448
707-431-1691

# Frequently Asked Questions

## WHAT ARE COVER CROPS AND GREEN MANURES?

Cover crops are used primarily to protect fallow (unused) soil. In the North, gardeners usually plant them at the end of the season so their soil is not bare over the winter. Cold-hardy crops such as vetch and winter rye are best for overwintering. They will begin growth again in spring, and need to be tilled in before you can plant your garden. Green manures can also be planted on a new garden area the year before you plan to use it. They will choke out weeds and add a wealth of organic matter. Legumes, including field peas, soybeans, and alfalfa, will contribute both nitrogen and organic matter to the soil. Fast-growing grains and buckwheat produce the most organic matter and will smother competing weeds as they grow.

If your soil will be fallow for more than one growing season, you can plant perennial or biennial green manures, such as clover or alfalfa. All cover crops should be tilled-in at least three weeks before the area is to be replanted, so the organic matter will already be partially decomposed at planting time.

## WHAT ARE LIQUID SOIL CONDITIONERS?

Liquid soil conditioners typically contain a blend of humic acid and catalytic enzymes, which are produced in a controlled environment by the same sort of microorganisms that are at work in your compost pile. When applied to your soil, their effect is similar to the effect you get when you add compost. Clay soils become easier to

work and nutrients become more available; sandy soils are able to retain more water and nutrients.

Researchers have now isolated specific organic substances that solve specific soil problems. Soon you will be able to buy organic soil conditioners that have been specially selected for their effectiveness in opening up heavy soils or dislodging salts and other elements that have become tied up in the soil.

## WHAT IS HARDPAN?

Hardpan is a dense layer of soil that restricts root growth and the movement of moisture, air, and beneficial organisms through the soil. Hardpan is usually created by glacial action, heavy rain, or heavy equipment, and typically lies between 6 and 25 inches below the soil surface. Farmers often cope with hardpan by using a chisel plow to cut and break up this dense layer of soil.

Home gardeners can break up and mix the hardpan layer by "double digging" the soil. This involves removing 10 to 12 inches of topsoil, and then working organic matter into the 12-inch layer of material that lies below. If the hardpan layer is not too deep, you can use a digging fork to puncture it and open up passages for air and water. (See products section.)

## WHAT DOES CHELATED MEAN?

Chelation is a process that joins a nutrient, such as iron, to a non-nutrient compound that can be easily absorbed by your plants.

## WHAT DOES 5-8-3 MEAN?

The numbers refer to the percentage

fruits. Too much nitrogen in the soil will produce lush foliage instead of fruit, and it can burn plant tissues. Organic sources of nitrogen include aged animal manure, dried blood, fish emulsion, bird or bat guano, cottonseed meal, alfalfa meal, cocoa bean or peanut shells, bone meal, tankage, hoof and horn meal, feather meal, wool waste, human hair, fish meal or scraps, seafood meal, and soybean meal.

by net weight of total nitrogen (N; always the first number), available phosphorus (P; the second number), and soluble potash (K; the third number). In other words, a 5-8-3 fertilizer contains 5 percent nitrogen, 8 percent available phosphorus, and 3 percent soluble potash. Labeling laws allow only the immediately available nutrients to be listed. That is why the nutrient analysis for organic fertilizers tends to be low. Most organic fertilizers actually have a higher nutrient content, but these nutrients gradually become available to plants over a period of months or even years.

## WHAT ARE THE BENEFITS OF SEAWEED?

Seaweed contains at least sixty micronutrients, including iron, copper, zinc, boron, and manganese. Seaweed also contains a high concentration of natural growth hormones which allow it to grow rapidly in its natural environment. When applied to plants, these growth hormones stimulate root growth, reduce transplant shock, promote more rapid fruit set, increase frost resistance, and improve storage life. Research has also revealed that seaweed contains antitoxins that help plants fend off bacteria, viruses, and pests.

Powdered seaweed (kelp meal) releases its nutrients gradually through the soil. Liquid seaweed makes these nutrients immediately available. Seaweed is not a complete fertilizer because it doesn't provide adequate nitrogen and phosphorus for most plants. But it is an excellent part of a balanced soil-building program and it has some very definite benefits for growing plants.

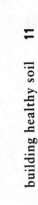

> A double handful of good garden soil contains more organisms, mostly microscopic, than there are people on earth."
>
> —from *Step By Step Organic Vegetable Gardening* by Shepherd Ogden (HarperCollins, 1992)

**PHOSPHORUS.** Plants use phosphorus to flower, fruit, and set seed. Phosphorus promotes strong root growth, makes stems strong, and improves disease resistance. Most soils are deficient in phosphorus, and when the soil pH is too high or too low, phosphorus becomes even less available. Phosphorus is not very water-soluble, so it doesn't move through the soil. For best results, it should be incorporated into the root zone where it can be utilized. Microorganisms convert phosphorus into a form that is available to plants, which is why phosphorus deficiencies are often apparent in the spring when soil microbes are not very active. Symptoms of a phosphorus deficiency include purplish leaves; pale, dull leaves with yellow, streaked margins; stems that are thin and hard; fruit that sets late or drops early; and stunted plants and roots. Organic sources of phosphorus include rock phosphate, colloidal phosphate, bone meal, dried blood, cottonseed meal, basalt rock powder, and langbeinite (usually sold as SulPoMag).

**POTASSIUM.** Potassium helps plants grow strong root systems and promotes disease resistance. It also regulates the uptake of other nutrients. Most soils have an adequate reserve of potassium, but in a form that is unavailable to plants. Symptoms of potassium deficiency include lower leaves being spotted, mottled, or curled; scorched leaf margins; weak stems; shriveled fruit; reduced disease resistance; and poor storage quality. Organic sources of potassium are seaweed extract or kelp meal, granite dust, greensand, leaf mold, and wood ashes.

**SECONDARY ELEMENTS AND TRACE MINERALS.** You can avoid most trace mineral deficiencies by adding organic matter and by using organic fertilizers that contain trace elements. To identify and correct specific deficiencies relating to secondary or trace elements, see one of the recommended soil books such as *Start with the Soil* by Grace Gershuny, *Rodale's Improving the Soil,* or *Fertile Soil* by Robert Parnes. Organic sources of trace minerals include seaweed, kelp meal, fish scraps, greensand, and rock powder.

## Organic versus Synthetic Fertilizers

Organic fertilizers contain naturally occuring nutrients derived from plants, animals, or minerals. They have not been chemically

# Products for Improving Your Soil

**Pelletized Hydrated Lime**

**Pelletized Sulfur**

**NO-WAIT SOIL TEST KIT**

and potassium. A slight odor requires out-door use. Mix with water to make 4 gal-lons of fertilizer.
#30-038 Sea Cure 1 pt. $4.95
#30-037 Sea Plus 1 pt. $4.95

**ROOTS Plus** is a complete (5-3-4) blend of organic ingredients and fast-activating fertilizers. It builds richer soil while ensuring that your plants have the nutrients they need for vigorous growth. Safe to apply as often as you like, at any time of year. 32 oz treats 4,000 square feet.
#07-276 ROOTS Plus All-Purpose $10.95
#07-274 ROOTS Sprayer $5.95

**Green Magic** stimulates plants and builds healthy soil with a blend of kelp, humic acids, vitamins, and amino acids plus beneficial soil bacteria. Mix powdered concentrate with water and apply in conjunction with a complete fertilizer. Covers approx. 5,000 sq. ft.
#30-263 Green Magic, 2.5 oz $9.95

sand, black rock phosphate, liquid phosphorus, kelp meal, trace minerals and a new line of biostimulants. Please call for more information and a cur-rent catalog.

Get a quick read on the pH level of your soil with this simple **pH Test Kit.** It lets you conduct 10 tests, and includes full instructions. The **NPK Test Kit** includes 10 tests each for pH, nitrogen, phosphorus, and potassium. You receive 4 color-coded test tubes and complete instructions.
#07-202 pH Test Kit $9.95
#07-104 NPK Test Kit $16.95

**Liquid Lime** is a con-centrated solution of ultra-fine dolomitic limestone. Sprayed directly on the soil, it works faster and pene-trates deeper than powdered limestone. One quart covers 5,000 square feet.
#07-222 Lime Plus 1 qt. $14.95

**Sea Cure** is a seaweed-based formula that contains over sixty trace ele-ments and compounds that aid in root develop-ment and overall vigor. Mix with water to make 8 gallons. **Sea Plus** (3-2-2) combines seaweed and fish emul-sion to provide nitrogen, phos-phorus

**AGGRAND Natural Lime Plus**

**SEA PLUS**

**SEA CURE**

Specially formu-lated for Gar-dener's Supply, these all-organic granular fertiliz-ers contain slow-release nutrients that feed your plants through-out the growing season. Applied regularly, they will improve the fertility of your soil for years to come. Apply 5 lbs per 200 square feet.
#07-300 All-Purpose Fertilizer, 5 lbs $5.95
#07-304 All-Purpose Fertilizer, 25 lbs $24.95
#07-200 Tomato Fertilizer, 5 lbs $5.95
#07-316 Flower Fertilizer, 5 lbs $5.95

Many other organic soil amendments are available from Gardener's Supply, including alfalfa meal, green-

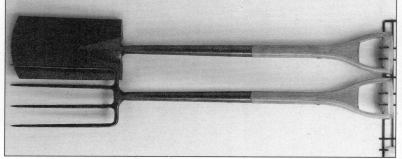

**ALL PURPOSE FERTILIZER** 5-5-5 GARDENER'S SUPPLY COMPANY

A set of high-quality digging tools makes gardening chores easier and more enjoyable. This fork and spade have extra-long hardwood handles and heat-treated, carbon steel heads that will stand up to a lifetime of heavy use. 32" overall. Made in England.
#02-225 Digging Spade $57.95
#02-226 Digging Fork $57.95

processed, and they have not been combined with any synthetic materials. Organic fertilizers are typically less soluble than synthetic fertilizers, which means nutrients are released more gradually, over a longer period of time. If you apply a granular organic fertilizer at planting time, you may want to also apply a liquid or foliar spray that will provide immediately available nutrients during the first few weeks of the growing season.

Organic fertilizers usually contribute some organic matter to the soil. This benefits microorganisms and, in turn, improves soil structure. But adding too much of these fertilizers even though they are organic, can cause problems. For example, chicken manure can provide too much nitrogen, and cause succulent growth and poor flower and fruit production. Some organic soil amendments are potent enough to injure tender plant tissues. For best results, always follow label instructions. Organic fertilizers include dried blood, fish or feather meal, rock phosphate, bone meal, seaweed, cottonseed meal, and animal manures.

Synthetic fertilizers are produced by chemically altering raw materials to convert them into a form readily absorbed by plants. Synthetic fertilizers are usually very water-soluble and are immediately available to plants. If you apply too much of these fertilizers, or if environmental conditions (such as a very wet spring) make them available too quickly, your plants and soil organisms will suffer. Examples of synthetic fertilizers include urea, ammonium sulfate, superphosphate, muriate of potash, and sulfate of potash.

> Several years ago, we watched a television program about agriculture as it was being practiced in the province of Quebec. The program focused on how farmers couldn't make much money because the prices they received for their crops were too low when compared to their costs. These Canadian farmers were barely making a living despite the long, hard hours of physical labor they put in seven days a week. Part of the show featured an interview with a man whose family had been farming the same piece of land since they had first settled in Quebec. It was hard to tell the age of the farmer, since he was slightly stooped and had such a weathered face. The interviewer asked him the obvious question of why he had stuck with farming, even though it clearly was a hard life with little or no profit. The farmer reached down with a large, bony hand, picked up a handful of black, rich soil, and said, 'J'aime la terre assez pour en manger,' or, 'I love the soil enough to eat it.'"
>
> —from *Solar Gardening* by Leandre Poisson and Gretchen Vogel Poisson (Chelsea Green, 1994)

# composting

**B**uilding and maintaining a compost pile is the surest, easiest way to become a better gardener. Not only will you be producing the best possible food for your garden, but by watching leaves, eggshells, orange rinds, and grass clippings become transformed into rich compost filled with earthworms and other soil creatures, you'll be learning what healthy soil is all about.

## What's so Special about Compost?

So what is compost and why is it so special? Compost is a rich and crumbly blend of partially decomposed organic material that does wonderful things for your garden.

**COMPOST IMPROVES SOIL STRUCTURE.** Most gardeners don't start with great soil. Whether yours is hard and compacted, sandy, stony, heavy, or wet, adding compost will improve its texture, water-holding capacity, and fertility. Your soil will gradually become fluffy and chocolatey brown — the ideal home for healthy plants.

**COMPOST PROVIDES A BALANCED SOURCE OF PLANT NUTRIENTS.** Even if you are lucky enough to have great soil, you can't expect that soil to remain rich and productive without replenishing the nutrients that are consumed each growing season. No commercial fertilizer, even one that is totally organic, provides the full spectrum of nutrients that you get with compost. The nutrients are available gradually, as your plants need them, over a period of months or years. The microorganisms in the compost will also help your plants absorb other fertilizer nutrients more efficiently.

**COMPOST STIMULATES BENEFICIAL ORGANISMS.** Compost is teeming with all kinds of microorganisms and soil fauna that help convert soil nutrients into a form that can be readily absorbed by your plants. The microorganisms, enzymes, vitamins, and natural antibiotics that are present in compost actually help prevent many soil pathogens from harming your plants. Earthworms, millipedes, and other macro-organisms tunnel through your soil, opening up passageways for air and water to reach your plants' roots.

**COMPOST IS GARDEN INSURANCE.** Even very experienced gardeners often have soil that is less than perfect. Adding compost moderates pH and fertility problems, so you can concentrate on the pleasures of gar-

## Guest Expert
## Andy Harper

The most critical factor in making consistent, high-quality compost is management. Like anything worth doing, the composter must make a commitment to constructing and maintaining the compost pile throughout the year. Develop a system of compost production that works for you, whether bins, piles, or windrows, and commit to the task of caring for your compost.

Balancing your recipe is the next most critical step in successful composting. A proper ratio of carbon and nitrogen (or browns and greens), blended with moisture and kept aerated, especially during the early stages of decomposition, will produce compost quickly and consistently. If you can easily squeeze water from your "blend," the material is too wet. If you don't see any moisture or the material easily flakes apart, it is too dry. When choosing ingredients to compost, remember your goal. You can't make filet mignon from hamburger — you must start with the best materials to get the best end-product. Turn your pile at least every other week, especially during earlier stages: homogenizing your material will help it break down quickly. Use a long-stemmed thermometer to monitor the progress of your pile. If temperatures do not exceed 110°F, your recipe needs some refinement.

Like fine wine, good compost cannot be rushed. With active management and a good recipe, you can have stable, finished compost every year from the previous year's organic waste. Although winter can substantially decrease microbial activity, you can jump-start the pile in the spring and do serious composting during the summer. Even when you have lots of other things to keep you busy, don't forget to tend your compost pile. The rewards far outweigh the effort!

Natalie Stultz

*Andy Harper is director of the Inter-vale Compost Project in Burlington, Vermont.*

## Favorite Books

**Let It Rot** *by Stu Campbell* (Garden Way Publishing, 1990). A fun, non-technical classic that demystifies the composting process and convincingly argues that everyone can — and should — make compost. 160 pages, paperback, $8.95.

**The Rodale Book of Composting** *by Deborah Martin and Grace Gershuny* (Rodale, 1992). A comprehensive guide that clearly explains how the composting process works. Detailed information about how to utilize dozens of kinds of organic matter. Almost 100 pages on different composting methods and structures. An excellent reference whether you are an apartment dweller, suburban dabbler, or master gardener. 278 pages, paperback, $14.95.

**Worms Eat My Garbage** *by Mary Appelhof* (Flowerfield Press, 1997). The hows and whys of setting up an indoor worm composting system. The author's enthusiasm about worms is contagious, and she covers every possible question with a blend of science, practical experience, and fun. 110 pages, paperback, $10.95.

Grass clippings

Leaves

Bacteria are single-celled and can be shaped like spheres, rods, or spiral twists. They are so small that it would take 25,000 bacteria laid end to end to take up 1 inch on a ruler, and an amount of garden soil the size of a pea may contain up to a billion bacteria. Bacteria are the most nutritionally diverse of all organisms, which is to say, as a group, they can eat nearly anything. Usually, they can produce the appropriate enzyme to digest whatever material they find themselves on.”

—from *Rodale's Book of Composting*
by Deborah Martin and Grace Gershuny (Rodale, 1992)

## How Compost Happens

Organic matter is transformed into compost through the work of microorganisms, soil fauna, enzymes, and fungi. When making compost, your job is to provide the best possible environment for these beneficial organisms to do their work. If you do so, the decomposition process works very rapidly — sometimes in as little as two weeks! If you don't provide the optimum environment, decomposition will still happen, but it may take from several months to several years. The trick to making an abundance of compost in a short time is to balance the following four things:

**CARBON.** Carbon-rich materials are the energy food for microorganisms. (Just like carbohydrates are the energy food for humans.) You can identify high-carbon plant materials because they are dry, tough, or fibrous, and tan or brown in color.

Compost is the perfect thing to spread around when you are creating a new garden, seeding a new lawn area, or planting a new tree. Compost can be sprinkled around plants during the growing season or used as a mulch in your perennial gardens. You can add compost to your flower boxes and deck planters. You can also use it to enrich the potting soil for your indoor plants.

Can a gardener ever have enough compost? It's doubtful. Unlike organic or inorganic fertilizers, which need to be applied at the right time and in the right amount, compost can be applied at any time and in any amount. You can't really over-apply it. Plants use exactly what they need, when they need it.

dening, not the science of your soil's chemical composition. Unlike

# Other Good Books

**Backyard Composting** (Harmonious Technologies, 1995). A simple little handbook with basic how-to information and a broader ecological context. 96 pages, paperback, $6.95.

**Composting to Reduce the Waste Stream** by *Ithaca NY Cooperative Extension Service.* An excellent publication covering all the basics. Includes plans for 9 kinds of home-made compost bins, and a good set of references. Available from N.E. Regional Agricultural Engineering Service, 152 Riley-Robb Hall Cooperative Extension, Ithaca, NY 14853-5701. E-mail: NRAES@cornell.edu. Phone: 607-255-7654. $8.00 plus $3.50 S&H.

**Composting: A Recipe for Success** by *Cort Sinnes.* A 21-minute video showing what materials to gather and how to combine them to produce finished compost in 14 days. $17.95 postpaid. 815-363-0909.

## COMMON COMPOST INGREDIENTS

### BROWN (HIGH-CARBON MATERIALS)
corncobs and stalks

paper

pine needles

sawdust or wood shavings

straw

vegetable stalks

dry leaves

### GREEN (HIGH-NITROGEN MATERIALS)
coffee grounds

eggshells

fruit wastes

grass clippings

feathers or hair

fresh leaves

seaweed

kitchen scraps

fresh weeds

rotted manure

alfalfa meal (or rabbit/hamster pellets)

## Composting Tips

❧ Keep a stash of straw, kitty litter, dry leaves, or peat moss near your compost pile. Sprinkle a little on the top of the pile each time you add fresh weeds or kitchen scraps. These high-carbon materials will help keep the C/N ratio in balance.

❧ Try burying your kitchen scraps right in the garden. Just dig a 12- to 15-inch-deep hole in the pathway, pour in the scraps, and cover with soil.

❧ Hunt around your town for a plentiful source of free organic material. You might try a horse farm, food processing plant, local wood shop, or grounds maintenance service.

❧ Cover your pile for best results. It will deter pests, hold in heat, and keep the moisture level more constant. A pile that's dry or too water-logged takes a very long time to break down. You can use a tarp, piece of plastic, hunk of old carpet, or piece of metal roofing.

❧ In northern states, you should cover your pile in late fall to avoid leaching nutrients and to prevent the pile from becoming water-logged. A drier pile will thaw more quickly the following spring.

❧ Don't add compost to a seed-starting mix unless you are sure that the pile got hot enough to be sterilized (140°–160°F). Seedlings are very susceptible to bacteria that are harmless to more mature plants.

❧ Shredded materials compost very rapidly. The more surface area for microbes to attack, the sooner you'll have usable compost. You can chop your materials with a machete or shovel, run them through a shredding machine, or run over them with your lawn mower.

❧ Compost piles that are smaller than 3 feet by 3 feet will have trouble heating up — especially in cool climates. Piles larger than 5 feet by 5 feet may not allow enough air to reach the center.

❧ If fruit flies are a problem indoors, your compost container is probably not airtight. Make sure it has a tight-fitting lid that gets sealed shut after being opened. You can also try emptying the container more frequently (every day or two).

❧ If skunks and burrowing rodents are hanging around your compost pile, you can try using a powdered or spray repellent (see "Tools and Composting Accessories," page 22). You can also bury hardware cloth up and around the bottom of your compost bin. Avoid putting meat or fatty foods in your pile: they attract all sorts of curious animals.

Examples are dry leaves, straw, rotted hay, sawdust, shredded paper, and cornstalks.

**NITROGEN.** High-nitrogen materials provide the protein-rich components that microorganisms require to grow and multiply. Freshly pulled weeds, fresh grass clippings, over-ripe fruits and vegetables, kitchen scraps, and other moist green matter are the sorts of nitrogen-rich materials you'll probably have on hand. Other high-protein organic matter includes kelp meal, seaweed, manure, and animal by-products like blood or bone meal.

**WATER.** Moisture is very important for the composting process. But too much moisture will drown the microorganisms, and too little will dehydrate them. A general rule of thumb is to keep the material in your compost pile as moist as a well-wrung sponge. If you need to add water

# SAMPLE COMPOST RECIPES

1 part fresh grass clippings
1 part dry leaves
1 part good garden soil

*Spread the ingredients in 3-inch-deep layers to a height of 3 to 4 feet.*

2 parts fresh grass clippings
2 parts straw or spoiled hay
1 part good garden soil

*Spread the ingredients in 4-inch layers, sprinkling about 1 inch of garden soil and adding water to the layers.*

2 parts dry leaves
1 part fresh grass clippings
1 part food scraps

*Spread ingredients in 4-inch layers, adding water if needed.*

(unchlorinated is best), insert your garden hose into the middle of the pile in several places, or sprinkle the pile with water next time you turn it. Using an enclosed container or covering your pile with a tarp will make it easier to maintain the right moisture level.

**OXYGEN.** To do their work most efficiently, microorganisms require a lot of oxygen. When your pile is first assembled, there will probably be plenty of air between the layers of materials. But as the microorganisms begin to work, they will start consuming oxygen. Unless you turn or in some way aerate your compost pile, they will run out of oxygen and become sluggish. (See the section "To Turn or Not to Turn" for more details about aerating your pile.)

## Do I Need a Recipe?

Microorganisms and other soil fauna work most efficiently when the ratio of carbon-rich to nitrogen-rich materials in your compost pile is approximately 25:1. In practical terms, if you want to have an active compost pile, you should include lots of high-carbon "brown" materials (such as straw, wood chips, or dry leaves) and a lesser amount of high-nitrogen "green" materials (such as grass clippings, freshly pulled weeds, or kitchen scraps). If you have an excess of carbon-rich materials and not enough nitrogen-rich materials, your pile may take years to decompose (there is not enough protein for those microbes!). If your pile has too much nitrogen and not enough carbon, your pile will also decompose very slowly (not enough for the microbes to eat!), and it will probably be soggy and smelly along the way.

But don't worry about determining the exact carbon content of a material or achieving a precise 25:1 ratio. Composting doesn't need to

---

# Troubleshooting

**COMPOST PILE WON'T HEAT UP**

The materials may be too dry. This can happen quickly during the summer months. Try to keep your compost materials moist to the touch. Cover the pile.

The pile may be low in nitrogen. Fast-working microorganisms can quickly consume all the nitrogen and leave undecomposed carbon materials behind. Replenish the nitrogen content of your pile with fresh green grass clippings, garden weeds, kitchen scraps, manure, or an activator like SuperHot.

Your pile may also be too small. Collect more materials and mix everything into a pile that measures 3 feet on each side, and is at least 3 feet high.

**SMELLY COMPOST**

If your pile smells like ammonia, it may contain too much nitrogen. Add carbon materials such as straw, leaves, or hay to correct the balance.

**SOGGY COMPOST**

Dense or water-logged compost piles don't contain enough oxygen for the microorganisms to survive. Often these piles give off an unpleasant odor. The solution is to aerate the pile and add more dry materials.

**FINISHED PRODUCT IS TOO ROUGH**

Some materials like eggshells and corncobs take a very long time to break down. If you want a more finely textured compost, shred or chop up the materials before putting them into the bin. You can also sift out these crumbs and throw them back into the next pile.

be a competitive, goal-oriented task. All organic matter breaks down eventually, no matter what you do. If you simply use about 3 times as much "brown" materials as "green" materials, you'll be off to a great start. Take a look at the sample recipes at left, and check the ingredients chart on page 17 for a list of common compost materials. With experience, you'll get a sense for what works best.

## Why Does a Compost Pile Get Hot?

A compost pile gets hot because of intense microbial activity. The heat is a by product of this activity, and an indicator that the microorganisms are happy and hard at work, munching on organic matter and converting it into finished compost. The temperature of your compost pile does not in itself affect the speed or efficiency of the decomposition process. But temperature does determine what types of microbes are active.

There are primarily three types of microbes that work to digest the materials in a compost pile. They each work best in a particular temperature range. The *psychrophiles* work in cool temperatures — even as low as 28°F. As they begin to digest some of the carbon-rich materials, they give off heat, which causes the temperature in the pile to rise. When the pile warms to 60°–70°F, *mesophilic* bacteria take over. They are responsible for the majority of the decomposition work. If the mesophiles have enough carbon, nitrogen, air, and water, they work so hard that they raise the temperature in the pile to about 100°F. At this point, *thermophilic* bacteria kick in. It is these bacteria that can raise the temperature

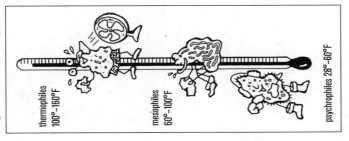

thermophiles
100°–160°F

mesophiles
60°–100°F

psychrophiles 28°–60°F

high enough to sterilize the compost and kill disease-causing organisms and weed seeds. Three to five days of 155°F is enough for the thermophiles to do their best work.

Getting your compost pile "hot" (140°–160°F) is not critical, but it does mean that your compost will be finished and usable within a month or so. These high temperatures also kill most weed seeds, as well as harmful pathogens that can cause disease problems. Most people don't bother charting the temperature curve in their compost pile. They just try to get a good ratio of carbon to nitrogen, keep the pile moist and well aerated, and wait until everything looks pretty well broken down. If you want to get a little more scientific about it, you might want to invest in a compost thermometer.

Commercial activators like SuperHot (see product section) can help raise the temperature in your compost pile by providing a concentrated dose of microorganisms and protein. Other effective activators

## *Web Sites*

**Rot Web**
http://www.intra.com/~topsoil/compost_menu.html
*Basic tips and how-to information with good links to other sites. Information on subscribing to an on-line composting newsgroup. Resource list.*

**Cornell University**
http://www.cals.cornell.edu/dept/compost/
*Good information on projects for school composting, how to compost some weird stuff like dead turkeys and zebra mussels; good information and links to other sites.*

**The Composting Resource Page**
http://www.oldgrowth.org/compost
*Good basic information on composting with links to other sites.*

**Compost Happens**
http://www.composthappens.com
*A good source for composting bins, accessories, general composting information, and links.*

**The Composting Council of Canada**
http://www.compost.org/
*FAQs, membership, publications, links, and other resources.*

## COMPOST MATERIALS TO AVOID

weed seeds and invasive weed roots
oil, meat scraps, grease, and bones
too much lime or wood ashes
fresh manure
cat, dog, or human waste (may contain pathogens)
too much sawdust or wood chips
plywood or pressure-treated lumber
coal ashes and charcoal
diseased plants
anything treated with a chemical pesticide or herbicide
anything that an earthworm won't eat

**Trash Can Bin.** To convert a plastic trash can into a composter, cut off the bottom with a saw. Drill about 24

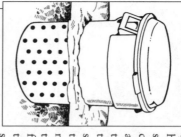

quarter-inch holes in the sides of the can for good aeration. Bury the bottom of the can from several inches to a foot or more below the soil surface and press the loosened soil around the sides to secure it. Partially burying the composter will make it easier for microorganisms to enter the pile.

**Block or Brick or Stone Bin.** Lay the blocks, with or without mortar, leaving spaces between each block to permit aeration. Form three sides of a 3- to 4-foot square, roughly 3 to 4 feet high.

**Wood Pallet Bin.** Discarded wooden pallets from factories or stores can be stood upright to form a bin. Attach

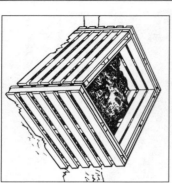

the corners with rope, wire, or chain. A fourth pallet can be used as a floor to increase air flow. A used carpet or tarp can be placed over the top of the pile to reduce moisture loss or keep out rain or snow.

**Plastic Stationary Bins.** These bins are for continuous rather than batch composting. Most units feature air vents

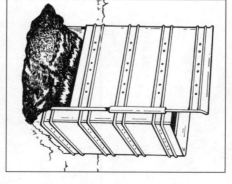

removable (lift out slats) for easy access. Lift-up lids are nice.

**Wire Bin.** Use an 11-foot length of 2-inch x 4-inch x 36-inch welded, medium-gauge fence wire from your local hardware or building supply store. Tie the ends together to form your hoop. A bin this size holds just over one cubic yard of material. Snow fencing can be used in a similar fashion.

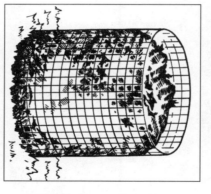

**Tumbling or Rotating Bins.** These composters are for making batches of compost all at one time. You accumulate organic materials until you have

along the sides and are made from recycled plastics. Look for a lid that fits securely, and doors to access finished compost. Size should be approximately 3 feet square.

enough to fill the bin, then load it up and rotate it every day or two. If materials are shredded before going into the bin, and you have plenty of nitrogen, you can have finished compost in as little as 3 weeks.

For more ideas on composting systems, see the "Other Good Books" section, or contact Seattle Tilth (see "Resources" page 23).

Other composting systems are available from Gardener's Supply. See "Tools and Composting Accessories," page 22.

**Two- or Three-Bay Wood Bin.** Having several bins allows you to use one section for storing materials, one for active composting, and one for curing or storing finished compost. Each bin should be approximately 36" x 36" x 36". Be sure to allow air spaces between the sidewall slats, and make the front walls

that can help to get your pile cooking include humus-rich soil, rotted manure, finished compost, dried blood, and alfalfa meal.

## To Turn or Not to Turn

Unless speed is a priority, frequent turning is not necessary. Many people never turn their compost piles. The purpose of turning is to increase oxygen flow for the microorganisms, and to blend undecomposed materials into the center of the pile. If you are managing a hot pile, you'll probably want to turn your compost every 3 to 5 days, or when the interior temperature dips below about 110°F. After turning, the pile should heat up again, as long as there is still undecomposed material to be broken down. When the temperature stays pretty constant no matter how much you turn the pile, your compost is probably ready. Though turning can speed the composting process, it also releases heat into the air, so you should turn your pile less frequently in cold weather.

There are several ways to help keep your pile well aerated, without the hassle of turning.

- Build your pile on a raised wood platform or on a pile of branches.
- Make sure there are air vents in the sides of your compost bin.
- Put 1 or 2 perforated 4-inch plastic pipes in the center of your pile.

## Worm Composting

Employing worms to make compost is called *vermiculture*. Manure worms, red worms, and branding worms (the small ones usually sold by commercial breeders) are dynamos when it comes to decomposing organic matter — especially kitchen scraps. The problem is that these worms cannot tolerate high temperatures. Add a handful of them to an active compost pile and they'll be dead in an hour. Field worms and night crawlers (common garden worms with one big band) are killed at even lower temperatures.

If you would like to maintain a separate worm bin for composting food scraps, you need a watertight container that can be kept somewhere that the temperature will remain between 50° and 80°F all year-round (the same temperatures humans find comfortable). A ready-made worm bin is described in the "Tools and Accessories" section. Red worms are also available by mail. For complete instructions about how to build and use an indoor worm bin, we recommend *Worms Eat My Garbage* by Mary Appelhof (see "Favorite Books").

## CONDIMENTS TO SPICE UP YOUR PILE

The following materials can be sprinkled onto your compost pile as you build each layer. They will add important nutrients and will help speed up the composting process:

garden soil or finished compost (high in microorganisms)
½ shovelful on each layer

bone meal, blood meal, or alfalfa meal (high in nitrogen)
½ shovelful on each layer

fish waste or manure (high in nitrogen)
shovelful on each layer

woodstove or fireplace ashes (high in potash and carbon)
shovelful on each layer

crushed rock dust (rich in minerals/feeds microbes)
shovelful on each layer

# Tools and Composting Accessories

The **Soil Maker Composter** is designed for continuous composting. You can add food scraps and garden refuse into the top of the bin as you have them, and remove finished compost from the bottom of the bin as it is ready. This composter has a special lid that captures rainwater to help keep the material inside moist. Measures 34" H x 28" W x 28" L, and holds 12 cubic feet. Thick, UV-protected plastic helps absorb and retain heat.

#30-367 Soil Maker Composter $79.95

The **Rolling Compost Machine** is a 30 inch diameter recycled plastic orb. Fill it up with leaves, grass clippings, or any other organic matter, and roll it around to mix the contents. Eight internal vanes help mix and separate material. 16-inch opening with locking lid. Holds 11 cubic feet.

#30-146 Rolling Compost Machine $99.95

With a supply of red wiggler worms and the special **Worm Bin**, you can compost up to 7 lbs of food scraps each week — all year-round. Line the bin with shredded newspaper or a soilless growing mix, add the worms, and kitchen scraps as you have them. Keep in a 40° to 80°F location. Comes with special aeration grid, foam filter, and moisture tray. 24" L x 19" W x 13½" H. Dark green plastic.

#02-233 Worm Bin $49.95
#02-232 Red Wigglers, 2 pounds (available seasonally) $29.95

includes a lid and three side panels for creating two side-by-side bins.

#02-275 Wire Bin Composter $39.95
#02-268 Extension Kit $34.95

A **Compost Aerating Tool** is handy for managing an enclosed bin. This one is made of galvanized steel, and has "wings" that lift material up from the interior of the bin.

#02-255 Compost Aerator $14.95

Since it's almost impossible to move compost with a shovel, you'll need a **Dished Manure Fork.** This one has a 52"-long wood handle and durable nylon tines. It weighs just over 2 lbs.

#30-687 Compost Fork $29.95

As much as half of the material for your compost pile may be kitchen scraps. These scraps can be stored indoors in an air-tight container. This container should be sized to accommodate the amount of food scraps that you generate in a two- or three-day period. To avoid fruit fly problems, the container must have a snug-fitting lid. Two popular options are a 1½-gallon plastic bucket with a carbon filter inside, and a 4-gallon **Jumbo Compost Pail** with a lift-off lid. If you get fruit flies, non-toxic, citric acid lures will usually control the problem.

#30-435 Odor-Free Compost Pail $16.95
#02-208 Jumbo Compost Pail $18.95
#05-243 Natural Fruit Fly Traps, set of 2 $14.95

The **Green Magic Tumbler** is a recycled plastic barrel mounted on a steel frame. You fill the bin with a batch of organic matter, water well, and then spin the barrel each day for several weeks. Can produce finished compost in just 21 days. Tumbler holds 6 to 7 cubic feet. Measures 27" W x 34" D x 48½" H assembled.

#02-257 Green Magic Tumbler $119.95

A **Wire Bin Composter** is a simple and inexpensive alternative. Made of heavy-gauge steel with a green PVC coating, it has pull-out corner rods for easy access, and a lid to keep out pesky animals. 36" square x 30" high. Holds 22 cubic feet. Extension Kit

Compost activators can help raise the temperature in your compost pile by providing a concentrated dose of microorganisms and protein. **SuperHot Compost Starter** contains a 100% organic blend of nitrogen-enriched peanut meal, microorganisms, alfalfa, cocoa meal, and other ingredients. 8 pounds activates up to 10 bushels of material.

#02-175 SuperHot Compost Starter $10.95

**Ropel Animal Repellent** imparts a foul taste to anything it's sprayed on. Spray on composter, plants, or trash cans.

#05-131 Ropel Animal Repellent, 8 oz $12.95

> Although nearly any organic material can contribute to good compost, there are some that should be avoided, and others to be used only in limited amounts. A truckload of grape pomace or a ton of wet hops from the brewery will be hard to handle, as will be the neighbors if your heap's odor wafts their way. Strive for a commonsense balance in the materials you select, and be sure to add a layer of soil over the heap every time you add materials that might cause odor or attract vermin.
>
> "Be very careful about diseased plants. You may be better off burning them and adding the ashes to your compost than risking inoculating your whole garden with them. Weeds can generally be composted, but be careful to ensure hot composting temperatures if they have produced seed. A few species, such as quack grass and Canada thistle, reproduce readily from the tiniest bit of surviving rhizome and should be avoided entirely.
>
> —from *The Rodale Book of Composting* by Deborah Martin and Grace Gershuny (Rodale, 1992)

## Resources

The Composting Council
114 S. Pitt St.
Alexandria, VA 22314
703-739-2401

Harmonious Technologies
P.O. Box 1865-100
Ojai, CA 93024
*Resource list of composting products ($1).*

Master Composter Program
Seattle Tilth
4649 Sunnyside Ave. N.
Seattle, WA 98103

The Rodale Institute
611 Siegfriedale Road
Kutztown, PA 19530

## Community Composting

Gardener's Supply began composting yard waste for the City of Burlington, Vermont back in 1988. The program has expanded over time to accept all sorts of organic materials, from grass clippings to food waste from local hospitals, restaurants, and even the Ben and Jerry's ice cream factory. The program is now a joint project between the county's solid waste district and the non-profit Intervale Foundation. In 1996, over 2,500 tons of waste was converted into high-quality compost that was sold to backyard gardeners, landscaping companies, and market gardeners.

If you would like to learn more about how to get a composting program started in your own community, please contact Andy Harper at the Intervale Compost Project, 128 Intervale Rd., Burlington, VT 05401. 802-660-4949.

## Kids and Composting

Composting is a great way to get kids interested in recycling and gardening. Check out the Cornell University web site (see page 19) for some interesting project ideas for home and school. Mary Appelhof's book, *Worms Eat My Garbage*, is a helpful and inspiring guide for setting up a classroom-based worm composting program. For a free bulletin entitled "Kids and Composting" contact Gardener's Supply.

# water-efficient gardening

WATER-EFFICIENT GARDENING

Water-efficient gardening makes the most of a precious natural resource. It also saves time and money, and will help you grow a more beautiful and more productive garden. This is true whether you garden in rainy northern Maine or the deserts of Arizona. It is actually surprisingly easy to reduce your water consumption by 50 percent or more, while also reducing the amount of time you spend watering. In some places, mulches, proper siting, and proper plant selection can eliminate the need for irrigation entirely. The way to start using water more efficiently is to begin thinking about your soil, your site, and the way you deliver water.

## Good Soil Requires Less Water

The type of soil in your garden determines how much moisture is available to your plants. All plants must extract the moisture they need from the thin layer of water that clings to each little soil particle. In sandy soils, the particles of soil and the pore spaces between them are so large that water moves through very quickly, and plant roots rarely have time to make good use of the moisture. Conversely, in clay soils, the pore spaces are very small and water moves very slowly, so that roots may be unable to absorb the water they need. Your goal should be to build a crumbly, water-retentive soil that can absorb and release water as it's needed by your plants. Adding organic matter, building raised beds, and breaking up compacted soil layers are all techniques that will make it easier for your plants to absorb water. (See "Building Healthy Soil.")

## Creating Planting Zones Conserves Water

Another way to reduce your garden's need for water is to take advantage of the microclimates within your site. Even a small yard and garden will usually contain several different microclimates: a steep and sandy slope by the road; a damp and shady spot near the downspout; a hot and sunbaked strip along the garage. If you think about your yard and divide it into several different microclimates, or "zones," you can

*Guest Expert*

### Robert Kourik

Drip irrigation is beneficial for most gardens, in most climates. It has more universal applicability than generally recognized where rains are sporadic enough that some form of irrigation is needed.

Healthy soil breathes through tiny pore-spaces, "inhaling" oxygen to stay aerobic and "exhaling" toxic fumes generated by soil life and roots. Scientific studies of vegetables and tree crops consistently show that the top foot of soil, with its abundance of eating-and-excreting life-forms, is the most important area for water and nutrient absorption. Unlike sprinklers, which can easily flood these pore spaces and stress microorganisms or drown tiny root hairs, drip irrigation oozes moisture out so slowly that most of the soil pores remain aerobic. It also concentrates watering in the upper two feet of soil without wastefully flooding deeper soils.

The typical wrong approach to drip irrigation is to place a single emitter at the base of each plant; this will actually dwarf growth because it waters only a fraction of the roots. Since the roots of a plant grow much wider than its foliage and are found mostly in the upper one to two feet of soil, current drip-irrigation wisdom dictates the use of multiple emitters, to cover all of the root zone. Properly done, this produces yields equal to and often greater than with sprinkler use, with substantial water savings.

*Robert Kourik is the author and publisher of* Drip Irrigation for Every Landscape and All Climates, Gray Water Use in the Landscape, *and* Designing and Maintaining Your Edible Landscape—Naturally *(all Metamorphic Press). Kourik's latest book is* The Lavender Garden *(Chronicle Books). He resides on a ridge five miles from the ocean in Occidental, California, where fog drip adds 36 inches to the annual rainfall.*

**Xeriscape Gardening: Water Conservation for the American Landscape** *by Connie Lockhard Ellefson, Tom Stephens, and Doug Welsch* (Macmillan, 1992). A good overview of the topic, with plant recommendations for all regions of the country. Includes information on water-conserving lawn grasses. 324 pages, paperback, $30.00.

**Drip Irrigation for Every Landscape and All Climates** *by Robert Kourik* (Metamorphic Press, 1992). Kourik is the country's leading expert on drip irrigation. This book contains more technical information than most people would ever want, but it is presented in a friendly and accessible manner. 118 pages, paperback, $12.00.

**Xeriscape Plant Guide** *by Rob Proctor* (Fulcrum, 1996). Detailed descriptions of 100 low-water-use plants with photos, illustrations, plant form, range, culture, and recommended landscape usage. 182 pages, paperback, $34.95.

> A water-thrifty garden doesn't mean that you cannot use what are usually thought of as water-thirsty plants, such as azaleas, camellias, roses, or others. The trick is to place these plants in areas where the most effective watering can be used and where these plants will naturally receive more water. These oasis areas will be watered more often than the rest of the landscape, but, since these plants are concentrated in the same area, you will not be wasting water. In a more traditional garden, you have to water the entire yard often just to satisfy the demands of the water-hungry plants that are scattered throughout the yard."
>
> —from *The Water-Thrifty Garden* by Stan DeFreitas (Taylor, 1993)

plants that have similar water needs. For example, lavender, perovskia, and coreopsis will all thrive in a hot, sunny spot, and actually prefer fairly dry soil. Foxgloves, roses, and delphiniums, on the other hand,

locate plants where they are best suited to growing. For example, if you plant primroses in a sunbaked strip by the garage, you'll have to water them every day just to keep them alive, and it is doubtful that they will ever be happy. Imagine the water you would save, not to mention the time and frustration, if you were to substitute coreopsis, yarrow, or creeping zinnias — all sun-lovers that thrive in hot, dry conditions.

Another way to reduce water consumption is to group together

## WATER IS OUR MOST ABUNDANT, YET MOST PRECIOUS RESOURCE

The surface of the Earth is 71% water.

People are 71% water.

Plants are up to 90% water.

Soil is 25% water.

---

# The Seven Principles of Xeriscaping

The word Xeriscape is derived from the Greek word *xeros* meaning "dry." Xeriscape gardening usually means water-thrifty gardening. The following seven Xeriscape Principles can be applied by gardeners throughout the country:

1. **Planning and Design** takes into account the regional and micro-climatic conditions of the site, existing vegetation and topographical conditions, intended use and desires for the site, and the zoning or grouping of plant materials by their water needs.

2. **Soil Analysis** enables proper selection of plants and soil amendments as needed. Organic soil amendments such as compost and kelp meal can enhance the health and growing capabilities of the landscape by improving water drainage, moisture penetration, and the soil's water-holding capacity.

3. **Appropriate Plant Selection** means grouping plants according to their respective water needs, and selecting plants that require a minimal amount of supplemental watering.

Choosing locally adapted plants is one of the easiest ways to ensure success.

4. **Practical Turf Areas** are a planned element of the Xeriscape landscape. Limiting how and where turf is used can result in a significant reduction in water use.

5. **Efficient Irrigation** means watering only when plants need water and watering deeply to encourage deeper root growth for a healthier and more drought-tolerant landscape. Water can be conserved through the use of a properly designed irrigation system.

6. **Use of Mulches** helps soils retain moisture, reduces weed growth, moderates soil temperatures, and prevents erosion. Mulch, stone, pavers, and other "hardscaping" materials can be used where conditions are not conducive to growing quality turf or ground covers.

7. **Appropriate Maintenance** uses a minimal amount of water, fertilizers, and pesticides.

(For more information about Xeriscaping, see "Resources," page 30.)

must have a moist, humusy soil. If you were to plant the delphiniums with the lavender and coreopsis, you would need to irrigate the whole area, just to keep the delphiniums happy. But if you grouped the moisture-lovers together, and put them in a naturally moist area, then grouped the sun-lovers together and put them where the soil is dry, you could easily cut your irrigation requirements in half.

## Water-Wise Lawn and Garden Maintenance

Lawns are usually the thirstiest plants in the home landscape. Besides consuming more than their fair share of water, most lawns also require fertilizers, pest controls, fungicides, and at least weekly maintenance with power equipment. Reducing the amount of lawn area in your yard can save an astonishing amount of water — especially if you live where summers are hot and dry. Ask yourself how much lawn you really need. Can you imagine reserving a modest area of lawn for croquet, badminton, and picnicking, and converting the rest into a combination of deck areas, paths, ground covers, hosta glades, naturalized shrub plantings, and daylilies? (See "Backyard Biodiversity.")

When you want to water your yard and garden, do so when the wind is calm and the sun is not at its hottest. Otherwise 30 to 40 percent of the water you apply will be wasted. Once the growing season is underway, cover all exposed soil areas with a thick layer of mulch. Mulch gives gardens and landscapes a neat, finished look; it also reduces watering chores significantly. Mulch keeps soil temperatures cooler, and prevents moisture loss from the soil surface. By absorbing rain and overhead irrigation, mulches also help to reduce erosion and runoff problems. If you are using a drip irrigation system or soaker hose, position the hose beneath the mulch so the mulch doesn't absorb the irrigation water.

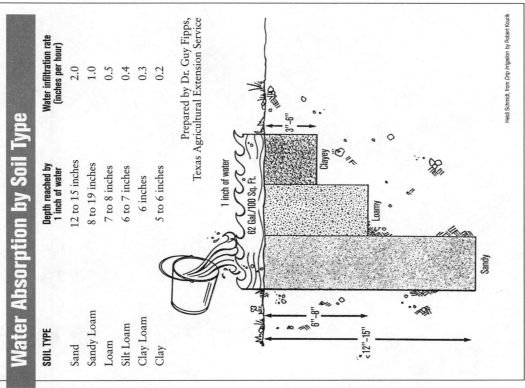

## Water Absorption by Soil Type

| SOIL TYPE | Depth reached by 1 inch of water | Water infiltration rate (inches per hour) |
| --- | --- | --- |
| Sand | 12 to 15 inches | 2.0 |
| Sandy Loam | 8 to 19 inches | 1.0 |
| Loam | 7 to 8 inches | 0.5 |
| Silt Loam | 6 to 7 inches | 0.4 |
| Clay Loam | 6 inches | 0.3 |
| Clay | 5 to 6 inches | 0.2 |

Prepared by Dr. Guy Fipps, Texas Agricultural Extension Service

Heidi Schmidt, from *Drip Irrigation* by Robert Kourik

## HOW MUCH TO WATER

The type of soil in your yard and garden determines how frequently and how long you should water. As a general rule:

Loamy soil — water moderately and evenly

Sandy soil — water for short periods, more frequently

Clayey soil — water for short periods, less often

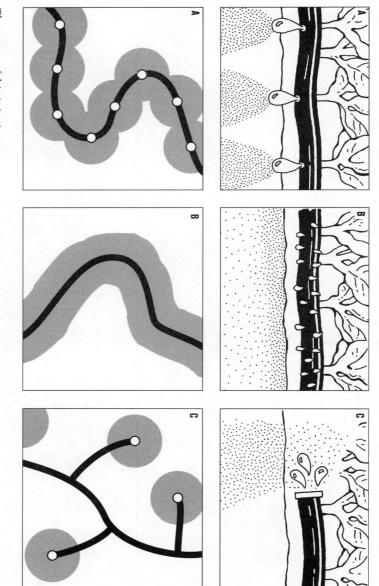

*Three types of drip irrigation systems: A) in-line drippers are factory-extruded at regularly spaced intervals; B) soaker hose emits water along its entire length; C) emitters are inserted as needed into non-porous hose or at the end of feeder lines from the main hose.*

# Smart Alternatives for Delivering Water

There are a variety of sensible, efficient ways to deliver water to your plants.

**RAINWATER.** Cisterns for collecting rainwater used to be common throughout rural America. Today, gardeners are rediscovering their practical good sense. By simply directing the rain gutters from your roof into an old wine cask, pickle barrel, or modern plastic rainbarrel, you can collect hundreds of gallons of free, naturally soft rainwater. If possible, you can use gravity to deliver the water right to your garden; otherwise you can dip your watering can right into the barrel. Just ¼ inch of rain falling on a 1000-square-foot roof will yield 150 gallons of clear, soft rainwater for your garden.

**OVERHEAD SPRINKLERS.** People who water on a windy day, or who allow their sprinklers to drench the street or sidewalk, have given overhead sprinklers a bad name. When not used wisely, overhead sprinklers can waste 50 to 70 percent of the water they emit. But used correctly, overhead sprinklers can be an inexpensive and relatively efficient watering solution. You can choose from impulse sprinklers, oscillating sprinklers, revolving or rotating sprinklers, stationary sprinklers, and traveling sprinklers. Each type has its advantages — you'll need to choose based on what's most appropriate for your own lawn and garden. The key is to position the sprinkler carefully, and to monitor how much water you are delivering.

For best results, attach an automatic timer to your overhead sprinkler, and adjust your watering schedule to the weather and season. Most water waste happens when people program their irrigation system for midsummer conditions as soon as they turn it on in the spring, and then don't reset the timer until fall. By just paying attention to the weather, watching your plants, and looking at the soil, you can reduce water consumption dramatically.

**SOAKER HOSES.** Soaker hose is "leaky" or porous hose that weeps water along its entire length. These hoses are easy to use — just snake them through plantings and turn on the water. Foliage stays dry, and water is delivered directly to the root zone for greatest efficiency. Depending on soil type, these hoses usually wet a 2- to 3-foot-wide band of soil. Some can be left in place year-round, buried as much as a foot deep. They are typically made of foam, vinyl, or recycled rubber. For best results, you should use a timer, a water pressure regulator, and a filter to screen out debris that may clog the pores of the hose.

**SUBSURFACE IRRIGATION SYSTEMS.** Underground irrigation systems are usually installed by a professional landscaping or irrigation firm. Steel, brass, copper, or plastic piping is installed below grade, and pop-up sprinkler heads are permanently attached at specific sites. Sizing the system for proper water coverage, and taking into account water pressure and elevation changes, is a task best handled by a professional. Consult *The Complete Irrigation Workbook* by Larry Keesen (Franzak & Foster, 1995) for details on design, installation, and maintenance of a professionally installed subsurface irrigation system. If you want to design and install your own system, take a look at *Watering Systems for Lawns and Gardens* by R. Dodge Woodson (see "Other Good Books").

**DRIP IRRIGATION.** There are two basic types of drip irrigation systems: blank hose with emitters that you insert where needed, and in-line dripper tape that has emitters molded right into the hose at one- or two-foot intervals. Both of these systems are easy for the homeowner to install

## Other Good Books

**The Water-Thrifty Garden** by *Stan DeFreitas* (Taylor, 1993).
A good overview of Xeriscape gardening. Focused on Southern and Western gardens. Plant list scribes and recommends best trees, shrubs, and perennials. 160 pages, paperback, $19.95.

**Watering Systems for Lawn and Garden** by *R. Dodge Woodson* (Storey, 1996).
Written by a master plumber, this is a do-it-yourselfer's guide to using sprinklers, drip and soaker systems, alternative water sources, and pumps. 144 pages, paperback, $16.95.

**Water-Conserving Gardens and Landscapes** by *John M. O'Keefe* (Storey, 1992).
Based on the author's landscaping experience in California, this is a clear and straightforward overview of low-water-use landscaping. It covers soil management, hardscaping, irrigation systems, and more. Plant recommendations have a west coast orientation. 160 pages, paperback, $12.95.

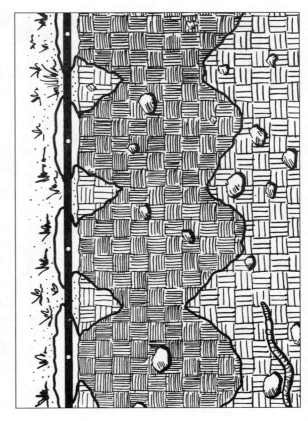

*Drip irrigation creates a zone of continuous moisture just below the soil surface.*
- Gardener's Supply Company

# Water-Smart Tips

and drooping leaves is normal on a hot, sunny day. If plants look that way in the mornings, though, it's time to water.

🌿 Your watering efforts should be focused on the upper 12 to 18 inches of soil, where the root systems of your plants are concentrated.

🌿 Cultivate before watering, so hard-baked surfaces absorb rather than shed water.

🌿 Plant thickly and in wide rows to keep the soil shaded. This will reduce evaporation and help collect dew.

🌿 Block the wind with netting or trees to reduce moisture loss.

🌿 Use shade netting or natural shade to help young plants get established.

🌿 Keep your garden weeded to reduce competition for moisture.

🌿 Don't be too quick to water. Wait for signs of water stress. Dull foliage

## Resources

**The National Xeriscape Council, Inc.**
P.O. Box 767936
Roswell, GA 30076
*Offers educational information, various programs, and a quarterly newsletter.*

and maintain. Because water is delivered directly to the root zone, foliage stays dry, and there is little or no water lost to evaporation or runoff.

Though drip irrigation systems have emitters that "leak" water at specific points, the water spreads out underground into a continuous zone of moisture. This encourages deep root systems, which help plants to maintain their vigor, even in times of drought. Because drip irrigation systems concentrate moisture below

ground, the soil surface remains fairly dry, which reduces evaporative moisture loss as well as weed growth.

Drip irrigation systems that have solid delivery tubing and emitters that are inserted where needed are ideal for container plantings, or if you only need to water a few plants within a large area. As a general rule, factory-extruded in-line dripper hose is the easiest and most foolproof system for gardens and landscaping. This type of hose is manufactured with drippers spaced at regular intervals right in the hose. You simply choose the dripper spacing and emitter rate that suits your plantings, soils, and climate. Though dripper line with 1/2-gallon-per-hour drippers, spaced at 12-inch intervals, is most popular, you can also get

One of the key elements in Xeriscape [water-efficient] garden design is the integration of plants with hardscapes and the extensive use of gravel, stone, pebbles, or organic mulches to define and set off different garden zones. Hardscapes of brick, stone, and vine-covered arbors . . . require no watering and very little maintenance, while providing practical user-oriented spaces. When thoughtfully incorporated into the overall garden design, they tie the garden together into a unified house and garden landscape of charm and practicality. A landscape designer may describe it as tonal contrasts or the contrast between inert and organic. Nevertheless, the combination of drought-resistant plants and hardscapes creates a soothing and pleasing effect that defies accurate description. The closest description would be the word 'harmony.' The surprising thing about water-conserving landscaping is that you can use a great deal of hardscape and still achieve the effect of a lush, natural-looking landscape."

—from *Water-Conserving Gardens and Landscapes*
by John M. O'Keefe (Storey, 1992)

## Garden Gear

**Netafim Dripper Line** is the drip irrigation system of choice at Gardener's Supply Company. This dripper line has emitters that are pre-manufactured right inside the tubing so that there are no external devices to be damaged or knocked off. The tubing is rugged, UV-stabilized, and can be left outdoors all winter. The emitters are pressure compensating so the dripper line can be installed on steep slopes with no leak rate fluctuations. The water pressure compensation range is 7 to 70 psi. Emitters have a filter, turbulent water flow path, and a floating pressure control diaphragm which combine to dislodge debris and prevent clogging. Netafim Techline has a 20-year life expectancy.

The expandable **Netafim Starter Kit** gives you 50' of dripper line (12" emitter spacing, .6 GPH) which can be cut to suit your garden. The **Hardware Kit** includes 5' of blank tubing, one spin lok "T", and one spin lok line end. You need one Hardware Kit for each run or row. The **Tap Kit** connects the system to a standard faucet and ends the system with a spin lok line end. For on/off control, you will need one spin lok zone control valve for each row.

#06-421 50' Dripper Line $24.95
#06-472 Hardware Kit $3.95
#06-423 Tap Kit $2.50
#06-438 Spin Lok Zone Control Valve $5.50

Direct your downspout into a **Deluxe Rainbarrel**, and you will have a plentiful supply of naturally soft rainwater to refresh thirsty plants. This one is dark green, and holds 75 gallons of water. Comes with an overflow hose, safety grid for the top, and a removable debris screen.

#06-323 Deluxe Rainbarrel $99.95

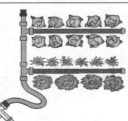

**Electronic Water Timers** can be complicated, but this one is not. Set it once, and your yard or garden will get the water it needs, even if you are away. Uses four AA batteries (not included).

#06-125 Electronic Water Timer $59.95

The **RainTower Sprinkler** features a fold-out tripod base and telescoping pole that adjusts to the height of your crops: 41" or 72". It waters in full or partial circles, up to 80' in diameter.

#06-324 RainTower Sprinkler $54.95

**PermaFlow Hose** is reinforced with a dual radial knit mesh for high burst resistance. It is also wrapped with a premium rubber and vinyl casing for all-weather flexibility. ⅝" diameter.

#06-144 PermaFlow Hose, 50' $28.95

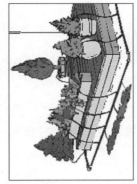

Attach a **4-Tap Distributor** to your outdoor faucet, and you can connect four different hoses at one time. Each tap has its own on/off valve. Includes click-on connectors.

#06-132 4-Tap Distributor $29.95

A long-reach **Spray Wand** lets you extend your reach into flower beds or across garden rows. This one has an adjustable head with 4 different spray patterns, and a thumb valve to adjust water flow. 24" long.

#30-234 Multi-Function Spray Wand $24.95

**Hydro-Grow Soaker Hose** leaks water slowly and evenly along its entire length, watering a 3-foot band of soil. Place it on the soil surface, or bury it 2" to 4" underground. Comes with an end cap and hose fittings. Extra fittings and longer lengths are available.

#06-361 Hydro-Grow Soaker Hose, 50' $19.95

Keeping track of natural rainfall lets you adjust your watering schedule for optimum efficiency. This **Rain Gauge** has a big red float indicator that can be read from 25 feet away. Mounting bracket is included.

#06-107 Rain Gauge $12.50

You can water as many as 10 patio containers from one hose line with this inexpensive **Container Irrigation System**. Attach a water timer, and your plants will be tended automatically for weeks at a time. Includes 60' of microtubing and 10 drippers.

#30-235 Container Irrigation System $19.95

*The test shown above (and described on page 5) will help you determine how easy or difficult it is for water to reach the root zone of your plants.*

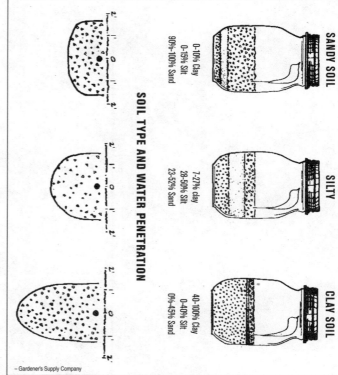

**SOIL TYPE AND WATER PENETRATION**

**SANDY SOIL**
0-10% Clay
0-15% Silt
90%-100% Sand

**SILTY**
7-27% clay
28-50% Silt
23-52% Sand

**CLAY SOIL**
40-100% Clay
0-40% Silt
0%-45% Sand

– Gardener's Supply Company

¹/₂-gallon- or 1-gallon-per-hour emitters spaced 12, 18, 24, or 36 inches apart.

When using dripper line to irrigate a wide garden bed, you simply run the hose in parallel rows. As a general rule, the spacing between the dripper lines is usually the same interval as the emitters are spaced in the line itself. (A dripper line with 12-inch emitter spacing can be laid out in parallel rows 12 inches apart to create a grid of continuous moisture.) This spacing may need to be somewhat closer in sandy soils, or further apart in heavy soils.

## Determining How Much to Water

Though you may have heard the old adage that lawns and gardens should receive an inch of water a week, this is really far too simplistic an answer. In fact, this figure will vary greatly depending on the crop, competition from neighboring plants, temperature and humidity, wind, whether the ground is mulched or not, how much natural rainfall you have had, and what type of soil the plants are growing in. Water-efficient gardening requires you to keep an eye on all of these environmental factors. It also asks you to consider how much water your plants really need for good health and peak performance.

---

Most irrigation specialists agree that gardeners should strive to maintain a relatively consistent moisture content in the soil — similar to that of a well-wrung sponge. If the soil is allowed to become too dry, plants are stressed and delicate root hairs are often injured. If the soil gets too wet, both roots and soil life can be suffocated. The goal should be to replace soil moisture as it is lost through plant growth, transpiration, and evaporation. For best results, this should happen before the soil becomes parched and hard. Soil that is already moist absorbs water much more quickly (without runoff) and that water spreads out quickly through capillary action.

The best way to ensure that you water only when necessary is to simply dig down into the top 12 inches of soil and take a look. Some gardeners may prefer to be more routine about watering, and like to follow the one-inch-a-week schedule. Start by using a rain gauge to keep track of natural rainfall, and subtract that figure from your weekly watering schedule. If you are using overhead irrigation (a sprinkler), you can figure out how much water you are applying each week by putting a plastic bucket in the garden (away from obstructions), and measuring how much water has accumulated in the bucket after each watering session.

If you have a soaker hose or drip irrigation system, it is relatively easy to figure out how long you need to operate your system in order to deliver one inch of water per week. Start with the fact that it takes 625 gallons of water to cover a 1000-square-foot garden with 1 inch of water. To determine the number of gallons of water required to put 1 inch of water on your garden, multiply 625 by your square feet of garden area, then divide by 1000 to get the number of gallons per week. Then determine how much water your system puts out in an hour (the leak rate and total footage of soaker hose, or the number of emitters in your irrigation system and the leak rate). Last, divide the number of gallons per week you need to deliver, by the amount of water your irrigation system distributes per hour. For a more complete explanation of how to calculate water delivery for different kinds of irrigation systems, consult *Drip Irrigation for Every Landscape and All Climates* by Robert Kourik (see "Favorite Books").

The best time of day to water depends on the situation. If you are in a hot, dry climate and water is precious, water in the evening (or the very early morning) so losses to evaporation are kept to a minimum. In humid areas it is a good idea to water only on sunny days, and always by lunchtime so that the plant leaves have a chance to dry off before evening; otherwise you are creating a good environment for bacterial and fungal infections to develop . . . .

In cold climates like ours it makes sense to water early in the day for another reason: the soil is cooled down by the irrigation water — especially in early spring, when soil and water are at their coldest — and if the sun has a chance to heat the soil right back up, the plants will suffer that much less. This is even more important when watering seedlings: professional nurserymen often heat their greenhouse irrigation water to avoid temperature shock on their seedlings."

—from *Step by Step Organic Vegetable Gardening* by Shepherd Ogden (HarperCollins, 1992)

## Web Sites

Water Wise Gardening
http://www.ebmud.com/wateron/garden.html
*Tips from the East Bay Municipal Water District in Oakland, California. Links to agencies, universities, and research groups.*

Northwest News Home & Garden
http://www.nwnews.com/nwissues/v2om23/home2.html
*Seven steps to the water-wise garden.*

# starting
# plants
# from seed

When mail-order catalogs and local garden centers are bursting with an astonishing variety of plants of all kinds, why would anyone want to bother starting their own plants from seed? But millions of gardeners do, and here are a few of the reasons why:

**IT'S LESS EXPENSIVE.** A packet of seeds usually costs about $2.00. Depending on the type of seeds you plan to grow, you will usually get from fifteen to three hundred seedlings from each packet of seeds. That same $2.00 would buy one six-pack of transplants from the local nursery. With a $20 investment in seeds, you can plant a 12-by-12-foot garden and have a whole summer's worth of food and flowers.

**MORE TO CHOOSE FROM.** In the tomato category alone, you will find hundreds of varieties to choose from, including cherry tomatoes, yellow tomatoes, plum tomatoes, patio tomatoes, heirloom tomatoes, and even tomatoes that are bred for drought resistance. Most of these special varieties are not available at your local nursery.

**HIGHER-QUALITY PLANTS SUITED TO YOUR SCHEDULE.** Your seedlings will thrive on your individual attention and tender loving care. With a healthier, stronger start, they will yield a bigger and earlier harvest. By growing your own, you can also have seedlings whenever you want them. Start your tomatoes early to harvest the first ripe tomato in the neighborhood. Stagger your plantings of petunias to maintain a fresh-looking windowbox display all summer long. Plant a second crop of broccoli in midsummer for a long fall harvest, or a succession of hardy salad greens that can be harvested until Thanksgiving.

**PRIDE AND SATISFACTION.** Beyond these practical reasons for starting your own seedlings, you will enjoy the simple satisfaction of nurturing tiny seedlings into beautiful and productive plants. There is nothing quite like it — especially in the dead of winter!

## Planning Ahead

Mail-order seed catalogs provide a wealth of important information that can help you select the plant varieties that are best suited to your location and interests. Cold-climate gardeners should look for melon varieties that are ready eighty days after planting rather than one hundred twenty days. Flower gardeners may want to find a certain shade of pink zinnias or a heat-tolerant variety of pansies. Southern gardeners can look for tomato varieties that set fruit at high temperatures and withstand drought.

## *Guest Expert*
## Carolyn Ormsbee

Many gardeners have heard about planting by the moon, and I'm often asked what this really means. Gardening by the moon phases and zodiac signs is an ancient tradition, and there are many gardeners who still plant their seeds on "moon favorable" days. The goal is to synchronize your sowing with the rhythmic powers exerted by the lunar phases.

When the light of the moon is *waxing* (growing in size from a quarter phase to full moon), sow seeds that produce above-ground crops (broccoli, beans, tomatoes, or squash). When the moon is *waning* from full to half, plant root crops such as beets, carrots, and turnips. Generally, no planting is done on the day of a new or full moon. Serious moon gardeners also take into account the 12 astrological signs of the moon for planting, harvesting, and even weeding. Most calendars show the moon phases, and you can find detailed charts on lunar and zodiac signs in farmers' almanacs and astrological books.

*Carolyn Ormsbee is the Gardener's Supply Staff Horticulturalist.*

## *Favorite Books*

**The New Seed-Starter's Handbook** by *Nancy Bubel* (Rodale, 1988). The best all-around seed-starting handbook. Comprehensive enough to satisfy the master gardener, yet the friendly tone is not intimidating for beginners. Covers all the basics for starting flowers and vegetables, as well as planting by the moon, growing wildflowers, starting woody plants from seed, collecting and storing seeds, and more. Illustrations throughout. 385 pages, paperback, $15.95.

**From Seed to Bloom** by *Eileen Powell* (Garden Way Publishing, 1995). The essential book for anyone who starts flowers from seed. Also addresses herbs. Describes each plant's germination requirements, time of bloom, growth habit, soil preferences, hardiness, and more for over 500 different plants. Easy to read, with line drawing of each plant. Good coverage of seed-starting basics. 312 pages, paperback, $19.95.

**Burpee Seed Starter: A Guide to Growing Flower, Vegetable, and Herb Seeds Indoors and Outdoors** by *Maureen Heffernan* (Macmillan, 1997). A valuable new guide with easy-to-follow sowing and growing information for 300 different plants. General instructions for indoor and outdoor germination, plus tips for specific types of plants. 272 pages, paperback, $19.95.

# GLOSSARY

**Cotyledon** — The first leaf or set of leaves that emerge when a seed sprouts. These leaves often look completely different from the plant's "true" leaves, which will emerge next.

**Dormancy** — A somewhat mysterious phenomenon that prevents a seed from sprouting until conditions are right to allow it to reach maturity. Some seeds need to be "fooled" into breaking dormancy.

**Scarification** — Scratching or notching the seed coat to hasten germination. This is not necessary for most garden seeds.

**Stratification** — Exposing seeds to a period of cold temperatures in order to break dormancy. Not required for most garden seeds.

---

If you are a beginning seed starter, start with "easy seeds" that are quick to germinate and that don't require a lot of extra fussing (see page 37 for some recommendations). It's easy to get carried away and buy too many different seed packets (especially when you are ordering in the middle of winter!) If you are starting seeds for the first time, you may want to limit yourself to no more than ten different types of seedlings.

## Choosing the Right Containers

You can start your seeds in almost any type of container as long as it is at least 2 to 3 inches deep and has some drainage holes. There are many different seed-starting containers on the market, including peat flats, jiffy pellets, and flats with individual growing cells. (The products and supplies section on page 42 offers some suggestions.) For tomatoes and peppers, you may want to start your plants in small containers and then "pot up" to larger containers. Some gardeners always plant their seeds in little rows in a larger flat. Once they're up, the tiny seedlings get separated and replanted into individual containers.

## The Best Growing Medium

To provide the optimum growing conditions, and to avoid disease and insect problems, seeds should be started in a soilless growing mix, not in garden soil. A good soilless mix is a moist and spongy blend of sphagnum moss, vermiculite, and perlite. The finer the texture the better. You can purchase a ready-mixed blend, or mix your own, using 1/3 vermiculite, 1/3 perlite, 1/3 milled sphagnum moss. Remember that soilless mixes contain few, if any, nutrients. You will need to start feeding your seedlings with a weak fertilizer solution as soon as they germinate, and continue to feed them weekly until you transplant them into the garden.

Once your seedlings are up and growing, you can transplant them into a coarser growing medium that contains some garden soil or sifted compost. A standard blend may contain 1/3 compost, 1/3 perlite or vermiculite, and 1/3

---

# What is in a Soilless Growing Medium

**Sphagnum moss.** Sphagnum moss is a dehydrated bog plant that is able to absorb ten to twenty times its weight in water. It is used to retain water and provide texture. For seed starting, look for moss that has been "milled" to remove debris and achieve a fine consistency. Sphagnum moss is naturally acidic (pH 3.5), so if you are creating your own soil blend, you should add some limestone to counteract the acidity. Sphagnum moss also has some fungus-inhibiting properties.

**Vermiculite.** Vermiculite is mica rock that has been heated until it expands into what look like tiny multi-paged books. It is used to retain water and provide texture for strong root growth. Vermiculite is pH neutral, sterile, and insoluble. It contains some magnesium and potassium, and also has a high cation exchange capacity, which means it is able to absorb fertilizers and release them to plant roots when needed.

**Perlite.** Perlite is made from crushed lava that has been heated until the particles "pop" into white, sponge-like kernels. It is used to retain water and provide good aeration. Perlite is sterile and pH neutral. It holds three to four times its weight in water.

**Sharp sand.** Coarse builder's sand is the best type of sand to use in a growing mix. Do not use beach or riverbed sand. The purpose of sand is to add texture, provide aeration, and improve drainage.

**Sifted compost.** If you are not an experienced seedstarter, and are unable to sterilize your compost, stick with a soilless growing medium. Most compost and garden soil contains pathogens that are not harmful to established plants, but can be harmful to tender seedlings. Once your seedlings are several weeks old, and you are transplanting them into larger containers, you can add compost or garden soil to your soilless blend. This will provide some beneficial nutrients, and will help your seedlings get used to the bacteria and other microorganisms they will soon experience in the garden.

> Seeds don't spring to life when you plant them. Seeds are alive. Inside even the most minute, dust-like grain of seed is a living plant.
>
> True, it's in embryonic form, possessing only the most rudimentary parts, but it lives, and it is not completely passive. At levels we can't see, but laboratory scientists can measure, seeds carry on respiration. They absorb oxygen and give off carbon dioxide. They also absorb water from the air. Thus, seeds maintain their spark of life — dim though it may be — until conditions are right for them to complete their destiny as germinated plants."
>
> —from *The New Seed-Starters Handbook* by Nancy Bubel (Rodale, 1988)

sphagnum moss. This will help ensure that your plants have access to some soil nutrients, and it will also help prepare them for life in the garden.

## Timing Your Planting

Seeds sprout and plants grow at different rates, so timing is very important. Some seeds, such as celery and leeks, need to be started twelve weeks before they are transplanted into the garden. Others, including cucumbers and sunflowers, need only three or four weeks (and will suffer if started too early). Check the back of the seed packet to find the recommended seed-starting times. If you plan to start more than a packet or two of seeds, it helps to chart out a weekly seed-starting schedule, counting back from the date you plan to set out the transplants.

If you will be growing your seedlings in a greenhouse or a very warm room, you should subtract at least a week from the recommended planting date. Heat promotes faster growth, and you may find yourself with giant plants that are ready to be put out into the garden before warm weather arrives.

Seedlings that are started very early may need to be transplanted into larger containers after three or four weeks. This is especially true if you broadcast your seeds in flats rather than planting them in individual growing cells. The sooner your plants are put into individual cells with plenty of root space, the happier they will be.

## Planting Your Seeds

The growing medium should be thoroughly moistened before it is placed in your seed-starting containers. (Warm water works best.)

### EASY SEEDLINGS TO START INDOORS

| | |
|---|---|
| broccoli | pansies |
| cabbage | peppers |
| coleus | petunias |
| eggplant | sunflowers |
| impatiens | tomatoes |
| marigolds | zinnias |

### Small or More Difficult Seeds

| | |
|---|---|
| aster | lupin |
| celery | lobelia |
| cleome | parsley |
| columbine | primrose |
| larkspur | snapdragon |

# How to Plant Very Tiny Seeds

1. Fill a clean pot or seed flat with a well-moistened, finely-textured soilless growing medium.
2. Add a teaspoon of granulated sugar to the seed packet and shake to mix.
3. Tap the packet gently over the soil surface to disperse seeds evenly, soon as seeds sprout.
4. Do not cover seed with soil. Establish good soil contact by misting from above or by pressing seeds into the soil with the back of a dry spoon.
5. Set pot or flat in a shallow tray of water until the soil becomes fully moistened.
6. Cover pot or flat with a piece of glass or clear plastic and put under lights. Remove covering as soon as seeds sprout.

—from *Greenhouse Gardener's Companion*, by Shane Smith (Fulcrum, 1993)

Fill the flats or containers to within ¼ to ½ inch of the top. You are now ready to sow your seeds. But before you do so, take another look at the seed packet for any special information about pre-chilling, pre-soaking, a preference for light or darkness, or special temperature requirements.

Seeds can either be scattered on the soil surface or placed individually into each growing cell. Resist the temptation to sow too thickly! Most seeds should be covered with a fine layer of soil. Unless the seeds require light to germinate (such as snapdragons), or are too tiny to tolerate being covered (such as petunias), you should cover the seeds to about three times their thickness. Gently moisten the growing medium (using a mister or with dribbles of water) to ensure good contact between the seeds and the soil. Label each flat, row, or container with a wood or plastic marker so you can identify them later. Save the seed packet for reference.

**TEMPERATURE.** The temperatures for optimum germination listed on seed packets refer to soil temperature, not air temperature. Though some seeds germinate best at a soil temperature of 60°F, and some at 85°, most prefer a temperature of about 78° (see page 43). Remember that the soil temperature in a drafty 65° room will be even colder than 65°. If the soil is too cold, seeds may take much longer to germinate, or they may not germinate at all. To provide additional warmth, you can place the containers on top of a warm refrigerator, television, or heat

## *Other Good Books*

**Park's Success With Seeds** *by Ann Reilly* (Scribner, 1982).
This book may be a bit dated, but to our knowledge, it is the only one that has closeup photos of each type of young seedling. The focus is about four-fifths flower, one-fifth vegetables. 364 pages, hardcover, $16.95.

**Secrets of Plant Propagation** *by Lewis Hill* (GardenWay Publishing, 1985).
The author covers seed-starting basics, but this book will be of greatest value if you are attempting to grow woody plants from seed or cuttings. 168 pages, paperback, $16.95.

**Plant Propagation Made Easy** *by Alan Toogood* (Timber Press, 1994).
Good technical information from a popular British author, presented in a very easy-to-read format. Covers seeds, cuttings, air layering, fern spores, and more. Uses both Latin and common names. 300 pages, paperback, $15.95.

## What to Feed Your Seedlings

**Seaweed/kelp extracts.** Kelp's almost magical effect on plants has been well documented. It seems to be especially effective on seedlings, promoting vigor, cold hardiness, and pest and disease resistance. Apply a dilute amount to the soil or foliage several times during seedling development and at transplanting time. Kelp is not considered a fertilizer, because it does not provide any major nutrients. It should always be used in combination with a complete organic fertilizer.

**Fish emulsion.** An excellent source of trace minerals, as well as micro- and macronutrients. It can be smelly, so be cautious about using it indoors. Ideal for young seedlings during their first few weeks in the garden.

**Complete organic fertilizers.** These specially formulated blends contain plant nutrients and organic compounds that promote strong root growth and overall vigor. They ensure that your plants get off to a strong start by providing a balanced supply of micro- and macronutrients including the Big Three: nitrogen, phosphorus, and potassium.

## Common Questions about Seed Starting

**Q** Only one-quarter of my seeds germinated. What went wrong?

**A** There are a number of factors that affect seed germination. Check the seed packet to determine if all the requirements for temperature and light were met. If the soil was cold and excessively wet, the seeds may have rotted. Dig up one of the seeds and examine it. If it is swollen and soft, the seed has rotted and you will need to start over. If the soil was too dry, the seeds may not have germinated or may have dried up before their roots could take hold.

**Q** My seedlings are spindly. What can I do?

**A** Plants grow tall and leggy when there is insufficient light. Use grow lights as recommended in the section on lighting (below). You can also try lowering the room temperature and reducing the amount of fertilizer you apply.

**Q** The leaves on my tomatoes are starting to look purple along the veins and on the underside of the leaves. What's happening?

**A** Purple leaves are an indication that the plant is not receiving enough phosphorus. If you have been using a dilute fertilizer for the first three to four weeks of the seedling's life, it may be time to increase the fertilizer to full strength. The phosphorus content (the middle number on the fertilizer analysis) should be at least a three.

**Q** My seedlings were growing well until all of a sudden they toppled over at the base. What happened?

**A** When the stems of young seedlings become withered and topple over, they have probably been killed by a soil-borne fungus called "damping off." This fungus is difficult to eradicate once it is present in the soil, but you can avoid it by using a sterile, soilless growing medium, and by providing good air circulation. If you see signs of this fungus, transplant the healthy plants out of the container and throw away the diseased plants and soil. Water less and improve the air circulation.

**Q** Mold is growing on the top of the soil surface. It doesn't appear to be hurting my plants, but should I be concerned?

**A** Mold is an indication that the growing medium is too wet. It will not harm your plants as long as you take quick action. Withhold water for a few days and try to increase air circulation around the containers by using a small fan. You can also scrape some of the mold off or try transplanting the seedlings into fresh growing medium.

---

mat, or keep them in a warm room until the seeds germinate. Just be sure to get your seedlings to a sunny window or under lights as soon as you see little sprouts emerging through the soil surface.

After germination, most seedlings grow best if the air temperature is below 70°F. If temperatures are too warm (over 75°), the seedlings will grow too fast and get weak and leggy. Most seedlings grow fine in air temperatures as low as 50°, as long as soil temperature is maintained at about 65°–70°. You can keep the soil warm by using a heat mat, and can monitor the temperature with a soil thermometer (see products, page 42).

**LIGHT.** Most seeds don't require light to germinate, but as soon as they sprout, they need to be placed in a south-facing window or under lights. Check your seeds daily. Seeds that germinate and start to grow without adequate light will become tall and leggy — a condition that is almost impossible to correct.

Most seedlings require twelve to fourteen hours of direct light to manufacture enough food for healthy stems and leaves. The characteristic legginess that often occurs when seedlings are grown on a windowsill indicates that the plants are not receiving enough light intensity, or enough hours of light. (For more information see "Growing Under Lights.") If your seedlings are in a south-facing window, you can enhance the incoming light by covering a piece of cardboard with aluminum foil and placing it in back of the seedlings. The light will bounce off the foil and back onto the seedlings.

- Seeds have their own internal timeclocks. Even with the right conditions, some seeds take one day to germinate (turnips), some take twelve days (parsley), some take fifty (astilbe), and some take two or three years!

- The "number of days" listed on a seed packet refers to the time between transplanting into the garden and your first harvest. It does not include the time period between germination and viable transplant.

- The most crucial time in the life of a seedling is the period when it is sprouting. It must find adequate moisture, light, and warmth when it emerges from the seed coat.

## SEEDLINGS THAT HATE TO BE MOVED

The following plants do not like to have their roots disturbed. For best results, plant these seeds directly in the garden.

| | |
|---|---|
| Beans | Cucumbers |
| Beets | Dill |
| Carrots | Melons |
| Chervil | Poppies |
| Chinese | Portulaca |
| cabbage | Pumpkins |
| Coriander | Squash |
| Corn | |

If you do not have a south-facing window, you will need to use artificial lights. When growing seedlings under lights, you can use a combination of cool and warm fluorescents, or full-spectrum fluorescent bulbs. The familiar incandescent bulb that lights our homes produces too much heat in relation to the light given off. It also lacks the blue spectrum light that keeps seedlings stocky and dark green.

Seedlings need a high intensity of light. The bulbs should be placed very close to the plants — no more than three inches away from the foliage — and should be left on for twelve to fourteen hours per day. If you are growing your

- Avoid using peat moss in a seed-starting mix. It is very acidic, rough-textured, and difficult to keep moist. Sphagnum moss is what you are looking for.

seedlings on a windowsill, you may need to supplement with a few hours of artificial light, especially during the winter months.

**MOISTURE.** Germination requires consistent moisture. It is important that the soil be kept moist but not soggy to prevent the seeds from rotting. There are different ways to achieve this. Some gardeners cover their flats with clear plastic until the seeds germinate. Some seed-starting systems have a plastic cover to help retain moisture.

As soon as your seeds have sprouted, you should remove any plastic covering to reduce moisture and humidity levels. Check the soil every day to ensure that it is moist, not wet. Too much moisture will retard root growth and lead to disease problems. Letting the soil dry out a bit between waterings helps prevent molds and fungus from growing on the soil surface.

Your seedlings will be much happier if you water them with room-temperature water rather than ice-cold tap water. If your water supply is chlorinated, fill some plastic jugs or your watering can and let the water sit overnight so the chlorine dissipates. Don't use water that has been through a water softener. The sodium may kill your seedlings. Try to make sure that the moisture reaches the bottom of the growing container. You want your seedlings to stretch their roots out and create a nice, fat rootball. You might want to fill the sink or a waterproof tray with an inch or two of water and set your containers right in the water. Just be sure to remove them from the water when the soil surface feels fully moist to the touch.

**AIR AND HUMIDITY.** Most seedlings like a humidity level of 50 to 70 percent. Higher humidity levels and poor air circulation can lead to fungus growth on the soil surface and disease problems. If the air in your house is very dry, you can keep your seedlings happy by setting them on capillary matting, or in a waterproof tray filled with small stones and a little water. If your plants are in a small room, you may consider running a small fan to keep the air circulating.

**FERTILIZING.** Once your seedlings develop their second set of true leaves, it is time to start feeding them. Young seedlings are very tender and can't tolerate a full dose of fertilizer. Baby them with a half-strength dose until they are three or four weeks old. After that, you should start full-strength fertilizing every week or two. Since your seedlings are growing in a sterile, soilless medium, fertilizing them is absolutely critical. For best results, use an organic fertilizer that contains trace elements to ensure that you are providing all the major and minor nutrients.

**THINNING AND POTTING-UP.** You may need to transplant your seedlings into larger pots if they start to get crowded and it's still too early to put them outdoors. Don't wait until the plants are a tangle of foliage and roots. The less you rip and tear, the better your plants will survive the move. When handling tiny seedlings, grasp them by their leaves or roots. Avoid holding them by their stems, which are fragile and can be easily crushed or bent.

Stems and roots are easier to separate when the soil is dry rather than wet. You can remove a clump of seedlings and separate them as you go, or use a spoon or your fingers to remove individual plants. Most seedlings should be repotted at the same depth or just a little deeper. The exception is tomato seedlings. When transplanting tomatoes, you should remove all but the top few leaves, and bury the rest of the stem. New roots will form along whatever part of the stem is underground. When your seedlings have been repotted, water them well, fertilize them, and return them to the grow light or sunny windowsill.

**TRANSPLANTING.** Once the weather has warmed up, you can start "hardening off" your seedlings by gradually exposing them to the great outdoors. They have been pampered with warm temperatures, plenty of light, and consistent water. The weather outside is not so kind — especially in the spring! At least one week before you plan to put your plants into the garden, begin reducing the

---

## Dealing with Damping Off

### How to Avoid It

- Sterilize all seed containers and any instruments used in the process of sowing.
- Use only sterile growing media or sterilized soil.
- Sow seeds thinly to allow air circulation between seedlings. Promptly thin overcrowded containers.
- Water seed trays from below.
- When growing plants that are particularly susceptible to damping-off, keep soil on the dry side.
- Damping-off can be stimulated by the presence of nitrogen. Always allow seedlings to develop two sets of true leaves before applying fertilizer.

### What to Do if You Detect It

- If even one of your seedlings exhibits signs of damping-off (stems wither at the soil level and tip over), remove it and, for caution's sake, its immediate neighbors, from the container at once.
- If the soil appears to be too moist, take immediate action by moving the containers away from other plants in order to increase air circulation. Crushed charcoal or perlite can be placed on the soil surface to absorb excess moisture.
- Return the containers to their normal location and resume cautious watering (only from below) once the soil has dried out sufficiently.

*—from From Seed to Bloom*
*by Eileen Powell*
*(Garden Way Publishing, 1995)*

---

The Accelerated Propagation System (APS) was developed by commercial growers in England. It has a plastic cover to retain moisture and warmth, capillary matting and a water reservoir for consistent moisture, and individual growing chambers for good root development. Seeds germinate rapidly, and seedlings can be grown without daily attention. There are 5 models to choose from. All are reusable. Recommended for use with the APS.

#03-234 APS-40 (40, 1½" x 1½" cells) $10.95
#03-235 APS-24 (24, 2" x 2" cells) $10.95
#03-231 APS-12 (12, 2" x 2" cells), set of 2 $10.95
#03-230 APS-30 (30, 1" x 1" cells), set of 2 $10.95
#03-239 APS-6 (6, 4" x 4" cells – no plastic cover) $10.95

**Professional Germinating Mix** is a finely textured blend of sphagnum moss and vermiculite. Excellent for tiny seedlings.
#03-199 Germinating Mix, 9 quarts $4.95

**Transplant Mix** contains sphagnum moss, perlite, and vermiculite. It has a coarser texture than the Germinating Mix. Good for larger pots or transplanting.
#03-215 Transplant Mix, 30 quarts $6.50

**ROOTS Plus for Seedlings** is specially formulated to stimulate strong root growth without leggy top growth. Contains liquid humus and a balanced 2-4-2 fertilizer. Apply every 2 weeks.
#07-257 ROOTS Plus for Seedlings, 8 oz $4.95

**PaperPots** are a honeycomb of paper pots joined together with water-soluble glue. Pots have open bottoms for air pruning, and fit snugly together to reduce moisture loss. They promote dense, fibrous root systems. Each set expands to fit the (optional) 16" x 21" reusable plastic tray.

#03-238A Small PaperPots (130, 2" x 1½" pots) $3.95
#03-238D Medium PaperPots (80, 3" x 2½" pots) $3.95
#03-238G Large PaperPots (30, 4" x 3½" pots) $3.95
#30-062 PaperPot Tray (16" x 21") $6.95

The **PolySprayer** holds 2½ pints of water. It can be pressurized with just a few quick strokes and sprays for over a minute. Great for misting and foliar feeding. Nozzle is adjustable. Made in England.
#05-231 PolySprayer $19.95

Most seeds germinate best at a soil temperature of 60°–70°F. This **Soil Thermometer** lets you monitor soil temperatures both indoors and out. Plastic sleeve and pocket clasp. 6" L.
#03-110 Soil Thermometer $12.95

The **Soil Block Maker** forms soil into 2" cubes. Eject the cubes into a tray and plant seeds. Entire block can go right into the garden. Use a heavy mix to ensure blocks hold together.
#03-193 Large Soil Block Maker $24.95
#03-375 Container Mix, 20 qts. $6.95

A **Root Zone Heat Mat** provides gentle bottom heat to promote fast germination. Waterproof mylar mat measures 9" wide x 24" long. Includes 6' power cord.
#03-228 Root Zone Heat Mat $49.95

**Capillary Matting** draws up water like a wick to provide potted plants with continuous moisture. Lasts for years.
#03-232 Capillary Matting, 21" x 3' $4.95

**SeaCure** is a seaweed-based fertilizer that provides over 60 trace elements and compounds that benefit seedlings. **Sea Plus** (3-2-2) combines seaweed with fish emulsion to provide the macronutrients nitrogen, phosphorus, and potassium. It has a slight odor.
#30-038 Sea Cure, 16 oz $4.95
#30-037 Sea Plus, 16 oz $4.95

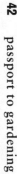

## Optimum Soil Temperatures for Germination of Common Vegetable Seeds

| CROP | Min. °F | Optimum °F | Max. °F | CROP | Min. °F | Optimum °F | Max. °F |
|------|---------|------------|---------|------|---------|------------|---------|
| Asparagus | 50 | 75 | 95 | Onions | 35 | 75 | 95 |
| Beans, Lima | 60 | 85 | 85 | Parsley | 40 | 75 | 90 |
| Beans, Snap | 60 | 80 | 95 | Parsnips | 35 | 65 | 85 |
| Beets | 40 | 85 | 95 | Peas | 40 | 75 | 85 |
| Cabbage | 40 | 85 | 100 | Peppers | 60 | 85 | 95 |
| Carrots | 40 | 80 | 95 | Pumpkins | 60 | 95 | 100 |
| Cauliflower | 40 | 80 | 100 | Radish | 40 | 85 | 95 |
| Celery | 40 | 70 | 85 | Swiss Chard | 40 | 85 | 95 |
| Corn | 50 | 95 | 105 | Spinach | 35 | 70 | 85 |
| Cucumbers | 60 | 95 | 105 | Squash | 60 | 95 | 100 |
| Eggplant | 60 | 85 | 95 | Tomatoes | 50 | 85 | 95 |
| Lettuce | 35 | 75 | 85 | Turnips | 40 | 85 | 105 |
| Muskmelon | 60 | 90 | 100 | Watermelon | 60 | 95 | 105 |
| Okra | 60 | 95 | 105 | | | | |

Note: Celery must have daily fluctuation to 60°F or lower at night.

—from Prof. J.F. Harrington, Dept. of Vegetable Crops, University of California at Davis

amount of water and fertilizer you give them. Place your plants outdoors for one hour each day on a protected porch or under the shade of a tree. Bring them inside at night, and gradually increase the amount of time they spend outdoors. Be sure to protect them from too much wind and hot sun.

If at all possible, try to transplant your seedlings on an overcast or drizzly day when the wind is relatively calm. A polyethylene row cover or shade fabric can help ease the transition, and will protect your plants from cats, flea beetles, and other threats as well. Be sure that you water well, so the roots establish good soil contact.

# seed saving

PASSPORT TO GARDENING
SEED SAVING

Reprinted courtesy of Judith Ann Griffith, Seed Savers Exchange

S aving seeds is a practice that's as old as agriculture itself—older, in fact, because early humans used many seeds as food long before they ever thought of planting them. The human race has, in essence, co-evolved with plants. Corn, for example, has been gradually transformed, through selection and hybridization, from an insignificant wild grass with small grainlike heads into the tall, heavy-eared food plant we know today.

It isn't difficult to harvest the seeds of many flowers and vegetables, and more and more home gardeners are getting into seed saving every year. Growing a plant to maturity represents an honors-level course for gardeners: it's amazing what you can learn about nature when you "complete the cycle," growing and observing a plant from seed to seed.

## Seeds and Plants

The obvious first question is "Why should I bother saving seeds?" After all, many seed companies cater to home gardeners, and the range of varieties they offer is impressive. Also, although the price of a packet of seeds has gone up in recent years, growing your own plants from seed is still a bargain when you compare it to the cost of buying flats of greenhouse plants.

However, the business of seeds has changed over the past few decades. Many smaller regional or family-owned seed suppliers have either gone out of business or have been bought up by large multinational companies that specialize in one-size-fits-all hybrid seeds. When we use the term "hybrid" in this chapter, we're referring to a plant that has been developed by cross-breeding two known, carefully controlled parent varieties. The genetic mixing of these parent strains results, in the next generation, in so-called F₁ hybrid plants (see "A Plant Breeder's Glossary," page 47).

There's nothing inherently wrong with these hybrids; often they grow vigorously and are fairly well adapted to a wide range of climates and growing conditions. The main problem is that most hybrids don't come "true to type" from seed; in other words, the saved seeds don't produce a new plant that is genetically similar to the hybrid parent plant. To grow the same variety, gardeners have no choice but to keep buying hybrid seed year after year. Fortunately, with the renewed interest in heirloom plants, several new seed companies have sprung up that offer both old and new varieties of "open-pollinated" (nonhybrid) flowers and vegetables (see "Resources," page 49).

## *Guest Expert*
## Kent Whealy

Today's plant breeders use the genetic traits of older plant varieties to incorporate disease and pest resistance into modern crops. Sometimes, though, a potentially important variety has become extinct. For example, the best source of resistance for ringspot — a disease affecting the cabbage family — vanished some 50 years ago when 'Old Cornish', an English variety of cauliflower, disappeared.

In addition to compelling genetic

*Kent Whealy is the director of Seed Savers Exchange (see "Resources," page 49). He lives in Decorah, Iowa.*

arguments, our lives would be equally impoverished by the historical and cultural loss of traditional plant varieties. Members of the Seed Savers Exchange are currently maintaining more than 20,000 rare vegetables, including; beans that came over on the *Mayflower*; corn and beans carried by the Cherokee over the Trail of Tears (1838–39); lettuce grown in Thomas Jefferson's gardens at Monticello; and tomatoes that General Lee sent home during the Civil War.

From every corner of the world, immigrant gardeners and farmers brought the best of their seeds with them to America. To the incredible diversity of this melting pot, add the richness of both the past and the future: ancient varieties from native tribes and civilizations spread throughout the Americas, and the rich flow of seeds from Eastern Europe and the former Soviet Union, whose countries have only recently opened their borders. We are truly blessed to be gardeners living here, in this time.

Why should we care? Because seeds represent our gardening heritage, our rapidly disappearing birthright, and the richness on the dinner plate of life. When any of this fragile, beautiful diversity is lost, it's gone for good. Extinction is forever.

## *Favorite Books*

**Seed to Seed** *by Suzanne Ashworth* (Seed Saver Publications, 1991).

The best and most comprehensive book available on saving seeds of crop plants.

You'll find all the usual garden vegetables, plus wonderful but little-known plants such as orach and skirret. 224 pages, paperback, $20.00.

**Saving Seeds: The Gardener's Guide to Growing and Storing Vegetables and Flower Seeds** *by Marc Rogers* (Storey Publishing, 1990).

Ideal for beginning seed savers, this great little guide covers all of the common vegetables and also has a section on saving seeds of popular flowers. Includes a useful glossary. 192 pages, paperback, $9.95.

**Garden Seed Inventory, 4th Edition,** *eds. Kent Whealy and Joanne Thuente* (Seed Savers Publications, 1995).

An exhaustive reference listing all of the open-pollinated vegetable varieties offered by U.S. and Canadian seed companies. While this might be more information than novices need, the GSI is the bible of serious home gardeners and seed savers. 632 pages, paperback, $24.00.

## Seed-Saving Tips for Beginners

- Start with easy crops. The easiest seeds to save are those from plants with self-pollinating flowers, such as beans, peas, tomatoes, and peppers, lupines, and snapdragons.

- Plan to grow only one variety of a cross-pollinated crop each year. Advanced seed savers can isolate (in bags or cages), hand-pollinate, and separate different varieties, but even easier is to let nature take its course and grow, say, only one kind of melon or sweet corn every year.

- Be aware of wild plants that can cross with your crops. Some common wildflowers can cross with related garden plants if they happen to flower at the same time. For instance, Queen Anne's lace (*Daucus carota* var. *carota*) is simply a wild form of the cultivated garden carrot, and the two will cross-pollinate. Many wild and cultivated members of the *Brassicacaea*, or Mustard Family, will also cross with one another.

- Select the best plants for seed saving. Look for the healthiest, most vigorous plants or fruits and mark them with colored yarn, tape, or ribbon, so you and others will know not to harvest them for eating.

- Select for desired characteristics. For instance, by saving seeds from your earliest beans year after year, you can develop a strain that matures early. The same goes for heat tolerance, disease resistance, and other desirable traits. This kind of selection is plant breeding at its most basic — gardeners and farmers have been doing it for millennia.

## Benefits of Saving Seeds

There are many reasons people decide to save their own seeds, but some of the more common include:

**AVAILABILITY.** Saving seeds ensures that you can continue growing your favorite varieties, even if seed companies drop them from their catalogs.

**ADAPTABILITY.** Over several seasons, saving seeds of a particular plant variety can result in a strain that is especially well suited to your garden's unique microclimate and growing conditions,

**PRESERVATION.** Many fine heirloom varieties are not sold through the seed trade, but instead have been passed down from generation to generation by families, tribes, or ethnic groups. Saving seed from these plants helps preserve our common plant heritage, not to mention our own family histories. America is a nation of immigrants, after all, and seeds provide living links to our past.

**DIVERSITY.** By saving many different varieties of seed, home gardeners encourage crop biodiversity and a broad genetic base. This has become especially important in these days of agribusiness farming, when, for instance, only two varieties of peas account for 96 percent of the entire U.S. crop. Backyard seed savers can make a difference, especially when they work together through seed exchanges (see "Seed Trusts and Exchanges," page 49).

## Getting Started in Seed Saving

There are plenty of specific tips that will help you become a successful seed saver (see "Seed-Saving Tips for Beginners," left), but the most important general rule is: "Know your plant, and know its sex life." It might sound a little kinky, but this basic information is crucial for successful seed saving.

Plants fall into three general categories based on life expectancy in a particular growing region — annual, biennial, and perennial. Seed savers are generally not that interested in perennials, since most of these long-lived plants can be propagated vegetatively (by root division, cuttings, or layering) more easily than by seed. Also, seeds saved from many perennial garden vegetables, such as rhubarb and asparagus, will — like hybrids — not necessarily result in a plant that resembles its parent.

Annuals, of course, are those plants that flower and produce seed in one growing season. Most common vegetables are treated as annuals in temperate climates, because they are killed by freezing temperatures. Tomatoes and peppers, for instance, are perennial plants in the wilds of Central and South America, but in our gardens we treat them as annuals and harvest seed from their fruits to replant the following year.

Biennial plants flower and produce seed in their second growing season, often following a period of dormancy. Common garden biennials include onions, carrots, hollyhocks, and sweet William. The most common way to save seed from biennial vegetables involves harvesting them from the garden in fall, wintering them over in cold (but not freezing) storage conditions, then replanting a few roots or plants in the spring garden, where they will then send up a flower stalk and set seed. Depending on the plant's cold hardiness and the severity of your winter climate, saving seed from biennials can prove tricky for northern gardeners, and some, like cauliflower, are for advanced seed savers only.

As far as your plants' sexual habits go, the most basic distinction is between "self-pollinators" and "cross-pollinators." Self-pollinating plants have perfect flowers (see "A Plant Breeder's Glossary," above) and can fertilize themselves, whereas cross-pollinators need to have their pollen transferred to the flowers of other plants by wind, water, insects, or animals. Cross-pollinated plants include corn, spinach, squash, carrots, sunflowers, and zinnias.

The easiest plants to start with for beginning seed savers are self-pollinating annuals like peas, beans, lettuce, tomatoes, peppers, snapdragons, lupines, sweet peas, and stock. These plants will sometimes cross-pollinate, but you don't have to worry as much about isolating similar varieties, as you do with different varieties of cross-pollinated plants.

Saving seeds from $F_1$ hybrids (see above) is possible, but the plant that grows from a hybrid's seeds won't resemble its parent, and in many cases the seed itself is sterile. It is possible to "grow out" some hybrids, saving seeds over four or more generations, until you obtain a variety

## A Plant Breeder's Glossary

**Cross-pollination.** The transfer of pollen from the anther of the flower of one plant to a stigma of the flower of another plant.

**$F_1$.** An abbreviation for "first filial generation"; in other words, the direct offspring of any given set of parents.

**$F_1$ hybrid.** The seed or plant that results from the cross between two genetically different plant varieties of the same species. $F_1$ plants often exhibit a great deal of hybrid vigor (see below), but the seed they themselves produce will generally not produce similar plants in the following ($F_2$) generation.

**Heirloom.** An older, open-pollinated plant variety, usually one that has been selected, preserved, and handed down outside of the commercial seed trade within a particular family or a regional, ethnic, or tribal group.

**Hybrid.** A product of a cross or mating between any two plants or animals that are not genetically the same. In the common and legal sense, a plant variety whose parents are known and whose breeding has been strictly controlled.

**Hybrid vigor.** A term coined by the naturalist Charles Darwin to describe the increased vitality of growth that often occurs in the $F_1$ generation after two genetically dissimilar plant varieties are crossed with one another. This is also known as *heterosis*.

**Open-pollinated (OP).** Refers to those plant varieties that have the ability to cross-pollinate among themselves by natural means and produce plants that are "true to type" (resemble the parent variety). The term is also used loosely to include varieties of plants whose flowers normally self-pollinate, such as peas, beans, lettuce, and tomatoes.

**Perfect flower.** A flower that contains within itself both male and female reproductive organs. An imperfect flower contains either male or female sex parts, but not both.

**Self-pollination.** The transfer of pollen from the male sex organs of one flower to the female sex organs of the same flower, or to those of another flower on the same plant.

## Other Good Books

*Taylor's Guide to Heirloom Vegetables by Benjamin Watson* (Houghton Mifflin, 1996). Profiles more than 500 outstanding heirloom varieties, giving origins and descriptions; glorious color photos. 352 pages, paperback, $19.95.

*Breed Your Own Vegetable Varieties by Carol Deppe* (Little, Brown, 1993). A basic course in plant breeding for backyard gardeners and budding Luther Burbanks. 320 pages, paperback, $18.95.

# Other Good Books

**Heirloom Vegetable Gardening** *by William Woys Weaver* (Holt, 1997). An encyclopedic guide to the history and cultivation of heirloom vegetables. Rather esoteric for the average gardener, but a delight for heirloom aficionados. 464 pages, hardcover, $45.00.

**Seeds: The Definitive Guide to Growing, History and Lore** *by Peter Loewer* (Macmillan, 1995). While "definitive" may be an exaggeration, this book is a worthy overview of the science and culture of seeds. 240 pages, hardcover, $25.00.

## Garden Gear

Most garden seeds will remain viable for several years if properly stored. This **Seed Saver Storage System** is perfect for protecting and organizing leftover seed packets and storing seeds harvested from your own plants. The durable, waterproof box comes with 15 resealable, airtight plastic bags in a convenient hanging file system; multicolored labels to organize and identify your seeds; and a large plastic file folder to hold plans, notes, and other gardening information. Measures 13½" W x 12" H x 10" D. **#03-301 Seed Saver Storage System $34.95**

**Drierite Desiccant Bags** remove moisture from the air, and so are useful for placing in storage containers with packets of seed. They are manufactured by the W.A. Hammond Drierite Co. of Xenia, Ohio, and are available through several sources, including The Cook's Garden catalog (see "Resources," page 49).

---

that has the characteristics you want, and comes reliably true from seed. But this kind of stabilization and selection is more for amateur plant breeders than beginning seed savers. Also, it is against the law to propagate some hybrid varieties (from seed or otherwise) that have been developed and registered by seed companies. Varieties protected by law are usually listed in seed or nursery catalogs with the abbreviation PVP, which stands for "Plant Variety Protection."

## Seed Storage and Shelf Life

Specific instructions for when and how to harvest and process mature seeds vary by plant; see "Favorite Books" on page 45 for references that will give you all the information you need to get started.

After harvesting, seeds should be dried for a time before storage; ideally, their moisture content should be around 5 to 8 percent. If the weather is dry and sunny, you can dry seeds on wire mesh screens in a place with good air circulation. A small fan is good for moving air over seeds that need to be soaked and fermented, such as those of tomatoes, melons, and cucumbers. For final drying before storage, place small amounts of seed in envelopes and put them in a coffee can or plastic container with a tight-fitting lid, along with an equal weight of silica gel crystals (available at craft shops or from some mail-order seed companies; see "Resources"). These desiccant crystals, which are dyed cobalt blue, continue to absorb excess moisture from the seeds, until the silica has eventually turned pink in color. Plan on leaving each batch of seeds in the container for only a few days, to avoid overdrying them. Silica gel can be reused indefinitely, by placing pink crystals into a 200°F oven until they turn blue again.

The length of time a particular kind of seed remains viable (with good germination) varies according to the plant and the storage conditions. Seeds store best in a dry, dark, and cool (45° to 50°F) location in an airtight container. Unheated barns or garages are not good places to store seeds because humidity and temperature are likely to fluctuate. To ensure dry storage conditions, you can throw into the storage container one or two small "desiccant bags." These packs contain Drierite, a chemically inert material that absorbs moisture from the air. Most kinds of vegetable seeds have a shelf life of three to five years in normal storage. The chief exceptions are parsnips, salsify, scorzonera, and members of the onion family.

# Resources

## SEED COMPANIES

All of the following companies offer a good selection of open-pollinated (nonhybrid) seeds well suited to home gardeners, and many specialize in heirloom varieties that are over fifty years old.

**Bountiful Gardens**
18001 Shafer Ranch Rd.
Willits, CA 95490
707-459-6410
*Also sells silica gel desiccant.*

**The Cook's Garden**
P.O. Box 535
Londonderry, VT 05148
800-457-9703
*Fine selection of salad greens and flowers; catalog $1.00.*

**Fox Hollow Seed Company**
P.O. Box 148
McGrann, PA 16236
412-548-SEED
*Herbs, vegetables, flowers, and heirlooms; catalog $1.00.*

**Garden City Seeds**
778 Hwy. 93 N.
Hamilton, MT 59840
406-961-4837
*Seeds for short-season gardeners; catalog $1.00.*

**Johnny's Selected Seeds**
Foss Hill Rd.
Albion, ME 04910
207-437-9294

**Nichols Garden Nursery**
1190 North Pacific Hwy.
Albany, OR 97321
541-928-9280

**Pinetree Garden Seeds**
P.O. Box 300
New Gloucester, ME 04260
207-926-3400
*Vegetable and flower seed in small, cost-efficient packets.*

**Santa Barbara Heirloom Nursery**
P.O. Box 4235
Santa Barbara, CA 93140
805-562-1248
*Seedlings of heirloom vegetable, herb, and edible flower varieties; overnight shipping.*

**Seeds Blüm**
HC 33, Idaho City Stage
Boise, ID 83706
800-528-3658
*Good selection of heirlooms; informative catalog is $3.00.*

**Seeds of Change**
P.O. Box 15700
Santa Fe, NM 87506-5700
888-762-7333
*Gorgeous color catalog; organically grown seeds.*

**Seeds of Distinction**
P.O. Box 86, Sta. A
Toronto, Ontario M96 4V2
416-255-3060
*Hard-to-find annual and perennial flower seeds.*

**Select Seeds — Antique Flowers**
180 Stickney Hill Rd.
Union, CT 06076-4617
*Heirloom and fragrant varieties of flowers and herbs; catalog $1.00.*

**Shepherd's Garden Seeds**
30 Irene St.
Torrington, CT 06790
860-482-3638
*Catalog $1.00.*

**R.H. Shumway**
P.O. Box 1
Graniteville, SC 29829
803-663-9771
*Great old-timey catalog; many heirlooms.*

**Territorial Seed Co.**
P.O. Box 157
Cottage Grove, OR 97424
541-942-9547

**Tomato Growers Supply Company**
P.O. Box 2237
Fort Myers, FL 33902
941-768-1119
*Large catalog of tomato and pepper varieties.*

## SEED TRUSTS AND EXCHANGES

**Abundant Life Seed Foundation**
P.O. Box 772
Port Townsend, WA 98368
360-385-7192
*Nonprofit seed company and preservation project; operates the World Seed Fund, which sends seeds all over the world to groups working to reduce hunger. Catalog $2.00; annual membership $30.00.*

**Eastern Native Seed Conservancy**
P.O. Box 451
Great Barrington, MA 01230
413-229-8316
*Northeast regional seed conservation group that offers organically grown rare and heirloom seeds, many Native American varieties. Free catalog; call for membership brochure and information.*

**Flower and Herb Exchange**
3076 North Winn Rd.
Decorah, IA 52101
319-382-5990
*Annual membership is $7.00.*

**Heritage Seed Program**
RR 3
Uxbridge, Ontario L9P 1R3
*Dedicated to preserving heirloom and endangered plant varieties. Regular membership is $18.00 per year and includes HSP magazine and seed list.*

**Landis Valley Museum**
Heirloom Seed Project
2451 Kissel Hill Road
Lancaster, PA 17601
*One of many historical sites that now operates its own heirloom seed project. Seed list includes more than 100 varieties with background information; available for $2.50.*

**Native Seeds/SEARCH**
2509 North Campbell Ave., #325
Tucson, AZ 85719
*Nonprofit organization dedicated to preserving traditional crops of the U.S. Southwest and northern Mexico, and their wild relatives. Great selection of native beans, corn, melons, and chilies. Seed catalog $1.00; annual membership $18.00.*

**Seed Savers Exchange**
3076 North Winn Rd.
Decorah, IA 52101
319-382-5990
*Founded in 1975, SSE has grown to more than 8,000 members, and works to preserve heirloom and endangered plants. Members share some 12,000 varieties of rare seeds with each other through an annual Yearbook. Annual membership is $25.00; call for free color brochure.*

**Southern Exposure Seed Exchange**
P.O. Box 170
Earlysville, VA 22936
804-973-4703
*Informative catalog features many traditional Southern varieties. Catalog $2.00.*

# extending the season

**EXTENDING THE SEASON**

Few gardeners are content with the growing season they're dealt by Mother Nature. In the North, that season can be as short as 90 days — barely enough time to ripen tomatoes or melons. In the South, drought and intense heat often limit gardening activity to the spring and fall months. The good news is that by using a few simple season-extending techniques and plant protection devices, you can shield your plants from extremes of weather, and stretch your gardening season by two, three, or even six months.

## Contending with the Elements

Extending your growing season requires protecting your plants from wind, frost, cold soil, heat, and too much sun.

**WIND.** If the plants in your garden must battle the wind, they will end up using most of their energy simply to survive, rather than developing strong root systems and putting on healthy growth. A permanent solution, which may be a worthwhile investment if you live in a windy spot, is to enclose your garden. You can build a wood fence, plant some shrubs, or put up windbreak netting (see "Garden Gear," page 54). Creating dead calm is not the goal. Your objective is to reduce the wind speed. If there's a prevailing wind direction, a fence on that side of the garden may be all that's needed. If a permanent fence or hedge requires more of a time or financial commitment than you are ready to make, you can try covering your plants with a polypropylene garden fabric (see product section). Seedlings grown under the shelter of garden fabric will often put on twice as much growth as control plants.

**COLD SOIL.** If you protect your garden over the winter with a thick layer of mulch, be sure to pull the mulch off the planting beds in early spring to expose the soil to the sun. Building raised beds is another way to warm the soil more quickly. Covering cold spring soil with black plastic can boost soil temperature by several degrees. The plastic can be left on all season, or removed prior to planting.

Combining black plastic mulch with a clear, slitted plastic tunnel will raise soil temperatures enough to get melons and other heat-lovers off to a fast start. In the fall, polypropylene fabrics will retain heat and keep soil temperatures several degrees warmer. This can give heat-loving crops such as peppers, okra, and tomatoes a couple extra weeks to ripen.

## Favorite Books

**The New Organic Grower's Four-Season Harvest** *by Eliot Coleman* (Chelsea Green, 1992).
A how-to manual from an intrepid Maine gardener who has learned how to coax fresh vegetables from his garden all year-round. Practical, low-tech ideas with construction techniques, specific recommendations for varieties, planting and harvest schedules, and more. 224 pages, paperback, $19.95.

**Solar Gardening** *by Leandre Poisson and Gretchen Vogel Poisson* (Chelsea Green, 1994).
These two New Hampshire gardeners use an assortment of tunnels, pods, and other easy-to-build structures to grow more than 90 crops beyond their normal harvest season. 288 pages, paperback, $24.95.

**Efficient Vegetable Gardening: Getting More Out of Your Garden in Less Time** *by Paul Doscher, Timothy Fisher, and Kathleen Kolb* (Globe Pequot, 1993).
A substantive, highly useful book that features practical advice on intensive growing methods and season-extending techniques gleaned from more than 40 gardeners. Excellent material on building soil, making intensive beds, insect and disease control, and cold weather gardening. Recommended especially for northern growers. An updated version of their long out-of-print best-seller, *Intensive Gardening Round the Year*. 216 pages, paperback, $15.95.

## Guest Expert
### Eliot Coleman

It is the middle of January on the coast of Maine, and I'm harvesting crops for dinner. Despite the typically frigid New England weather, I can choose from 18 garden-fresh vegetables. Not bad for fresh garden harvesting in Zone 5. I haven't done a lot of extra garden work to be able to eat this well. I planted all these crops during the summer and early fall. I provided them with protective covers once the cool weather arrived. That slight protection allows me to harvest them all winter long. . . . None of the crops are the typical heat lovers of the summer garden. And therein lies the secret.

Hardy plants don't mind cold, but they are affected by those alternating freeze/thaw, wet/dry, and gale/calm conditions. Such extremes are as stressful to plants as they are to humans. The aim of crop protection in the winter garden is to lessen those climatic extremes and consequently lessen plant stress. The first step toward lessening plant stress is to cover the plants.

*Eliot Coleman is the author of* The New Organic Grower's Four-Season Harvest *(Chelsea Green, 1992) and* The New Organic Grower *(Chelsea Green, 1995).*

# Other Benefits of Horticultural Fabrics

Floating row covers do much more than extend the growing season. They moderate temperature, wind, sunlight, humidity, and even rain. In this way, they create a favorable climate, giving seeds, seedlings, and transplants a head start, a better chance to mature into healthy, high-yielding vegetable plants. They also reduce soil heaves in the spring and fall due to thawing and freezing — an important bonus when you're growing strawberries and other over-wintering plants. Row covers protect plants from birds, squirrels, chipmunks, ground hogs,

and deer; and they reduce the need for pesticides by creating a barrier against insects. Covers also delay or reduce diseases transmitted by cucumber beetles and aphids.

—from *Extend Your Garden Season: Row Covers and Mulches* by Fred Stetson (Storey, 1996).

*Lightweight fabric cover is breathable.*

from *Rodale's Illustrated Encyclopedia of Gardening & Landscaping Techniques*

**SUN AND HEAT.** Hot weather can be just as challenging as cold weather, especially for people who garden in the South. Young plants can be stressed and stunted by too much direct sunlight, and once the weather gets hot and soil temperatures rise, getting seeds to germinate becomes very difficult. Cool-weather plants, such as most salad greens, turn bitter and go to seed in hot weather. Shade netting (see "Garden Gear") can be laid right over wire hoops or a movable wooden frame; by reducing the amount of sun reaching the plants, it can keep soil temperatures cooler and reduce moisture loss from the foliage. A piece of wood lathe attached to a frame can serve the same purpose.

**FROST.** For most gardeners, frost is a limiting factor in both spring and fall. One 32°F night will usually put an end to all but the hardiest of garden crops. Sheets, blankets, and cardboard boxes are a good emergency solution, but polypropylene row covers are far easier to handle and much more effective. These row covers are available in a variety of thicknesses, and some will protect to temperatures as low as 25°F. Cold frames and portable greenhouse structures can offer even greater cold protection, allowing you to extend your harvest season of cold-weather crops right through the winter.

## Stretching Your Harvest Season

In determining which sort of season extending device to use, you need to consider your local climate, how much longer you want to stretch the season, and how much extra time you are willing to invest. If you live in a cold climate and want to extend your harvest season year-round, you will probably need to invest in a portable greenhouse and be prepared to provide daily attention. On the other hand, if you would be happy with a few extra weeks of red tomatoes in the fall, and salads a couple of weeks earlier in the spring, the solution is easy and inexpensive.

## The 30-Day Stretch

You should be able to extend your harvest season by at least a month, if you provide your plants with a sheltered growing environment that minimizes stress. When transplanting your seedlings, try to keep them covered with a horticultural fabric for the first couple of weeks. With protection from hot sun, cold wind, frost, and even insects, your plants will

## Other Good Books

*Rodale's Illustrated Encyclopedia of Gardening and Landscaping Techniques* ed. *Barbara W. Ellis* (Rodale, 1995).
Jam-packed with how-to information and step-by-step instructions. Lavishly illustrated. Includes a short, yet very thorough section on extending the season. 432 pages, paperback, $17.95.

*Cold-Climate Gardening* by *Lewis Hill* (Garden Way Publishing, 1987). 308 pages, paperback, $14.95.

*Extend Your Garden Season: Row Covers and Mulches* by *Fred Stetson* (Storey Publishing, Bulletin #A-148, 1996). 32 pages, paperback, $2.95.

_A variety of season-extending devices._

Kathleen Kolb, from _Intensive Gardening Round the Year._

get off to a much faster start. Horticultural fabrics made of spun polyester or polypropylene are sun-, air-, and water-permeable, which means excess heat can escape and rainwater can pass through. Checking your plants weekly, for water and weeds, is all the attention that's required. Individual plants can also be covered with plastic milk jugs, coffee cans with the bottom cut out, or tomato cages encircled with clear plastic. Just be sure that the cover is vented, and that you stay on the lookout for signs of overheating.

## The 60-Day Stretch

Using horticultural fabrics in both spring and fall can add a full two months to your harvest season. Use them in the spring as described above, but plan to use a heavier fabric in the fall to retain soil heat and prevent frost from damaging the foliage.

Choosing the right plant varieties can make a significant difference too, since some varieties are specially suited to early- or late-season production. There are some varieties of broccoli, for instance, that thrive in cold spring soils, but go to seed quickly once warm weather arrives. There are other varieties that will tolerate heat, and still others that thrive in the low light conditions and cold temperatures of late fall.

## A Stretch of 3 to 4 Months

This is the point at which structures come into play. In many parts of the country, cold frames, Solar Pods, and movable greenhouses can extend your harvest almost

> Cold-tolerant plants can have a prolonged harvest period even with cold temperatures, so long as they have sufficient light and heat to mature before freezing weather arrives. A few notable cold-tolerant vegetables, such as kale, leeks, and parsnips, can actually freeze solid and still remain harvestable (and edible) after they have thawed. Spinach and many types of leaf lettuce can also survive freezing temperatures and will continue to grow later on once they thaw out. Other cold-tolerant vegetables like carrots can be mulched over the winter and will withstand several light freezes to remain tasty, and possibly even sweeter than before. If you plan a crop's maturity to coincide with conditions that are favorable for a prolonged harvest period, you can make the most out of that vegetable's fresh harvest."
>
> —from _Solar Gardening_ by Leandre and Gretchen Poisson (Chelsea Green, 1994).

# Garden Gear

**Garden Cover** is a polypropylene fabric that provides frost protection down to 28°F. It transmits 85% of the possible sunlight. Excellent as a windbreak for transplants, and for speeding growth in cool weather.
#09-130-50 All-Purpose Garden Cover, 6' x 50' $11.95
#09-131-20 All-Purpose Garden Cover, 12' x 20' $9.95
#30-122 All-Purpose Garden Cover, 83" x 164' $44.95

**Garden Quilt** is a thicker version of the fabric described above. It protects to 24°F. The thick, 1.5 oz. fabric can be used in early spring and late fall, or for overwintering. 50% light transmission.
#09-132-20 Garden Quilt, 6' x 20' $10.95

**Tri-Tough** garden fabric has added wind and tear resistance due to an inner layer of thermally bonded polypropylene threads. It protects to 28°F. Admits 70% of available sunlight.
#09-120 Tri-Tough, 6' x 25' $14.95

**Summerweight Cover** is designed for warm-weather pest protection. It also protects crops from wind damage. Transmits 90% of sunlight.
#09-259-20 Summerweight Cover, 6' x 50' $12.95

**Shade Netting** is a knitted polyethylene netting that lets air and moisture through, yet provides 50% shading to shield plants from too much sun and heat. Cuts easily, lasts for years.

**Support Hoops** are pre-formed, galvanized wire hoops used to support horticultural fabrics. **Regular Hoops** are 63" long and are designed for 2'- to 3'-wide beds. **High-Rise Hoops** are 70" long, and are designed for 3'-wide beds.
#09-905B Wire Support Hoops, 6 $7.50
#09-104 High-Rise Hoops, 6 $17.95

**Earth Staples** are 11-gauge wire staples that are inserted into the soil to hold fabrics or plastic mulches in place. Optional black rubber discs help keep fabric from tearing.
#09-213 Earth Staples, 15 $2.95
#09-217 Easy-Out Earth Staples, 15 $4.95
#09-209 Earth Discs, set of 15 $2.95

The **Super Tunnel** provides everything needed to construct a 4' H x 5' W x 12' L tunnel. You get six, 11'-long hoops, 12' x 22' of GardenQuilt, and 15 Earth Staples.
#09-106 Super Tunnel $49.95

**Garden Net** is a woven, UV-stabilized polypropylene fabric that reduces wind speed by 50%. Netting is 6' high, and protects a 40–50' area

#09-242 5' x 5' Shade Net $7.95
#09-248 10' x 15' Shade Net $39.95
#09-247 5 x 15' Shade Net with 7 Wire Hoops $24.95

behind it. Secure to wood or metal posts. Lasts 5–10 years.
#09-107 Garden Net, 6' x 25' $59.95
#09-108 Garden Net, 6' x 50' $110.95

The **Wall O'Water** is a teepee made from water-filled plastic tubes. It is used to surround individual plants, and provides protection down to 10°F. Each Wall O'Water holds 3 gallons of water and will last 3–5 years.
#09-216B Wall O'Waters, 6 $16.50

**A cold frame** creates a cozy micro-climate for early spring or late fall greens, for growing seedlings, or for forcing bulbs. This one is made from weather-resistant cypress, and has two clear acrylic panels that lift up for easy access and venting. 53½" L x 26½" W x 14½" H.
#30-641 Cypress Cold Frame $199.00

The **Grow House** is an affordably priced commercial-style greenhouse constructed from PVC ribs and standard lumber. Kits range in size from 12' x 12' to 12' x 24'. Prices start at $299. Call Gardener's Supply for details 800-863-1700.

year-round. Managing a protected growing environment in the face of widely fluctuating weather extremes is actually easier than you might imagine. The rewards — salad greens in February and tomatoes right through Thanksgiving — far outweigh the investment.

The key to success in this showdown with Mother Nature is to concentrate your energies on one small section of your garden. This area should be as accessible to the house as possible, and you should be prepared to see it under cover for at least half of the year. Focusing on a few crops is another way to increase your success. Salad greens and root crops are easiest. You'll find that a 3-foot-by-4-foot bed of greens, well managed, will provide many months' worth of salads. Choosing the right varieties and following a continuous planting schedule is essential. (See "Favorite Books" for more information.)

Like greenhouse gardening, growing under cover is an exciting new world with big rewards. Imagine having a salad bar with fresh, organic produce right outside your door, eight or ten months a year. And imagine the pride and satisfaction you would get from this degree of self-sufficiency!

> Temperature control is the real key to successs. Cloches, lights, cold frames, pods, or any solar-intensive device must be ventilated to prevent excessively high temperatures on warm days. This ventilation is also necessary to reduce dampness, which could otherwise lead to mildew or fungal disease problems. Excessively high temperatures cause stress and wilting in some plants because photosynthesis increases with temperature. Your objective should be to obtain daily temperatures that approximate the optimum growing conditions of the individual species. For most early spring crops, this means no higher than 80°F and no lower than 40°F. Most gardeners worry more about cold temperatures than hot, but excess heat is actually more harmful to plants than cold."
>
> —from *Intensive Gardening Round the Year* by Paul Doscher, Timothy Fisher, and Kathleen Kolb (reprinted as *Efficient Vegetable Gardening* by Globe Pequot, 1993)

## Cold Frame Crops for Zone 5

### Crops for Fall and Winter Consumption

| CROP | Planting Dates | Harvest Dates |
| --- | --- | --- |
| Arugula | 8/1–8/21 | 10/1–spring |
| Endive | 7/10–7/20 | 9/15–11/30 |
| Escarole | 7/10–7/20 | 9/15–11/30 |
| Italian dandelion | 8/1–8/15 | 10/1–spring |
| Lettuce | 7/21–9/7 | 9/15–11/30 |
| Mizuna | 8/1–8/15 | 9/15–11/30 |
| Parsley | 6/1–7/15 | 10/1–spring |
| Radish | 9/1–10/15 | 10/1–spring |
| Scallion | 7/1–7/15 | 10/1–spring |
| Spinach | 8/1–3/30 | 10/15–11/30 |
| Swiss chard | 7/1–8/1 | 10/1–spring |

### Crops for Winter and Spring Consumption

| CROP | Planting Dates | Harvest Dates |
| --- | --- | --- |
| Carrot | 8/1 | 12/1–spring |
| Claytonia | 8/1–9/1 | 11/1–spring |
| Italian dandelion | 8/1–8/15 | 10/1–spring |

| CROP | Planting Dates | Harvest Dates |
| --- | --- | --- |
| Kohlrabi | 8/1–8/15 | 11/1–spring |
| Mache | 9/15–11/15 | 12/1–spring |
| Parsley | 6/1–7/15 | 10/1–spring |
| Radicchio | 7/15–8/1 | 11/1–spring |
| Scallion | 7/15–8/1 | 11/1–spring |
| Sorrel (perennial) | transpl 9/1 | 11/1–spring |
| Spinach | 9/15–10/15 | 12/1–spring |
| Sugarloaf chicory | 7/1–7/15 | 11/1–spring |

### Overwintered Crops for Spring Eating

| CROP | Planting Dates | Harvest Dates |
| --- | --- | --- |
| Dandelion | 7/1–7/15 | 2/15–4/15 |
| Lettuce | 9/15–10/15 | 3/1–5/1 |
| Onion | 8/1 | 4/1–7/1 |
| Spinach | 10/1–10/15 | 2/15–4/15 |

—from *Four Season Harvest* by Eliot Coleman. (The book explains how to adjust for different growing zones, and provides information about other vegetables as well.)

# pest and disease control

W e all know that feeling: strolling out to the garden on a beautiful spring day, excited and expectant, wondering how those seedlings you transplanted yesterday have held up overnight — only to experience the horror of seeing a whole line of lovingly nurtured plants mowed down at the base by cutworms. Or a midsummer check on the potatoes, a couple of days ago lush with dark green leaves — now completely defoliated! Or preparing to cut some flowers for an indoor arrangement, only to discover black spot and mildew running rampant in your perennial bed. The scourges of insect pests and plant pathogens are a challenge for every gardener and the temptation to wipe them out is strong.

We encourage you to resist the urge to declare total war and reach for an arsenal of chemical weapons. Doesn't it seem like overkill to use powerful poisons to protect your garden from insects and diseases? In the short term they may provide a quick knock-down to the attackers, but they may also kill beneficial organisms. In the long term, you expose yourself and the landscape to toxic chemicals, and risk disrupting the natural ecosystem that you and your garden inhabit. All things considered, an organic approach is both safer and more effective. By applying the simple principles of ecological plant protection, you can work with nature to control pests and diseases, and enjoy a healthier garden and harvest.

## Your Garden Is an Ecosystem

Organic methods of pest and disease control mean a healthier garden for you, your plants, and the insects, birds, and animals around you.

## Favorite Books

The Organic Gardener's Handbook of Natural Insect and Disease Control eds. Barbara W. Ellis and Fern Marshall Bradley (Rodale, 1996). The bible of organic pest control. Comprehensive, up to date, easy to read, with excellent beautiful drawings and illustrations. 544 pages, paperback, $17.95.

The Gardener's Bug Book by Barbara D. Pleasant (Storey, 1994). A beautifully written, philosophical, and comprehensive introduction to earth-safe insect control and garden protection. Provides home remedy recipes and offers frank assessments of the effectiveness of various controls, based on personal experience. 160 pages, paperback, $9.95.

Rodale's Flower Garden Problem Solver by Jeff and Liz Ball (Rodale, 1990). Covers annuals, perennials, bulbs, and roses, and the most likely pests and diseases to affect them. Plant-specific (five pages just on snapdragons!): how to recognize the symptoms, identify underlying problems, and what to do. Highly recommended. 422 pages, paperback, $14.95.

## Guest Expert
## Barbara D. Pleasant

We are living in an age of blindingly bright enlightenment of the natural forces that make a garden tick. If you've noticed how some plots of soil support robust, pest-resistant crops year after year, you've seen a glimpse of the future of ecological gardening.

Many of the good garden practices we take for granted, like rotating crops, enriching the soil with compost, and providing habitat for beneficial insects, are finally giving up their secrets to scientific inquiry. Ten years from now, you might water every seedling you set out with a natural bacterial brew that doubles its ability to fend off both insects and diseases overnight. Your garden will change sooner than that, for every season will show you more about the unique tapestry of life in your own backyard.

Solving pest problems, whether today or tomorrow, will always be a combination of science and attitude. The garden will forever be a dirty place full of idiot insects and fearless fungi that require action. Thoughtful intervention comes from science, but respect for the garden's natural earthly essence is a matter for the heart.

*Barbara D. Pleasant is the author of The Gardener's Guide to Plant Diseases (Storey, 1995), The Gardener's Bug Book (Storey, 1994, and Warm-Climate Gardening (Garden Way Publishing, 1993), and a contributor to many magazines and newspapers. She lives in Huntsville, Alabama.*

*Colorado
potato beetle*

**Bugs, Slugs, and Other Thugs** by *Rhonda Massingham Hart* (Storey, 1991). Lively, accessible, and concise, this book contains a lot of good information, including a section on big game (deer, coyotes, etc.) and plans for traps. 224 pages, paperback, $9.95.

**Natural Insect Control** ed. *Warren Schultz* (Brooklyn Botanic Garden, 1994). Has a good historical introduction tracing the trends in insect control over the past half-century. Another "encyclopedia of pests," with chapters on cultural, physical, and biological controls. Excellent photographs and illustrations. 112 pages, paperback, $6.95.

Organic pest controls do not try to eradicate all insects — that would upset the natural balance of life in your garden, and perhaps endanger birds and other animals by exposing them to poisons and depriving them of an important food source. Instead, the organic approach requires that you spend a bit more time in your garden, take extra good care of your plants, and keep an eye out for early signs of insect attack or disease symptoms. As gardeners, we can learn to tolerate some damage to our plants, and we should use such damage as a signal that our plants need more attention.

Not every insect is an enemy. Some are pollinators, some break down organic matter, and some are beneficial predators that feed on the real enemies. You want to be able to identify your friends and foes, and then encourage the friends and frustrate the foes. Effective and appropriate technologies, such as physical barriers, traps, and specific biological agents, are available to assist in your efforts to protect your garden and at the same time maintain a safe, harmonious natural environment.

## Take Good Care of Your Plants

Insects and diseases usually attack unhealthy plants, so the key to preventive control is taking good care of your plants. That means paying close attention to them and providing them with the conditions they need for healthy, vigorous growth. Those steps include the following:

- Grow your plants in healthy soil. Build healthy soil by adding organic matter to your garden every year to improve nutrient levels, soil structure, and water-holding capacity.

- Make sure your plants are getting the right amount of water and all the nutrients they need, supplemented with organic fertilizers if necessary.

- Don't force plants to compete with masses of weeds for water and nutrients. Minimize weeds by using mulches, such as landscape fabric or plastic, and by pulling a few weeds every time you visit the garden, rather than waiting until they are so thick you can't see your seedlings and it becomes a big problem to get rid of them.

- Thin your seedlings so the plants are not overcrowded and there is good air circulation between them; check seed packets for thinning instructions.

Complement attentive plant care with several other ecological gardening strategies that employ Mother Nature to enhance the health of your garden.

**GARDEN CLEAN-UP.** Leaving old squash vines, tomato plants, and similar debris in your garden after the harvest ends is like putting out a welcome mat for pests and pathogens. Many insects overwinter in such debris, and they will get an early start nibbling on your plants the following spring. Many plant pathogens also live in the soil year-round. Remove and dispose of any diseased or infested plants. Till other debris into the soil or put it in your compost pile. Then cultivate the soil so that

*Mole*

any remaining eggs, larvae, or pupae will be exposed to birds and cold winter temperatures. Keep on top of the weeds around your garden, since they can also harbor insect pests.

Make garden clean-up a part of your yearly routine. It may take a bit of extra work when the season is winding down and you're looking ahead to different activities, but you'll significantly reduce next year's pest and disease problems, and you'll appreciate the satisfaction of completing a job well done.

**CROP ROTATION.** This principle serves two important purposes. First, many insects and disease-causing organisms overwinter in the soil near their host plants. If you grow the same plant (or a related one) in the same place the next year, you give those pests a big head start. Crop rotation can thus reduce insect damage and minimize exposure to soil-borne disease organisms. Wait at least two years before you plant the same or related crops, such as broccoli and cauliflower, in the same spot. Brassicas, potatoes, tomatoes, and onions are particularly vulnerable to problems when planted in the same place year after year.

Second, crop rotation is beneficial because it helps to keep soil nutrients in balance over time. Heavy feeders, such as tomatoes and lettuce, can be followed the next year by legumes, such as peas and beans, which actually return nitrogen to the soil through microorganisms on their roots. The third year, you could let the soil "rest" by planting light feeders in that spot, such as carrots or beets.

**COMPANION PLANTING.** This technique takes advantage of the various ways different plants complement or protect one another, thereby promoting each others' healthy growth. Marigolds, for example, have a natural resistance to insects, and planting marigolds as a border around the garden, or among vegetables, seems to discourage both insect and animal pests in colorful fashion. Other examples: basil is said to be beneficial to tomatoes; carrots grow well with leaf lettuce, and their roots exude a substance that helps peas; and members of the allium family, such as onions and garlic, effectively deter pests that attack roses. You also need to be aware of certain plants that hate each other and inhibit each other's growth. For example, tomatoes and members of the brassica family (broccoli, cabbage, etc.) do not grow well when planted together.

Consider planting an assortment of flowers or wildflowers in the fields, meadows, or formal beds that surround or adjoin your vegetable garden. Ornamental alliums, such as nodding onion (*Allium cernuum*), make especially good insectary plants, as do most members of the Api-

> " You may use suggested companion plants as a starting point, but effective companion planting is something that must be learned through experience in your own garden. The assortment of insects present in your garden is not like that in any other, so the relationships that exist or develop between the plants and insects in your yard are unique by nature."
>
> —from *The Gardener's Bug Book* by Barbara D. Pleasant (Storey, 1994)

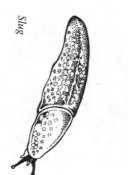

Slug

You can use highly efficient poisons to destroy entire communities of insects with a single squirt or spray. But in so doing you may be tainting the environment in ways we barely understand and inviting the emergence of more sinister enemies than the one you just killed. Worst of all, you will risk turning the fun and fascination of gardening into a never-ending, unwinnable war. The plants you so desperately attempt to protect will always be rooted in the ground and will never be able to fly into the sky to do battle with moths, flies, and winged beetles. It makes more sense to assist plants on their own terms, by giving them good soil in which to grow, allowing them the companionship of friendly neighbors, and offering security from insects whose talents for destruction far exceed what seems reasonable or right. . . . Every garden method you use that helps keep plants happy, from enriching your soil to staking your peas, contributes to the defensive capabilities of your garden where insects are concerned."

—from *The Gardener's Bug Book* by Barbara D. Pleasant

(Storey, 1994)

## Identify the Pest

Your first job when you discover an insect problem is to identify the pest and/or the damage it causes. This will allow you to determine the least toxic, yet most effective solution. There are two types of insect pests.

**RESISTANT VARIETIES.** Sometimes certain varieties or cultivars show a strong natural resistance to pests and/or disease. Seed catalogs are a good guide for selecting these resistant varieties. Why not experiment and try some along with your old standby favorites!

chart of some common insect emergence times can be found in *The Encyclopedia of Natural Insect and Disease Control* (see "Favorite Books"). You could also keep records to gain familiarity with these patterns in your own region and microclimate.

*Caterpillar*

aceae (Celery Family), Asteraceae (Aster Family), and Lamiaceae (Mint Family). Growing insectary plants near the garden provides important habitat for many beneficial insects, which in turn help control pest populations around your other plants.

Intercropping on the basis of growth characteristics can also be advantageous. Deep-rooted plants and shallow-rooted plants grow well together in a group, because they draw water and nutrients from different layers of soil. Examples include Swiss chard and beans, or lettuce and carrots. Corn and cucumbers have another symbiotic relationship: both like heat and well-drained soil, but cukes like the shade provided by corn plants.

Consult one of our recommended books for more information about good companion-planting combinations.

**MIXED CROPPING.** If you place smaller groups of plants throughout the garden, rather than planting all of your potatoes, say, in one place, it will be more difficult for pests to converge on the whole lot. Mixing marigolds and strong-smelling herbs in among your plants can deter insect pests by masking the smell of the plants they want to eat.

Interplanting herbs and flowers that attract beneficial insects, such as dill or fennel, is another effective way to give the "good guys" an edge.

**TIMED PLANTING.** Insects usually appear at about the same time every year, so you can schedule your plantings to avoid the heaviest feeding stages. An excellent

**SUCKING INSECTS.** Aphids, leafhoppers, and harlequin bugs insert their long mouth parts into plants and suck out the juices. As they feed, some of these insects can also transmit plant viruses. Typical signs of sucking damage include a weakening of the plant; yellowed, brown, or wilted leaves; and a sticky substance or sooty black mold covering the leaves (this is especially common with aphids). Unlike most insect pests, these look like adults as soon as they hatch from the egg.

**CHEWING INSECTS.** This group includes caterpillars and beetle larvae, such as the Colorado potato beetle, cabbage worms, and tomato hornworms. They are voracious feeders that tear and mash plant tissue, nibbling on leaf margins or making holes through leaves, and they are capable of completely defoliating a plant. Most chewing insects go through a complete metamorphosis, from eggs to larvae to pupae to adults, changing appearance at each stage. Different insects cause damage at different points in this cycle, sometimes in more than one stage (the Colorado potato beetle, for example, is destructive as a grub and as an adult).

In general, insects are easiest to control during the egg stage. Simply remove the eggs from the underside of leaves and dispose of them. Since many insects reproduce more than once during a season, you should keep your eyes open for eggs all summer long. Larvae and nymphs often overwinter in the soil or in plant debris, so garden cleanup in the fall is a good means of prevention.

Consult the recommended books for tips on how to recognize the symptoms of various insect attacks, and for detailed information on the life cycles of your problem pests.

## Encourage Beneficial Insects

In addition to the pests, it's important to be able to identify insects that are beneficial to your garden, and to encourage them to take up residence. When nature is in balance, the good guys usually keep the bad guys in check. You may already know about ladybugs. They (and their larvae) feed on aphids, mites, and other soft-bodied insects, as do the larvae of green lacewing flies. If these

*Ladybug*

predators find plenty of food in your garden they will lay eggs and stick around for several generations. So if you buy ladybugs, be sure to release them in the garden, near their source of food.

Other beneficial insects include trichogramma wasps, braconid wasps, pediobius wasps, tachinid flies, and syrphid flies, which all lay eggs on insect pests and parasitize them. Certain kinds of beneficial nematodes (microscopic worms that are naturally present in healthy soil) attack soilborne pests such as Colorado potato beetle larvae, Japanese

## Other Good Books

**Carrots Love Tomatoes** *by Louise Riotte* (Garden Way Publishing, 1975).
A classic encyclopedia of the lore of companion planting. Easy to use, but tends to accept all the lore on faith. 224 pages, paperback, $9.95.

**The Gardener's Guide to Plant Diseases** *by Barbara D. Pleasant* (Storey, 1995).
Organized by category of disease (airborne, soilborne, viruses, nematodes) and very readable. Tells you how to recognize a disease and what immediate and future action to take. Nice first chapter on the gardener as plant physician. 192 pages, paperback, $12.95.

**Rodale's Color Handbook of Garden Insects** *by Anna Carr* (Rodale, 1979). Excellent photographs accompanied by brief information on life cycles, host plants, feeding habits, and natural controls. 260 pages, paperback, $16.95.

**Rodale's Garden Insect, Disease, and Weed Identification Guide** *by Miranda Smith and Anna Carr* (Rodale, 1988).
Informative general compendium, with a short section of good photographs, and a nice glossary. 336 pages, paperback, $16.95.

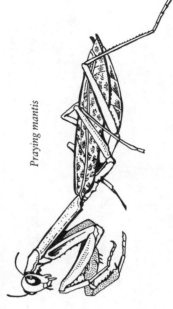

*Praying mantis*

beetle grubs, and cutworms. These nematodes can be sprayed in solution on the soil, or in planting holes.

Ladybugs, trichogramma wasps, and lacewings can be purchased from garden stores and mail-order companies. You can encourage these beneficial insects by limiting your use of insecticides (chemical and natural). You can also attract them to your garden by growing pollen-rich flowers and weeds such as Queen Anne's lace, lamb's-quarters, evening primrose, and goldenrod in the surrounding landscape.

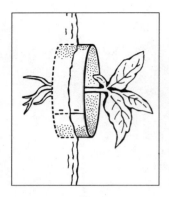

*Cutworm (top) and simple cutworm collar.*

## Barriers, Traps, and Other Deterrents

Many types of pests can effectively be deterred with physical barriers and traps. You can protect young seedlings from cutworms by making a simple collar. Just cut out a 3-inch strip of cardboard or ring of plastic from a yogurt container, encircle the stem, and push it an inch or two into the soil. Row covers, such as Tri-Tough, are an effective deterrent to flying insects that want to lay eggs on your plants. If you use row covers, you may need to remove them to allow pollination to occur, and then replace them after the flowers have disappeared. You should also be aware of the life cycle of the insect you are trying to control; be careful not to trap overwintering larvae *inside* a row cover!

SilKaBen is a blend of finely ground rock powders that can be used to coat plant stems. It deters chewing and sucking insects, and inhibits fungus growth.

You can also buy traps that attract insects by using color, taste, and sex hormones. Examples include commercially available traps for aphids, whiteflies, and thrips, and another for Japanese beetles. Follow the manufacturer's instructions about how far away from your garden to place these traps. Slugs have a particular affection for stale beer and will drown in a shallow saucer of it placed in the garden.

Our animal friends can be garden pests too. The Golden Rule here is: don't harm them, just make them want to leave your garden alone. A simple fence will keep out dogs and possibly cats. Deer are great jumpers, and it generally takes a 7-foot fence to deter them. There are several fencing systems for deer on the market, and also a variety of organic repellents that can be quite effective. One key with deer is to periodically change the location of the repellent, because they become bolder if something becomes familiar.

Electric fence systems can prevent rabbits, woodchucks, sometimes deer, and perhaps your own chickens from getting into the garden. A variety of products are available that will drive away burrowing animals such as moles, voles, mice, and gophers by creating harmless sounds or vibrations that bother them but not you. Deer, raccoons, and skunks can also be deterred with sonic devices.

You can try to keep birds away from your vegetables with scarecrows and other homemade noise- and commotion-makers; many garden books provide creative suggestions. Netting can also protect some plants from birds, especially fruits and berries.

## HOMEMADE REMEDIES

Many people make their own natural pesticides at home. The measurements are rarely exact, and neither are the results, but they are inexpensive, easy to make, and safe to use. Most popular are botanical sprays containing:

* members of the allium family (garlic, onions, chives)
* hot peppers (cayenne, jalapeño)
* herbs (basil, coriander, peppermint, wormwood)
* mildly soapy water (especially good against aphids and spider mites)

Simply steep in hot water or mix in a blender, and strain before spraying. Wet both sides of leaves and repeat after a rain, or as often as necessary. Flour and salt can be used to suffocate or dehydrate many kinds of caterpillars. Wood ashes sprinkled around the base of plants can discourage cutworm attacks.

# Garden Gear

## INSECT AND DISEASE CONTROL SOLUTIONS

Lady Beetles will quickly rid your garden or greenhouse of aphids, white-flies, spider mites, and mealy bugs. 1,000 will effectively patrol 1/8 acre. Shipped priority mail; allow 2 to 3 weeks for delivery.
#05-239 1,000 Adult Ladybugs $17.50

An abrasive powder made from the mineral remains of single-cell aquatic plants, **Diatomaceous Earth** kills by abrading and dehydrating crawling insects such as slugs, cockroaches, earwigs, and fleas.
#30-123 Diatomaceous Earth, 1½ lb. box $7.95

**Bt**, or *Bacillus thuringiensis*, is the most widely used bacteria for garden pest control. Safe for humans, animals, and beneficials, Bt causes insects to stop eating and die within a few days. "Regular" Bt acts against caterpillars such as army worms, gypsy moths, hornworms, and loopers. The Bt strain "San Diego" is effective against Colorado potato beetle larvae.
#05-176 Bt, Caterkil Insecticide, 8 fl. oz. $14.95
#30-243 Bt "San Diego," Colorado Potato Beetle Beater, 16 oz. $15.95

We've had our best success controlling Japanese beetles with a 3-part strategy. 1. Reduce the grub population with **Grub Guard**, beneficial nematodes that attack many grubs, including Japanese beetles, Colorado potato beetles, and cutworms. Mix with water and apply to moist soil with a sprayer or watering can. 2. Lure and trap adult beetles with **Catch-Can.** Holds up to 400 beetles and is vented to prevent "beetle soup" smell. 3. Use **Neemachtin™**, an organic insecticide extracted from the seeds of the neem tree, to repel adult Japanese beetles (and other pests) without harming honey bees and ladybugs. 8 oz. makes 2½ gallons of spray.
#05-292 Grub Guard, treats 2,000 sq. ft. $19.95
#05-298 Grub Guard, treats 12,000 sq. ft $69.95
#05-268 Catch-Can with bait $18.95
#05-270 Optional 64" Metal Stand $5.95
#05-196 Japanese Beetle Repellent $9.95

**Milky Spore** is a naturally occurring bacteria that kills grubs, including Japanese beetle larvae, before they turn into ravenous adults. Especially good for lawns: simply apply the powder in a grid pattern. Safe for people, animals, and beneficial insects.

Works for up to 20 years.
#05-153 Milky Spore 10 oz. $29.95

**Liquid Rotenone/Pyrethrin** is an all-purpose control for many destructive adult beetles, including striped cucumber beetles, Japanese beetles, and Colorado potato beetles. Great for potatoes, cucumbers, tomatoes, and eggplants.
#30-244 Rotenone/Pyrethrin, 16 oz. concentrate makes at least 24 gallons $16.95

**Organic Garden Dust** is especially good for controlling a wide variety of flower pests, including aphids, harlequin bugs, stink bugs, thrips, and more. It also controls diseases such as bacterial spot, blights, and powdery mildew. 1 lb. covers 1,000 sq. ft.
#05-277 Garden Dust $8.95

**Summerweight Garden Cover** is designed for warm-weather pest protection. It also protects crops from wind damage. Transmits 90% of sunlight.
#09-259-50 Summerweight Cover, 6' x 50' $12.95

## BIRD AND ANIMAL CONTROL SOLUTIONS

This **Instant Garden Fence** can be attached to posts or stakes in minutes to create a temporary barrier against deer and other animals. Rolls up at the end of the season. The tough, UV-stabilized black polypropylene mesh netting is almost invisible in place and will last for years of seasonal use. Comes in a 7' x 100' roll that can be cut to length.
#05-345  Instant Garden Fence  $24.95

Ravenous deer can strip the foliage from shrubs, nibble hostas to the quick, and wreak havoc in your vegetable garden. One taste of **Deer Off** will leave them wincing. Sprayed on foliage, it imparts the taste of egg solids, hot pepper, and garlic, without leaving a visible residue. Will not rinse off in rain. Not for use on edible crops.
#05-627  Deer Off, 1 qt  $18.95

Another way to keep deer off your property, as well as raccoons, skunks, and dogs, is with sound waves. **Crop Gard** is an ultrasonic device that emits

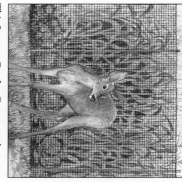

highly amplified sounds that are inaudible to humans but intolerable to most animal pests. Unlike other ultrasonic devices, Crop Gard can be adjusted, aimed, moved, and tuned, allowing you to keep affected animals confused and unnerved. Coverage of 10,000 sq. ft. Plugs into standard AC outlet.
#05-499  Crop Gard  $159.95

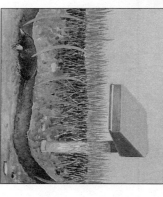

The **Mole Mover** uses harmless, underground vibrations to drive moles and voles from your yard and keep them away. Fully adjustable for volume, duration, and interval of vibrations. Depending on your soil type and obstructions like buildings and driveways, can protect up to 1/4 acre. Comes with an unconditional money-back guarantee. Uses four C-cell batteries (not included).
#30-134  Mole Mover  $115.00

Marlene's **Mole Control** is a castor-oil based mix that can be used year-round, directly on mole holes and tunnels, or to create a barrier around your garden. One quart treats 10,000 square feet. Master Gardener Marlene Hansen says "moles and voles won't cross a castor oil barrier," and independent research has confirmed its effectiveness.
#30-015  Mole Control  1 quart  $19.95

Catch furry garden pests unharmed with a **Havahart™ Trap**. It's a humane way to remove squirrels, chipmunks, rabbits, young woodchucks, and other small animals from your yard and garden. Simply place bait in the trap and set the spring-loaded trap door to respond to the weight of the animal you want to catch. When tripped, the door locks securely and you can safely transport the animal to a remote area and set it free.
#30-337  Small Animal Havahart™ Trap, 24" x 8" x 8"  $42.00
#30-338  Squirrel/Chipmunk Havahart™ Trap, 16" x 6" x 6⅜"  $25.00

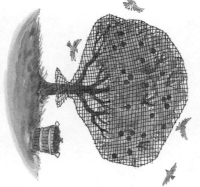

This soft, no-tangle **Bird Netting** is fine enough to keep birds off, yet it allows good air circulation. It lasts several seasons, and the green color blends into the garden. Place 1/4" x 1/4" mesh directly on plants such as corn, raspberries, and strawberries; use 1/2" x 1/2" mesh for trees, bushes, and grapes. (Multiply height of tree or bush by 2 and order closest size.)
#05-315  1/4" x 1/4" Netting, 4½' x 40'  $8.95
#05-316  1/4" x 1/4" Netting, 9' x 15'  $7.95
#05-317  1/4" x 1/4" Netting, 14' x 25'  $16.95
#05-318  1/2" x 1/2" Netting, 14' x 14'  $8.95
#05-319  1/2" x 1/2" Netting, 28' x 28'  $29.95
#05-329  1/2" x 1/2" Netting, 45' x 45'  $84.95
#05-328  Bird Net Clips, pack of 35  $1.95

*Japanese beetle*

For specific information on products that can deter animal and insect pests, consult "Garden Gear" and our recommended books.

## Biological Insect Control

No matter how well you care for your plants and maintain your garden, you will inevitably have to deal with pest problems at some point. Fortunately, many very effective biological pest controls have become available during the past twenty years. These naturally occurring pathogens destroy specific insects but do not harm other creatures that inhabit the same environment.

The biological control most commonly used in gardens is *Bacillus thuringiensis* (Bt). This bacterium kills many kinds of insect larvae by paralyzing the digestive system. Bt is sold as a dust or liquid under such trade names as Dipel and Thuricide. A new strain that is effective against Colorado potato beetle larvae (Bt "San Diego") is sold under trade names such as Beetle Beater. Milky spore (*Bacillus popillae*) is another example of a biological pest control. By killing Japanese beetle grubs, it can effectively control the Japanese beetle population in your yard for up to twenty years.

## Organic Insecticides

As a last resort, you can pull out the big guns. Most natural insecticides are less toxic than synthetic chemicals. They don't accumulate in the environment or in animal tissues, and most insects don't readily develop resistance to them. Still, they can upset the ecological balance in your garden because some of them will also kill beneficial insects and honeybees. They should be used with caution and care. Be aware of any specific toxicities indicated on the label, and spray late in the day when honeybees have returned to their hives. Always wear a mask and remove contact lenses when applying dusts, and wear gloves and protective clothing when applying any kind of insecticide. Follow label directions carefully.

**DIATOMACEOUS EARTH (DE).** This is made from the fossilized skeletons of marine creatures known as diatoms. The razor-sharp particles pierce soft-bodied creatures such as slugs, beetles, aphids, spider mites, cabbage loopers, and hornworms (but not earthworms),

## Resources

**Gardener's Supply**
**Pest Control Hotline:**
802-660-4620

### SUPPLIERS

**BioOrganics Supply Center**
http://www.bio-organics.com
*On-line catalog for organic pesticides and fertilizers; also carries beneficial microorganisms.*

**The Bug Store**
http://www.bugstore.com
*Order beneficial insects on-line.*

**Gardens Alive**
5100 Schenley Place
Lawrenceburg, IN 47025
812-537-8650

**Harmony Farm Supply**
P.O. Box 460
Graton, CA 95444
707-823-9125

**Necessary Trading Company**
One Nature's Way
New Castle, VA 24127
703-864-5103

**Peaceful Valley Farm Supply**
P.O. Box 2209
Grass Valley, CA 95945
916-272-4769

**Planet Natural**
P.O. Box 3146
Bozeman, MT 59772
406-587-0223
http://www.planetnatural.com

**Worm's Way**
3151 South Hwy. 446
Bloomington, IN 47401
812-331-0300
http://www.wormsway.com
*Free catalog; on-line ordering.*

*Field mouse*

killing them by dehydration. The trace minerals found in diatomaceous earth also enhance soil fertility. However, DE is not selective and will also kill some beneficial insects, such as ladybug larvae.

**INSECTICIDAL SOAPS.** Like DE, these work by inducing dehydration, but they are less toxic to bees and other beneficials. They are made from potassium salts of fatty acids. The foliage of some plants is sensitive to insecticidal soaps, so avoid spraying on a hot, sunny day.

**BOTANICAL INSECTICIDES.** This category of products derived from plants includes pyrethrum, rotenone, nicotine, sabadilla, and ryania. These substances break down easily when exposed to light, heat, or water, so they are less likely to contaminate soil or groundwater. Most states allow certified organic farmers to use these agents. However, they are some of the most toxic substances used in organic pest control, so use them as a last resort, and with discretion.

## Common Plant Diseases

The following table describes the symptoms of most common garden diseases.

| Symptom | Description | Agent |
|---|---|---|
| Damping-off | Stem rots at soil line, seedlings topple over | Fungi |
| Root rots | Attack older plants; stunting and wilting | Fungi |
| Wilts | Leaves and/or stems wilt and die due to lack of water | Fungi, bacteria |
| Club root | Common in brassicas; swellings on roots; stunted growth | Fungi |
| Leaf spots | Many types, spots on leaves | Fungi, bacteria |
| Rusts | Orange or white spots on leaves and stems; weakens plant, reduces yield | Fungi |
| Mildews | Spots or white patches on leaves and shoots | Fungi |
| Blights | Dead or damaged leaves; rotten fruit or tubers | Fungi |
| Galls | Swollen masses of abnormal tissue | Fungi, insects, bacteria |
| Cankers | Usually on woody stems; cracks, sunken or raised tissue; may ooze; cause withering | Bacteria |
| Soft rot | Small water-soaked spots that turn mushy and smelly | Bacteria |
| Blisters and curls | Yellow bumps, curled or puckered leaves; sometimes pale or reddish leaves | Virus |
| Mosaic | Leaves become mottled with light green, yellow, or white areas; breaks in flower color | Virus |
| Rosetting | Causes short, bushy growth, stunting; leaves or branches grow too close together | Virus |
| Ring spot | Pale or yellow spots on leaves | Virus |

—from *The Organic Gardener's Handbook of Natural Insect and Disease Control* by Barbara W. Ellis and Fern M. Bradley (Rodale, 1996)

*Plant pathogens can be spread in many ways: by leaving plant debris in the garden; on dirty tools and clothes; and by insects or animals.*

As with other insecticides, take proper precautions when applying botanical pest controls. Wear gloves and protective clothing, and avoid using any insecticides near waterways, because they could be harmful to fish.

## Plant Pathogens and Disease

Blight. Rust. Fusarium wilt. Botrytis. Smut. Scab. The names we give to plant diseases are unpleasant and downright ominous. But then again, so are their consequences. Diseases often appear very suddenly, and can severely weaken or kill a plant within days. Plant diseases can be caused by fungi, bacteria, viruses, or nematodes, which can be soilborne, carried through the air, transmitted by insects, or lodged within dead plant cells. As with insect pests, as soon as you notice a disease problem your first job is to make a diagnosis and identify the culprit. Treatment usually involves removing the infected parts of a plant, or the whole plant, and destroying them.

The same good cultural practices that prevent insect pest infestations are the first line of defense against disease-causing plant pathogens. Build healthy soil, use compost, keep your flowers and vegetables appropriately watered, and clean up garden debris.

A few other practices are particularly important to preventing disease problems.

• Choose disease-resistant varieties. Many ornamental plants and vegetables have proven resistance to diseases such as canker,

## Web Sites

**Iowa State Entomology Index of Internet Resources**
http://www.ent.iastate.edu/List
*A superb directory and search engine; lots of links to ecological pest control sites.*

**Biological Control: A Guide to Natural Enemies in North America**
http://www.nysaes.cornell.edu/ent/biocontrol
*Set up by Cornell University, this site features excellent photographs and detailed information about natural pest and disease control; includes a section on controlling problem weed species, especially those not native to North America.*

mildew, and rust. These will be identified in catalogs and books and on nursery tags.

- Don't overcrowd your plants. Good air circulation prevents the damp conditions that promote the growth of fungi and other disease organisms.

- Watch moisture levels. Notice if the soil is too wet or too dry and correct these conditions. Try to keep foliage dry. Moving susceptible crops from year to year is excellent preventive medicine.

- Practice crop rotation. Even more than insects, disease pathogens can persist in the soil from one season to the next.

- Inspect your plants and regularly prune leaves or stems that you suspect may be diseased. Destroy the cuttings.

- Be sanitary. Humans are effective, if innocent, vectors of plant disease: pathogens can be spread by your footwear, hands, and clothes. Wash your hands before and after working with your plants, and clean your clothes if you think you have come in contact with sick plants.

- Clean your tools. Soil clinging to tools may harbor disease organisms. Similarly, clean out pots and flats before reusing them. A 10 percent bleach solution (1 part bleach to nine parts water) makes a good disinfectant.

You should also be aware that sometimes what looks like disease is really a nutritional problem. Improper pH, deficiencies or excesses of certain micro- or macronutrients in the soil, or temperature extremes can cause plants to appear diseased, and in a sense they are. Always check your reference books first to rule out nutritional problems. Often, such problems can easily be addressed by adding lime, compost, fertilizer, or specific soil amendments. Foliar feeding, especially with organics like seaweed and fish emulsion, can be very helpful for boosting your plants' general health (see the chapters on "Building Healthy Soil" and "Vegetables").

As you continue year by year to build healthy soil in your garden, to understand the nuances of your own ecosystem, and to learn more about insects, animal pests, disease pathogens, and their habits, organic prevention and control will become second nature. You'll find that you have fewer and fewer pest and disease problems, and it will become easier every year to control them without chemicals.

# PART II

## edibles

PASSPORT TO GARDENING · HERBS

THE KITCHEN GARDEN

PASSPORT TO GARDENING · FRUIT

PASSPORT TO GARDENING · VEGETABLES

# the kitchen garden

Robin Wimbiscus, *Solar Gardening*

THE KITCHEN GARDEN

The words "kitchen garden" conjure up images of late-summer harvest and abundance: tomatoes ripening on the vine; baskets full of fresh vegetables, herbs, and flowers; boxes of blueberries and raspberries for a fancy dessert or a simple breakfast. Yet the fresh harvest is not limited to high summer alone. From "spring tonic" perennial plants like rhubarb and asparagus to the frost-hardy vegetables of fall (kale, leeks, Brussels sprouts, and root crops), the well-planned kitchen garden can provide a wide range of crops that are perfect for seasonal cooking.

With its dual emphasis on beauty and practicality, the kitchen garden nourishes both body and soul. This chapter introduces some basic principles behind the kitchen garden tradition, and lists resources that can help you start your own traditions.

## A Royal Legacy

A kitchen garden implies a degree of planning, style, and design that isn't evident in just any backyard vegetable patch. In fact, the kitchen garden needn't be relegated to the backyard at all, but should be treated like any other display garden, with the exception that most or all of the plants that grow in it are edible. It stresses the use of neatly edged, intensively planted beds of vegetables, herbs, and edible or ornamental flowers. It often includes small fruits like strawberries, dwarf fruit trees, or vine and tree fruits pruned and trained in espalier fashion to a wall, trellis, or other support.

Perhaps the most famous kitchen garden of all time was created by the gardener of France's Louis XIV at Versailles. The Sun King's kitchen gardener was a former lawyer named Jean-Baptiste de La Quintinye, who in 1678 began transforming a swampy, uninviting plot of land near the palace (known as *le marais puant*, "the smelly marsh") into the paradigm for all formal kitchen gardens to come. Ever since that time, the French tradition of the *potager*, or kitchen garden, has remained strong (hardly a surprise considering the Gallic passion for good food). In 1690 La Quintinye published his "Instructions pour les jardins Fruitiers et Potagers," a book that stayed in print for 150 years. Even today, the

## Guest Expert
### Lyndon Virkler

Nothing says fresh seasonal cooking like herbs and edible flowers, just picked from the garden. From the first chives in spring, to starry blue borage blossoms in midsummer, to frost-hardy thyme in the late fall: every season is enhanced by their appearance in the garden and on the plate.

Fresh herbs and flowers add incredible flavor to foods — sometimes subtle, but just as often spicy and intense. Plus they lend a touch of elegance to the simplest of dishes. Your mealtime options suddenly expand from "Chicken again?" to Lemon Thyme Chicken, Stir-Fry with Cilantro, and Blanquette with Tarragon. Low-fat food becomes a delight, not deprivation, when fresh herbs and flowers are added.

While they are always best when fresh-picked, herbs and edible flowers can also be preserved in a number of ways, to be enjoyed throughout the year. Flavored vinegars make salads and marinades something special, and can be used to deglaze sauté or roasting pans to make a savory sauce.

Experiment with herb and flower vinegars made from chive blossoms, thyme, opal basil, or nasturtiums, or mix herbs and fruits together, such as lemon and dill or chili and lime (great for making salsa).

If you're tired of the traditional basil pesto, try using other green herbs like arugula or sage; or make a Moroccan charmoula — a spicy lemon, garlic, and cilantro paste that's great as a marinade for grilled fish or to finish a soup.

In short, there are no limits when cooking with fresh herbs and flowers, and the satisfaction of growing them in your own garden makes the possibilities all the more exciting.

*Lyndon Virkler is a Chef Instructor at New England Culinary Institute in Vermont and an avid gardener and compost maker.*

## Favorite Books

**Cooking from the Garden: Creative Gardening and Contemporary Cuisine** *by Rosalind Creasy* (Sierra Club Books, 1988). This rich, fascinating book is a treat for cooks and gardeners alike. Unfortunately, it is also currently out-of-print. The author describes lots of actual theme gardens (some featuring chilies, grains, herbs, and edible flowers), includes profiles of master chefs and growers, and sprinkles 180 recipes throughout. An encyclopedia of superior vegetables in the back gives good growing information. Highly recommended. 562 pages, paperback, $20.00.

**The New Kitchen Garden** *by Anna Pavord* (DK Publishing, 1996). A colorful, well-conceived book that features sample garden designs, as well as good growing information on many edible plants (fruits, vegetables, herbs, and flowers). A comprehensive section on planning and cultivating techniques is particularly useful. 208 pages, hardcover, $29.95.

**The Complete Kitchen Garden: The Art of Designing and Planting an Edible Garden** *by Patrick Bowe* (Macmillan, 1996). This book is for people who want to create kitchen gardens that are as beautiful as they are useful. The text offers a lot of information on ornamental design, and profiles 14 decorative gardens in North America and Western Europe. 224 pages, hardcover, $35.00.

## TIPS FOR COOKING FRESH HERBS AND EDIBLE FLOWERS

➤ When buying edible flowers, make sure they have been organically grown (not sprayed with pesticides). Don't use flowers from a florist for cooking.

➤ Pick herbs and flower blossoms in the morning, just after the dew has dried and before the heat of the day has made them limp.

➤ When herbs start to blossom the flavor of the herb itself often fades. Keep some plants well cut for their leaves, and allow others to flower if you want to use the blossoms. Harvest buds and blossoms to prevent plants from bolting or going to seed.

➤ Both flowers and herbs should be gently washed and well dried before use.

➤ Large flower blossoms, unless you are stuffing them, should be cut into slivers for easier eating and a more pleasant texture. Remove the stems of the flower, and the stamen if it is large or tough.

➤ Fresh herbs contain volatile oils that are easily cooked out. Add them toward the end of cooking time (in the last ten minutes or so).

➤ Variety in planting means variety on the table. Experiment with different herbs and flowers from the same species and you'll be rewarded with a full range of tastes and colors.

—from Chef Lyndon Virkler,
New England Culinary Institute

*The best site for a kitchen garden is near the house, sunny, and shielded from the wind.*

---

Potager du Roi (king's kitchen garden) is still growing at Versailles on more than 20 acres of land, still producing 60 tons of pears and apples each year, and yielding a similar abundance of vegetables.

Fortunately, you don't need 20 acres of land or a staff of gardeners to create your own kitchen garden. All it takes is desire and a little thoughtful planning. Also, you don't need to stick to ordered, geometric designs. A more informal style, with plants in a sunny, cottage-garden setting, is just as much a kitchen garden as a fancy French potager, with its serried ranks of cabbage and leeks, or its hedgelike borders of herbs and flowers.

## Siting and Planning

When designing a kitchen garden, start with a site that is sunny and open but not exposed to harsh winds, which will stress plants and reduce their yield. Planting a living hedge as a windbreak or building a rock or masonry wall around the garden are two classic approaches to creating a warmer, sheltered microclimate for plants and thus extending the growing season. Don't place a solid windbreak or wall at the down-slope side of the garden, though, since cold air flows downhill on frosty nights. If this side of the garden needs to be enclosed for animal protection, use an open fence that doesn't restrict air flow. For the same reason, try to site the garden in the middle of a sloping piece of ground, rather than at the bottom of a slope. If you can, add a south-facing greenhouse or cold frame bed to the garden, for starting seeds, hardening-off young plants, or growing hardy winter greens like mâche and arugula. (See "Greenhouse Gardening" and "Extending the Season".)

A few other basic rules of vegetable gardening apply to kitchen gardens as well. For instance, they should be sited fairly close to the house, for both aesthetic and practical reasons. Aesthetic because the kitchen garden is meant for display as well as for food production. Practical because water sources are normally located close to the house, and access to water is crucial in most areas during the summer months.

The whole purpose of the kitchen garden is to provide an abundance of fresh vegetables, herbs, flowers, and fruit for the table. In other words, you want to be able to run outside while you're cooking or preparing food, snipping off a few sage leaves or harvesting a couple of pattypan squash as needed. You don't want to go on safari to some distant garden, one which will probably be neglected, haphazard, and overgrown with weeds. Relegate space-hogging crops such as winter squash and large block plantings of corn to that more distant site. But keep specialty vegetables, culinary herbs, salad greens, and edible flowers close at hand for easy picking.

Another important concept in kitchen gardening is maximizing space through succession planting — sowing seeds and setting out plants frequently to take the place of crops that you're harvesting for the table.

For more information on succession planting for a continuous harvest, turn to the "Vegetables" chapter.

## Making Your Beds

The size and shape of your kitchen garden beds can vary, but in general formal gardens use some type of neatly edged, permanent raised beds. Raised beds warm up more quickly in the spring, thus allowing you to get a jump on the growing season. What's more, they usually can accommodate more plants than either regular or wide-row plantings.

Plan to build your raised beds up to twelve inches high. You can either hill up the beds, giving them a slightly crowned or sloping surface, or enclose them with permanent sides. Some gardeners use old railroad ties, which are generally treated with creosote to discourage rot. Other people prefer using pressure-treated lumber. Be aware that most chemically treated woods appear to have an adverse effect on the soil life surrounding them (though how much of an effect is still an open question). A thoroughly modern (and ecologically correct) compromise would be to use "lumber" made out of recycled plastic. Untreated wood is another option. Depending on your climate, it may last three to ten years.

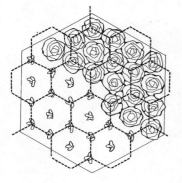

*Hexagonal planting enables efficient use of space.*

## Other Good Books

**The Kitchen Garden Month-by-Month** *by Andi Clevely* (David & Charles, 1996). Stresses the continuous kitchen garden, with very practical, month-by-month instructions on when to sow, transplant, and harvest crops for a full year's succession of produce. A British book, but one that Americans also will find extremely useful. 144 pages, hardcover, $24.95.

**The Kitchen Garden** *by Sylvia Thompson* (Bantam, 1995). Consists mainly of A–Z plant listings that are descriptive and include recommended varieties. A "gardener's notebook" section provides lots of growing tips. 416 pages, hardcover, $27.95.

### SALAD GARDENING GUIDES

**The Salad Garden** *by Joy Larkcom* (Penguin, 1996). A great resource that covers

basic garden techniques, but more importantly introduces readers to the wide range of salad vegetables — some common, others little-known (Abyssinian cabbage, sea-kale, etc.). Also covers herbs, flowers, and wild salad plants. Color photos by Roger Phillips are botanically useful, not merely decorative. Includes a chapter on salad preparation. 168 pages, paperback, $19.95.

**The Harrowsmith Salad Garden: A Complete Guide to Growing and Dressing Fresh Vegetables and Greens** *by Turid Forsyth and Merilyn Simonds Mohr* (Camden House, 1992).
A beautiful and well-researched book on salad plants of all types, from exotic greens to root vegetables. Good growing information and excellent recipes. Highly recommended, especially for cool-climate

gardeners. 160 pages, paperback, $19.95.

### COOKBOOKS FOR GOURMET GARDENERS

**Recipes from a Kitchen Garden** *by Renee Shepherd and Fran Raboff* (Ten Speed Press, 1993).
No fluff, just creative and delicious recipes for both common and unusual varieties of garden vegetables. Renee Shepherd is the founder of Shepherd's Garden Seeds (see "Resources," page 76) and her talent for using homegrown produce is obvious. Try a Crustless Spinach Pie, a Summer Squash Chowder, or the Orange-Calendula Drop Cookies. Highly recommended. 176 pages, paperback, $11.95. Also by the same authors is **More Recipes from a Kitchen Garden** (Ten Speed Press, 1995).

**Potager: Fresh Garden Cooking in the French Style** *by Georgeanne Brennan* (Chronicle Books, 1992).
This mouth-watering book takes readers through the four seasons of a *potager*, or kitchen garden, reflecting the French passion for fresh ingredients and offering 60 recipes like Sorrel and Potato Soup, Leek and Cod Gratin, and many more. 144 pages, paperback, $18.95.

**Edible Flowers: From Garden to Palate** *by Cathy Wilkinson Barash* (Fulcrum Publishing, 1995).
A beautiful book featuring background and growing information for 67 edible flowers, plus 280 recipes, many developed by noted North American chefs. For something different, try Lilac Chicken or Sweet Woodruff Ice Cream. 264 pages, paperback, $22.95.

# How to Force Belgian Endive

The pale, elongated little heads of Belgian endive that you find in the market are actually fairly simple to force at home, in a cool cellar or similar location, to provide fresh greens during the winter. In fact, this is common practice in the French countryside, where the heads are known as *chicons*. The other name for Belgian endive is witloof ("white leaf") chicory.

Sow seeds around midsummer in cooler climates, in early fall in warmer regions. Plant seeds ½-inch deep in rows spaced 12 to 18 inches apart; thin seedlings to stand 12 inches apart in the row.

After the first light frosts, dig up the parsnip-like roots, which should measure about 10 inches long.

Store the roots in a cool root cellar or other location (35° to 40°F) in a box of moistened sand or peat moss, just as you would carrots or other root vegetables. Then, around the middle of winter, cut off the bottom of the roots so that they measure about 8 to 10 inches in length, and stand them upright, neck to neck, in their storage boxes or other containers, surrounded by moistened sand or peat moss.

Move the boxes into a completely dark, warmer location (around 50° to 60°F). Begin watering lightly and regularly, to keep the humidity high, around 95 percent. One way to create these conditions is to place the forcing containers inside a plastic bag that has one or two holes punched in it.

Harvest the chicons (endive heads) when they are 4 to 6 inches long by cutting them off just above the crown of the plant. With proper care, you should be able to force a second and even a third crop of heads from each of the roots.

Radicchio is another kind of chicory that you can force during the winter, in the same way as Belgian endive.

Also, seed companies now carry hybrid witloof chicories that can be forced without the sand or peat moss. The Cook's Garden (see "Resources," page 76) currently offers two such chicories: 'Zoom,' which produces the distinctive pale yellow-white chicons, and 'Robin,' whose heads are an attractive pale pink.

Kathy Bray, *Four-Season Harvest*

The best bed width is one that is narrow enough to allow you access to plants from either side. Four feet is a comfortable reach for most people, with two feet of bed accessible from either side. Beyond that, the size and shape of the bed will depend on your own site and sense of design. You might decide to make square, circular, or hexagonal beds to achieve a formal look, or just run a few 4-foot-wide row beds as far as your garden allows. The main advantage to smaller beds is that it gives you more control over the design and "look" of the garden, with manageable plantings of one to three crops that can be tended, harvested, and replanted as necessary in a clearly defined way. It also makes crop rotation a simple process. (See "Vegetables," page 78.)

Keep in mind that, as with perennial flower beds, the beds of your kitchen garden should be designed to be fairly permanent. Edging beds with railroad ties, bricks, or stones gives the garden a neat, formal appearance. Another possibility involves defining the edges of beds with low-growing perennial plants such as alpine strawberries, or annual flowers such as signet marigolds or compact nasturtiums.

Sow seeds or place transplants in a diagonal (hexagonal) grid pattern when planting the beds (see illustration, page 73). This maximizes growing space, giving each plant just the right amount of shoulder room it needs — nothing more, nothing less. Of course, if you plant this intensively, and if you plan on growing a succession of crops for fresh harvest in the same bed throughout the season, you will need to continually build up and fertilize your soil, so plants get the nutrients they need to grow. Add plenty of organic matter to the beds (compost, well-rotted manure, etc.) between crops and at the beginning and end of the growing season. Apply other minerals such as rock phosphate and lime as needed after your soil has been tested by a professional soil laboratory. (See "Building Healthy Soil.")

## Choosing Plant Varieties

Since the kitchen garden, in its highest form, does double-duty as both an ornamental and a food garden, try to select plants that will enhance the overall design. Annual flowers (whether edible or simply ornamental) make beautiful edgings for beds and work well as companion plants with vegetables. In addition, some vegetables (squash, okra) and herbs (basil, borage) also have attractive flowers that add to their appeal in the kitchen garden.

The predominant color of a vegetable garden is green, of course, but within that one color are an almost infinite number of shades and variations: blue-green, gray-green, green leaves with colorful veins or spots. Also, many vegetables have a red- or purple-leaved form, which contrasts remarkably well with the green foliage and fruits of other garden plants. You can achieve very decorative and striking effects, for example, by interplanting different-colored varieties of lettuce. And the wine-dark leaves of purple basil mix well with almost any other plant. The possibilities for stunning color displays are endless: picture a fall garden with delicate, ruffly pink lavatera growing among sturdy red cabbage heads.

Edible flowers and flowering herbs are an important component of any kitchen garden. Not only are they useful in light cooking and salads, but they add immeasurably to the beauty and color of the garden. (For details on a few of the more popular edible flowers, see below.) Finally, don't exclude nonedible plants from consideration when planning the

## Top Ten Edible Flowers

| BOTANICAL NAME | COMMON NAME | VARIETIES | GROWING NOTES |
|---|---|---|---|
| *Allium schoenoprasum* | garden chives | species | perennial (hardy to Zone 3); 12"; sun to part shade; moist soil |
| *Borago officinalis* | borage | species | annual; 18" to 36"; sun |
| *Calendula officinalis* | calendula, pot-marigold | Kablouna, Pacific Beauty, Touch of Red | annual; 12" to 24"; sun |
| *Lavandula angustifolia* | English lavender | Hidcote, Munsted | perennial (hardy to Zone 5); 12" to 36"; sun |
| *Ocimum basilicum* var. *purpurescens* | basil (purple) | Dark Opal, Osmin, Purple Ruffles | tender annual; 18"; sun; warm soil |
| *Phaseolus coccineus* | runner bean | Painted Lady (bicolor), Scarlet Runner, Dutch White | grown as annual; 6 to 18 feet (climbing forms); sun |
| *Salvia viridis* | annual clary sage | species | annual; 12"; sun |
| *Tagetes signata* (*T. tenuifolia*) | signet marigold | Golden Gem, Lemon Gem, Tangerine Gem | annual; 6" to 12"; sun |
| *Tropaeolum majus*; *T. minus* | nasturtium | Empress of India, Gleam Mix, Whirlybird (*T. majus*; trailing form); Alaska Mix, Jewel Mix (*T. minus*; compact form) | annual; 6" (*T. minus*); to 6 feet (*T. majus*); sun; light soil |
| *Viola tricolor*; *V. x Wittrockiana* | Johnny-jump-up, pansy | Helen Mount, King Henry (*V. tricolor*); Imperial Antique, Super Swiss Mix (*V. x Wittrockiana*) | short-lived perennial (*V. tricolor*; hardy to Zone 4); annual (*V. x Wittrockiana*); 6" to 12"; sun/part shade/shade |

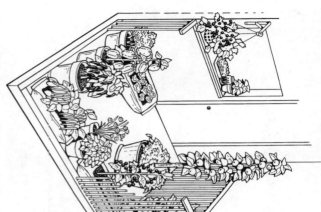

*You can grow a kitchen garden in pots on your patio or deck.*

kitchen garden. The main emphasis may be on culinary plants, but if you have space there's no reason to overlook other worthy annuals, such as globe-amaranth (*Gomphrena globosa*) or zinnias (*Zinnia elegans*). Any flowers that are good for cutting and arranging, like these, definitely belong in the kitchen garden.

## Container or Patio Gardens

Not everyone has the yard space necessary to grow even a small salad or herb garden. Urbanites and apartment dwellers can take heart, though, because a kitchen garden can certainly be accommodated on a sunny patio or balcony.

First, select varieties of plants that are compact in form and will grow well in containers. Most kinds of herbs grow well in pots, as do greens like leaf lettuce and Swiss chard. Any kind of vegetable that has a bushy growing habit (determinate tomatoes, almost all kinds of peppers, even bush snap beans) can be grown in containers. Read seed catalog descriptions and select the best varieties. For instance, you might want to choose varieties that bear a succession of smaller fruits rather than putting lots of effort into two or three enormous eggplants, tomatoes, or peppers.

Even if you already have a separate kitchen garden, you might want to take advantage of a warm, sheltered courtyard or patio for certain kinds of container plants. Growing citrus fruit, for instance, becomes a possibility even for northern growers if the trees are planted in large containers that can be brought indoors for the winter. One excellent, hardy, and naturally dwarf citrus tree is the 'Meyer' lemon, which rarely exceeds 6 feet in height.

## Resources for Kitchen Gardeners

### MAGAZINES

**Kitchen Garden** is a terrific magazine launched in 1996 by Taunton Press, the people who publish *Fine Gardening* and other high-quality periodicals and books. Each issue strikes a nice balance between vegetable gardening how-to and cooking techniques and recipes. A one-year subscription (6 issues) is $24; the toll-free order number is 800-888-8286.

**Cook's Illustrated** magazine isn't about gardening, but kitchen gardeners who want to make the most out of their homegrown produce should check it out. CI is one part culinary arts class, one part

*Consumer Reports,* with just a pinch of high-school chemistry lab thrown in for good measure. Articles usually focus on a single technique (the best way to roast sweet peppers, thicken a fruit pie, etc.). A one-year subscription (6 issues) is $24.95; the toll-free order number is 800-526-8442.

### SEED SUPPLIERS

**The Cook's Garden**
P.O. Box 535
Londonderry, VT 05148
800-457-9703
*In addition to a full range of vegetables and flowers, Cook's Garden features an astounding array of lettuces and other salad greens,*

*including several salad mixes, or mescluns.*

**Le Jardin du Gourmet**
Box 75K
St. Johnsbury, VT 05863
Catalog $1.
*Specializes in small, inexpensive packets of seed especially for people who have small or indoor/patio gardens. Over 200 kinds of herb seeds, plus imported vegetable and flower seeds and excellent shallots, garlics, and herb plants.*

**The Gourmet Gardener**
8650 College Blvd.
Overland Park, KS 66210
913-345-0490
*Varieties offered in this catalog have been tested at the*

*company's trial garden in northern France, then grown in the U.S. to see how well they adapt to North American growing conditions. Listings include herbs, vegetables, and edible flowers, and the catalog features many French heirloom varieties.*

**Shepherd's Garden Seeds**
30 Irene St.
Torrington, CT 06790
860-482-3638
*Choice selection of vegetables, herbs, and flowers for home gardeners. The catalog stresses cooking, and each year includes several terrific recipes. (See also the "Cookbooks" box, p. 73.)*

# Garden Gear

Flowers add an extra dimension to your cooking. Not only are they visually striking on a plate, but they lend unique and different flavors to ordinary dishes. Use flowers as garnishes, or in salads, flavored butters, sorbets, and many other dishes. The Cook's Garden offers this **Ornamental Edibles Seed Collection** to kitchen gardeners. The collection includes one packet each of 'Kablouna', calendula, 'Gem Mix' marigold, 'Tip Top', and 'Alaska', nasturtiums, annual clary, 'Emperor' runner bean, borage, and 'Purple Ruffles' basil. *Ornamental Edibles Seed Collection (8 packets), $13.50; available from The Cook's Garden (see "Resources," page 76).*

From the salad experts at The Cook's Garden comes this **Year-Round Lettuce Collection,** which will keep kitchen gardeners in salads throughout the growing season. It features eight outstanding varieties of lettuce, plus a detailed planting guide. Selection contains one packet each of: 'Four Seasons', 'Reine des Glaces', 'Red Grenoble', 'Kinemontpas', 'Royal Oak Leaf', 'Salad Bowl', 'Winter Density' and 'Rouge d'Hiver' lettuces. *Year-Round Lettuce Collection (8 packets), $13.25; available from The Cook's Garden (see "Resources").*

Wash your favorite salad greens in the bowl of this high-capacity Zyliss Salad

**Spinner,** then transfer them to the colander section, replace the lid, and pull the cord. The special yo-yo action spins the greens first one way, then the other, to remove moisture without damaging delicate leaves. *Zyliss Salad Spinner, $30.00; available from The Cook's Garden (see "Resources").*

This compact **Italian Tomato Press** is the ideal tool for many purée jobs. Just place halved or quartered ripe tomatoes in the top, turn the handle, and the screen

separates tomato pulp from skins and seeds.

It will also process cooked apples for applesauce. Attaches in seconds to any table or countertop.

A suction cup base holds it firmly in place. Red polypropylene body with stainless steel strainer and durable plastic blades. 9¼" high. *#08-207 Italian Tomato Press $24.95*

The hardest part about building a raised bed from wooden planks is figuring out how to secure the corners. These heavy-duty recycled plastic **Raised Bed Connectors** make the job easy. Simply drive the connector stakes into the ground, slip on the brackets, and slide your lumber right into place. The brackets adjust to any angle so you can create a variety of bed shapes. Accommodates 2" x 6", 2" x 8", or 2" x 10" milled lumber in lengths up to 4'. *#03-192  Raised Bed Connectors, set of 2  $12.00  Buy 3 or more sets  $11.50 each*

Lightweight and durable, **Recycled Plastic Lumber** fits perfectly into the Raised Bed Connectors described above. It can be nailed, drilled, or bolted just like regular wood. Each plank measures 2" x 5½" x 4' L. *#03-194  Recycled Plastic Lumber, set of 2  $17.95  Buy 2 or more sets  $17.50 each*

This handsome **Cold Frame** is crafted from weather-resistant cypress. The two clear acrylic panels lift up for easy access and venting, and they can be secured at two different heights for controlling interior temperatures. 53½" L x 26½" W x 14½" H. Optional **Vent Openers** automatically lift the panel to vent excess heat. Simple installation. *#30-081  Cold Frame  $199.00* *#11-229  Automatic Vent Opener  $49.00*

This **Raised Bed Kit** is an inexpensive way to create an extra-deep bed for plants such as tomatoes, potatoes, greens, and flowers. It has a 4' by 8' planting area, enclosed by 11"-high, UV-stabilized polyethylene walls. A center brace adds strength. Sets up in minutes. *#30-279  Double-Deep Raised Bed Kit  $175.00*

# vegetables

Every few years, it seems, the popularity of vegetable gardening surges, often due to economic or social forces (the Victory Gardens from World War II, the back-to-the-land movement of the 1970s, and so on,). But regardless of your lifestyle or income, growing your own vegetables can be fun and rewarding. In fact, vegetable gardening has many benefits beyond the production of great tasting, organically grown food. It teaches children that lettuce and carrots do not come from the produce aisle. It provides good exercise for adults of all ages. It offers a meditative escape from the stress of work and the demands of daily life. And it affords everyone in the family the opportunity to observe nature close at hand, to work with her forces, and to feel a sense of pride in bringing crops to harvest.

All you really need to begin growing vegetables is some decent soil and the information on the back of a seed packet. But once you've started gardening, you will find that growing vegetables well is a real art, one that in its highest form integrates much of the information found in other chapters of this book ("Composting," "Building Healthy Soil," "Pests and Diseases Control," "Extending the Season," "The Kitchen Garden," and others). In this chapter, we'll discuss some basic concepts for growing vegetables organically and introduce you to some of the best sources for more detailed information.

## Join the Crowd

It is estimated that more than 5 million Americans grow at least part of their own food each year. At first this number seems impressive: 5 million of anything sounds like an awful lot. But it also means that some 245 million Americans (around 98 percent) do *not* grow any food for themselves or their families. Suddenly, the number of home vegetable gardeners seemed pathetically small.

One main reason for this is our industrialized society, which values specialization over self-reliance. No one would ever contemplate doing brain surgery at home, and by the same token many people feel that growing vegetables is best left to farmers, the food specialists. But not everyone needs brain surgery, whereas food is a basic commodity that each of us requires every day.

Advice for the would-be organic gardener abounds in the form of magazine articles and books written by a wide array of garden gurus and personalities. Everyone, it seems, has his or her own "system" for

## Guest Expert
## Shepherd Ogden

There are three good ways to gain a big harvest from a small space: grow quick, grow tight, or grow up. Quick crops like salad greens and mesclun are ideal for small gardens because they grow from seed to maturity in little over a month and can be replanted frequently for a continuous harvest. A bed three feet by twelve feet can keep a family of four in salads for 9–12 months, depending on climate. Other crops, such as carrots, turnips, and beets (especially the thin-rooted kinds like 'Cylindra') can be planted densely in raised beds and will produce high yields by making the most of space both above and below ground. Fall crops can be left in the ground for an extended harvest.

The final way to wrest big crops from small gardens is to plant vining crops such as tall peas (in cool weather) and indeterminate tomatoes or pole beans (in warm weather), and then train them up on trellises so that you get the maximum amount of plant for the minimum amount of soil. This is also an excellent solution for shady lots, where the plants can climb into the sun or be housed in containers.

*Shepherd Ogden is founder and president of The Cook's Garden, a mail-order seed and supply house in Londonderry, Vermont (http://www.cooksgarden.com). He is the author of more than 40 magazine articles, and Step by Step Organic Vegetable Gardening and Step by Step Organic Flower Gardening (HarperCollins, 1992 and 1995, respectively).*

## Favorite Books

**Step by Step Organic Vegetable Gardening** *by Shepherd Ogden* (HarperCollins, 1992).
One of the finest books on organic gardening: practical, thoughtful, and readable. Ogden, the co-founder of The Cook's Garden seed company, updates the garden wisdom of his grandfather and draws from his own considerable knowledge and experience. Highly recommended. Currently out of print, but available from The Cook's Garden (see "Vegetable Seed Companies," page 87). 320 pages, paperback, $16.00.

**How to Grow More Vegetables** *by John Jeavons* (Ten Speed Press, 1995).
The fifth edition of this popular work on biointensive gardening from John Jeavons includes a lot of good information on double-digging garden beds and building healthy soil. Lots of useful charts and illustrations. For gardeners who have some growing experience and an interest in sustainable methods. 232 pages, paperback, $16.95.

**Square Foot Gardening** *by Mel Bartholomew* (Rodale, 1981).
A bonafide classic that is must reading for people with small gardens. In addition to intensive planting methods, the book provides some valuable information on trellising crops to maximize growing space. 352 pages, paperback, $16.95.

growing vegetables, and the available information runs the gamut from traditional folk wisdom (planting by the moon, companion planting, etc.) to the latest scientific research.

So, do you really need to keep up on all this information, or subscribe to a particular system or philosophy to have a great vegetable garden? Of course not. In fact, much of the knowledge found in books and articles tends to cover much of the same ground. There are only a few basic rules to good organic vegetable gardening, with the first one being *Do what works for you.* The following sections highlight some of what we consider to be key concepts in vegetable gardening. Much of the specific information has been adapted from *Solar Gardening* by Leandre Poisson and Gretchen Vogel Poisson (Chelsea Green, 1994) and is used with permission; see review, page 51.

## "Feed the Soil, Not the Plant"

This phrase is like a mantra for organic gardeners, and with good reason. In conventional chemical agriculture, crop plants are indeed "fed" directly using synthetic fertilizers. When taken to extremes, this kind of chemical force-feeding can gradually impoverish the soil, turning it

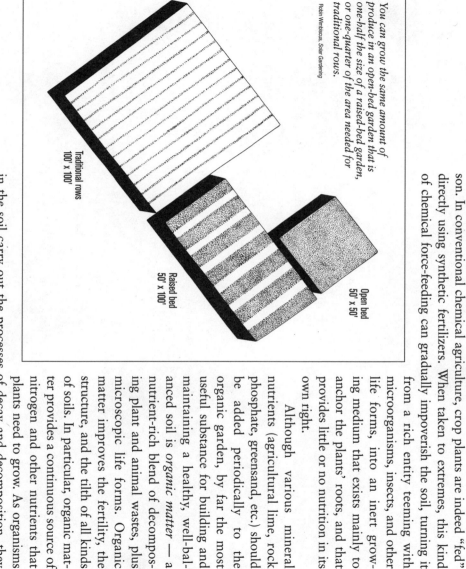

Robin Wimbiscus, *Solar Gardening*

*You can grow the same amount of produce in an open-bed garden that is one-half the size of a raised-bed garden, or one-quarter of the area needed for traditional rows.*

Traditional rows
100' x 100'

Raised bed
50' x 100'

Open bed
50' x 50'

from a rich entity teeming with microorganisms, insects, and other life forms, into an inert growing medium that exists mainly to anchor the plants' roots, and that provides little or no nutrition in its own right.

Although various mineral nutrients (agricultural lime, rock phosphate, greensand, etc.) should be added periodically to the organic garden, by far the most useful substance for building and maintaining a healthy, well-balanced soil is *organic matter* — a nutrient-rich blend of decomposing plant and animal wastes, plus microscopic life forms. Organic matter improves the fertility, the structure, and the tilth of all kinds of soils. In particular, organic matter provides a continuous source of nitrogen and other nutrients that plants need to grow. As organisms in the soil carry out the processes of decay and decomposition, they make these nutrients available to plants.

For more on this subject, see the chapter on "Building Healthy Soil."

## Make Efficient Use of Space

A particular site and its characteristics (the amount of sunlight it receives, proximity to a source of water, and protection from frost and wind) are important considerations for any kind of garden. In the chapter on "The Kitchen Garden" we outline some of the guidelines for choosing and modifying a garden site. Yet just as crucial for vegetable growers is making the most of available garden space once you've decided on a site.

Lots of people dream of having a huge vegetable garden, a sprawling site that will be big enough to grow everything they want, including space-hungry crops like corn, dried beans, pumpkins and winter squash, melons, cucumbers, and watermelons. If you have the room and, even more importantly, the time and energy needed to grow a huge garden well, then by all means go for it. But gardens that make efficient use of growing space are much easier to care for, whether you're talking about a few containers on the patio or a 50-foot-by-100-foot plot in the backyard.

**GET RID OF YOUR ROWS.** The first way to maximize space in the garden is to begin converting from traditional row planting to 3- or 4-foot-wide raised beds. Single rows of crops, while they might be efficient on farms that use large machines for planting, cultivating, and harvesting, are often not the best way to go in the backyard vegetable garden. In a home-sized garden, the fewer rows you have, the fewer paths between rows you will need, and the more square footage you will have available for growing crops. An even more efficient use of space involves the intensive or "open bed" concept, in which practically the entire garden surface is treated as potential growing space (see illustration, page 80).

If you are already producing the amount of food you want in your existing row garden, then by switching to raised beds or open beds you will actually be able to downsize the garden. By freeing up this existing garden space, you can plant green manure crops on the part of the garden that is not currently raising vegetables and/or rotate growing areas more easily from year to year. Or you might find that you now have

## How to Grow Inside-Out Tomatoes

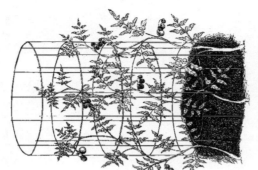

Robin Wimbiscus, Solar Gardening

No, inside-out doesn't mean that your tomatoes will have all their seeds and pulp out where the skin should be. It refers to an unusual method of trellising or caging tomatoes recommended by garden authors Lea and Gretchen Poisson in their book *Solar Gardening* (Chelsea Green, 1994).

First, make a circular tomato cage out of heavy-duty wire; concrete-reinforcing mesh is ideal for this job because it's sturdy, will last for years, and has large square openings that make reaching inside easy. Cut the wire mesh in lengths of 30 to 36 inches, using a good pair of wire cutters, and (wearing work gloves) twist the cut ends of the wire together to form the cage cylinder.

Next, place the cage out in the garden and fill the interior space halfway to the top with well-rotted hay. The hay serves two purposes: it anchors the cage and provides nutrients for the tomatoes as it decays.

Finally, plant four or five indeterminate (vining) tomato plants around the *outside* of the cage. As the tomato plants vine upward, gently weave their stems through the wire mesh to train the plants to their support.

This neat method makes the ripening tomatoes easy to see and easy to harvest. Give it a try and see how it works for you.

# Succession Planting for Fresh Harvest

In the first column, this table indicates how many succession plantings you can make of various vegetable crops during an eight-month growing season. Of course, not all gardeners have eight months during which they can grow vegetables in the open garden, but there are many ways to give plants some early- and late-season protection and make the most of your climate (see the chapter "Extending the Season," for some ideas).

The second column shows the length of the harvest period for each crop of the vegetable grown, and the third column suggests how many plants you'll need per planting to feed one person.

| VEGETABLE | Number of Added Succession Plantings in 8-Mo. Period | Harvest Period (in weeks) | Plants per Person for Each Planting |
|---|---|---|---|
| Amaranth | 6 | 3 | 10 |
| Asparagus | 1 | 8 | 5 |
| Artichoke (globe) | 1 | 8 | 1 |
| Artichoke (Jerusalem) | 1 | 8–16 | 4 |
| Beans (snap) | 2 | 6–10 | 15 |
| Beans (shell) | 1–2 | 6–10 | 20 |
| Beans (dried) | 1 | 2 | 20 |
| Beets | 4 | 3–6 | 15 |
| Bok choi (pak choi) | 3–4 | 4 | 5 |
| Broccoli | 2 | 6 | 5 |
| Brussels sprouts | 1 | 6–10 | 2 |
| Bunching onions | 1 | 6–12 | 20 |
| Cabbage (round) | 2 | 4 | 2–3 |
| Cardoons | 1 | 4–8 | 2 |
| Carrots | 3 | 9–11 | 50 |
| Cauliflower | 2 | 2 | 1 |
| Celeriac | 2 | 6 | 4 |
| Celery | 2 | 11 | 5 |
| Celtuce | 4 | 6 | 3–5 |
| Chicory | 3 | 2–3 | 5–10 |
| Chinese broccoli (gai lohn) | 6 | 2 | 6 |
| Collards | 2 | 8–16 | 5 |
| Corn salad (mâche) | 8 | 1–2 | 10 |
| Corn (sweet) | 3 | 1 | 10–15 |
| Corn (dried) | 1 | 2 | 20–30 |
| Cucumber | 2 | 8 | 3 |
| Daikon radish | 4 | 5 | 6 |
| Dandelion greens | 6 | 1 | 6–8 |
| Eggplant | 1 | 10 | 3 |
| Escarole (endive) | 3 | 6 | 6 |
| Florence (bulb) fennel | 3 | 6 | 10 |
| Flowering cabbage or kale | 1 | 12–15 | 3 |
| Garlic | 2 | 4 | 1–3 |
| Gobo (edible burdock) | 1 | 10–15 | 2 |
| Good King Henry | 1 | 4 | 5 |
| Hamburg (root) parsley | 2 | 6 | 8 |

| VEGETABLE | Number of Added Succession Plantings in 8-Mo. Period | Harvest Period (in weeks) | Plants per Person for Each Planting |
|---|---|---|---|
| Horseradish | 1 | 12–15 | 1 |
| Kale | 2 | 6–15 | 5 |
| Kohlrabi | 2 | 2 | 6 |
| Leeks | 1 | 6–15 | 10–25 |
| Lettuce | 4 | 3–6 | 8 |
| Melons | 1 | 6–10 | 3 |
| Mizuna | 6 | 2 | 6 |
| Mustard greens | 3 | 6–12 | 5 |
| New Zealand spinach | 1 | 6–12 | 3 |
| Okra | 1 | 6–12 | 5 |
| Onions (bulb) | 1 | 6 | 20 |
| Parsnips | 1 | 6–15 | 12 |
| Peas (snap and shell) | 2 | 4–8 | 30–50 |
| Peanuts | 1 | 2–3 | 5–10 |
| Peppers (sweet) | 1 | 8–12 | 3 |
| Peppers (hot) | 1 | 8–12 | 1 |
| Potatoes (Irish) | 2 | 2–3 | 5 |
| Pumpkins | 1 | 4–6 | 1 |
| Purslane | 3 | 3 | 5 |
| Radicchio | 1 | 5 | 10 |
| Radish (round) | 8 | 1–2 | 12 |
| Roquette | 4 | 2–4 | 5 |
| Rutabaga | 1 | 3–6 | 3 |
| Salsify | 1 | 6–15 | 12 |
| Scallions | 2 | 10–12 | 20–25 |
| Scorzonera | 1 | 6–12 | 4 |
| Sea kale | 1 | 3 | 5 |
| Shallots | 2 | 4–6 | 3 |
| Spinach | 4 | 3–6 | 10 |
| Summer squash | 2 | 6–12 | 1–2 |
| Sunflower | 1 | 2 | 2 |
| Sweet potatoes | 1 | 4–8 | 5 |
| Swiss chard | 2 | 6–20 | 3 |
| Tomatillos | 1 | 6–12 | 1–2 |
| Tomatoes | 1 | 6–15 | 3 |
| Turnip greens | 4 | 2–4 | 3–5 |
| Turnips | 4 | 2–6 | 2–3 |
| Watermelon | 1 | 6–10 | 1 |
| Winter squash | 1 | 2–4 | 2 |
| Zucchini | 2 | 6–12 | 1 |

—from *Solar Gardening* by Leandre Poisson and Gretchen Vogel Poisson (Chelsea Green, 1994).

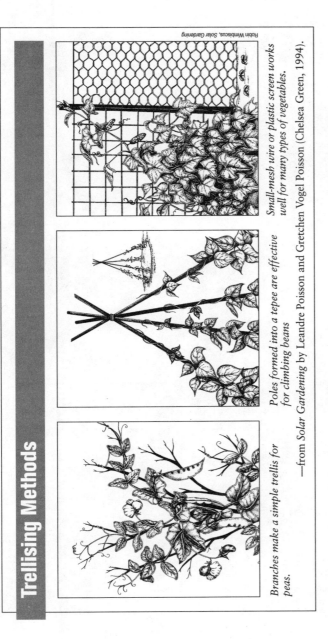

## Trellising Methods

*Branches make a simple trellis for peas.*

*Poles formed into a tepee are effective for climbing beans*

*Small-mesh wire or plastic screen works well for many types of vegetables.*

—from *Solar Gardening* by Leandre Poisson and Gretchen Vogel Poisson (Chelsea Green, 1994).

Robin Wimbiscus, *Solar Gardening*

room for planting new crops — rhubarb, asparagus, small fruits, or flowers for cutting — in the newly available space.

Other good reasons to convert from rows to an intensive garden system like raised beds or open beds include:

**Less effort.** When vegetables are planted intensively (with just enough elbow room between plants) they shade and cool the ground below and require less watering, less weeding, less mulching — in other words, less drudge work for the gardener.

**Less soil compaction.** The more access paths you have between rows or beds, the more you and others will be compacting the soil by walking in them. By increasing the width of the growing beds and reducing the number of paths, you will have more growing area that you won't be walking on, and this untrammeled soil will be fluffier and better for plants' roots.

**GROW UP, NOT OUT.** Next to intensive planting, trellising represents the most efficient way to use space in the garden. People who have tiny gardens will want to grow as many crops as possible on vertical supports, and gardeners who have a lot of space will still need to lend physical support to some of their vegetables, such as climbing varieties of peas and pole beans. Other vegetables that are commonly trellised include vining crops such as cucumbers and tomatoes.

The fence surrounding your garden may well do double-duty as a trellis, so long as the crops grown on the fence can be rotated in different years. Other kinds of trellises are generally constructed from either wood or metal (see the illustrations above for some typical examples). However, no matter which design or materials you use, be sure to have your trellis up and in place well before the plants require its support —

## *Video Picks*

### Dig It!

Watching a videotape of somebody digging for an hour or so may not sound too scintillating, but when your host is John Jeavons, you're sure to learn a lot about building and maintaining great garden soil. Jeavons demonstrates the proper way to double-dig a planting bed, following the methods outlined in his book *How to Grow More Vegetables* (see page 79). VHS format, 60 minutes; $20.00. Available from John Jeavons, 5798 Ridgeweed Rd., Willits, CA 95490, or from Bountiful Gardens; phone: 707-459-6410.

### "The Victory Garden" Vegetable Video

Master gardeners Bob Thompson and Jim Wilson take viewers on a comprehensive crash course in vegetable gardening. An excellent video from the producers of the still-popular PBS gardening show. Includes on-screen indexing by subject matter. VHS format, 60 minutes; $19.95. Available from A.C. Burke & Co.; phone: 310-574-2770.

# THREE-YEAR CROP ROTATION

Robin Wimbiscus, Solar Gardening

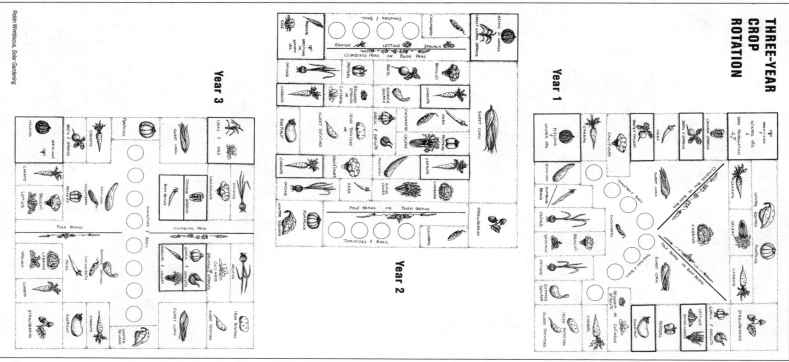

**Year 1**

**Year 2**

**Year 3**

## Keep Crops Moving

Crop rotation within the vegetable garden means planting the same crop in the same place only once every three years. This policy ensures that the same plants will not deplete the same nutrients year after year. It can also help foil any insect pests or disease pathogens that might be lurking in the soil after the crop is harvested.

To use a three-year crop rotation system, make a plan of the garden on paper during each growing season, showing the location of all crops (as an example, see the illustrations at left). If, like most people, you grow a lot of different vegetables, these garden plans are invaluable, because it can be difficult to remember exactly what you were growing where even last season, much less two years ago. Saving garden plans for the past two or three years means that you don't have to rely on memory alone.

## A Continuous Harvest

This advice could as easily belong under the heading of "space efficiency," since planting crops in succession is yet another way to maximize growing area in the garden. All too often, though, gardeners will prepare their seedbeds and plant or transplant

preferably even before you plant the crop. With some vegetables, such as tomatoes or melons, you may also have to tie the plants gently to the support, or carefully weave them through the trellis as they grow.

Many gardening books provide information on trellising. One excellent reference is *Square Foot Gardening* by Mel Bartholomew (see "Favorite Books," page 79).

all their crops on only one or two days in the spring, usually after the last frost date for their location.

While there is nothing wrong with planting a garden this way, wouldn't it be easier to plant a few seeds or transplants at a time, throughout the course of the whole growing season, rather than facing the herculean task of "getting in the garden" all at one time? After all, a job almost always becomes easier the more you divide it up. Plan to plant something new in the garden almost every week of the season, from the first cold-hardy greens and peas in late winter or early spring, to heat-loving transplants such as tomatoes, peppers, and eggplant once the weather becomes warm and settled. Then start all over again, sowing frost-hardy crops from midsummer through mid-fall, depending on your climate. Keep cleaning out beds as you harvest crops to make room

## Other Good Books

**Vegetable Gardening** by *David Chambers and Lucinda Mays, with Laura Martin* (Pantheon, 1994). Part of the America's Garden Guides series, this book was assembled by the staff of Callaway Gardens in Georgia. Particularly good for its recommended varieties, many of which are shown in color photos. 224 pages, paperback, $25.00.

**The Random House Book of Vegetables** by *Roger Phillips and Martyn Rix* (Random House, 1993). Large color photographs show many varieties of common and unusual vegetables. Includes information on history, growing, and pests and diseases. 272 pages, paperback, $25.00.

**Vegetables** by *Patricia Michalak and Cass Peterson* (Rodale, 1993). A well-designed, easy-to-use book that contains both general organic growing information and an A–Z gallery of vegetable crops. 160 pages, paperback, $14.95.

## STORING AND PRESERVING BOOKS

**Root Cellaring: Natural Cold Storage of Fruits & Vegetables** by *Mike and Nancy Bubel* (Storey, 1991). The best book on building and using a root cellar, with profiles and illustrations showcasing a variety of designs — from simple to more sophisticated — used by gardeners across North America. 318 pages, paperback, $12.95.

**Stocking Up** by *Carol Hupping and the staff of the Rodale Food Center* (Simon & Schuster, 1990). Probably the most comprehensive book on the subject, with lots of recipes and general information. In addition to vegetables and fruits, the book gives instructions for

preserving meat and fish, making homemade cheese and ice cream, and much more. 640 pages, paperback, $17.95.

**Canning and Preserving without Sugar, 4th Edition** by *Norma M. MacRae, R.D.* (Globe Pequot, 1997). A must for diabetics, or for health-conscious people who want to avoid refined sugar. Each recipe comes with a calorie count, as well as listing protein, fat, carbohydrate, and cholesterol content. Recipes include Spicy Blueberry-Plum Jam, Dilled Mushrooms, and Cucumber Catsup. 304 pages, paperback, $14.95.

**Ball Blue Book, Vol. 1** (Ball Corporation, 1995). A valuable guide published by the folks who make all those canning jars. Loaded with recipes for pickles, preserves, relishes, chutneys, jams and jellies — you name it. 120 pages, paperback, $5.95. Available at Agway and other retail outlets, or direct from Ball (phone 800-240-3340).

**Keeping the Harvest: Preserving Your Fruits, Vegetables & Herbs** by *Nancy Chioffi and Gretchen Mead* (Storey, 1991). Covers canning, pickling, freezing, and drying. Lots of recipes, tables, and sidebars with useful tips. 208 pages, paperback, $12.95.

Robin Wimbiscus, *Solar Gardening*

# Vegetable Crops List

| VEGETABLE | Plant Spacing in 4 x 8 Bed (inches) | Maximum Number of Plants per 4 x 8 Bed | Average Yield per 4 x 8 Bed (pounds) |
|---|---|---|---|
| Amaranth | 6 | 133 | 9 |
| Asparagus | 24 | 8 | 8 |
| Artichoke (globe) | 18 | 14 | 7 |
| Artichoke (Jerusalem) | 15 | 18 | 35 |
| Beans (snap) | 6 | 133 | 22 |
| Beans (shell) | 6 | 133 | 9 |
| Beans (dried) | 6 | 133 | 5 |
| Beets (round and greens) | 6 | 133 | 35 |
| Beets (cylindrical) | 8 | 75 | 50 |
| Bok choi (pak choi) | 8 | 75 | 30 |
| Broccoli | 12 | 33 | 16 |
| Brussels sprouts | 15 | 18 | 10 |
| Bunching onions | 8 | 75 | 15 |
| Cabbage (round) | 15 | 18 | 25 |
| Cardoons | 30 | 5 | 10 |
| Carrots | 4 | 300 | 35 |
| Cauliflower | 15 | 18 | 20 |
| Celeriac | 10 | 48 | 16 |
| Celery | 10 | 48 | 25 |
| Celtuce | 8 | 75 | 15 |
| Chicory | 10 | 48 | 16 |
| Chinese broccoli (gai lohn) | 9 | 59 | 15 |
| Collards | 10 | 48 | 45 |
| Corn salad (mâche) | 4 | 300 | 9 |
| Corn (sweet) | 12 | 33 | 11 |
| Corn (dried) | 15 | 18 | 6 |
| Cucumber | 15 | 18 | 30 |
| Daikon radish | 8 | 75 | 50 |
| Dandelion greens | 9 | 59 | 15 |
| Eggplant | 8 | 75 | 15 |
| Escarole (endive) | 10 | 48 | 15 |
| Florence (bulb) fennel | 10 | 48 | 16 |
| Flowering cabbage or kale | 9 | 59 | 15 |
| Garlic | 12 | 33 | 8 |
| Gobo (edible burdock) | 15 | 18 | 6 |
| Good King Henry | 15 | 18 | 8 |
| Hamburg (root) parsley | 12 | 33 | 12 |
| Horseradish | 15 | 18 | 9 |

| VEGETABLE | Plant Spacing in 4 x 8 Bed (inches) | Maximum Number of Plants per 4 x 8 Bed | Average Yield per 4 x 8 Bed (pounds) |
|---|---|---|---|
| Kale | 15 | 18 | 18 |
| Kohlrabi | 8 | 75 | 15 |
| Leeks | 6 | 133 | 60 |
| Lettuce | 8 | 75 | 18 |
| Melons | 18 | 14 | 12 |
| Mizuna | 6 | 133 | 15 |
| Mustard greens | 10 | 48 | 35 |
| New Zealand spinach | 12 | 33 | 22 |
| Okra | 15 | 18 | 8 |
| Onions (bulb) | 6 | 133 | 30 |
| Parsnips | 6 | 133 | 50 |
| Peas (bush shell) | 6 | 133 | 10 |
| Peas (bush snap) | 6 | 133 | 15 |
| Peanuts | 12 | 33 | 5 |
| Peppers (sweet) | 15 | 18 | 14 |
| Peppers (hot) | 15 | 18 | 4 |
| Potatoes | 12 | 33 | 19 |
| Pumpkins | 30 | 5 | 25 |
| Purslane | 6 | 133 | 6 |
| Radicchio | 8 | 75 | 12 |
| Radish (round) | 3 | 533 | 18 |
| Roquette | 4 | 333 | 8 |
| Rutabaga | 9 | 59 | 48 |
| Salsify | 8 | 75 | 37 |
| Scallions | 4 | 300 | 32 |
| Scorzonera | 12 | 33 | 15 |
| Sea kale | 18 | 14 | 8 |
| Shallots | 8 | 75 | 22 |
| Spinach | 6 | 133 | 14 |
| Summer squash | 24 | 8 | 40 |
| Sunflower | 18 | 14 | 12 |
| Sweet potatoes | 15 | 18 | 45 |
| Swiss chard | 9 | 59 | 25 |
| Tomatillos | 18 | 14 | 56 |
| Tomatoes | 15 | 18 | 42 |
| Turnips | 9 | 59 | 22 |
| Turnip greens | 8 | 75 | 20 |
| Watermelon | 24 | 8 | 28 |
| Winter squash | 24 | 8 | 18 |
| Zucchini | 24 | 8 | 35 |

NOTE: There are many variables that will affect plant yield, including weather, soil quality, insect damage, and variety grown. The average yields included in this chart are conservative ballpark figures for an intensive growing area with good soil quality. The poundage listed represents only the edible part(s) of the plant.

—from *Solar Gardening* by Leandre Poisson and Gretchen Vogel Poisson (Chelsea Green, 1994).

Robin Wimbiscus, *Solar Gardening*

for new vegetables that will take their place. You can even interplant crops that grow quickly (radishes) alongside other vegetables that require a long season (carrots or parsnips), sowing their seeds together. This makes thinning out the bed an easier chore later on, since you will have already harvested the quick-growing crop and given the long-season vegetables that remain some much-needed elbow room.

Another benefit of succession planting, of course, is that your harvest season lasts longer for every crop. This means that, instead of getting buried in snap beans or summer squash as your plants mature all at once, you can stagger plantings to ensure a steady, but more manageable supply of fresh vegetables. To get an idea of just how productive your garden can be over the course of an entire growing season, refer to the table, "Succession Planting for Fresh Harvest," on page 82.

## Keep Good Records

Finally, we end up where we started — with the realization that, although vegetable gardening can be rewarding even for beginners, there is an art to doing it well. There is also a mountain of good information and advice from other gardeners available to you. Yet one of the most important ways of improving your garden from year to year is to pay close attention to how plants grow, and note your successes and failures in a garden notebook or journal.

Just as drawing a garden plan each year helps you remember where things were growing, so taking notes can help you avoid making the same mistakes again, or ensure that your good results can be reproduced

## *Resources*

### VEGETABLE SEED COMPANIES

**General Suppliers**

W. Atlee Burpee & Co.
300 Park Avenue
Warminster, PA 18991-0001
800-888-1447

The Cook's Garden
P.O. Box 535
Londonderry, VT 05148
800-457-9703

Garden City Seeds
778 Hwy. 93 North
Hamilton, MT 59840
406-961-4837

Johnny's Selected Seeds
Foss Hill Road
Albion, ME 04910-9731
207-437-9294

Nichols Garden Nursery
1190 North Pacific Hwy.
Albany, OR 97321-4580
541-928-9280

George W. Park Seed Co.
Cokesbury Rd.
Greenwood, SC 29647-0001
864-223-7333

Pinetree Garden Seeds
Box 300
New Gloucester, ME 04260
207-926-3400

Seeds of Change
P.O. Box 15700
Santa Fe, NM 87506-5700
888-762-7333

Shepherd's Garden Seeds
30 Irene St.
Torrington, CT 06790
860-482-3638

R.H. Shumway Seedsman
P.O. Box 1
Graniteville, SC 29829
803-663-9771

Willhite Seed Inc.
P.O. Box 23
Poolville, TX 76487
800-828-1840

**Specialty Suppliers**

Filaree Farm
182 Conconully Hwy.
Okanogan, WA 98840
*Huge selection of garlics from all over the world.*

Ronniger's Seed Potatoes
P.O. Box 1838
Orting, WA 98360
*Excellent source of virus-free seed potatoes; also sell onions and garlic.*

Tomato Growers Supply Co.
P.O. Box 720
Fort Myers, FL 33902
(941) 768-1119
*Over 300 varieties of tomatoes, and over 100 different peppers.*

# Web Sites

**W. Atlee Burpee & Co.**
http://garden.burpee.com
*Burpee's colorful, well-designed home page features not only on-line catalog and order information, but lots of terrific recipes and gardening tips that are updated weekly.*

**The Garden Gate**
http://www.prairienet.org/garden-gate/
*Information and links to many other sites.*

**Illinois Cooperative Extension Service**
http://www.ag.uiuc.edu/~robsond/solutions/hort.html
*The Horticulture Solutions Series provides not only good information on a variety of vegetable crops, but also on topics such as soils, fertilizers, garden pests, and other horticultural subjects.*

**National Gardening Association**
http://www.garden.org/nga
*The NGA site includes a library search engine, useful for finding topics covered in National Gardening magazine, which features lots of articles on growing vegetables, new and better varieties, and much more.*

**Nichols Garden Nursery**
http://www.pacificharbor.com/nichols
*Nichols' web page features an on-line catalog, a Garden Tip of the Week, and a Recipe of the Week, such as Three-Minute Cilantro-Artichoke Pesto, or Swiss Chard with Tomatoes and Anchovies.*

in future years. For instance, write down all the names of different vegetable varieties, and compare them from year to year, so you will know which ones have done well in your garden. Many people keep a book in their car to record when they change their oil and perform other routine maintenance. In the same way, get in the habit of jotting it down whenever you apply organic matter or fertilizer to the garden, or the dates on which you plant or begin to harvest a crop.

Over time this kind of careful observation and record-keeping will probably teach you more about growing vegetables than any single book or authority. That's because the notes you make will be based on your own personal experience and observations, and will reflect what works best for you in the unique conditions of your own garden. As in so many other pursuits, so it is in the art of vegetable gardening: practice does make perfect.

## Time-Tested Pepper-Growing Tips

**Got a Light?** Peppers like growing in warm, well-drained, slightly acidic soil. If your garden soil's pH isn't low enough, try placing three or four matches from a pocket matchbook at the bottom of the planting hole when you're setting out your pepper plants. Dick Raymond, a well-known garden authority, recommends this method in his book, *Down-to-Earth Gardening Know-How for the 90s* (Storey, 1991).

**Oh, My Aching Leaves!** Another interesting tip from Dick Raymond involves spraying the leaves of pepper plants after they blossom with a solution of Epsom salts (1 tablespoon per 16-ounce spray bottle will do). The chemical name for Epsom salts is magnesium sulfate, and the magnesium helps turn leaves a darker green and ensures a good crop of peppers.

**Everybody Must Get Stoned.** Master gardener Eliot Coleman reports that cool-climate growers can enhance pepper growth by placing flat stones around the plants as a mulch. The stones absorb heat to warm the soil and the air around the peppers in their early growth, before summer temperatures climb. The stones also help conserve soil moisture, just like an organic mulch.

Robin Wimbiscus, *Solar Gardening*

# Garden Gear

Made of foam-coated stainless steel wire, these soft **Cushioned Plant Ties** support your plants gently without injuring stems or branches. The 30-foot roll may be cut to desired lengths. Weather-resistant and reusable.
#03-250 Cushioned Plant Ties, 30' roll $6.95

The slow-release granules of this **Organic Tomato Fertilizer** (5-6-5) will provide your tomatoes with all the major nutrients they need, including plenty of phosphorus, to produce an abundant crop of big fruit. For a healthy start, mix small handfuls into the soil at transplant time and again when tomatoes begin to set fruit. Contains peanut and whey meals, sulphate of potash/magnesia, and Chilean nitrate. Five pounds covers 200 square feet.
#07-200 Gardener's Supply Tomato Fertilizer, 5 lbs. $5.95

**ROOTS Plus for Tomatoes and Vegetables** (3-5-6) is a specially formulated blend of organic ingredients plus quick-release fertilizers that can help you produce a big tomato harvest. It's also excellent for other heavy feeders like eggplants and peppers. One 32-ounce bottle feeds 40 plants all season long. Apply with a watering can, garden sprayer, or with a special ROOTS hose-end sprayer.
#07-278 ROOTS Plus™ for Tomatoes and Vegetables, 32 oz. $10.95
#07-274 ROOTS™ Sprayer $5.95

Developed by the USDA and Clemson University, this specially engineered red **Tomato Booster Mulch** reflects far-red light wavelengths upward into

your tomato plants. This triggers the release of a natural plant protein that stimulates more rapid growth. Your plants will mature faster and give you a more abundant harvest.
#30-005 Tomato Booster Mulch, 4' x 50' $9.95

These heavy-duty galvanized steel **Tomato Cages** are strong enough to support full-grown vines loaded with tomatoes. The 8-inch square openings make it easy to reach in and pick ripe fruit. You can even stack one cage on top of another to support the tallest tomato plants. The hinged panels fold flat for compact storage. 14⅜" x 14⅜" x 32" high, with 7" legs.
#03-249 Tomato Cage $8.95
#03-248 Set of 4 Tomato Cages $27.50

Many folks mark their garden rows with empty seed packets. Unfortunately the packets usually disintegrate after a few weeks of rain and wind. These rust-proof galvanized steel **Crop Markers** have a protective vinyl sleeve to keep seed packets legible all season long. The bracket is angled for easy viewing, and the markers can be reused for years. 18¼" overall.

Developed for outdoor use in nurseries and trial gardens, reversible vinyl **Nursery Cards** allow you to record plant names, varieties, and planting dates. Use a grease pencil or waterproof marking pen for best results. 4½" x 3".
#03-450 Crop Markers, set of 6 $14.95
#03-271 Nursery Cards, set of 24 $3.99

Tiny lettuce, carrot, and flower seeds are notoriously difficult to plant by hand; they often clump together and require time-consuming thinning later on. The **Seed Sower** lets you control the flow rate of small seeds as you plant, spacing them correctly and eliminating clumping. Just place seeds inside the chamber, dial one of five different openings, and jiggle the Seed Sower to begin the flow.
#30-000 Seed Sower $4.95

**Bamboo Stakes** have long been favored as plant supports by the nursery industry because they are strong, attractive, weather-resistant, and last for many years. The hard outer shell repels water and resists rot, yet the stakes are flexible enough to withstand high winds and support heavy loads. Taller canes are great for staking tomatoes, or making teepees and trellises for climbing plants. Shorter canes are ideal for supporting bushy plants as well as large potted plants. Two lengths: 70" x ¾" diameter and 36" x ⅜" diameter.

**Bamboo connectors** join bamboo canes together to quickly create custom A-frames or teepees. These durable, plastic interlocking connectors are made in England.
#03-162 70" Bamboo Stakes, set of 12 $14.95
#30-226 7' Bamboo Stakes, set of 50 $44.95
#03-275 36" Bamboo Stakes, set of 25 $7.50
#03-269 Bamboo Connectors, set of 5 $2.95

The **Bamboo A-Frame Kit** contains everything you need to build a sturdy A-frame trellis for your vine crops: twelve 70" bamboo stakes, five universal connectors, a 5' x 30' length of soft netting (7" mesh) and 15 Earth Staples. Just insert the stakes through the ridge clips, drape the netting over the frame, and secure with the Earth Staples. Vines grow fast, and harvesting is easy.
#03-160 Bamboo A-Frame Kit $24.95

# herbs

*Mullein*

W here would humans be without herbs? Considering how many centuries we have used plants for their culinary or healing properties, our world would certainly be a poorer place without them. Gardeners would be especially destitute: no longer would we enjoy the clean, heady fragrances of mint or lavender, the intense flavors of basil or rosemary, or the healing balm of comfrey or calendula. Herbs are beautiful plants, and their easy care and deep historical significance only adds to their lasting charm.

Fortunately, herbs are here to stay, and they remain as popular today as ever — perhaps even more so. Cooks love the unique flavors that herbs — fresh or dried — lend to all kinds of food and drink. Herbal crafters preserve the beauty and fragrance of flowers and leaves in potpourri, wreaths, sachets, and dried arrangements. And gardeners value herbs for all their excellent qualities, including their vigor, low maintenance, and resistance to pests. In this chapter we'll explore a few of the major themes in herb gardening and direct you to a host of other resources that will help you to expand your knowledge and appreciation of herbs and their many uses.

## What Is an Herb?

When most of us think of herbs, we picture the ones we commonly use as kitchen seasonings — basil, rosemary, sage, thyme, and so on. Yet in the broadest sense of the word, an herb is any plant that is considered "useful" in some respect to humans. The leaves, roots, seeds, stems, or flowers of an herb might be important as a source of flavoring, medicine, fragrance, dye, or some other product. And just as we might consider any aggressive plant a "weed" when it is growing someplace where we don't want it, so an "herb" is any type of plant — annual, perennial, tree, shrub, or vine — that has some practical value beyond looking beautiful in the garden.

Not that good looks don't count. In fact, gardeners regularly grow many useful herbs not so much for their culinary or medicinal properties, but simply because they work so well in the landscape. Unless you are a devoted herbalist, you probably don't use dried peony roots as a remedy for cold sores, or pick the leaves of betony (*Stachys* spp.) to use as a natural bandage (its other common name is woundwort). Instead, we grow these "herbs" because we like having them in the garden as ornamentals. Yet exploring the useful properties of many of our favorite plants, though little appreciated in this modern consumer age, can add a whole new dimension to gardening and inspire a lifelong fascination with herbs.

## Guest Expert

### Jo Ann Gardner

With a little attention, it is easy to keep your herbs thriving all summer long, even under adverse conditions. Cool and rainy weather is good for hardy perennials like sweet cicely, but awful for tropical plants like basil. Once in the ground, it's difficult to protect plants from cool, wet conditions: the best defense is a deep, humusy soil that drains well.

Good air circulation, as in a sunny, exposed site, will discourage fungus disease. If plants are close together, they should not be touching. Keep them trimmed to avoid this situation.

If you are growing herbs primarily to use them, frequent cutting will keep plants healthy, encouraging fresh growth. If your aim is to produce lots of foliage, pinch off buds or cut plants back before they flower, and they will grow more leaves.

Don't feel guilty if you don't use every one or even any of the herbs you grow. You may just want to admire their beauty, their green-hued foliage and enticing scents. But *do* pick them for bouquets. Virtually every herb has value in a vase of flowers. Cool green mint leaves, for instance, look lovely in an arrangement. Once you get in the habit, you will want fresh bouquets all summer so you can enjoy the beauty of herbs indoors at your leisure.

*Jo Ann Gardner is an author and herbalist whose books include* Living with Herbs, The Heirloom Garden, *and* Herbs in Bloom. *She lives on Cape Breton Island, Nova Scotia.*

## Favorite Books

Living with Herbs *by Jo Ann Gardner* (Countryman Press, 1997). Jo Ann Gardner's style is personal and appealing as she introduces readers to the wide range of useful plants she has grown on her backcountry farm in Nova Scotia. This book features excellent chapters on growing, harvesting, drying, and crafting with herbs, plus 74 herb portraits that talk about each plant like an old, familiar friend. Highly recommended. 288 pages, paperback, $17.00.

**Your Backyard Herb Garden**
*by Miranda Smith* (Rodale, 1997). Probably the best all-around herb book for beginners. Color illustrations and tables enhance the text, which provides much useful material in a concise way. Individual entries for over 50 herbs, plus sections on using herbs in cooking, crafts, and personal care products. 160 pages, hardcover, $27.95.

**The Encyclopedia of Medicinal Plants**
*by Andrew Chevallier* (DK Publishing, 1996). More than just a reference, this big, colorful book is fascinating to read or browse through. Entries for more than 550 medicinal plants discuss traditional and current uses; the latest research into health benefits and claims; the parts of the plant used and how to prepare them; and cross-references to ailments and self-help remedies. Highly recommended. 336 pages, hardcover, $39.95.

## Site and Soil Considerations

Most herbs grow best in a well-drained, moderately rich garden soil. However, some of the most popular herbs, such as rosemary, lavender, bay, and winter savory, are woody plants native to the Mediterranean region. These herbs prefer a gritty, sharply drained soil. Good drainage is extremely important because standing water around the root crown of plants can cause them to rot. To keep these plants happy in garden soil that is particularly heavy or clayey, you will need to improve drainage either by adding lots of organic matter like compost, or by growing herbs in raised beds or containers.

Another crucial factor to consider is the amount of sunlight a plant needs to "see" every day. Most common herbs thrive in full sun conditions (six or more hours of direct sunlight per day). Don't despair, though, if you have a garden site that receives only partial sun (two to six hours per day). Many herbs will thrive with less sunlight; you just need to select the right types based on the amount of light they can expect to get in your garden (see "Shade-Tolerant Herbs," page 94).

## Flowering Herbs

| Common Name | Botanical Name | Plant Type | Height | Light | Flower Color |
|---|---|---|---|---|---|
| Anise hyssop | Agastache foeniculum | perennial | 2–3' | sun | purple |
| Bee balm | Monarda didyma | perennial | 3–4' | sun, part shade | red, pink, blue |
| Borage | Borago officinalis | hardy annual | 18–36" | sun | blue |
| Calendula | Calendula officinalis | hardy annual | 2' | sun, part shade | yellow, orange |
| Chamomile, German | Matricaria recutita | hardy annual | 1–2' | sun | white, yellow center |
| Chives | Allium schoenoprasum | perennial | 8–12" | sun, part shade | pink-purple |
| Clary sage | Salvia sclarea | biennial | 2–3' | sun | white and light purple |
| Comfrey | Symphytum caucasicum | perennial | 2–3' | sun, part shade | blue |
| Dame's rocket | Hesperis matronalis | perennial | 2–3' | sun, part shade | pink, purple, white |
| Elecampane | Inula helenium | perennial | 4–8' | sun, part shade | yellow |
| Evening primrose | Oenothera biennis | annual/biennial | 3–4' | sun, part shade | yellow |
| Feverfew | Chrysanthemum parthenium | perennial | 2–3' | sun, part shade | white, yellow center |
| Garlic chives | Allium tuberosum | perennial | 2–3' | sun | white |
| Hyssop | Hyssopus officinalis | perennial | 16–24" | sun, part shade | blue-violet |
| Lavender | Lavandula spp. | perennial | 12–30" | sun | light purple |
| Love-in-a-mist | Nigella damascena | hardy annual | 1–2' | sun | blue, pink, purple, white |
| Mealy-cup sage | Salvia farinacea | half-hardy annual/ tender perennial | 1–3' | sun | blue |
| Mullein | Verbascum thapsus | biennial | 2–8' | sun, part shade | yellow |
| Nasturtium | Tropaeolum majus; T. minor | tender annual | 6"–6' | sun | red, orange, yellow |
| Purple coneflower | Echinacea purpurea | perennial | 2–3' | sun | purple |
| Spilanthes, para cress | Spilanthes oleracea | annual | 8–12" | sun | yellow and red |
| Tansy | Tanacetum vulgare | perennial | 3–4' | sun, part shade | yellow |
| Valerian | Valeriana officinalis | perennial | 3–5' | sun, part shade | pale pink |

Many herbs require full sun and warmth to grow well and to develop the essential oils that give them their pungent aroma and flavor. Raised beds are a good way to provide not only better drainage, but warmer soil, especially early in the season. Using stone or brick as edging for raised beds helps to reflect and retain heat in and around the herb garden. Paving also works well to create a warmer microclimate for heat-loving herbs that are often grown in pots or planters, such as rosemary or bay, and for low-growing ground covers such as creeping thyme. For more information, see the design section below.

Like other plants, herbs can become stressed on an especially windy or exposed site. Growing herbs in beds near the house or next to other buildings or walls provides the plants with a warm, sheltering microclimate and increases a gardener's chances of success with tender perennials like rosemary, which is hardy only to Zone 8. Even if, like most American gardeners, you grow rosemary in containers and bring it indoors for the winter, it's still a good idea to set it out in a sunny, sheltered area, one that duplicates as closely as possible its native growing conditions.

## Pest and Disease Control

For the most part, herbs are not much affected by insect pests. The same essential oils that give herbs their appealing flavor and aroma (to us) make the plants unpalatable to bugs. This is why you'll see herbs touted as good companions for all kinds of vegetable crops and other plants. Some herbs, such as pennyroyal and tansy, can even be used as natural insect repellents in the home.

If necessary, handpick any insects you see damaging leaves, or remove any leaves that have become infested. Control aphids, spider mites, or whiteflies, if they appear, by spraying leaves (including the undersides) with an insecticidal soap.

Diseases are also rather rare with herbs, and are most often the result of plants being stressed — either because the plant isn't growing in the kind of conditions it needs (amount of sunlight, water requirements, adequate drainage, etc.), or because the plants are crowded together too closely. In the case of downy or powdery mildew, remove and destroy any infected leaves and try spraying plants with a compost tea.

> " Part of our delight in the good fragrance of herbs comes from their being in relation to mankind. For some odors are subhuman, being contrived and distilled for insects and such small deer, and others are overpowering, being meant for genii, so overpowering are they and cloying. The fragrance of herbs is a thing of the human scale which lies between. Like all other manifestations of life, it is a thing of change, the scents varying subtly with the growth of the plants, the time of the year, and even the time of the day. There are herbs which are best in daytime, and others which are best in the early morning when even the dew upon their leaves is fragrant. Now and then it comes to pass that an herb will have one fragrance in one part of the garden and quite another elsewhere (Hyssop does this), and plants of the same herb all growing together may have marked individualities of odor. With some herbs, Rue, for instance, there is an underfragrance which is almost a separate thing."
>
> —from *Herbs and the Earth* by Henry Beston (1935; reprint Godine, 1990)

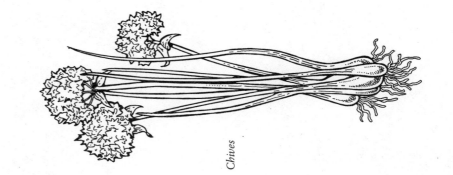

*Chives*

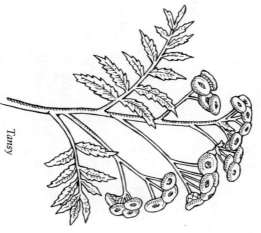

Tansy

## Shade-Tolerant Herbs

| Common Name | Botanical Name | Plant Type |
| --- | --- | --- |
| Agrimony | Agrimonia eupatoria | perennial |
| Angelica | Angelica archangelica | biennial |
| Bee balm, bergamot | Monarda spp. | perennial |
| Boneset | Eupatorium perfoliatum | perennial |
| Bronze fennel | Foeniculum vulgare | tender perennial |
| Chervil | Anthriscus cerefolium | hardy annual |
| Comfrey | Symphytum caucasicum | perennial |
| Dame's rocket | Hesperis matronalis | perennial |
| Evening primrose | Oenothera biennis | annual/biennial |
| Feverfew | Chrysanthemum parthenium | perennial |
| Lady's-mantle | Alchemilla mollis | perennial |
| Lemon balm | Melissa officinalis | perennial |
| Lovage | Levisticum officinale | perennial |
| Mints | Mentha spp. | perennial |
| Mugwort, white | Artemisia lactiflora | perennial |
| Mullein | Verbascum thapsus | biennial |
| Parsley | Petroselinum crispum | biennial |
| Pennyroyal | Mentha pulegium | tender perennial |
| Rue | Ruta graveolens | perennial |
| Stinging nettle | Urtica dioica | perennial |
| Sweet cicely | Myrrhis odorata | perennial |
| Sweet woodruff | Galium odoratum | perennial |
| Tansy | Tanacetum vulgare | perennial |
| Valerian | Valeriana officinalis | perennial |
| Viper's bugloss | Echium vulgare | annual/biennial |
| Wormwood | Artemisia absinthium | perennial |

## Propagating Herbs

Some herbs are easy to start from seed, whereas others take a long time to germinate and grow and usually are either purchased as plants from a nursery or propagated vegetatively from existing plants (by stem cuttings, layering, or root division). Popular herbs that are easy to grow from seed include basil, borage, calendula, chervil, coriander, dill, lemon balm, parsley, and sage. Before sowing any herb, whether in flats or directly in the garden, check its specific germination requirements to see how early you'll need to start it and whether it requires any special handling (a period of cold dormancy, or *stratification*; light or darkness for germination; soil temperature; etc.). Like other plants, most herb seeds should be planted at a depth of only about twice their thickness: with very small seeds, this means sowing on top of moistened soil in flats and gently pressing them in. (For more information on starting plants from seed, see the "Starting Plants from Seed" chapter.)

If you want to start new herbs from plants that you already have growing in your garden, there are several ways to do it, all of them variations of *vegetative propagation*.

**ROOT DIVISION.** For many hardy perennial herbs, root division is the simplest means of propagation. Using a garden fork, dig up the plant's root system and either pull the roots apart by hand (as with chives), or cut the root mass into several pieces and replant them elsewhere in the garden.

The best time to divide plants is in the fall, when they are winding down for the year. If divided and replanted at this time, new plants will establish themselves and get off to a good start the following spring. Placing transplants on a small mound of soil or compost in the bottom of the planting hole helps to prevent settling. Firm down the soil around the plants and water them well after planting to eliminate any large air pockets around the roots. Laying a thick organic mulch around plants in the late fall will help insure against crown heaving, which may otherwise occur as a result of freeze/thaw cycles over the winter.

Herbs that respond well to root division include bee balm, chives, garlic chives, horehound, lovage, marjoram, oregano, pennyroyal, sorrel, tansy, thyme, and sweet woodruff.

CUTTINGS. Stem cuttings of various herbs (hyssop, lavender, mints, oregano, sage, thyme) should be taken during the spring or summer, when plants are healthy and growing vigorously. Rosemary and

## Other Good Books

**Herbs and the Earth** by *Henry Beston* (David R. Godine, 1990).
A literary gem first published in 1935. Beston's prose is at once descriptive and lyrical. He weaves intimate observations of plants and nature with fascinating historical and mythical details about herbs. A timeless gardening book, and a reader's delight. Highly recommended. 160 pages, hardcover, $17.95.

**The Herb Gardener: A Guide for All Seasons** by *Susan McClure* (Garden Way Publishing, 1996).
With loads of brief tips and boxes, this general book is accessible and useful for beginning herb growers. Design information is strong, as is the section on seasonal tasks in the herb garden. 240 pages, hardcover, $29.95.

**Growing and Using Herbs Successfully** *by Betty E.M. Jacobs* (Garden Way Publishing, 1981).
Not a slick color coffee-table book, but one that has been around for years and still has lots of relevant and useful material. Good lists and charts, plus chapters on growing and marketing herbs and herb products. 240 pages, paperback, $10.95.

### HERB REFERENCE BOOKS

**The Herb Society of America Encyclopedia of Herbs and Their Uses** *by Deni Bown* (Dorling Kindersley, 1995).
Comprehensive, with entries for more than 1,000 plants. Entries are brief and pithy, with descriptions of plants and notes on growing and using them. Lots of color photos aid in identification. Highly recommended. 424 pages, hardcover, $39.95.

**Taylor's Guide to Herbs** *ed. Rita Buchanan* (Houghton Mifflin, 1995).
Like all the Taylor guides, this book's encyclopedic listings of 400 herbs give good plant identification and growing information. General chapters provide an overview of growing and using herbs. Good color photo section. 464 pages, paperback, $19.95.

**Rodale's Illustrated Encyclopedia of Herbs** *eds. Claire Kowalchick and William H. Hylton* (Rodale, 1987).
A to Z entries on 139 herbs, both common and unusual, are interspersed with more general entries on growing and using herbs. Plant histories and cultural tips are especially good. 550 pages, hardcover, $24.95.

### HERBAL CRAFT BOOKS

**The Pleasure of Herbs** *by Phyllis Shaudys* (Garden Way Publishing, 1986).
A nice mix of general how-to on growing, drying, and using herbs, along with an impressive number of specific projects like herbal sachets, pomanders, potpourri, and recipes. Highly recommended. 288 pages, paperback, $14.95.

**Herb Drying Handbook** *by Nora Blose and Dawn Cusick* (Sterling, 1993).
Complete information on drying more than 60 herbs, plus notes on how to use the dried herbs in crafts and cooking. 96 pages, paperback, $9.95.

**Herbal Treasures** *by Phyllis Shaudys* (Garden Way Publishing, 1990).
A month-by-month guide to using herbs in seasonal cooking and crafts. Tons of valuable tips, from making holiday wreaths to herbal weddings and showers. Highly recommended. 320 pages, paperback, $16.95.

tarragon tend to root better in the fall, so use them for cuttings at that time and grow them indoors over the winter.

1. Select stem segments that are tender (not woody) and about 3 to 6 inches long, with at least five leaves along the stem. Make an angled cut, just above an outward-facing leaf node.

2. Remove the lower leaves on the stem, dip the cut end in rooting hormone powder, and plant it deeply in a pot containing a soilless seed-starting medium mixed with moistened vermiculite or perlite.

3. Cover the cuttings loosely with a plastic bag to create humid conditions and place them in a cool (70°F) location away from direct sunlight.

## Other Good Books

### HERBAL COOKBOOKS

**Herbs in the Kitchen: A Celebration of Flavor** by Carolyn Dille and Susan Belsinger (Interweave Press, 1992). An attractive cookbook with more than 200 recipes, organized by herb. Recipes are simple but elegant, as befits herb cookery, and include Sage Apple Cake and Rosemary Biscuits. 336 pages, hardcover, $26.95.

**The Herb Companion Cooks** (Interweave Press, 1994). Recipes taken from the pages of *Herb Companion* magazine, organized by course type (appetizers to desserts). Tasty-sounding entries include Borage Fritters with Capers and Nectarine and Plum Cake with Bergamot. 128 pages, paperback, $16.95.

**The Herb Garden Cookbook** by Lucinda Hutson (Gulf Publishing, 1992). Organized by herb, with descriptive introductions to each plant that give growing and harvesting tips. Over 150 recipes have a generally Tex-Mex flair and feature some nifty drink recipes. 240 pages, paperback, $21.95.

**The Herbal Tea Garden: Planting, Planting, Harvesting & Brewing** by Marietta Marshall Marcin (Garden Way Publishing, 1993). A simple, straightforward guide that gives good information on selecting, growing, and brewing tea from 70 herbs, from agrimony to yarrow. 224 pages, paperback, $12.95.

### REGIONAL HERB BOOKS

**The New England Herb Gardener: Yankee Wisdom for North American Herb Growers** by Patricia Turcotte (Countryman Press, 1990). A good general work for gardeners in Zones 3–6. Chapters include growing information, recipes, and beauty uses of herbs, and herbal crafting. 256 pages, paperback, $15.00.

**Growing Herbs: For the Maritime Northwest Gardener** by Mary Preus (Sasquatch Books, 1994). Especially good information on designing an herb garden, plus 24 portraits of individual herbs well suited to the Pacific Northwest. 96 pages, paperback, $9.95.

**Herb Gardening in Texas** by Sol Meltzer (Gulf Publishing,

1997). The third edition of this popular book deals with propagation, container growing, and more. Some terrific recipes from Texas restaurants. 208 pages, paperback, $16.95.

### HERB BUSINESS BOOKS

**The Potential of Herbs as a Cash Crop** by Richard Alan Miller (Ten Speed Press, 1992). A must-have book for anyone interested in growing herbs on a commercial scale. Sections discuss drying and processing herbs in bulk, direct marketing, financial planning — even foraging herbs in the wild. 240 pages, paperback, $14.95.

**Herbs for Sale: Growing and Marketing Herbs, Herbal Products, and Herbal Know-How** by Lee Sturdivant (San Juan Naturals, 1994). Lots of profiles of herb farmers and herbalists make this book very useful for gardeners looking to turn a passion for herbs into money. 256 pages, paperback, $14.95.

### HERBAL DESIGN BOOKS

**The Herb Garden: Decorative Ways to Grow Herbs in the Garden** by Malcolm Hillier (DK Publishing, 1996),

A colorful, beautifully designed picture book. Shows how herbs can be used as design features in the garden, from low edgings to containers and topiary. 120 pages, hardcover, $24.95.

**Using Herbs in the Landscape** by Debra Kirkpatrick (Stackpole Books, 1992). Provides lots of ideas through plant lists, profiles, and a large section on herbal theme gardens. 240 pages, paperback, $16.95.

**Creative Herb Gardening** by Geraldene Holt (Conran Octopus, 1993). This colorful, inspiring British book shows different styles and themes of herb gardens, such as formal, scented, medicinal, culinary, and container. Lots of useful design and growing tips. 96 pages, hardcover, $19.95.

**Artistically Cultivated Herbs: How to Train Herbs as a Decorative Art** by Elise Felton (Woodbridge Press, 1990). Especially good for gardeners with limited space, this book shows how to grow herbs as bonsai, in window boxes and hanging baskets, and as espaliers. 144 pages, paperback, $16.95.

4. Monitor the plants and water if needed, or remove the plastic bag if there seems to be too much moisture. After a few weeks, start checking for new leaf growth, which indicates that the plants are rooting well. Repot the plants into larger containers filled with regular potting soil and gradually expose the plants to full light.

**LAYERING.** Layering involves burying a trailing stem of an herb plant, encouraging it to form roots, and ultimately creating a new plant. It works well with perennial herbs such as marjoram, rosemary, sage, and winter savory. The best time to do this kind of propagation is in spring (on last year's growth) or in summer (on this year's growth).

1. Select a stem that is long and trailing and that you can bend down easily to touch the ground.

2. Make a slanted cut halfway through the stem (or, with slender stems, scrape the outer surface). Place the cut part of the stem in a shallow depression just below the soil surface, holding down the stem on either side with lengths of metal wire (unbent paper clips are good for this). Cover the cut part of the stem with a little soil, and water well.

3. After six to eight weeks, brush away the soil and check to see whether the stem has begun to form a new root system. If it has, cut the stem that connects the new plant to the mother plant and transplant the new plant elsewhere in the garden.

For more detailed information on propagating herbs, see *Growing Herbs from Seed, Cutting, and Root* by Thomas DeBaggio (Interweave Press, 1994).

*Chamomile*

## Designing an Herb Garden

As a group, herbs are extremely versatile plants and lend themselves to a variety of garden styles and settings. The monasteries of the Middle Ages were famous for their medicinal herb or "physic" gardens, which in addition to leafy herbs included many flowering plants such as roses and irises. By the 16th century in England, the "knot garden" had become a popular design for a formal herb planting, with a rectangular bed laid out in an intricate geometrical pattern. Inside the interlacing lines of herbs or miniature box (*Buxus*) hedges, small beds or compartments were each planted with a single variety of herb, often selected for its ornamental foliage.

**FORMAL DESIGN ELEMENTS.** The intricate knot garden is still a beautiful way to grow herbs, but today most home gardeners find the heavy maintenance required to keep it weeded, pruned, and looking good too formidable and time-consuming. However, if a formal herb garden fits with your house and landscape, you can incorporate some traditional design elements that will lend the appeal of a formal appearance without the high maintenance.

The most basic characteristic of all formal herb gardens is their use of a "focal point," something that draws the eye to the center of the design. This center point is typically an architectural feature, such as a sundial, pedestal, column, birdbath, fountain, or a decorative or distinc-

# suppliers

## MAIL-ORDER PLANT AND SEED SOURCES

tive pot. When planning an herb garden, start with this central focal point and work outward, defining beds with radiating paths that divide the garden into quarters (for a square or rectangle) or into pie-shaped sections for a circle or wheel design (see illustrations). The point of these formal designs is to set off each individual herb, rather than merging different types into an indistinct hedge or border.

Many kinds of perennial plants — both herbaceous and woody — can be used for edging in the formal herb garden, from shrubs such as

**Edgewood Farm & Nursery**
RR 2, Box 303
Stanardsville, VA 22973-9405
804-985-3782
*Herb plants and perennials; large selection; catalog $2.*

**Fox Hill Farm**
P.O. Box 9
Parma, MI 49269-0009
517-531-3179
*Herb plants and supplies; large selection; catalog $1.*

**Fox Hollow Seed Co.**
P.O. Box 148
McGrann, PA 16236
412-548-7333
*Herb and heirloom vegetable seeds; catalog $1.*

**Good Hollow Greenhouse & Herbarium**
50 Slate Rock Mill Rd.
Taft, TN 38488
615-433-7640
*Herb plants and perennials.*

**The Herb Barn**
HC 64, Box 435D
Trout Run, PA 17771
717-995-9327
*Herb plants; send long SASE for catalog.*

**The Herb Garden**
P.O. Box 773
Pilot Mountain, NC 27041-0773
*Herb plants and supplies; good selection; catalog $4.*

**It's About Thyme**
11726 Manchaca Rd.
Austin, TX 78748
512-280-1192
*Herb plants, including Southwestern herbs; catalog $1.*

**Johnny's Selected Seeds**
Foss Hill Rd.
Albion, ME 04910-9731
207-437-9294
*Seeds for culinary and medicinal herbs; good selection.*

**Lily of the Valley Herb Farm**
3969 Fox Ave.
Minerva, OH 44657
216-862-3920
*Herb plants and supplies; dried herbs and flowers; catalog $1.*

**Mountain Valley Growers**
38325 Pepperweed Rd.
Squaw Valley, CA 93675
209-338-2775
*Herb plants, including some new or hard-to-find varieties.*

**Nichols Garden Nursery**
1190 North Pacific Hwy. NE
Albany, OR 97321-4580
541-928-9280
*Herb plants and seeds; good selection.*

**Papa Geno's Herbs**
1951 South 25th
Lincoln, NE 68502
402-423-5051
*Herb plants; large selection.*

**Rasland Farm**
Rte. 1, Box 65C
Godwin, NC 28344-9712
910-567-2705
*Herb plants and products; catalog $3.*

**Renaissance Acres Organic Herb Farm**
4450 Valentine Rd.
Whitmore Lake, MI 48189
313-449-8336
*Herb plants and seeds.*

**Richters Herbs**
357 Hwy. 47
Goodwood, ON, Canada
L0C 1A0
416-640-6677
*Herb plants and seeds; herbal products; catalog $2.*

**Sandy Mush Herb Nursery**
316 Surrett Cove Rd.
Leicester, NC 28748-9622
704-683-2014
*Herb plants and seeds; catalog $4.*

**Sleepy Hollow Herb Farm**
568 Jack Black Rd.
Lancaster, KY 40444-9306
606-792-6183
*Organically grown herb plants and perennials; catalog $1.*

**Taylor's Herb Gardens**
1535 Lone Oak Rd.
Vista, CA 92084
619-727-3485
*Herb plants and seeds; catalog $3.*

**Thyme Garden Seed Co.**
20546 Alsea Hwy. 34
Alsea, OR 97324
503-487-8671
*Herb and flower seeds; catalog $1.50.*

**Tinmouth Channel Farm**
RR 1, Box 428B
Tinmouth, VT 05773
802-446-2812
*Herb plants and seeds; catalog $2.*

**Well-Sweep Herb Farm**
317 Mt. Bethel Rd.
Port Murray, NJ 07865
908-852-5390
*Herb plants and perennials; very good selection; catalog $2.*

**Winstead Farms**
105 Romanshorn
Interlachen, FL 32148
(904) 684-2448
*Herb plants: culinary, medicinal and ornamental.*

**Wrenwood of Berkeley Springs**
Rte. 4, Box 361
Berkeley Springs, WV 25411
304-258-3071
*Herb plants and perennials; large selection; catalog $2.*

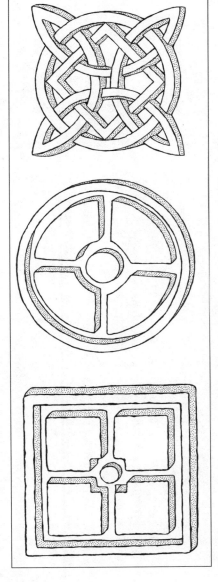

*Formal herb garden designs.*

southernwood (*Artemisia abrotanum*) and various evergreens to low ground covers such as creeping thyme (*Thymus praecox*). Another idea, especially if your soil is heavy or clayey, is to grow herbs in a number of neatly sided raised beds, organized in a geometrical pattern.

Paths or edgings made of bricks or other paving materials such as Belgian blocks add a nice formality to the herb garden. Paved paths provide easy access to the beds for maintenance and serve as walkways — plus, they are easier to maintain than traditional boxwood hedges. Another benefit of bricks is that they soak up and retain the warmth of the sun, something that is appreciated, especially in the cooler climates, by heat-loving Mediterranean herbs.

**INFORMAL GARDEN IDEAS.** Formal gardens are beautiful, but many people prefer to incorporate herbs into their existing garden spaces, among either ornamental or edible plants. Annual herbs such as basil and summer savory are natural partners for tomatoes and beans in the vegetable garden, while purple-leaved basil or calendula make good choices in an annual or mixed flower bed. Perennial herbs such as creeping thyme feel right at home in a rock garden, while taller plants such as hyssop (*Hyssopus officinalis*) and silvery wormwood (*Artemisia absinthium*) fit nicely into an ornamental border.

Another way of using herbs in the landscape is to combine fragrant plants to make a "scented garden." First, find a sunny spot where you might enjoy sitting with your morning cup of coffee, or in the evening after dinner. Reserve a spot in or next to the garden for a wooden garden bench, or a table and chairs for outdoor dining and entertaining. Then select herbs of various heights and growing habits, whose scents will turn this spot into a pleasant area for reading, socializing, or private meditation. So many herbs have a delightful fragrance that it's hard to limit yourself to just a few. Some excellent choices for the scented garden include English lavender (*Lavandula angustifolia*), lemon balm (*Melissa officinalis*), all kinds of mints, oregano, rosemary, scented geraniums (*Pelargonium* spp.), costmary (*Chrysanthemum balsamita*), and dame's rocket (*Hesperis matronalis*), whose flowers release a delightful clove-like aroma in the evening. Plant fragrant ground covers such as creeping

# Resources

## MAGAZINES

**The Herb Companion**
Interweave Press, Inc.
201 East Fourth St.
Loveland, CO 80537-5655
Bimonthly; $24/year in U.S.,
$31/year in Canada.

**The Herb Quarterly**
Long Mountain Press, Inc.
P.O. Box 689
San Anselmo, CA 94960
Quarterly; $24/year.

## ORGANIZATIONS

**American Herb Association**
P.O. Box 1673
Nevada City, CA 95959
Emphasis on medicinal herbs
and herbal healing; $20

annual dues include quarterly
AHA newsletter.

**The Flower and Herb
Exchange**
3076 North Winn Rd.
Decorah, IA 52101
319-382-5990

A grassroots organization
dedicated to preserving and
distributing heirloom varieties
of flowers and herbs. FHE's
annual yearbook features
seed listings of rare plant
varieties from participating
members, from whom other
members can request seeds.
Annual membership is
$7/year in the U.S., $10/year
in Canada.

**Herb Research Foundation**
1007 Pearl St., Suite 200
Boulder, CO 80302
800-748-2617

The Herb Research Founda-
tion is a nonprofit research
and educational foundation
focusing on the worldwide
use of herbs for health, environmental conservation, and
international development.
Annual $35 membership
includes the newsletter Herb
Research News, as well as
subscriptions to HerbalGram
or Herbs for Health maga-
zines. Also offers customized
information research and
public access to over 100,000
studies on thousands of

herbs; by mail and online services available.

**The Herb Society of America**
9019 Kirtland Chardon Rd.
Kirtland, OH 44094
216-256-0514

Founded in 1933, the HSA
has over 2,500 members and
is dedicated to promoting the
knowledge, use, and delight
of herbs. Regional chapters
or "units" are located across
the U.S.; annual dues are
$35, which includes the soci-
ety's bimonthly newsletter
and its annual publication,
The Herbarist.

---

thyme (*Thymus praecox*) and Roman chamomile (*Chamaemelum nobile*), perhaps in gaps between flagstones or other large, flat paving stones set around the area.

Gardeners who are interested in naturalizing herbs in a somewhat wilder setting can select from a wide range of hardy plant species. Certain herbs are aggressive and vigorous, fitting better into the landscape at large than in a mixed bed or border, where they can quickly crowd out other plants. Examples include various mints (*Mentha* spp.), elecampane (*Inula helenium*), comfrey (*Symphytum caucasicum*), tansy (*Tanacetum vulgare*), and soapwort or bouncing-bet (*Saponaria officinalis*). Look around your property and see what kinds of sites and soils you have; you're sure to find niches that offer the perfect conditions for some of these wilder herbs to thrive and spread.

## Growing Herbs in Containers

Growing different types of herbs in containers is a great idea for several reasons. First of all, you can grow tender perennials like rosemary and flowering sages all year long, bringing the pots indoors as days shorten and temperatures dip in the fall. Secondly, growing in containers gives you the flexibility to move plants around outside and display them to best effect. Containers also are a boon for gardeners who have poorly drained soil or limited growing space.

The soil you use in containers should be well-drained; regular potting soil amended with perlite and vermiculite will suit most plants. As with other plants in containers, herbs require regular watering and fertilization throughout the growing season. Plants like rosemary can tolerate fairly dry soil between waterings, but other herbs with broader

*Some long-lived herbs can be trained and pruned into a tree-like form known as an herbal standard.*

leaves need more attention to watering when grown in pots. Adding finished compost or peat moss to the soil mix when you are potting plants will help the soil retain moisture.

During the outdoor growing season most potted herbs can be fertilized as frequently as once a week. Use a liquid fish or seaweed emulsion or a complete liquid fertilizer. Once you bring plants inside for the winter, they require much less fertilization; once or twice a month is sufficient. Especially after plants are inside, it's important to practice "flush watering" regularly; in other words, keep adding liquid until you see water running out of the bottom hole in the pot and into the tray beneath. This prevents fertilizer salts from building up in the soil.

Herb plants that can live for several years in pots include rosemary, lemon verbena, bay laurel, and scented geraniums. Check plants periodically to see whether they need to be repotted into a larger container.

During the winter, the best place for herbs is inside the house next to a cool, sunny window, where they can get about three or four hours of direct sunlight every day. Conditions inside most houses during the winter months are dry, so mist plants or place them in trays on top of watered pebbles to increase the humidity level.

Plants that you bring inside for the winter invariably experience some insect problems. This is frequently due to the stress of being moved into an indoor environment and new growing conditions. The best way to minimize this stress is to dig and pot up plants at least a couple of weeks before the first frost, then acclimate them gradually to indoor conditions, perhaps by moving them to a porch or breezeway (a reverse process to the hardening-off that you do in the spring with plants started indoors). Watch the plants closely for the first few weeks inside, and pamper them by providing plenty of water and misting them.

Even given this tender loving care, some herbs will become infested with insects. If you shake a plant and see a cloud of whiteflies, it's a good idea to set the plant in the shower briefly and wash the insects off the leaves. Then spray the plant with an insecticidal soap or hot pepper wax. Follow label instructions and repeat treatments as needed.

Some long-lived herbs can be pruned and trained into interesting topiary shapes or ball-headed "standards," which makes them valuable as formal accents on a patio, entrance, or walkway during the summer, and as houseplants during the cooler months of the year. For detailed instructions on how to grow herbal topiaries, standards, and espaliers, as well as on growing herbs in hanging baskets, window boxes, and other containers, refer to Elise Felton's book, *Artistically Cultivated Herbs* (see "Herbal Design Books," page 96).

For more information and resources about growing plants in containers, see the chapter on "Container Gardening."

## Harvesting and Preserving Herbs

The uses for herbs, and the number of products and recipes that can be made with them, are practically endless. Fortunately there is an almost

*Web sites*

**Algy's Herb Page**
http://www.algy.com/herb
*A large and well-designed site that features information on growing and using culinary and medicinal herbs; a seed exchange; an herb forum; a retail store; herbal lore, crafts, and rituals; and Algy's Herb News, an on-line newsletter.*

**American Botanical Council**
http://www2.outer.net/herbalgram/
*The ABC is a nonprofit organization that educates the public about herbs and beneficial plants. Their site includes an herb-related bookstore section, as well as information on research and findings concerning the safety and efficacy of herbs and plant medicines.*

**Herb Research Foundation**
http://www.herbs.org
*Public access to reliable herb information, featuring the latest herb news and updates. The Herb Research Foundation has scientific and historical materials on thousands of herbs and their uses, and this site provides a good introduction to the organization and its resources.*

**The Herb Society of America**
http://www.herbsociety.com
*Includes information on the Society's projects and programs, such as the member seed exchange and regional and national symposia. There's also an on-line shop that lists herb books and gift items, plus a calendar of events for regional chapters.*

**The Whole Herb**
http://www.wholeherb.com
*Developed and maintained by Storey Communications, a garden publisher, this site features an on-line bulletin board as well as information on herbal crafts, aromatherapy, recipes, and herbal body products. Articles are updated weekly, and the site profiles a different herb every month.*

# Garden Gear

equally large number of books that can give you ideas and instructions for making herbal recipes, crafts, gifts, and other items (for some recommended titles, see the books listed earlier in this chapter).

However, one topic of interest to gardeners, cooks, and crafters alike is when and how to harvest herbs, and how best to preserve them so that they retain as much of their flavor and fragrance as possible.

In almost all cases, the best time to harvest herbs is when the plants are forming buds, but before they have flowered. At this time, the plant's leaves contain the highest concentration of essential oils. A few exceptions

This special **Herbal Lawn Seed Mix** blends slow-growing dwarf grasses with fragrant herbs to spice up your lawn with a wonderful new look and texture. It requires less water and fertilizer than grass alone, and needs mowing just once every two to four weeks. Herbs such as chamomile, sweet alyssum, yarrow, and strawberry clover create a novel texture and give off a sweet fragrance when you mow. One pound of the herbal seed mix covers 700 sq. ft. Zones 4–8.
#16-280B Herbal Lawn Seed Mix, 1 lb. $29.95

Plant a fragrant herb garden, or a rainbow of colorful annuals in this sectional **Hexagonal Herb and Flower Planter.** The six pie-shaped planter pieces let you work with different soils and create a changing display of your favorite plants. Sections are joined at the center by a decorative finial. Corner foot supports keep the planter up off your deck. Drain holes can be plugged for indoor use. Made from rugged polypropylene with a textured terra-cotta finish. 24" W x 8" H.
#30-168 Hexagonal Herb and Flower Planter $24.95

Perfect for herbs or vegetables like chili peppers, this **Oven Drying Rack** can be used inside an ordinary home oven for low-heat food drying. The ash hardwood frames are fitted with nylon screening; four screens measure 14½" x 12" and slide out of the frame. Overall size is 13" x 17" x 7" H. Can also be used outside the oven for drying herbs.
Available for $50.00 (product #9297) from Johnny's Selected Seeds, Foss Hill Rd., Albion, ME 04910; 207-437-9294.

Seeds of Change has put together an **Heirloom Herbs Seed Gift Collection,** which contains ten packets of seed for starting a delightfully old-fashioned herb garden. Included are 'Lettuce Leaf' basil, German chamomile, chervil, cilantro, lemon balm, summer savory, clary sage, lovage, rue, and feverfew. A nice combination of annual and perennial herbs for culinary, medicinal, and ornamental uses.
Available for $17.18 (product #A1025) from Seeds of Change, P.O. Box 15700, Santa Fe, NM 87506; 888-762-7333.

Nichols Garden Nursery offers two nice herb garden plant collections for use in the home landscape. The **Shady Corner Collection** features lovage, bergamot, 'Forsgate' chives, sweet woodruff, angelica, sweet cicely, Corsican mint, and lady's-mantle. The **Sunny Border Collection** includes anise hyssop, 'Moonshine' yarrow, tarragon, English thyme, garlic chives, lavender, rosemary, dwarf sage, oregano, and green lemon thyme. Each collection includes ten plants and is available for $30.95 from Nichols Garden Nursery, 1190 North Pacific Hwy, Albany, OR 97321; 541-928-9280.

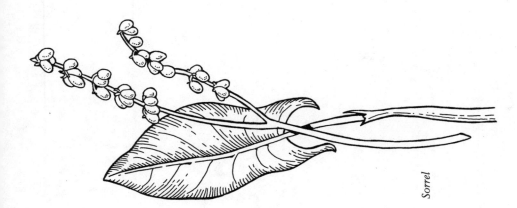

*Sorrel*

include lavender, which is valued mostly for its flower buds, and herbs like calendula and chamomile, which are harvested for their flowers.

Probably the easiest and most common method of drying various kinds of herbs is to cut back whole stems of plants and bunch a dozen or so together, securing them with a rubber band at the end. Then bring them into a warm, dry place out of direct light and hang the bunches up from hooks or rafters to air-dry. Leaves should be crisp and dry in seven to ten days, at which time you can take down the bunches and strip the leaves from the stems over a newspaper or large tray, discarding any debris or leaves that look discolored. Pour the herb leaves into tightly sealed jars or other containers, label them, and store them in a cool, dark place.

Not all herbs will air-dry successfully in this way. Basil, for instance, tends to turn brown and lose a lot of its pizzazz when hung up in bunches. An alternative to bunch drying is to place herbs on a drying rack in a just-warm oven, or in a dehydrator, which will dry leaves more quickly than simply hanging them up. Even faster is to spread herbs between paper towels in a single layer and place them in a microwave oven. In her book *Living with Herbs*, Jo Ann Gardner recommends zapping herbs in the microwave for two minutes, then taking them out and checking them. If the leaves aren't crisp-dry, she puts them back in the microwave and zaps them for additional 30-second intervals until they are done. Microwaves and leaf thickness may vary, so this method requires some experimentation.

Finally, a neat alternative to drying some herbs such as parsley, chervil, and basil for use as seasoning is to place two cups of fresh herbs in a blender with one cup of water and then process them. Pour the resulting slurry into ice-cube trays and freeze. Remove the cubes from the trays and put them in freezer bags. Then they can be taken out as needed and dropped as seasonings into soups, stews, and other recipes.

# fruits

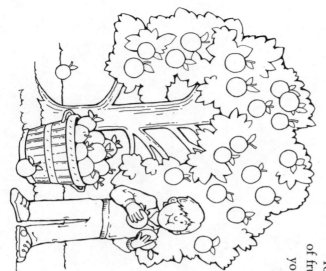

PASSPORT TO FRUIT GARDENING

For the home gardener, backyard fruit growing represents both luxury and practicality. Luxury because including apples, cherries, pears, raspberries, or other fruits in your landscape means years of harvests for fresh eating, preserving, and sharing with friends and neighbors. Practicality because fruit trees and bushes are long-lived and productive, and most require relatively little care once they are established. In years past, almost every American homestead included fruit — at the very least a few apple trees for fresh use and cidermaking. Today the interest in fresh, organic food and independent living means that home fruit-growing is enjoying renewed popularity.

You don't have to own a large estate to grow a wide variety of fruits at home. If you don't have space for full-sized trees, you can plant dwarf forms of apples, pears, and other fruits. If you don't have space for free-standing trees, try pruning and training trees on a trellis in the time-honored technique known as espalier. Grow a grape vine over an arbor or pergola. Plant lowbush blueberries or alpine strawberries in a bed near the house. Even container growing is a possibility, giving northern gardeners a chance to grow citrus, figs, and other frost-tender fruit trees outdoors in the summer, then moving them indoors when the weather turns cool (see "Growing Citrus and Other Tender Fruits" on page 108).

Of course, different fruits and berries have different cultural needs, and there is no way to cover the whole subject here. For further reference, we've listed a number of excellent books and resources. This chapter covers just a few of the basic points of home orcharding: selection, planting, and natural disease and insect control.

## Locating Your Orchard

Fruit trees have very specific site requirements. They don't like wet feet, so well-drained, loamy soil is a must. They should be located where there is good air circulation so their leaves will dry quickly, since moisture helps spread disease. Flower buds can be easily killed by late spring frosts, so avoid siting your orchard in a frost pocket. Cold air flows downhill, making flowering fruit trees located at the bottom of a slope especially vulnerable to frost.

## Michael Phillips

Fruits offer the perpetual promise of bearing year after year. Orchard trees and berry plantings are in place when winter snows melt and spring brings the swelling buds. Baby Grace and I delight in the pure ecstasy of a tree in flower. She teaches me how to taste plum blossoms. Time stands still as a father and daughter are caught up in the perfect fragrance of spring. Summertime brings delicious berries and peaches picked perfectly ripe. Apple-picking is a joy, picking fruit from the arms of tree friends that we've nurtured over the years. Family and neighbors gather round to help squeeze cider on the handscrew press. The smell of hot apple pie wafts from the kitchen as a gentle snow puts the orchard to bed for another season.

Some gardeners find the prospect of growing fruit trees daunting. Personally, I love a challenge and the chance to plumb Nature's depths. I grow along with my trees, learning the nuances of pruning, the fascinating balance of the insect world, and how to moderate my expectations in the inevitable off-years. Contrary to current recommendations, you don't need to spray with chemicals to grow good fruit. But you do need to understand what is taking place, and perform certain tasks in a timely manner. Too often, our culture opts for convenience over quality. For me, this is a straightforward choice: give me my own 'Honeycrisp' apples and 'Jefferson' plums over the meager offerings of the market any day.

*Michael Phillips grows apples organically at Lost Nation Orchard in Lancaster, New Hampshire, where he lives with his family. He is writing a book about orcharding, due in 1998 from Chelsea Green.*

**Fruits and Berries for the Home Garden** *by Lewis Hill* (Garden Way Publishing, 1992).
A clear, concise guide for the home orchardist. Features information on some small fruits, vine fruits, and nuts. Good photographs and material on common insects and diseases. 280 pages, paperback, $16.95.

**The Smart Gardener's Guide to Growing Fruit** *by Dr. Bob Gough* (Stackpole Books, 1997).
A concise yet comprehensive new book that covers all the basics, including planting, pruning, grafting, varieties, and much more. Mostly deals with trees, but also includes information for small fruits. 256 pages, paperback, $16.95.

**The Orchard Almanac: A Seasonal Guide to Healthy Fruit Trees,** 3rd ed. *by Steve Page and Joe Smillie* (agAccess, 1995).
The best book currently available on organic orchard practices. The month-by-month organization makes it easy to use. 176 pages, paperback, $12.00.

**Citrus: Complete Guide to Selecting and Growing More than 100 Varieties** *by Lance Walheim* (Ironwood Press, 1996).
An excellent introduction to all kinds of citrus fruits, including hardiness and harvest information. Great color photos and recipes. 112 pages, paperback, $16.95.

If you plant your orchard on a slope, avoid planting trees near the top where the winds are most severe. Mid-slope is the best location. There are conflicting recommendations about which direction the slope should face. Southern and southwestern slopes can be hot and dry, and can also cause trees to break dormancy too early, which makes them susceptible to damage from late frosts. Yet a southern slope can work well if it is protected from the prevailing winds by a windbreak on any side except the downslope one (which would block air circulation.).

A northerly slope will help delay bloom time and thus reduce frost damage to tender buds, but it may not provide enough solar exposure to evaporate moisture and promote good fruiting. In humid regions, easterly slopes are advantageous because they promote rapid drying of the morning dew.

# Other Good Books

**Taylor's Guide to Fruits and Berries** ed. *Roger Holmes* (Houghton Mifflin, 1996). Excellent reference. 464 pages, paperback, $19.95

**Citrus** *by the editors of Sunset Books* (Sunset, 1996). Good information on landscaping, microclimates, and frost protection. 96 pages, paperback, $9.99.

**Fruit Trees for the Home Gardener** *by Allan A. Swenson* (Lyons & Burford, 1994). 176 pages, paperback, $14.95

**The Gardener's Book of Berries** *by Allan A. Swenson* (Lyons & Burford, 1994). 144 pages, paperback, $12.95.

**The Backyard Orchardist** *by Stella Otto* (OttoGraphics, 1993). 268 pages, paperback, $14.95.

**The Backyard Berry Book** *by Stella Otto* (OttoGraphics, 1995). 300 pages, paperback, $15.95.

## REGIONAL FRUIT BOOKS

**Berries: A Firefly Gardener's Guide** *ed. Jennifer Bennett* (Firefly Books, 1996). A colorful little book especially for gardeners in Canada and the northern U.S. Chapters discuss row cropping, cane fruits, and wild berries. 96 pages, paperback, $10.95.

**The Harrowsmith Book of Fruit Trees** *by Jennifer Bennett* (Camden House, 1991). Very useful and attractive, with lots of hardy cultivars recommended for gardeners in the northern U.S. and Canada. 160 pages, paperback, $22.95.

**Growing Fruit in the Upper Midwest** *by Don Gordon* (University of Minnesota Press, 1991). A good reference work for fruit tree and small fruit growers in Minnesota, Iowa, Wisconsin, and the Dakotas. Lists the best cultivars for each area. 286 pages, hardcover, $24.95

**American Horticultural Society Pruning and Training** *by Christopher Brickell and David Joyce* (DK Publishing, 1996).

**Old Southern Apples** *by Creighton Lee Calhoun, Jr.* (McDonald & Woodward, 1995). The only comprehensive book on Southern apple varieties, of which more than 300 are still grown today. Variety descriptions feature historical information. 326 pages, paperback, $40.00.

## PRUNING GUIDES

**The Pruning Book** *by Lee Reich* (Taunton Press, 1997). A new and thorough treatment of the subject, with lots of color photos and clear illustrations. Chapters cover advanced techniques such as espalier, pollarding, bonsai, and topiary. 240 pages, hardcover, $27.95.

**Pruning Simplified** *by Lewis Hill* (Garden Way Publishing, 1986). Basics for beginners, covering both ornamental and fruit trees. 224 pages, paperback, $12.95.

## CIDER AND CIDERMAKING BOOKS

**The American Cider Book: The Story of America's Natural Beverage** *by Vrest Orton* (North Point Press, 1995). A new edition of this classic little book, filled with the history and the folk traditions of cider. 144 pages, paperback, $9.00.

**Sweet and Hard Cider: Making It, Using It and Enjoying It** *by Annie Proulx and Lew Nichols* (Garden Way Publishing, 1980). Complete information on equipment, procedures, and the best cider apple varieties. 192 pages, paperback, $9.95.

**The Art of Cidermaking** *by Paul Correnty* (Brewers Publications, 1995). A "home brewing" book for cidermakers, with several good hard cider recipes. 96 pages, paperback, $9.95.

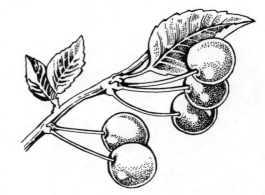

## Disease-Resistant Apples*

| VARIETY | Scab | Fire Blight | Cedar Rust | Powdery Mildew |
|---|---|---|---|---|
| Liberty | ✓ | ✓ | ✓ | ✓ |
| Prima | ✓ | ✓ | ✓ | |
| Priscilla | ✓ | ✓ | ✓ | |
| Nova Easy-Gro | ✓ | ✓ | | |
| Grimes Golden | ✓ | ✓ | | |
| Macfree | ✓ | | | ✓ |
| Freedom | ✓ | ✓ | ✓ | ✓ |
| Jonafree | ✓ | | ✓ | ✓ |

*Disease resistance varies from place to place and even within cultivars. For best success, try several varieties and see which work best for you.

Fruit trees need a lot of sun to grow healthy and be productive. If they are shaded by other trees or a building they will be less fruitful and more prone to insects and disease.

Now, most people don't have this many choices when it comes to sites; we've laid out their various advantages and disadvantages only to help you understand and work with what you have. Your best bet is to take all of these variables into account, select the most promising site on your property, and then plant a couple of trees to start with. Then, if they thrive in the first year or two, you'll know you can invest in more plants.

## Selecting Plants

In deciding which varieties to grow, consider trees and shrubs that have some natural resistance to disease. In apples and pears the common diseases include scab and fire blight. (See the box above on "Disease-Resistant Apples" for some good varieties.) With other fruits, such as raspberries, make sure you buy from a nursery that propagates from virus-free plants. Selecting disease-resistant plants doesn't mean that you will never experience any disease problems, but it greatly improves your chances for success.

Another crucial issue is hardiness. Most gardeners are well aware of their growing zone and savvy enough to make sure that the perennial plants they buy are hardy enough to survive there. The same applies to fruits and berries. You need to make sure that the plants you purchase won't be damaged over the winter, by checking hardiness information before buying. Bloom time is another factor to consider. Many fruits flower very early in the spring (like cherries) and crops can be diminished or entirely lost when blossoms are damaged by frost. If your specific area is prone to late frosts every spring, such early bloomers may survive, but they will never truly thrive or reliably set fruit. To grow these plants in a marginal area, you'll have to plant them in an especially favorable and protected site.

## Buying Plants: Locally or by Mail?

When purchasing fruit trees or bushes, you have the option of either ordering plants by mail or going to a local garden center or nursery. Local nurseries usually sell trees in containers or with the root mass wrapped in burlap. Mail-order nurseries usually sell trees as "bareroot stock," which means that they are shipped to you in a dormant state

# Growing Citrus and Other Tender Fruits

In this chapter, we've focused mainly on types of fruits that are reliably hardy when planted in most growing regions. But for gardeners who want to grow something a little different, various kinds of citrus fruits can make a wonderful addition to the home or garden, especially when grown in containers.

With few exceptions, citrus fruits are hardy only to around 20°F, so growing them outdoors year-round is not an option for people who live in areas colder than Zone 9. Fortunately, several kinds of citrus make good container plants, particularly the dwarf varieties, many of which are highly ornamental and ever-blooming. Good examples include dwarf sour oranges like 'Chinotto' and 'Bouquet des Fleurs' (7 to 8 feet at maturity), and the popular and hardy 'Meyer' lemon (which grows to about 6 feet); 'Meyer' bears fragrant, thin-skinned, good-tasting lemons. Lesser-known citrus relatives like the kumquat and the calamondin also make beautiful plants, bearing lots of small fruits that can be used in marmalades and other preserves.

Citrus fruits like growing in well-drained soil (regular potting soil is fine for containers). They need regular watering and, during the outdoor growing season, biweekly foliar feeding with a complete liquid fertilizer, one that contains the micronutrients zinc, manganese, and iron.

When you bring containers indoors or outdoors at the change of seasons, try to move the plants gradually to acclimate them to their new growing conditions. Once inside the house, it's good to mist the plants or to set them on trays of watered pebbles to raise the humidity level. When moving citrus trees outdoors, pick a sunny, protected spot, and paint any exposed areas of trunk with a white latex paint diluted with water, to prevent sunscald.

Other tropical or exotic fruits can be grown indoors, in containers or in a greenhouse. The shorter varieties of bananas like 'Dwarf Orinoco', make great container plants. They do, however, require uniform temperatures (above 60°F), and may need to grow for 20 or 30 months after planting before they will start flowering. For more information on growing bananas, an excellent reference is *The Complete Book of Bananas* by William O. Lessard, available from Lessard Nursery or Stokes Tropicals (see suppliers list, page 113).

Figs seem like an exotic fruit, but several varieties are quite hardy and fairly easy to grow, even as far north as Zone 5. The secret is to pick a cold-hardy type like the popular 'Brown Turkey' or 'Celeste', then plant it in a warm, sunny location — for instance, trellised on a south-facing masonry wall. Gardeners in Zones 5–7 will need to provide winter protection. One simple way to do this is to grow the fig tree in a large tub or container, moving it inside in the fall or early winter, before temperatures dip to 10°F.

Fresh figs are wonderful for table use or preserving, and varieties like 'Brown Turkey' are everbearing. See the suppliers list on page 113 for the names of some sources for tropical plants.

with their roots packed in damp wood shavings. The choice of where to buy is up to you: mail-order nurseries tend to offer more varieties than garden centers, so if you are looking for a particular cultivar or want a broad selection you should start with them. (See the suppliers list on page 113 for the names of some recommended mail-order companies.) However, if you're unsure about which variety to buy, a local nursery will carry plants that will thrive in your growing area.

If you do buy bareroot plants by mail, you will need to plant them in early spring, as soon as the ground can be worked, while the plants are still dormant and the water table is high. In most regions of the country, this spring planting is important because it gives the young plants a full growing season to get established before the onset of freezing weather in the fall. Trees and shrubs sold in containers by local nurseries are more forgiving in terms of planting time; they can be successfully transplanted in most areas either in the spring or early fall.

Whether you purchase bareroot or container plants, most fruit trees will be sold as grafted stock. This means that the tree consists of at least two sections. The top part is called the *scion* (sigh-on), and is a branch cutting that has been taken from the variety of fruit you want to grow. The bottom part is the *rootstock*, and it is usually selected either for hardiness or for the way it will determine the ultimate height and size of the tree. Standard rootstocks result in trees of full size (to 15 feet or more).

Dwarf rootstocks have less vigorous root systems and limit the size of mature trees to 6 to 8 feet or so. Semi-dwarfing rootstocks produce mature trees somewhere in between the two extremes.

Dwarf fruit trees are very popular among home orchardists because they result in space-efficient plants that begin bearing fruit quickly, usually two to three years after planting. There are, however, a few disadvantages to growing dwarf trees. For one thing, they have a shorter life expectancy than standard-sized trees — about 10 to 20 years on average. Because of their limited root systems, dwarf trees don't compete well with grasses and other plants, so you'll have to keep the area around them weeded and well mulched. Also, most true dwarfs are not suitable for regions with extremely cold winters (Zone 4 and colder). But for gardeners concerned with space limitations, or who live in relatively mild climates, dwarfs can be the ideal choice.

## Pollination

Many varieties of fruit trees and shrubs are self-fruitful: that is, they do not need to have a plant of another variety nearby with which to cross-pollinate. Other varieties (particularly those of tree fruits) need to have a partner in the orchard so that they will be pollinated and produce a good crop of fruit. In fact, even self-fruitful varieties often benefit from having a different variety of the same plant located nearby. The easiest way to determine whether the variety you want to grow is self-fruitful, or requires another pollinator, is to carefully check its specific description in a mail-order nursery catalog (or ask at a local nursery).

Cross-pollination doesn't mean that you will end up with weird-looking hybrid fruits. For example, a 'Cortland' apple tree will always produce 'Cortland' apples, even if its blossoms are visited by bees who carry pollen from another variety of apple or crabapple that is growing nearby. However, if you planted the *seeds* from that 'Cortland' apple, you would probably grow a tree that bore an entirely different kind of apple, one that was not "true to type," in plant-breeder's lingo.

Commercial orchards often rent honeybee hives to ensure good pollination during blossom time. Fortunately, there are also wild bees

## Pollination Tips

**Apples.** Crabapples will cross-pollinate with apples, and in fact are often grown near apple trees for just that purpose.

**Pears.** Most varieties of pears need to be cross-pollinated with a different variety. Two popular varieties, 'Seckel' and 'Bartlett,' will not pollinate one another.

**Raspberries.** Raspberries are self-fruitful and do not require another variety for good pollination.

**Blueberries.** Even though blueberries are self-fruitful, the size of the berries and the size of the crop will be improved by planting more than one variety.

**Cherries.** Sweet cherries and sour (pie) cherries are different species, rarely bloom at the same time, and will not cross-pollinate with one another. Unless you purchase a self-fruitful variety ('Montmorency', 'Star Stella', etc.) each type of cherry will need another pollinator from its own species.

**Plums.** Relatively few varieties of plums are self-fertile ('Mt. Royal', 'Stanley', etc.), so you'll need to plant at least two different varieties that can cross-pollinate. There are European plums, Japanese plums, American native plums, and a whole host of hybrids. Consult catalog descriptions to determine whether the varieties you want to grow will pollinate one another.

**Peaches, Nectarines, and Apricots.** Most varieties are self-fertile and do not require another pollinator.

**Citrus Fruits.** Most citrus fruits are self-pollinating, and some varieties will even set fruit without pollination (such fruits are seedless).

that do the same job, and who don't mind the sometimes cool spring weather that prevails when trees flower. For example, the orchard mason bee (*Osmia lignaria*) is a good pollinator, and is found throughout most of the United States, with the exception of the Deep South.

It's very important *never* to spray insecticides during the blossom time of either the fruit trees or the other groundcover plants (dandelions, clovers, etc.) that may be growing near them. These toxic chemicals can kill bees and other beneficial insects. Read on for more information on nonchemical methods of pest control.

Nursery catalogs and books usually provide good information on which varieties of plants need pollinators and which will produce fruit even if planted alone. Rules of thumb for various kinds of fruits are given in the "Pollination Tips" box on page 109.

## Planting and Fertilizing

Many nurseries supply good instructions on how to plant your trees or shrubs. You could also consult the books listed on pages 105 and 106. For the basic tree-planting procedure, see the box on the facing page.

After planting your trees, apply compost in a circular band around each plant, beginning under the branches and extending about a foot beyond the ends of the branches. Apply ½ to 1 inch of compost annually, working it into the top 2 inches of soil. Or mix in 3 to 4 inches of

# Resources

An exhaustive and valuable reference book for serious fruit growers is the *Fruit, Berry and Nut Inventory*, 2nd Edition, which is available for $22.00 from Seed Savers Exchange, 3076 North Winn Rd., Decorah, IA 52101; 319-382-5872. This book describes some 5,800 varieties of fruits, nuts, and berries that are currently being offered by more than 300 mail-order nurseries.

Another good resource for home orchardists is **Apple-source**, 1716 Apples Rd., Chapin, IL 62628. This service ships out apples during harvest season to people who would like to taste particular varieties before deciding which ones to grow. Owners Jill and Tom Vorbeck are involved with the North American Fruit Explorers.

**American Pomological Society**
102 Tyson Bldg.
University Park, PA 16802
814-863-6163
*Founded in 1848, the APS promotes the improvement of fruit varieties through breeding and testing; annual membership dues are $20 and include a subscription to the quarterly Fruit Varieties Journal.*

**California Rare Fruit Growers, Inc.**
9872 Aldgate Ave.
Garden Grove, CA 92641
*A nonprofit organization committed to the study and preservation of rare fruit varieties. Members receive "The Fruit Gardener," a bimonthly newsletter.*

**Fruit Testing Association Nursery, Inc.**
P.O. Box 462, North St.
Geneva, NY 14456
315-787-2205
*A cooperative fruit nursery established in 1918 to introduce the most promising varieties developed at the New York State Agricultural Experiment Station at Geneva. Annual membership is $10; members receive a newsletter and can purchase from a catalog of new fruit varieties.*

**Home Orchard Society**
P.O. Box 230192
Tigard, OR 97281-0192
*An educational organization formed to assist new and experienced fruit growers. Membership is $15 per year and includes a subscription to the quarterly journal Pome News.*

**North American Fruit Explorers (NAFEX)**
c/o Jill Vorbeck
1716 Apples Rd.
Chapin, IL 62628
*The best-known fruit group in North America, with more than 3,000 members committed to discovering and cultivating superior varieties of fruits and nuts. Membership is $8 for one year or $15 for two years. Members can borrow books from NAFEX's extensive library and they receive the quarterly journal Pomona.*

**Western Ontario Fruit Testing Association (WOFTA)**
Agriculture Canada Research Station
Harrow, Ontario N0R 1G0
*Canadian members can purchase new, sometimes unnamed, varieties of fruit trees. Annual membership $15.*

## How to Plant a Fruit Tree

1. If you've ordered bareroot nursery stock, soak the plant roots in water or manure tea up to 24 hours before planting. If you can't plant within a few days after receiving the shipment, repack the plant in the damp sawdust or wood shavings it came in and store it in a cold, dark location until the ground can be worked. Never expose the bare roots of plants to wind or sun.

2. Using a sharp, square-ended planting spade, dig a circle 2 feet in diameter and about 3 feet deep. Remove the sod and set it aside, and separate the topsoil and the lighter-colored subsoil into two piles. Remove any rocks from the planting hole.

3. Chop up the sod and put the pieces in the hole, grass side down, so that it doesn't come in contact with the tree roots. Cover the sod with a little topsoil.

4. Set the tree into the hole. For grafted trees grown on standard rootstocks, position the tree so that the *graft union*, the point at which the scion and the rootstock were joined together, is 1 to 2 inches below the surface of the ground. For dwarf and semidwarf rootstocks, the graft union should be 2 to 3 inches *above* the soil surface.

5. Fill in around the roots, using the topsoil first. Use your hands to firm the soil around the roots and eliminate any air pockets. Fill in about half the planting hole.

6. Pour water into the planting hole until the soil gets quite mucky. Then, using the heel of your foot, tamp down the soil.

7. Fill in the rest of the planting hole with the remaining topsoil and subsoil. Firm down the soil around the tree and make a "dish" or depression to encourage water to drain toward the tree.

8. Mulch around the tree with organic matter (leaves, compost, grass clippings, etc.). Don't use fresh manure, though well-rotted manure is fine. Line the mulch in the same dish shape around the tree.

9. Water the tree until the soil cannot readily absorb any more.

10. Drive one or two stakes into the ground outside the root zone to mark the tree. Fruit trees grafted to dwarf rootstocks develop smaller root systems than standard-size trees and require some support. After planting dwarf trees, attach the tree to the stake using some flexible tubing or other material.

11. Prune off any side branches and cut back trees by about one-third after planting. Balled or container trees do not need to be pruned.

12. Place wire-mesh "hardware cloth" or a plastic tree guard around the tree trunk to protect it from rodents and deer.

13. Post-Planting. During the first growing season, water the tree regularly, giving it 5 to 10 gallons per day for the first month or so, then watering two or three times a week for another couple of months, or during dry weather. In the late fall, paint the tree bark with white latex paint diluted with water, so the bark will reflect winter sunlight and not be damages by sunscald or cracking.

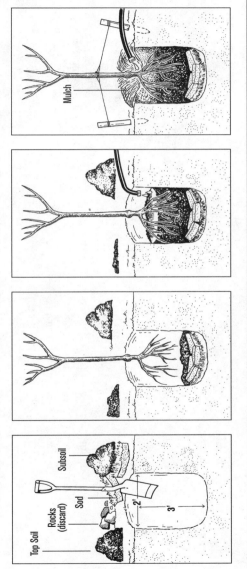

compost or composted manure every few years. However, don't spread uncomposted manure around fruit trees or shrubs, because fresh manure usually has too high a concentration of nitrogen, salts, and disease organisms.

## Web sites

**California Rare Fruit Growers**
http://www.crfg.org
*Members in 48 states and 29 foreign countries. Links to international sites; seed bank; fruit cultural data; FAQs.*

**Cornell University Cooperative Extension**
http://www.cce.cornell.edu/programs/ag/fruit.html
*Helpful information on all manner of fruits and vegetables.*

**Miller Nurseries**
http://www.millernurseries.com
*This colorful site features material on fruit varieties sold by Miller Nurseries, plus an on-line catalog.*

**St. Lawrence Nurseries**
http://www.sln.potsdam.ny.us
*St. Lawrence Nurseries in Potsdam, New York, specializes in hardy fruit and nut trees for cold-climate growers. Their web site features the nursery's extremely useful Planting Guide as well as their on-line catalog.*

**Usenet News Group**
cce.ag.small-fruit
cce.ag.tree-fruit

Have your soil tested periodically to check nutrient levels. Be careful not to overfertilize, though. Excess nitrogen promotes fast, succulent growth that is susceptible to damage from insects and diseases like fire blight. Also, don't fertilize plants after midsummer, because you can stimulate tender new growth that won't have time to harden-off before cold temperatures arrive.

## Orchard Maintenance

Maintaining a clean orchard means picking up after your trees. Fruit that drops to the ground can contain insect larvae, which burrow into the soil where they overwinter, to reemerge in the spring. These drops also attract voles and mice, which can damage trees by chewing on the bark. Pick up the dropped fruit and burn or bury it underground far away from your trees. Pick up the fruit as soon as possible after it drops to catch the larvae before they burrow into the ground. It's especially important to collect the spring drops, which are still quite small but can contain a large number of larvae.

While you're picking up dropped fruit in the fall, also clean up fallen leaves, which can likewise harbor disease and insects. Removing apple leaves within 200 yards of your apple trees will reduce the number of scab spores the following spring.

Pruning is a subject all to itself. Certainly you will want to learn the basics and practice selective pruning of your fruit trees and shrubs on a yearly basis, removing crossing branches, suckers, and watersprouts; opening up and reinvigorating older plants; and allowing good air circulation to prevent disease. For complete information on pruning, consult one of the references listed under "Pruning Guides," page 106.

## Insect and Disease Control

If you follow good cultural practices and select disease-free trees and shrubs, you should be able to keep most common orchard pests and diseases in check without the use of chemicals. But to grow fruit organically, you will need to tolerate some degree of pest and disease damage. If you were to prevent all insect and disease damage, you would need an arsenal of toxic sprays — something no one wants to use around the home landscape.

One strategy for controlling insect pests is to attract beneficial insect predators to your orchard by planting wildflowers and herbs, including dill, buckwheat, tansy, yarrow, and goldenrod. Another way to reduce certain kinds of insect damage is to trap pests using simple, visual lures. These traps mimic the way leaves or fruits appear to insects. For example, the apple maggot fly can be lured by hanging in the tree small, dark red spheres that are covered with a sticky substance called Tangletrap (see "Garden Gear," page 114). Female flies get stuck as they jump from fruit to fruit, and then die.

There are also many biological or natural sprays that can be used in the orchard at key times to disrupt insect cycles. Dormant oil spray,

# Suppliers

These mail-order nurseries have been included for their longevity, reputation, customer service, or the number and range of varieties they offer. When requesting catalogs, check first with companies located in your own climate region.

## Alabama

Classical Fruits
8831 AL Hwy. 157
Moulton, AL 35650
205-974-8813

## California

Fowler Nurseries, Inc.
525 Fowler Rd.
Newcastle, CA 95658
916-645-8191

Greenmantle Nursery
3010 Ettersburg Rd.
Garberville, CA 95440
707-986-7504
*Catalog $3.00.*

Sonoma Antique Apple Nursery
4395 Westside Rd.
Healdsburg, CA 95448
707-433-6420
*Catalog $5.00.*

## Georgia

Lawson's Nursery
Rte. 1, Box 472
Yellow Creek Rd.
Ball Ground, GA 30107
404-893-2141

## Michigan

Newark Nurseries, Inc.
P.O. Box 578
Hartford, MI 49507
616-621-3135
*Catalog $5.00.*

Southmeadow Fruit Gardens
15310 Red Arrow Hwy.
Lakeside, MI 49116
616-469-2865
*Free price list; $9 for illustrated catalog.*

## Minnesota

Northwind Nursery & Orchards
7910 335th Ave., NW
Princeton, MN 55371
612-389-4920
*Catalog $1.00.*

## Missouri

Stark Brothers Nursery
Hwy. 54, P.O. Box 10
Louisiana, MO 63353
314-754-5511

## New York

Miller Nurseries Inc.
5060 West Lake Rd.
Canandaigua, NY 14424
716-396-2647

St. Lawrence Nurseries
325 State Hwy. 345
Potsdam, NY 13676
315-265-6739

## Oregon

Northwoods Nursery
27635 South Oglesby Rd.
Canby, OR 97013
503-266-5432

## Pennsylvania

M. Worley Nursery
98 Braggtown Rd.
York Springs, PA 17372
717-528-4519

## Tennessee

Cumberland Valley Nurseries
P.O. Box 471
McMinnville, TN 37110
615-668-4153

## Texas

Womack's Nursery
Rte. 1, Box 80
DeLeon, TX 76444
817-893-6497

## Virginia

Burford Brothers
Route 1
Monroe, VA 24574
804-929-4950
*Sales catalog $2.00; $12.00 for extensive international apple catalog.*

## Washington

Bear Creek Nursery
P.O. Box 411H
Northport, WA 99157
*Catalog $1.00.*

Raintree Nursery
391 Butts Rd.
Morton, WA 98356
360-496-6400

## Canada

Corn Hill Nursery
RR 5
Petitcodiac, NB E0A 2H0
506-756-3635
*Catalog $2.00.*

V. Kraus Nurseries Ltd.
P.O. Box 180
Carlisle, ON L0R 1H0
416-689-4022
*Catalog $1.00.*

Morden Nurseries Ltd.
P.O. Box 1270
Morden, MB R0G 1J0
204-822-3311
*Catalog $2.00.*

Tsolum River Fruit Trees
P.O. Box 1271
Ganges, BC V0S 1E0
604-537-4191
*Catalog $3.75.*

## Tropical Fruits

The Banana Tree
715 Northampton St.
Easton, PA 18042
215-253-9589
*Catalog $3.00.*

Exotica Rare Fruit Nursery
P.O. Box 160
Vista, CA 92085
619-724-9093
*Long SASE for catalog.*

Four Winds Growers
P.O. Box 3538
Fremont, CA 94539
510-656-2591
*Specializes in dwarf citrus; long SASE for catalog.*

Lessard Nursery
19201 SW 248th St.
Homestead, FL 33031
305-247-0397
*Specializes in bananas; catalog $2.00.*

Oregon Exotics
Rare Fruit Nursery
1065 Messinger Rd.
Grants Pass, OR 97527
503-846-7578
*Catalog $2.00.*

Pacific Tree Farms
4301 Lynwood Drive
Chula Vista, CA 91910
619-422-2400
*Catalog $2.00.*

Stokes Tropicals
P.O. Box 9868
New Iberia, LA 70562
800-624-9706
*Bananas and tropical plants.*

**Gardener's Supply's Home Orchard Kit** controls common fruit pests without chemicals. The red spheres lure insects like the apple maggot fly, which are caught on the sticky surface for easy removal. The red spheres are also effective for monitoring cherry fruit fly, blueberry maggot fly, and for controlling apple maggot fly on plums, pears, and crabapples. The red spheres are reuseable and must be covered with Tanglefoot to be effective.

On apple trees you'll need two red spheres per dwarf tree, two to four per semidwarf, and six or more for full-size trees.

The white rectangles can greatly reduce damage caused by tarnished plant bugs. Use three to four white rectangle traps per tree regardless of size.

For best results, hang both of these traps at blossom time.

#05-495 Home Orchard Kit (3 red spheres, 5.5 oz. Tangletrap, 4 white rectangles) $29.95
#12-320 Red Sphere $4.95 each
#12-217C Tangletrap, 5.5 oz. (covers 6 spheres) $4.95
#12-218 Tangletrap, 1 qt. $17.50
#12-217D White Rectangle $2.95 each

**SunSpray Oil** protects against aphids, thrips, mealy bugs, pear psylla, codling moths, and leaf rollers. For best results, the branches and trunk of the tree should be completely covered. One quart makes 25 gallons. EPA registered.

#05-287 SunSpray Oil, 1 qt. $12.95

**Liquid Sulfur** fungicide coats the leaves of fruit trees with a caustic solution that prevents the growth of apple scab, powdery mildew, and brown rot — and that irritates the membranes of mites. Apply in early spring. 16 ounces of liquid makes 3½ gallons of spray.

#05-106 Liquid Sulfur, 16 oz. liquid concentrate $10.95

The **Easy-Pump Garden Sprayer** requires only one or two pumps to reach optimum pressure — half that of other, similar-sized sprayers. The 22-inch spray wand comes with three spray tips (fan, hollow cone, jet stream). The high-density polyethylene tank resists damage from sunlight and corrosion and has a large 4½-inch fill opening. Includes a webbed nylon carrying strap.

#05-008 1½-Gallon Pump Sprayer $38.95

---

**Felco No. 2 Pruners** have become the standard by which all other pruners are measured. The original 1940 design has professional features like a sap groove on the blade, a wire-cutting notch, a cushioned shock absorber to prevent wrist fatigue, and a non-corroding spring mechanism. The precision-ground, hardened-steel blades produce a clean cut.

#04-230 Felco No. 2 Pruner $44.95
#04-221 Felco Holster $7.95

For smooth, precise, and effortless cuts, this **Folding Pruning Saw** can't be beat. The saw cuts on the pull stroke for maximum power and control. The 6½-inch blade locks open and folds back into the curved handle for easy carrying.

#04-306 Folding Pruning Saw $14.95

**Lac-Balsam** is the best-selling plant wound sealer in Europe. The patented compound forms a rubber-like seal that allows breathing. Antiseptic resins aid in the formation of healing callouses. Nontoxic and cleans up with soap and water.

#12-230 Lac-Balsam Tree Wound Dressing, 12 oz. $14.95

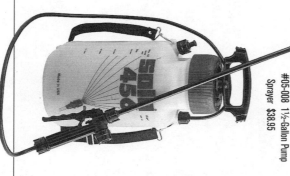

Ultra-fine **SunSpray Oil** can be sprayed on fruit trees during winter dormancy, before any buds swell, and during the spring season. It's effective against overwintering scale and mites, and

Bordeaux mixture, and other products of natural or elemental origin are relatively nontoxic to beneficial insects and to humans when used judiciously and according to the manufacturer's instructions.

Simple physical barriers serve to keep many animal pests from damaging trees and fruit. These range from wire mesh or plastic tree guards set around young trees to protect them from mice and rabbits, to smelly soap hung on branches or tall fences erected around the orchard to discourage deer.

By combining preventive measures with the least toxic controls, you can have a healthy orchard and still harvest lots of good-quality fruit for eating. See the references listed under "Favorite Books" for more in-depth information on dealing with insects, disease, and animal pests (page 105).

## Backyard Berries

Being a backyard fruit grower doesn't necessarily mean you have to plant fruit trees. Berries and other so-called small fruits generally don't require as much space as full-size trees, and growing several different types can extend your harvest from early summer through the end of the growing season.

Keep in mind, though, that the "small" in small fruits refers to the size of the fruit, not the plant. A full-size highbush blueberry may grow 12 feet tall and 6 feet wide — hardly appropriate for a patio. If you have limited space, a half-high cultivar like 'Northsky' or one of the lowbush blueberries (*Vaccinium angustifolium*) might be a better choice.

Much of the preceding information in this chapter relates to berries as well as to tree fruits. Buy from a local nursery or a regional mail-order supplier, and purchase plants that are disease-free and reliably winter-hardy in your growing zone. In most areas of North America, planting in early spring is recommended, whether you've purchased dormant bareroot stock or a plant that's growing in a container. Also when selecting plants, be sure to check whether the type of fruit you're growing is self-fruitful (requires only one variety for good pollination) or whether you need to plant two different varieties of the same fruit (see the "Pollination Tips" box on page 109). Rabbit-eye blueberries, muscadine grapes, and kiwis (*Actinidia* spp.) are all examples of small fruits that require two compatible varieties for successful pollination. In addition, kiwi plants are either male or female, so (as with hollies or ginkgos) you will need to plant at least one of each sex to ensure fruit set.

The ideal site and soil conditions will vary depending on the type of fruit. In many cases, these plants aren't fussy and will grow just fine in an average, well-drained garden soil. However, it's important to check the nursery catalog or a good book on berries before planting to make sure your conditions are suitable (see the recommended books in this chapter).

Blueberries, lingonberries, and other members of the genus *Vaccinium* require an acid soil (pH 4.5 to 5.5) to grow well. If your soil is not

that acidic, you can amend it organically a year or so in advance by digging lots of peat moss and pine needles into the planting site. Once the soil is acidic enough, plant the blueberries and maintain soil acidity by mulching heavily every year with pine needles and shredded oak leaves. If you want to lower your soil pH more rapidly, you can apply a fertilizer that's formulated for azaleas, hollies, and other acid-loving shrubs, or sprinkle some aluminum sulphate onto the soil before planting.

Raspberries, blackberries, and dewberries (*Rubus* spp.) are also known as brambles, and they are among the easiest and most popular backyard fruits. They all have perennial roots that send up biennial shoots, or canes. In the first year of growth, these canes are vegetative; in the second year they bear fruit, then die. But at the same time the plant is producing new vegetative canes, which will bear next year's fruit.

To lessen the chances of disease, avoid growing raspberries on ground that has recently been growing a member of the Nightshade Family (tomatoes, peppers, potatoes, eggplant), or where some other tree fruits or wild brambles have grown before. For the same reason, locate raspberries at least 500 yards away from any wild brambles.

Raspberries and other cane fruits have shallow root systems, so it's important to remove any weeds that will compete with them for nutrients. The most common way of growing raspberries is in rows spaced 6 to 12 feet apart. This spacing allows you to cultivate the rows with a rototiller, but also permits easy access from both sides and ensures good air circulation around the plants.

Consider planting a number of different varieties to ensure a continuous harvest of berries from early summer through late fall. A well-tended raspberry patch will produce for ten years or more before the plants start to decline.

It's impossible to give even sketchy instructions for all of the small fruits in this chapter. There are just too many wonderful choices, and each one has its own place in the backyard landscape. From strawberries and rhubarb, which are often grown in the vegetable garden, to vines like grapes and kiwis, which can be trained along a wire support or over a trellis or pergola, at least one type of small fruit is sure to be just right for your garden. And don't forget the ornamental possibilities of many lesser-grown fruits, such as the spicy-scented clove currant (*Ribes odoratum*) and the beautiful American persimmon (*Diospyros virginiana*). For more details, see the chapter, "The Edible Landscape."

> There is real value in blending different forms, shapes, and leaf patterns as part of a total outdoor scene. When you select furniture for a room, you look for pieces that complement each other but aren't necessarily identical. Some standout accent pieces always lend a special touch. The same is true with outdoor living rooms.
>
> "It has been you can't have your cake and eat it too. But with multipurpose landscaping, you can come close. You'll appreciate the blooms of trees each spring, their fruits in season, and foliage in the fall."
>
> —from *Fruit Trees for the Home Gardener* by Allan A. Swenson (Lyons & Burford, 1994)

PART III

ornamentals

BULBS

FLOWERS FOR CUTTING

GROWING ROSES

GARDEN DESIGN

PASSPORT TO GARDENING
ANNUAL FLOWERS

PERENNIAL FLOWERS

# garden design

Experienced gardeners have no problem deciding when to plant their peas, how deep to put their tulip bulbs, or how much to water their geraniums. But when it comes to garden design, even the most seasoned gardeners begin to sweat. We can spend weeks trying to find the perfect spot for a new shrub; spend an entire winter sketching plans for a new perennial garden; and agonize for years about how to reconfigure the front walk. Why do we find these decisions so paralyzing?

One reason may be that garden design is perceived as the work of experts: landscape architects, landscape designers, garden designers, and landscape contractors. Yet some of the most beautiful gardens in the world were not designed by experts. Sissinghurst, the home and gardens of Vita Sackville-West and Harold Nicolson, is a perfect example. So, too, are the gardens of Tasha Tudor and Thomas Jefferson. These gardens are the result of an attentive eye, a sensitive hand, and many years of experimentation — skills that are not the exclusive property of design professionals. Our goal in this chapter is to help you overcome the garden design jitters, and give you the confidence to finally remove that hedge of overgrown yews, install a flagstone path to your garden, or decide where to put a water garden.

## To Plan or Not to Plan
Some gardeners wouldn't dream of planting anything without having a comprehensive design and planting plan for their entire yard. Others don't think about "designing"

their gardens until several years down the road. And still other gardeners never develop a long-range or a short-range plan. They do their planning in the moment, poised with a shovel and a couple of homeless plants.

Which approach is right for you? It depends entirely on who you are and what you are comfortable with. If you have the confidence to forge ahead and follow your intuition, do so! If you feel the need to get some professional advice, then that's the best alternative for you. Both approaches are equally valid.

## Guest Expert
## Anne Rowe

For many gardeners, decorating their garden space is as important as planting it. Those wishing to achieve a personal look not provided by plastic pots and garden center ornaments need look no further than the dump. Salvage yards, flea markets, antiques fairs, and auctions offer an unending supply of garden treasures. Ancient stone and iron farm troughs can be used as alpine planters and birdbaths. Staddle stones — the mushroom-shaped stones once used to support graineries — make wonderful architectural accents. Chimney pots, planted up, and set on end, add height. And terra-cotta roof tiles can be used to edge a garden bed.

*Anne E. Rowe is a garden design and landscaping consultant who lives in Danbury, New Hampshire.*

These are especially desirable design ornaments. But don't overlook the possibilities of humbler (and cheaper) objects. My daughter, short of money and space, created a lovely herb garden in an ancient wheelbarrow. Fragments of gates can become trellises. Old boots destined for the trash make perfect planters to tuck in a corner, and buckets, lidless tea kettles, leaky watering cans — any container can be potted up as long as you provide proper drainage. A friend even took an old bicycle and, rather than tossing it, parked it in her garden, where it now proudly stands covered in morning glories.

Once you look at the Saturday morning dump run with new eyes, the possibilities are endless. Your garden will have its own personality, and you will be the ultimate recycler!

## Favorite Books

**The Garden Design Primer** *by Barbara Ashmun* (Lyons & Burford, 1993). A practical and unintimidating book that clearly explains the essential principles of design, and then applies them to all aspects of gardening. Accessible enough for beginners, and a valuable reference for the more experienced gardener. 226 pages, paperback, $16.95.

**Beds and Borders: Traditional and Original Garden Designs** *by Wendy B. Murphy* (Houghton Mifflin, 1993). A good book for beginners who want to get themselves oriented in the world of garden styles. 160 pages, hardcover, $22.95.

**Elements of Garden Design** *by Joe Eck* (Henry Holt, 1996). Eck's elegant prose is always a delight, but he is really in his element when addressing abstract concepts such as frame, harmony, contrast, symmetry, and scale. In this collection of thirty succinct essays he defines key design concepts and provides examples of their practical application. A treasure for the serious gardener. 164 pages, paperback, $14.95.

**The Inward Garden: Creating a Place of Beauty and Meaning** *by Julie Moir Messervy* (Little, Brown, 1995). A book about how to make a garden that is an outward expression of your individual memories, dreams, and desires. More philosophical than hands-on, it will appeal to more experienced gardeners. Beautiful writing and evocative photographs. Winner of the 1996 Quill and Trowel Award. 256 pages, hardcover, $40.00.

# Questions Designers Ask Their Clients

- What are the primary goals for your garden? Is it to look attractive to visitors and passing traffic, or are you a collector who needs to accommodate a wide assortment of plants? Is your garden a place to entertain friends and family, or is it a refuge for quiet contemplation? Are you trying to create a period garden that complements your home, or an informal collection of native plants to attract birds and wildlife?

- How many hours each week are you willing to invest in your garden? If it's only an hour or two, don't put in a thirty-foot perennial border, a water garden, or a large collection of hybrid roses.

- How much money are you willing to spend on your garden? Do you expect to have a finished project or will it be a work in progress?

- Where do you want to focus your energy? Start with an area that will have a significant impact — the entryway, the deck, the strip of lawn along the fence. You'll build confidence by tackling a manageable chunk and, along the way, learn a tremendous amount about your own style and tastes.

- What are the positive and negative features of your property? Using a garden to disguise or hide a negative feature usually backfires. If you need to hide an unsightly view, do it with something simple — trees, shrubs, or a fence. Then locate your garden where you can see it and enjoy it, and where it will relate to positive features of your landscape.

It is good to remember that there is no ultimate garden design for your property. There are as many different designs as there are gardeners. And even if you had a detailed plan that you executed to the "T", tomorrow would bring a new interest, a new challenge, and a whole new set of design decisions. The trees will mature and turn your sunny meadow into a shady glade. The weeping cherry that anchored your spring bulb garden will die and need to be replaced. You will tire of the cottage garden and develop a passion for dwarf conifers. In garden design there are no "right" decisions. It's a delightful (though sometimes unnerving) opportunity to express yourself. The hardest part may be trusting your own intuition, and allowing yourself to experiment as you evolve your own unique garden design.

## The Site Plan

One of the most valuable design tools is a site plan, or bird's-eye view of your yard. Seeing your garden on paper makes it much easier to identify underlying design elements such as traffic patterns, scale, and symmetry. A professional designer will give you a site plan that is precisely drawn to scale, but your own rough sketch or a survey map will be adequate

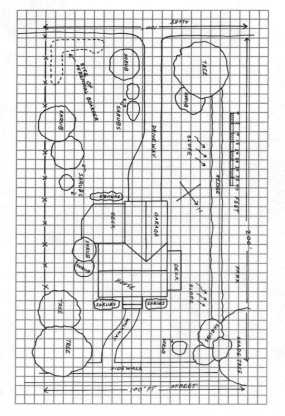

*Laying out your site plan on graph paper allows you to easily see design considerations such as traffic patterns, scale, and symmetry.*

for all but the most complex landscape designs. Once you have a plan to work from, you can start to indicate the positive and negative features of your yard (trees, shrubs, fences, outbuildings, pathways, views) and natural environmental factors such as light conditions and soil or drainage problems. Pathways and garden areas can be sketched right on the plan. If you enlarge sections of the plan, you can also use it to create your planting map.

Should you hire a professional landscaper or garden designer? If you have the means and desire to do so, it will probably be money well spent. Professional advice will always give you a valuable new perspec-

## *Other Good Books*

### BOOKS ABOUT USING COLOR

**The Gardener's Book of Color** *by Andrew Lawson* (Reader's Digest, 1996). Five hundred luscious photographs of inspiring plant combinations, including single-color plantings, harmonies, and stunning contrasts. Originally a British publication, it has been Americanized with hardiness zones and other information. 192 pages, hardcover, $32.95.

**Color Echoes** *by Pamela J. Harper* (Macmillan, 1994). A good discussion of color theory, followed by an explanation of how to repeat and complement colors as a way of creating unity in the garden. Of interest to the more experienced gardener. 228 pages, hardcover, $35.00.

**The Harmonious Garden** *by Catherine Ziegler* (Timber Press, 1996). 149 color photographs of successful plant combinations based on color, form, and texture, with explanations by the author about how and why they work. Combinations are simple, and limited to no more than four varieties of plants. Great inspiration for the experienced gardener or gar-

den designer. 292 pages, hardcover, $44.95.

### DESIGN BOOKS OF SPECIAL INTEREST

**The Lattice Gardener** *by William C. Mulligan and Elvin McDonald* (Macmillan, 1995). Great inspiration for all kinds of trellises, from simple to grand. Includes plans for many of the lattices shown, and plant recommendations. 192 pages, hardcover, $35.00.

**Japanese Garden Design** *by Marc P. Keane* (Charles P. Tuttle, 1996). Tantalizing images supported by a thorough explanation of the history and design concepts that are at work. Excellent. 186 pages, hardcover, $39.95.

**Decorating Eden** *by Elizabeth Wilkinson and Marjorie Henderson* (Chronicle, 1992). Over 1,000 line drawings, diagrams, and photographs depicting garden architecture and artifacts from seven centuries. A great source of inspiration for designers. 226 pages, paperback, $19.95.

**Garden Paths** *by Gordon Hayward* (Camden House, 1993). A garden designer shares insights and images that explain why garden paths are thought by many to be the single most important design element. Practical, yet thought provoking. 242 pages, paperback, $19.95.

**Gardening With Foliage Plants** *by Ethne Clarke* (Abbeville, 1996). 160 pages, hardcover, $29.95.

### HOW-TO DESIGN BOOKS

**Easy Garden Design** *by Janet Macunovich* (Garden Way Publishing, 1992). If you'd like to generate your own landscape plan and can proceed logically through the various steps, this is an excellent book. Learn how to assess the site, basic design considerations, choosing plants, and getting it all down on paper. 162 pages, paperback, $14.95.

**The Ultimate Garden Designer** *by Tim Newbury* (Ward Lock, 1995). 100 garden designs with site plans and planting schemes from a well-known British garden designer. 256 pages, paperback, $19.95.

**Penelope Hobhouse's Garden Designs** (Henry Holt, 1997). Twenty-three inspiring garden designs from a renowned British gardener. 168 pages, hardcover, $45.00.

**The Book of Garden Design** *by John Brookes* (Macmillan, 1991). 352 pages, hardcover, $45.00.

**Garden Style** *by Penelope Hobhouse* (Willow Creek, 1988). A visually satisfying overview of various garden styles with examples from famous gardens around the world. 216 pages, hardcover $35.00.

**The Education of a Gardener** *by Russell Page* (1962; Harvill Press, 1995). A classic from one of 20th-century Europe's greatest master gardener/landscape architects. Wonderful black and white photos of Page's gardens throughout the world. 382 pages, paperback, $15.00.

## The Golden Section

First identified by the ancient Greeks, the golden section is an aesthetically pleasing design guideline that can be used to site gardens, position plants, or design a temple. It is an asymmetrical proportion that is created by dividing a line in two so that the shorter part relates to the longer part as the longer part relates to the whole. If the whole length of a line is given a value of 1.0, the golden section falls at 0.618 on the line or 8/13 of its length.

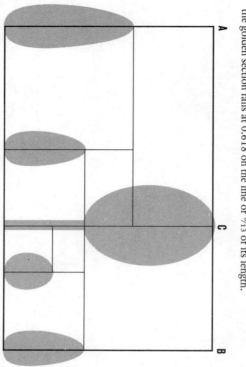

The length of line segment CB relates to segment AC in the same proportion that AC relates to AB. Further divisions of segments, following the same rule, can help you locate secondary plantings (as shown above). This can apply to

tive on your yard and gardens. You may follow their recommendations to the letter, or select only the elements that you find most appealing or most manageable. It is not necessary to contract for a full-scale site plan. Most designers will be very willing to focus their attention on a particular area (like the entryway). One well-conceived and well-executed feature may go a long way toward identifying a style that you can then carry forward yourself.

## Garden Design Basics

What follows is a list of design principles that are common to all the creative arts, whether it be painting, music, literature, or garden design. Don't let them intimidate you. Just use them as tools to help you see.

**STYLE.** Every garden has a style or personality to it. Unless you have a very large yard that is divided into distinct areas or "rooms," it will be hard to gracefully accommodate lots of different garden styles. Begin by thinking about whether you want your garden to have a formal or informal look. Consider your site, the style of your home, and your own personality. Though you don't have to be too rigorous about striving for a consistent style, you'll want to avoid a jumble of diverse and unrelated elements.

**FLOW.** A garden is more pleasing if there is a logical progression from one area to the next. Think about how you would like someone to view and move through your garden. Paths are one way to connect some of the various parts to achieve a sense of order and cohesiveness. Focal points, such as

a piece of sculpture, a distinctive tree, or a captivating view, can be used to draw the eye and pull us forward into a new space.

**SCALE.** Scale is about proportions — how the sizes and shapes of things relate to each other. A three-foot-by-six-foot island bed floating in a half-acre sea of lawn will be seriously out of scale. The same will be true of a dwarf cherry tree located in front of a two-story colonial house. Most scale problems are due to skimpiness, such as beds and paths that are too narrow, or plantings that are too small and tentative. If in doubt, err on the side of boldness and generosity.

**RHYTHM.** By repeating plants and materials, you can produce a sense of rhythm, order, and predictability. Too much repetition is monotonous, but, as in music, variations on a theme are pleasing. You may want to repeat certain distinctive plant materials, such as the spearlike foliage of Siberian iris, or the eye-soothing grey of lamb's-ears (*Stachys byzantina*). Repeating splashes of color will also establish a rhythm in the garden and help to guide the eye. But don't be a slave to repetition. The best gardens always leave room for the unexpected — a giant pot of agapanthus, a whimsical birdhouse in a tangle of morning glories, or a blood-red rose tumbling over a stone wall.

**SYMMETRY AND BALANCE.** Humans seem to be naturally attracted to symmetry — toward creating perfectly balanced features. Our bodies are symmetrical, as are the cars we drive, the arrangement of windows in our homes, and often the shrubs that flank the front door. Used judiciously, perfect symmetry can be a powerfully appealing design technique. But when overused it can become stiff and boring. The natural landscape, which we also find visually pleasing, is not governed by symmetry. In nature, something more subtle is at work, something artists and designers refer to as balance. Balance is an essential factor in garden design. It refers to visual weight: a birch clump balanced by a large bed of hosta; a brick pathway balanced by a wide swath of lawn; orange

## Designing My Garden

My garden began with a trunkful of perennials and an acre of mud. We finished building our house in the late fall, and the following spring, there was not a tree or a shrub or a blade of grass within 30 feet of the house. The pressure was on. In just 10 weeks we were expecting 150 people to arrive for our wedding and reception.

I worked like a dog on weekends, and every weekday after work, digging and planting and raking and mulching. Incredibly, it all came together into a flowery profusion that almost stole the show.

Today, twelve years later, I tend an acre of intensively managed gardens including trees, shrubs, spring bulbs, wildflowers, and hundreds of different perennials and annuals. My garden has even been on a local garden tour.

Did I start with a plan? No. Do I have a plan today? No. I'm one of those people who just wanders around with a garden fork and a couple of plants until I figure out what I'm going to do. It may sound odd, but I make most of my design decisions in the moment by tuning in to the scene and to the plants. This free-form approach suits me. In fact, it is one of the parts of gardening that I most enjoy.

—Katherine LaLiberte

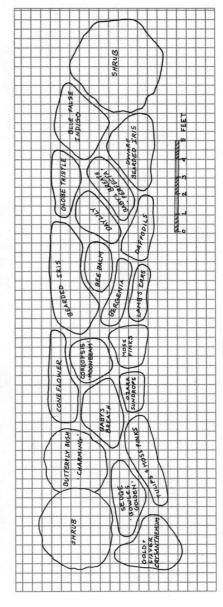

*Use a bubble diagram, with circles approximating the size and shape of a mature planting, to visualize how combinations of plants will look together.*

## Web Sites

GardenEscape
http://jgarden.com
Sample garden plans, a garden planner that can be customized and saved for you at the site, and a plant finder.

"

For most homeowners, I recommend planning in stages rather than tackling the entire garden. Perhaps a rough plan of the garden as a whole, a theme or style choice, or a rough sketch of areas and their uses is helpful. Then concentrating on one area at a time to plan thoroughly and plant is best. Unless you are highly experienced, you will learn much as you proceed, and your taste will develop and change . . . . Building your garden one section at a time will also increase your confidence as you see the results of your efforts."

— from *The Garden Design Primer* by Barbara Ashmun (Lyons and Burford, 1993).

---

Oriental poppies balanced by deep blue lupines. In these examples, the two elements are not identical in size, shape, or color, but there is a response from each side that balances the other. Successful garden design incorporates both symmetry and balance.

## Walls, Roofs, and Paths

One thing great gardens share is a sense of place. Entering them is like entering a home — you are wrapped in a particular environment that is very different from the world outside. As in a home, the walls, roof, and floor help give a garden its unique character. When designing your own garden, you can use these aspects to create "rooms" in which plants are arranged in a context rather than floating in space.

**WALLS.** English flower borders almost always have a background behind them. In England, this is usually a tall stone or brick wall or an evergreen hedge. The backdrop serves to stop your eye from roving and allows you to focus on the intended view. Most American gardeners don't make use of this very effective technique, and our gardens often get lost in the larger scene. Whenever possible, anchor your garden by placing something behind it: a structure, a fence, or a planting of shrubs. Remember to keep it simple. The objective is to direct the eye to the foreground, not create a competing element.

**ROOFS.** Though there are plenty of very successful gardens that are totally exposed to the sky, most of us are naturally attracted to more sheltered, intimate spaces: a garden that's been carved out of a woodland or is nestled beneath an ancient apple tree. We are, for the same reason, drawn to arbors, bowers, allees, and pergolas. The roof need not cover your entire garden. Including the experience of enclosure somewhere in your garden — it can be as simple as an arbor at the entrance — will help to create that sense of being in a special environment set apart from the rest of the world.

**PATHS.** Paths lead us through a garden and link one area to another. Paths in themselves are an age-old comfort, showing us the way we are to travel, assuring us of a progression that is safe and intentional.

The paving material and the way the paths are laid out can help define the style of the garden. A meandering pathway made of flat stones spaced several inches apart will have an intimate, informal feel; a wide brick path suggests neatness and order; a broad path of closely mown lawn conveys grandeur and expansiveness. Paths also create edges that suggest where new plants or even entire gardens could be located.

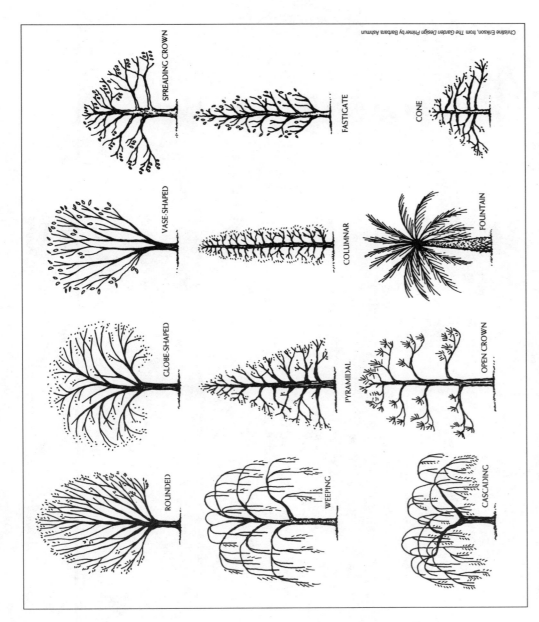

Christine Erikson, from *The Garden Design Primer* by Barbara Ashmun

LABELS IN IMAGE:
SPREADING CROWN — FASTIGATE — CONE
VASE-SHAPED — COLUMNAR — FOUNTAIN
GLOBE-SHAPED — PYRAMIDAL — OPEN CROWN
ROUNDED — WEEPING — CASCADING

*Trees (and all plants) have distinctive shapes or forms. By carefully combining the forms, you can create rhythm, balance, and harmony.*

## Plant Material as a Design Element

Plants themselves can be important design elements, though few gardeners actually use them this way. The arching branches of a well-pruned cherry tree can frame an entire garden. The repetition of soft, grey-leaved plants or the spiky foliage of Japanese iris can be used to unify a long border. If you take the time to notice and experiment with the form, texture, and color of plants, you will discover a whole new palette of design elements with which to work.

**FORM.** This is a three-dimensional consideration that takes into account the shapes and volumes of the plants in your garden. A variety of different forms makes a garden interesting, but too much diversity creates visual confusion. Trees and shrubs have characteristic forms that should be carefully combined to avoid clashing. Flowers, too, have characteristic shapes: the rounded heads of alliums, verbena, and globe thistle; the vertical spikes of delphinium, snapdragons, and veronica; the diaphanous look of baby's-breath and Queen Anne's lace; the strong architectural lines of a 5-foot martagon lily. Experiment by grouping plants with the same form into a drift, or by repeating a pleasing composition of different forms several times.

**TEXTURE.** Plants have a tactile quality that can be used as a valuable design tool. Think about how the glossy leaves of holly, magnolia, and roses contrast with the suede-like foliage of lamb's ears, heliotrope, and coleus. Or how the fat and fleshy leaves of a sedum differ from the needle-like foliage of rosemary or the quilted leaves of a blue-green hosta. Flowers also provide textural interest. They can be rich and velvety like a rose, or as thin and translucent as a poppy. Even tree bark contributes textural interest — especially during the winter months.

**COLOR.** Entire books have been written about using color as a design tool. You can approach color as a technician, using the color wheel to create harmonious combinations, or you can use your own eyes and emotions to guide you in creating the look and feel you want. Combining colors in new and interesting ways offers a lifetime of exciting possibilities.

As a general rule, red, orange, and yellow are colors that jump out at you. They are lively and stimulating, and give the impression that they are closer to the eye than they actually are. If you plant too many hot-colored flowers, and don't balance them with cool-colored, less assertive plants, your garden will be a jumble of blaring trumpets. Green, blue,

# Resources

## GARDEN DESIGN SOFTWARE

Several of the following software programs are reviewed on the internet at The Garden Gate site:
http://www.prairienet.org/garden-gate

### Sprout
This program allows you to lay out your vegetable garden, organize planting information, and print reports and shopping lists. For Windows and Mac. $59.95. From Abracadata: 800-451-4871.

### 3D Landscape
Lay out your entire garden with paths, fences, and over 2,200 different plants. Watch plants grow through the years. See spring and fall color. Windows $49.95. From Books That Work: 800-242-4546.

### Garden Companion CD
Available in Windows for $49.95 from Lifestyle Software. 800-289-1157. Their web site address is
http://www.lifeware.com/gardcd.htm

### Mum's The Word Plus
Available for Mac from Terrace Software. Call 617-396-0382.

### FLOWERscape
For Mac and Windows. Available from Voudette Software. 310-474-5840.

### Sunset's Western Gardening CD ROM
800-829-0113. Designed for the 11 western states.

## SOURCES FOR DECORATIVE ELEMENTS

### Robinson Iron
P.O. Box 1119
Robinson Road
Alexander City, AL 35010
*Decorative ironwork.*

### Seibert & Rice
P.O. Box 365
Short Hills, NJ 07078
*Italian terra-cotta pots.*

### Kenneth Lynch & Sons
P.O. Box 488
84 Danbury Road
Wilton, CT 06897
*New and recycled garden ornaments.*

### Haddonstone Ltd.
201 Heller Place
Interstate Business Park
Bellmawr, NJ 08031
*Imported English ornaments and stonework.*

### Trellis Structures
P.O. Box 380
60 River Street
Beverly, MA 01915
*Traditional and contemporary wood trellises.*

### Baker's Lawn Ornaments
Box 265
Somerset, PA 15501
*Gazing balls.*

### New England Garden Ornaments
P.O. Box 235
East Brookfield Road
North Brookfield, MA 01535
*Imported English statuary and architecture.*

### FrenchWyres
P.O. Box 131655
Tyler, TX 75713
*Wire garden furnishings.*

and violet are cool colors. In the garden these flowers create a more soothing, restful feeling, and tend to recede into the distance. See the books section on page 121 for more information about using color in the garden.

## Where to Go for Design Inspiration

Visiting other people's gardens may be the best source of design inspiration. Take along a camera or sketch pad to capture features that you find particularly successful or appealing. Notice when some of the design techniques described above are being used. Don't be afraid to ask questions about what the gardener was trying to achieve.

Glossy picture books of gardens run a close second for design inspiration. They have the distinct advantage of being available for perusal year-round. Use sticky notes to mark images that capture your attention, then go back and review your choices to see where the similarities lie. Comparing and contrasting different types of gardens can be very useful in helping you decide what sort of look attracts you. If you are gravitating toward a theme garden (colonial, Japanese, Southwestern, English cottage), you'll find dozens of books that illustrate the design features and techniques that distinguish these styles. See the "Favorite Books" section for some recommendations.

Plan books are another good source of design ideas. Most ready-made plans are theme-oriented, or are specific to a certain type of site. They usually include a site plan, a planting list, and an elevation drawing that shows what the garden will look like at eye level. You can follow the plan, or pick and choose the elements that appeal to you. See the books section for some recommendations.

---

## Tricks for Getting Yourself Unblocked

- Don't get caught up in a grand scheme or in executing the ultimate statement. Gardens evolve over time, as will your own gardening interests. No garden is ever finished.

- Pick a theme or a style you'd like to evoke and follow it through: calm and restive; exuberant and loud; simple and controlled. Stick with plants and materials that suit this theme.

- Ask a friend for help. An outside perspective can be incredibly valuable. "Why don't you just cut down that tree?" might be the solution that you were too stuck to see.

- Be bold and generous. Plant in groups of threes and fives and sevens rather than in ones and twos. Make your beds at least three or four feet deep. Skimpy gardens are rarely compelling.

- Use a hose or rope to outline new or expanded garden areas. You might also try using helium balloons, big branches, or step ladders to help you visualize how tall a plant or garden feature will be and where it should be located.

# Garden Gear

Permanent edging keeps weeds from encroaching and helps you maintain a nice clean line between grass and planting areas. **Pound-In Edging** comes in 6"-wide sections that lock together to create a weedproof barrier. Install with a rubber mallet. **Borderline Bricks** have a 2½" flange that creates a mowing strip for your mower. The 8"-long recycled plastic bricks link together and will pivot to follow a curve. **World's Best Edging** lets you install a 5½" deep, almost invisible weed barrier that will last 20 years or more. Comes in 20' lengths.

#13-283  Extra-Tall Pound-In Edging, 20 ft.  $18.95
#14-238  Borderline Bricks, Brown, 8 ft.  $19.95
#30-124  World's Best Edging, 20 ft.  $19.95

This **English-style furniture** has the elegant look of teak at half the price. Made of northern white cedar, it is durable and naturally resistant to rot and insects. Can be painted or will weather to a silvery gray. Mortised joints and zinc-plated hardware.

#10-054  Cedar Bench  $199.00
#10-055  Cedar Chair  $145.00
#10-056  Cedar Table  $85.00
#10-057  3-Piece Set  $389.00

Our **Red Cedar Arch** has lattice-work side panels and measures 7' H x 41" W x 24" D. It can be painted or stained, and assembles in 30 minutes. This **Red Cedar Obelisk** is adapted from a classic French design. It will create a bold statement in your flower or vegetable garden. Stands 81" H with a 23" square base.

#14-222  Red Cedar Arch  $225.00
#14-413  Red Cedar Obelisk  $79.95

Made of weather-resistant concrete, the **Garden Rabbit** has an innocent expression. 9½" H.

#30-183  Garden Rabbit  $34.95

Hide an unsightly view instantly with a 6' H **Reed Fence**. It weathers to a silvery-grey. Each of the two sections are 15' long.

#30-250  Reed Fence, 30 ft.  $125.00

**Latticework Cedar Panels** will hide a multitude of ills, including water heaters and grills. Each panel is 53" H x 31½" W. Set of two panels.

#30-192  Cedar Screen Panels  $169.00

The **Rose Arch** creates a strong architectural statement and looks charming wreathed with clematis or climbing roses. Fashioned in England from strong steel tubing, and

The **Solar Sensor Path Light** comes on automatically at dusk to softly illuminate a walkway or patio for up to 6 hours each night. It comes with a 12" H post.

#18-200  Solar Path Light  $49.95

protected from the weather with a durable black powder-coated finish. The arch is a full 8' H when installed. Measures 9' 4" H x 5' 2" W x 29" D.

#30-195  English Rose Arch  $169.00

A twining ivy pattern and 185 lbs. of heft give our cast **Stone Bench** a sense of permanence and timeless beauty. Impervious to weather. 38" L x 27" H x 13½" W

#30-170  English Stone Garden Bench  $225.00

Our forged steel **Scrollwork Fence Panels** can be positioned virtually anywhere, and can be easily moved to create a new look. The 60" W x 32" H panels attach to 56" H posts. The matching gate has a spring-operated latch and barrel-type hinge, and measures 43" H x 35½" W. A hardened oil finish inhibits rust.

#30-291  Iron Scrollwork Fence Panel  $129.00
#30-292  Wrought Iron Post  $20.00
#14-247  Wrought Iron Gate  $129.00

Popular in formal gardens since medieval times, this **Handblown Gazing Ball** attracts the eye to create a focal point for the flower or herb garden. The wrought iron pedestal is 24" H. Globe is 8" diameter. Available in silver or cobalt blue.

#14-012  Gazing Globe and Stand  $69.95

Creative gardeners read garden design books the way creative cooks read recipe books. You don't need to follow the garden design verbatim, but you can lift an idea here and there, and when you get back to the garden, you can combine them into your own unique expression.

> " Symmetry will always be more obvious than its kindred value, balance. But the point of both is the same. Both reflect the degree of calculation with which the seasonal and superficial beauties of the garden have been underlaid, achieving a deeper structure than the eye often registers and one more satisfying than the conscious mind acknowledges. For although both symmetry and balance must be consciously created in gardens, they reflect a preference buried below our minds and in our actual physical beings."
>
> —from *Elements of Garden Design* by Joe Eck (Henry Holt, 1996)

## Decorating Your Garden

Some purists believe that ornamentation — trellises, furniture, sculpture, and decorative planters — has no place in the garden. Others fill their gardens with so many decorative elements that it can be difficult to find the plants. Used judiciously, the furnishings and decorative features that you incorporate in your garden help give it style and character.

Decorative elements can be characterized as formal, informal, or somewhere in between. This has something to do with what the piece is (a whirligig versus a Japanese lantern), but also what the piece is made of. Fanciful wooden birdhouses and split-rail fencing have a casual, country feeling; whereas a bronze nude or a Grecian urn are more elegant and formal. When choosing decorative elements for your garden, the challenge is to select items that appeal to you, and that will also fit harmoniously with the style you are trying to achieve and any other decorative objects that you already own. See page 126 for a list of companies that specialize in garden ornamentation.

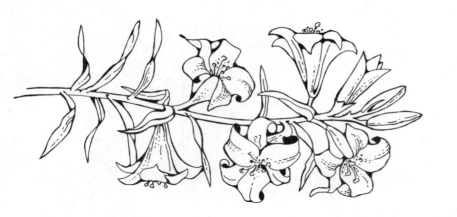

# bulbs

B ulbs are the epitome of nature's talent for packaging. Like other classic designs (the seed, the egg) bulbs contain within themselves all of the essentials they need to grow and flower. Some of them don't even require soil — just witness a paperwhite narcissus blooming happily indoors in nothing more than a bowl of marble chips.

But it is outdoors, in the garden and landscape, that bulbs really shine. Most bulbs are hardy and undemanding; some will even naturalize, multiplying and spreading to provide color year after year. Whether for borders, cutting gardens, containers, rock gardens, or naturalistic plantings, bulbs deserve a place in every garden scheme.

## Types of Bulbs

Perhaps the most important information about any kind of bulb relates to when the plant flowers and when you should plant it. Generally, bulbs are divided into one of two categories: the spring-flowering types, which are typically planted in the fall; and the summer-flowering bulbs, usually planted in the spring. Lilies (Asiatics, Orientals, tigers) are an exception to this rule; they can be planted in either spring or fall for summer blooms.

Another crucial consideration is whether the bulb is hardy or tender. Hardy bulbs (daffodil, crocus, hyacinth, tulip, lily, etc.) will survive the winter right in the ground to bloom again the following year. Tender bulbs (gladiolus, canna, dahlia, etc.), will also flower year after year, but in cold climates they must be dug up or "lifted" in the fall, stored indoors over the winter, then replanted the following spring.

## Naturalizing Hardy Bulbs

A naturalized planting is one of the most popular uses for bulbs in the landscape. Instead of planting the bulbs in a formal bed or border, you scatter them in irregular groupings across an area of lawn or meadow, or at a woodland edge. For the most natural effect, try not to plant bulbs in straight lines or discernible patterns.

Naturalizing bulbs in your lawn works well with the smaller, daintier flowers like crocuses, puschkinia, squill (*Scilla*), grape-hyacinth (*Muscari*), or snowdrops (*Galanthus*). These bulbs flower early in the season and their foliage dies back fairly quickly. If you plant such bulbs in a lawn, you have to hold off on mowing until the spent foliage has yellowed and died back. At this point, the plant will have stored all the food it needs in the underground bulb to produce next year's bloom. A sensible strategy is to plant bulbs in a less formal area of the lawn that you won't have to mow until later in the spring.

## *Guest Experts*
## Brent and Becky Heath

Bulbs reproduce and spread in two ways. Non-hybrid species bulbs self-seed, or "naturalize." Bulbs that "perennialize" flower year after year and multiply. Here are some favorites that you may not know.

*Brent and Becky Heath are third-generation bulb growers, the proprietors of The Daffodil Mart in Gloucester, Virginia, and the authors of Daffodils for American Gardens (Elliott & Clark, 1995).*

*Arum italicum* is a three-season, deer-proof plant. It produces deep green, variegated, arrow-shaped leaves that persist all winter, followed by a greenish-yellow Jack-in-the-Pulpit-type bloom in the spring. The leaves disappear and a stalk of bright red berries decorates the garden throughout the summer. It prefers shade to partial shade, and once established, a clump often naturalizes itself around the garden.

Two great daffodils are *N. Poeticus recurvus* and *N. 'Saint Keverne.' Poeticus* has white petals and a red-rimmed, yellow cup. It is a species narcissus that produces large clumps with lots of spicy/sweet flowers. It performs best in cooler climates and blooms in late spring. 'Saint Keverne' is an early-blooming, yellow, large-cup daffodil that grows anywhere. It is a true perennial bulb, producing tons of bright, highly visible flowers.

*Galanthus nivalis* (snowdrop) and *Leucojum astivum* (snowflake) both have white, hanging, bell-shaped flowers and strap-like leaves; both tolerate moist soils and are deer-resistant. *Galanthus* likes shade and blooms in early spring. *Leucojum* prefers sun and blooms in late spring.

## *Favorite Books*

**Bulbs: Four Seasons of Beautiful Blooms** *by Lewis and Nancy Hill* (Storey, 1994). The Hills manage to cover a lot of ground on this vast subject. Chapters on naturalizing, forcing, and summer-blooming bulbs are particularly useful. Includes color sections with plant photos. 224 pages, paperback, $18.95.

**Daffodils for American Gardens** *by Brent and Becky Heath* (Elliott & Clark, 1995). The definitive book for daff lovers, with chapters on anatomy, growing, companion planting, forcing, hybridizing, arranging, and more. Many color photos of recommended cultivars. 144 pages, hardcover, $24.95.

**John E. Bryan on Bulbs** *by John E. Bryan* (Macmillan, 1994). Part of the Burpee Expert Gardener series, and a great introduction to bulbs. Bryan's style is conversational, friendly, and very readable. Largely consists of an alphabetical listing of genera, with entries covering historical and growing information. 272 pages, hardcover, $20.00.

**The Random House Book of Bulbs** *by Roger Phillips and Martyn Rix* (Random House, 1989). Color photographs showcase plants with nearly the same detail and precision as botanical drawings. Includes over 1,000 bulbs and bulblike plants from around the world. A splendid reference. 256 pages, paperback, $24.95.

# Other Good Books

**Gardening with Bulbs: A Practical and Inspirational Guide** by Patrick Taylor (Timber Press, 1996). A good identification guide to bulbs currently available, with descriptions and color photos, plus origin and hardiness zone information. 256 pages, paperback, $17.95.

**The Complete Book of Bulbs, Corms, Tubers, and Rhizomes** by Brian Mathew and Philip Swindells (Reader's Digest, 1994). A big, beautiful book by two British authors. The book is organized by season, though gardeners north of Zone 6 will chuckle at the idea of winter-blooming outdoor bulbs. Still, most of the material translates well. 240 pages, hardcover, $30.00.

**The Indoor Potted Bulb: Decorative Container Gardening with Flowering Bulbs** by Rob Proctor (Simon & Schuster, 1993). Basic instructions on potting, followed by color plant profiles that feature historical and descriptive information. 128 pages, hardcover, $20.00.

**The Outdoor Potted Bulb: New Approaches to Container Gardening with Flowering Bulbs** by Rob Proctor (Simon & Schuster, 1993). Similar to the previous entry. 128 pages, hardcover, $20.00.

**Seasonal Bulbs** by Ann Lovejoy (Sasquatch Books, 1995). Part of the Cascadia Gardening Series for gardeners living in the Pacific Northwest. This little guide is organized by season, and the author's chatty, personal style is appealing. A nice regional book. 104 pages, paperback, $10.95.

Most bulbs appreciate well-drained soil and sunlight. Keep in mind, however, that bulbs that flower early in the spring will have bloomed and faded long before deciduous shrubs and trees have begun to leaf out. In other words, you can treat spring-blooming bulbs much like spring wildflowers. A fairly open woodland setting or orchard makes an ideal setting for spring bulbs, particularly long-stemmed showy ones like daffodils and early tulips, which can be seen and admired even at a distance.

Some bulbs need to be divided. For example, when happy, daffodils multiply enough to form dense clumps, which compromises the flowers. Dig after flowering (while you can still find them), divide the clumps,

## Tulips for Perennial Plantings

Although tulips are technically considered perennials, many gardeners find that their bulbs are relatively short-lived and begin to decline over two or three years, producing smaller flowers and eventually dying out altogether. Unless your climate and growing conditions are ideal (hot, dry summers, cold winters, and well-drained soil), it can be difficult to coax some varieties of tulips into making a long-term commitment to your garden. However, there are other types that, when given a little special care, will flower repeatedly and actually increase in size and beauty. These varieties are commonly known as "perennial tulips."

Although there are other tulips that will put in an appearance reliably for years, the following are among the most highly recommended varieties. One note: When buying Darwin hybrids, keep in mind that the ones with deep color will naturalize better than those with pastel colors.

To create the best conditions for perennial tulips, top-dress the planting bed with well-rotted cow manure, or add a slow-release fertilizer in the fall (9-9-6 or lower profile). After the flowers have finished blooming in the spring, deadhead the spent blossoms and allow the foliage to mature and wither naturally, so the bulbs can gather energy for next year's bloom.

| VARIETY NAME | TYPE | COLOR |
| --- | --- | --- |
| Apeldoorn's Elite | Darwin Hybrid | red with orange-yellow |
| Ballade | Lily-Flowering | violet with white edges |
| Beauty of Apeldoorn | Darwin Hybrid | orange-yellow & red striped |
| Candela | Fosteriana | yellow |
| Charles | Single Early | deep red |
| Couleur Cardinal | Single Early | violet-red |
| Golden Apeldoorn | Darwin Hybrid | yellow |
| Mayime | Lily-Flowering | bright violet, white edges |
| Orange Emperor | Fosteriana | orange |
| Oxford | Darwin Hybrid | vermilion red |
| Plaisir | Greigii | red with white edging |
| Purissima | Fosteriana | white |
| Red Emperor | Fosteriana | red |
| Red Riding Hood | Greigii | red |
| Stresa | Kaufmanniana | yellow with red markings |
| Tulipa tarda | Species | yellow/white |
| Toronto | Greigii | salmon pink-red |
| T. turkestanica | Species | white and cream |
| West Point | Lily-Flowering | yellow |

—from The Netherlands Flower Bulb Information Center

and replant immediately or store until fall. The same rule that applies to bulbs in the lawn holds true for other, larger plants like daffodils and tulips: don't remove or mow over the spent foliage until it has withered naturally. For this reason, it's best not to plant these long-standing bulbs in a lawn or other formal area, where the dying foliage can cause an unsightly mess. Try locating these bulbs in a field or meadow, or somewhere else that you might mow only once or twice a year. Or plant them at the base of deciduous shrubs or in mixed beds or borders, where other, later-blooming plants will draw attention away from the spent foliage.

## Prechilling and Forcing Bulbs

Nearly all hardy, spring-flowering bulbs require a period of "chilling" or cold dormancy before they will begin to grow and bloom. For gardeners in most regions of North America, providing this cold treatment is a no-brainer. Simply planting the bulbs in the fall and leaving them alone over the winter provides plenty of cold treatment. Just make sure to select bulbs that are hardy in your growing zone.

However, people who live in very mild winter regions (Zones 9 and 10) must select their bulbs very carefully. Daffodils should be planted in December or January (the coldest time of the year), but other hardy bulbs, such as tulips, crocuses, and hyacinths, may require special treatment in mild-winter areas. Gardeners in these regions of the country should select from among the many varieties that are rated best in warm spring and summer conditions. Many tulips will grow well as annuals in the South if the bulbs are prechilled. (See the Bulb Forcing Timetable above for more information on which types of bulbs require prechilling, and for how long.) Other good bulbs for warm climates include crocuses, hyacinths, lilies, muscari (grape hyacinth), colchicum (autumn crocus), and alliums (ornamental onions).

The easiest way to prechill bulbs is to store them in the refrigerator, where temperatures can be easily maintained at 40° to 45°F. Store them in breathable mesh bags, like the ones they are often sold in at garden centers. Then, when they have chilled for the requisite number of weeks, simply remove the bulbs from the refrigerator and plant them

## Bulb Forcing Timetable

The following table lists the number of weeks that different kinds of bulbs need to be chilled before being planted outdoors or forced into bloom in containers. Bulbs can be stored in the refrigerator, at a temperature between 40° and 45°F. For more specifics, see the discussion on "Prechilling and Forcing Bulbs" below.

| NAME OF BULB | WKS. OF COLD | WKS. TO BLOOM |
|---|---|---|
| Amaryllis/Hippeastrum | none | 6–8 |
| Chionodoxa luciliae (glory-of-the-snow) | 15 | 2–3 |
| Crocus chrysanthus | 15 | 2–3 |
| Crocus vernus | 15 | 2 |
| Galanthus nivalis (common snowdrop) | 15 | 2 |
| Hyacinth (prepared) | 10–12 | 2–3 |
| (unprepared) | 11–14 | 2–3 |
| Muscari armeniacum | 13–15 | 2–3 |
| Muscari botryoides alba | 14–15 | 2–3 |
| Narcissis | 15–17 | 2–3 |
| Narcissus tazetta (paperwhites) | none | 3–5 |
| N. tazetta orientalis | none | 3–5 |
| Scilla tubergeniana | 12–15 | 2–3 |
| Scilla siberica | 15 | 2–3 |
| Tulipa | 14–20 | 2–3 |

—from The Netherlands Flower Bulb Information Center

## Spring Bulbs for Container Planting or Forcing

| BOTANICAL NAME | COMMON NAME |
| --- | --- |
| Allium moly | golden garlic, lily leek |
| Allium neapolitanum | daffodil garlic, Naples garlic |
| Anemone blanda | windflower |
| Chionodoxa luciliae | glory-of-the-snow |
| Colchicum autumnale | autumn-crocus; meadow-saffron |
| Crocus ancyrensis | golden bunch crocus |
| Crocus chrysanthus | golden crocus |
| Crocus flavus; C. vernus | Dutch crocus |
| Hippeastrum | Dutch amaryllis |
| Hyacinthus | Dutch hyacinth |
| Muscari armeniacum | grape-hyacinth |
| Muscari botryoides | white grape-hyacinth |
| Narcissus | narcissus species and hybrids |
| Puschkinia libanotica | puschkinia, striped-squill |
| Scilla siberica | Siberian squill |
| Tulipa | tulip species and hybrids |

—from The Netherlands Flower Bulb Information Center

either outdoors in the ground or in containers.

If you have enough space in the refrigerator, you can even plant bulbs right in their containers and remove the whole pot at the end of the chilling period. Either way, place containers of bulbs that you're forcing into a warm, sunny spot and then sit back and wait for the bulbs to send up their green leaves. After their blooming period is over, you can continue to water the pots, letting the foliage die down naturally, then replant the whole mass of bulbs in the outdoor garden.

The most popular bulb for winter forcing is undoubtedly the paperwhite narcissus, which requires no period of prechilling before it will blossom. However, you can also add variety and color to your winter or early spring displays by prechilling many other types of bulbs, then forcing them in containers for indoor bloom.

It's common for florists to sell containers of forced bulbs that are all of one type, such as dark purple or pink tulips. This makes a smashing display, but you can also be creative by forcing several kinds of bulbs of different colors or even different species to make a mixed display. Unless you're using a large container or you have a good eye for natural design, it's best to experiment with only a couple of types of bulbs in each pot, ones that grow to roughly the same height and whose flowers will complement each other in form and color (pink alliums and white Dutch crocuses, for instance).

Pots sold for forcing bulbs tend to have no holes in the bottom, because many people grow paperwhite narcissus in a medium of small stones instead of soil, and so drainage is not an issue. It is possible to grow other bulbs this way as well, but keep in mind that you probably won't be able to replant them outdoors after they have blossomed unless you grow them in soil. When forcing bulbs in potting soil, make sure the container has drainage holes in its bottom and that you place a dish underneath it to catch the excess water, as with any other houseplant.

## The Lilies of the Field

Lilies are no more difficult to grow than other hardy bulbs, so long as you keep in mind a few of their important differences. For one thing, you should plan on planting lilies as soon as you get them, either in the fall or the spring, because the bulbs lack the papery covering (known as

## Web Sites

**American Daffodil Society**
http://www.mc.edu~adswww
*The home page for the American Daffodil Society; colorful and well-conceived.*

**The Geophyte Page**
http://agweb.clemson.edu/Hort/sctop/geophyte/webpage.htm
*A comprehensive source of information on bulbs, corms, tubers, and other geophytic plants. Primarily oriented toward commercial growers, forcers, and retailers. Beautiful photo gallery.*

**Netherlands Flower Bulb Information Center**
http://www.bulb.com
*One of the best garden web sites around, operated by the U.S. press office of the Dutch flower bulb industry. Contains lots of valuable material of interest to home bulb gardeners: how-to information on spring- and summer-flowering bulbs, charts and tables — even articles on the history and mythology of bulbs.*

a "tunic") that is common to other hardy bulbs, and thus can dry out quickly in storage.

Even more than other bulbs, lilies demand well-drained soil. It helps to dig the spot where you plan to plant lilies to a depth of at least 12 inches, removing rocks and adding organic matter such as leaf mold or peat moss to improve both the soil's structure and drainage. Like other bulbs, lilies appreciate a little bone meal scratched in at the bottom of the planting hole, but do not really require other fertilizers at planting time. Instead, wait until the bulbs send up green leaves and then sprinkle around them with a complete organic fertilizer and water it in (see "Garden Gear," page 136).

Spreading an organic mulch around lilies helps keep the soil moist and cool; use compost, well-rotted manure, or a longer-lasting mulch, such as wood chips or cocoa shells. As with other perennials, cover the bed over the winter with straw and/or evergreen boughs to help protect the bulbs from alternate freeze/thaw cycles. During the flowering season, remove spent blooms, but try not to cut off more than a third of the stem, which can reduce the plant's vigor and longevity. This can be difficult to observe if you're cutting stems for indoor arrangements: perhaps the best solution is to grow some lilies in perennial beds or borders, and others in a designated cutting garden.

## Growing Tender Bulbs

Tender bulbs tend to belong to the summer-flowering group and include such popular garden specimens as dahlia, gladiolus, tuberous begonia, canna, and calla-lily (*Zantedeschia*). Technically, these are not "true bulbs," because they don't contain a tiny flower and stalk inside of them. Instead, the plants grow from bulblike structures known as *corms* (gladiolus),

## Most Popular Flower Bulb Varieties

### TULIPS (*Tulipa*)

| Variety | Classification | Color |
|---|---|---|
| Parade | Darwin Hybrid | red |
| Oxford | Darwin Hybrid | yellow |
| Angelique | Double Late | blush pink |
| Apricot Beauty | Single Early | salmon |
| Pink Impression | Darwin Hybrid | rose |
| Red Emperor | Fosteriana | fire red |
| Queen of Night | Single Late | dark maroon |
| Shirley | Single Late | white, edged with purple |
| Attila (or Negrita) | Triumph | purple |
| Purissima | Fosteriana | white |

### DAFFODILS (*Narcissus*)

NOTE: The first color describes the perianth segments (the petals); the second color describes the corona (the trumpet or cup).

| Variety | Classification | Color |
|---|---|---|
| King Alfred | Trumpet | yellow-yellow |
| Salome | Large-Cupped | white-pink, yellow |
| Ice Follies | Large-Cupped | white-white |
| Tete a Tete | Cyclamineus | yellow-yellow |
| Minnow | Tazetta | yellow-yellow |
| Fortissimo | Trumpet | white-yellow |
| Tahiti | Double | yellow-red |
| Las Vegas | Trumpet | white-yellow |
| Barrett Browning | Small-Cupped | white-orange |
| Mount Hood | Trumpet | white-white |

### HYACINTHS (*Hyacinthus*)

| Variety | Color |
|---|---|
| Jan Bos | spiraea red |
| Delft Blue | soft lilac blue |
| Anne Marie | pale pink |
| L'Innocence | ivory white |
| City of Haarlem | soft yellow |

—from The Netherlands Flower Bulb Information Center

Of the dozens of different **bulb planters** tested by Gardener's Supply, this model is the clear favorite. Its sharp, hardened steel blade slices right through sod to penetrate even the toughest soils. An inner lip helps hold the soil, so you can remove a perfect, 3" x 7" plug.
#04-309 One-Step Bulb Planter $28.95

This handy **Bulb Planting Auger** bores a hole up to 6 inches deep, sending the soil up and out as you go. A rounded shank prevents kick-back if you hit a rock or root, and the soil-loosening tip promotes strong root growth. The 2½-inch auger makes holes for tulips and other smaller bulbs (use with a ⅜-inch power drill or larger). The 3-inch auger makes holes for large bulbs like daffodils (use with a ½-inch drill or larger).
#14-274 2½" Power Auger $26.95
#14-301 3" Power Auger $34.95

The **Easy Kneeler** lets you lower yourself down for planting or weeding, and push yourself up again without strain. Turn it over, and it becomes a portable bench. Tubular steel frame with foam cushion. Weighs less than 10 lbs.
#01-212 Easy Kneeler $49.95

This **All-Purpose Fertilizer** (5-5-5) was developed by Gardener's Supply. It contains minerals from naturally occurring deposits (including Chilean nitrate), and recycled agricultural

products, such as peanut meal and whey meal. It has no unpleasant odor and is guaranteed not to burn. Use 1 teaspoon per planting hole for bulbs. Also great for vegetables, shrubs, and trees.
#07-300 All-Purpose Fertilizer, 5 lbs. $5.50
#07-304 All-Purpose Fertilizer, 25 lbs. $24.95

**Bulb Insurance**™ is a low-cost, environmentally safe way to protect your flower bulbs from rodent damage. Composed of super-hard, sharp-edged crushed oyster shells, this natural product forms a barrier that burrowing rodents are reluctant to cross. Just sprinkle the ground-up shells liberally in the soil where you plant your bulbs. This homegrown remedy, suggested by a gardener from Maine, has been tested at Gardener's Supply. Rodent damage to bulbs was reduced by over 90 percent. Five pounds of Bulb Insurance™ will protect 80 to 100 bulbs.
#05-616 Bulb Insurance™, 5 lbs. $5.95

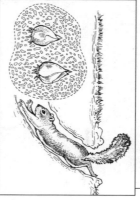

*tubers* (dahlia, caladium), and *rhizomes* (canna). However, they are just as dependable as true bulbs and can be grown in much the same way.

These exotic summer-blooming bulbs can be integrated into the perennial garden, but because they are so popular for arrangements, they're often planted right in the vegetable garden or in a special cutting garden. Plant tender bulbs about the same time as beans and other crops, after the last frost date in spring. Then, around the first fall frosts, when the garden's tender crops are winding down, dig up the bulbs and store them away for the winter.

These tender bulbs vary in hardiness, and it's impossible to give general growing instructions for all of them: different plants have distinct preferences about light, and soil structure and fertility. Gardeners living in Zone 8 or warmer regions can expect to successfully overwinter cannas, callas, and other types. However, by far the most popular way to grow these exotic tropical and subtropical natives is to dig up the plants around the time of the first fall frosts, allow the bulbs to dry for a short period, and then store them indoors until the following spring. In general, all of these bulbs can, once dried, be stored successfully over the winter, either in paper or mesh bags or placed in a shallow pan or box and covered with dry peat moss. Ideal storage conditions are dry, dark, and cool, around 40° to 50°F. Check the recommended books for detailed instructions concerning individual species.

# Resources

## MAIL-ORDER BULB SUPPLIERS

The following list of general and specialty bulb companies is, for space reasons, highly selective. For names of other suppliers, consult many of the books listed in this chapter, or check out the "Plant and Seed Sources" section of Barbara Barton's sourcebook, *Gardening by Mail* (Houghton Mifflin, 1994).

### General Suppliers

**Breck's**
US Reservation Center
6523 North Galena Rd.
Peoria, IL 61632
*Catalog $2.50.*

**Cruickshanks, Inc.**
1015 Mount Pleasant Rd.
Toronto, ON Canada
M4P 2M1
416-488-8292
*Catalog $3.00.*

**Dutch Gardens, Inc.**
P.O. Box 200
Adelphia, NJ 07710
908-780-2713

**Jackson & Perkins Co.**
60 Rose Lane
Medford, OR 97501
800-292-4769

**McClure & Zimmerman**
P.O. Box 368
108 W. Winnebago
Friesland, WI 53935
414-326-4220

**Charles H. Mueller Co.**
7091 N. River Rd.
New Hope, PA 18938
215-862-2033

**Park Seed Company**
Cokesbury Rd.
Greenwood, SC 29647
803-223-7333

**Van Bourgondien Bros.**
P.O. Box 1000
245 Farmingdale Rd.
Babylon, NY 11702
516-669-3500

**Van Engelen Inc.**
313 Maple St.
Litchfield, CT 06759
203-567-8734

**Veldheer Tulip Gardens**
12755 Quincy St.
Holland, MI 49424
616-399-1900

**The Waushara Gardens**
N5491 5th Drive
Plainfield, WI 54966
715-335-4462
*Catalog $1.00.*

**Wayside Gardens**
One Garden Lane
Hodges, SC 29695
800-845-1124

**White Flower Farm**
P.O. Box 50
Litchfield, CT 06759
860-496-9600

### Specialty Nurseries

**Amaryllis, Inc.**
P.O. Box 318
1452 Glenmore Ave.
Baton Rouge, LA 70821
504-924-5560
*Catalog $1.00.*

**B&D Lilies**
330 P St.
Port Townsend, WA 98368
206-385-1738
*Catalog $3.00.*

**Caladium World**
P.O. Drawer 629
Sebring, FL 33871
813-385-7661

**Cooley's Gardens**
P.O. Box 126
11553 Silverton Rd. NE
Silverton, OR 97381
503-873-5463
*Catalog $4.00.*
*Bearded iris.*

**The Daffodil Mart**
7463 Heath Trail
Gloucester, VA 23061
804-693-3966

**Dan's Dahlias**
1087 South Bank Rd.
Oakville, WA 98568
206-482-2607
*Catalog $2.00.*

**Kelly's Plant World**
10266 East Princeton
Sanger, CA 93657
209-294-7676
*Catalog $1.00.*
*Cannas and other summer-blooming bulbs.*

**Schipper & Co.**
P.O. Box 7584
Greenwich, CT 06836
800-877-8637
*Color blends of tulips.*

**Schreiner's Iris Gardens**
3625 Quinaby Rd., NE
Salem, OR 97303
503-393-3232
*Catalog $4.00.*

**Sister's Bulb Farm**
Rte. 2, Box 170
Gibsland, LA 71028
318-843-6379
*Heirloom (pre-1940) daffodils.*

**Skolaski's Glads & Field Flowers**
4821 County Hwy. Q
Waunakee, WI 53597
608-836-4822

**Swan Island Dahlias**
P.O. Box 700
995 NW 22nd Ave.
Canby, OR 97013
503-266-7711
*Catalog $3.00.*

# perennial flowers

PERENNIAL FLOWERS

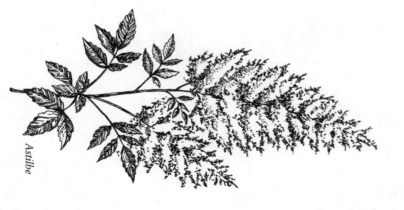

*Astilbe*

Perennial plants are the backbone of nearly every flower garden. Unlike annual plants, which must be replanted each spring, herbaceous perennials die to the ground at the end of the season, and then regrow from the same roots the following year. People grow perennial flowers because they are such easy-care, dependable performers, and because they offer an enormous variety of color, texture, and form. Perennials allow us to create gardens that are in bloom from the first breath of spring through the last sigh of autumn. Gardens that are bright and brassy or subdued and soothing. No artist has a more inspiring pallette.

All this variety makes perennial gardening both exciting and challenging. Go into a retail nursery, or page through a mail-order catalog, and you're faced with choosing among hundreds of different perennial plants. Consult a comprehensive book on perennials and you may see seven or eight hundred different species, and thousands of named cultivars. Even a very experienced gardener can be overwhelmed by so many choices.

To help you navigate the somewhat daunting world of perennial flowers, this chapter will explain a few basics, outline some key concerns, give you some places to start, and direct you to the best books and resources for further information.

## Dig into the World of Perennials

The lifespan, bloom time, culture, and form of perennial plants varies greatly. Some species, such as lupines and delphinium, are so called "short-lived" perennials, with a lifespan of just three or four years. Others may live as long as fifteen years, or even, in the case of peonies, a lifetime. Bloom time may last for only two weeks each year, or may extend over two or three months. Some perennials, such as primroses, require deep humusy soil and plenty of shade, while others such as threadleaf coreopsis and cushion spurge wither away unless they grow in well-drained soil and full sun. Some perennials contain themselves in a nice,

## Guest Expert
## Allan Armitage

The idea of "perennials for a lifetime" reminds me of the many plants that have teased me with a season or two of beauty, never to show their heads again after a particularly normal winter. The truth is, it's a good thing there aren't too many "plant and get out of the way plants." The essence of a garden is change, and if all plants lasted a lifetime, gardening would be rather boring. Here are two of my lifetime favorites.

False Indigo (*Baptisia*). Few plants provide so much enjoyment for so long as my blue baptisia, *B. australis*, and it's white-flowered cousin, *B. alba*. In early spring the green shoots emerge like asparagus and green pea-like foliage fills the plant. In late spring, hundreds of deep blue pea flowers appear on long stems. The resulting display always stops people in their tracks. Green pods follow in summer, turning from brown to black as fall commences. In full sun, the plant is a knockout. *B. alba* is also spectacular, with black stems, clean white flowers, and fine fruit. These plants have been beautifying my garden for 14 years now, and I expect they are only middle-aged.

Yellow Wood (or Celandine) Poppy (*Stylophorum*). Few flowering plants thrive and increase in our deep, shady woods. But the yellow wood poppy, *S. diphyllum*, relishes the darkness. The blue-green spring foliage is lovely, and sunshine-bright yellow flowers quickly follow, to bloom all spring and occasionally into summer. The plants reseed themselves with abandon, and soon the few original plants become large colonies. If watered, the plants will persist all summer. Ours have been in place for 8 years and the colonies keep getting better.

*Dr. Allan Armitage teaches in the Dept. of Horticulture at the University of Georgia in Athens. He recently published the 2nd edition of Perennial Herbaceous Plants (Stipes Press, 1997). Dr. Armitage has also produced a new Photographic CD of Herbaceous Plants, including over 6,000 images of annuals, perennials, bulbs, ferns, grasses, and wildflowers (available from PlantAmerica, http://www.plantamerica.com/).*

## *Favorite Books*

### For Beginners

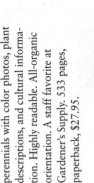

**Rodale's Illustrated Encyclopedia of Perennials** *by Ellen Phillips and C. Colston Burrell* (Rodale, 1993). The first half of this book is an accessible, yet comprehensive overview of design, planting, and culture. The other half profiles about 200 popular perennials with color photos, plant descriptions, and cultural information. Highly readable. All-organic orientation. A staff favorite at Gardener's Supply. 533 pages, paperback, $27.95.

**Better Homes and Gardens Complete Guide to Flower Gardening** *by Susan A. Roth* (Meredith, 1995). Another excellent choice. Covers annuals as well as perennials, with 200 pages on design and growing techniques followed by a color encyclopedia with photographs and complete descriptions of more than 450 plants. Dozens of sidebars categorize plants by color of blossoms, bloom time, region, and more. Captivating profiles of eight avid perennial gardeners. 408 pages, paperback, $29.95.

**Perennials for Dummies** *by Marcia Tatroe and the editors of the National Gardening Association* (IDG, 1997). Like the other books in the "dummies" series, this one does a good job of covering all the basics. A good way to help the neophyte get oriented, but not a long-term reference book. Only a handful of color photos. 325 pages, paperback, $16.99.

# What's In a Name?

Latin and Greek. The words sometimes refer to where the plant was first found ("canadensis" meaning Canada), who found it ("clarkei" for a Mr. Clark), or what it looks like ("roseum" meaning a rosy color).

Common names, such as "bleeding heart," are often used to refer to all the plants in a genus. Common names are useful unless you want to make sure that you are purchasing a 24-inch-high, old-fashioned, spring-blooming bleeding heart (*Dicentra spectabilis*) rather than the ever-blooming species known as the fringed bleeding heart, which is only 12 inches high (*Dicentra eximia*). If you are interested in learning more about botanical names, look for a copy of *Gardener's Latin* by Bill Neal (Algonquin Books, 1992).

Fellow gardeners are another great source of information about perennials. They can give you firsthand details about bloom time, height, hardiness, and cultural requirements, and, if you visit their gardens, you can also see for yourself what the plants really look like up close. Nothing beats seeing a plant in a garden setting, where you can observe how it is being used. You may even go home with some pass-along plants for your own garden.

Possibly the best way to learn about perennials is just to plant them in your garden and see how they grow. If there's a plant that you like, give it a try. Even though your next-door neighbor may not be able to grow iris, you may find that you have the ideal soil conditions and exposure. Though most books say that hostas are shade lovers, your climate may be cool enough or cloudy enough to keep them happy in full sun. Marginally hardy plants may survive for years if you can locate them in a sheltered spot. There's just no way to know how a plant will do for you unless you give it a try. If it turns out to be too tall, the color is wrong, or the plant doesn't thrive, you can always move it and try something different.

### Perennial Planting Styles

Few if any "perennial gardens" contain only herbaceous perennials. Woody plants, such as shrubs, roses, and trees, are often incorporated to

*Dicentra spectabilis* 'Alba' (old-fashioned white bleeding heart)

*Dicentra* — The first name is the genus. It is always capitalized.

*spectabilis* — The second name is the species. It is not capitalized.

'Alba' — The third name, which appears in single quotes, is the cultivar (cultivated variety).

It may be hard to believe, but scientific plant names are used to avoid confusion, not create it. They are developed by taxonomists to ensure that the same plant is called the same name throughout the world, regardless of language. Scientific plant names are usually a combination of

neat mound, while others, such as gooseneck loosestrife, will take over your entire garden. Some species should be cut back in mid-summer, while others, such as hybrid lilies, may die if you remove their foliage.

There are so many different species and cultivars of perennial flowers to choose from that few people ever become completely familiar with all the options. For the perennial gardener, books are an invaluable resource. They provide photographs for identification (and inspiration!), cultural information about soil preferences and propagation, a description of growth habits, bloom time, color, characteristics of special cultivars, and sometimes recommendations for complementary plants. Invest in a good how-to book that has cultural information, and a color encyclopedia to help you identify plants and plan your selections. (See the "Favorite Books" section on page 139.)

*Achillea* (common yarrow)

*Anthemis tinctoria* (golden marguerite)

*Chrysanthemum parthenium* (feverfew, matricaria)

*Coreopsis grandiflora* (coreopsis, tickseed)

*Coreopsis verticillata* (threadleaf coreopsis)

*Dicentra eximia* (fringed bleeding heart)

*Gaillardia x grandiflora* (blanket flower)

*Hemerocallis* 'Happy Returns' (dwarf daylily)

*Nepeta x faassenii* (catmint)

*Perovskia atriplicifolia* (Russian sage)

*Phlox paniculata* (garden phlox)

*Rudbeckia* (coneflower)

*Salvia x superba* (blue salvia)

*Sedum* (stonecrop)

*Veronica longifolia* 'Sunny Border Blue' (speedwell)

*Three types of perennial borders: A) with a brick or stone backdrop; B) mirroring beds on either side of a central path; C) an irregular backdrop of shrubs or trees.*

provide a backdrop for the perennial plants, or are used to fill in and give mass to the bed or border. Many gardeners include annuals in their perennial gardens to provide splashes of dependable color throughout the season. Favorite biennials (including foxgloves, sweet William, and Canterbury bells) are also incorporated, as are bulbs for early spring color, and ornamental grasses for their interesting textures and late-season beauty. Even wild plants (such as Joe-Pye weed, goldenrod, and asters) are finding their way into today's perennial gardens.

Traditionally, perennial gardens have been laid out in one of two ways: a border or an island bed. A border is typically a long, rectangular flower bed that is about two to four feet deep. The classic English perennial border, which was so popular in the first half of this century, maybe as much as eight feet deep and two hundred feet long. Borders on this scale are fine if you can afford to employ a small army of gardeners. But for most home gardeners, a good-sized perennial border might be three feet deep and about twelve to fifteen feet long. Borders are usually viewed from only one side, and are located in front of a backdrop. This backdrop may be created with shrubs, a hedge, a fence, or a stone wall. A well-defined front edge is another important feature. You may design a solo border, or a matched pair (see illustrations). When selecting plants for a border, keep in mind that borders usually look best when there is a repeating theme of plants and colors.

## Web Sites

**Cindi's Catalog of Gardening Catalogs**
http://www.oog.brown.edu:80/gardening/cat.html
*Over 1,000 gardening catalogs listed by subject. A good way to locate growers of specialty plants.*

**Perry's Perennials Pages**
http://moose.uvm.edu/~pass/perry/
*A top-rated site maintained by an enthusiastic professor of horticulture at the University of Vermont.*

**Time-Life Complete Gardener: Perennials**
http://pathfinder.com/@@jpWYbAUACdqbMI09/vg/Bookshelf/TLCG/Book01/choice.html
*A lengthy book excerpt with good information about gardening with perennials. More information is available from the Virtual Garden Home Page.*

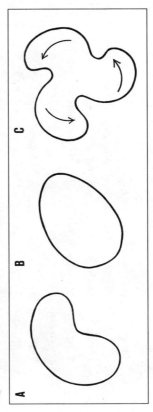

*Some pleasing shapes for an island bed. A) Kidney; B) egg-shape; C) irregular rotary shape with curves or bulges in the same direction.*

# LONG-SEASON FOLIAGE PLANTS

*Alchemilla mollis* (lady's-mantle)
*Artemisia*
*Baptisia* (false indigo)
*Cimicifuga* (bugbane)
*Heuchera* (coral bells)
Hosta
*Iberis* (candytuft)
Iris
*Macleaya* (plume poppy)
Ornamental grasses
*Paeonia* (peony)
*Pulmonaria* (lungwort)
*Santolina*
*Sedum* (stonecrop)
*Stachys* (lamb's ears)

# PERENNIALS FOR SOUTHERN GARDENS

*Achillea millefolium* (common yarrow)
*Asclepias tuberosa* (butterfly weed)
*Chrysanthemum x superbum* (Shasta daisy)
*Coreopsis grandiflora* (tickseed)
*Crinum* (crinum lily)
*Echinacea purpurea* (purple coneflower)
*Gaillardia x grandiflora* (blanket flower)
*Hemerocallis* (daylily)
Hibiscus
*Penstemon tenuis* (Gulf Coast penstemon)
*Physostegia virginiana* (obedient plant)
*Salvia leucantha* (velvet sage)
Verbena

An island is a garden that floats in a "sea" of lawn, sometimes among other island beds. The shape is irregular, with gentle curves and no sharp corners. It is usually designed to be viewed from all sides, with the tallest plants positioned along the center line of the bed, and the shortest plants around the edges. Island beds look best when they are generous in size. A good size for an island bed is eight feet wide by fifteen feet long, with the tallest plants reaching a height of about five feet.

Of course perennial flower gardens sometimes look nothing like a traditional border or island bed. Rock gardens break all the rules, for the objective is usually to create an irregular, natural-looking rock outcropping where tiny alpine plants can be featured. Shade gardens, too, are often irregularly-shaped, because they follow the natural shade patterns of the trees above. Another emerging style for perennial gardens is the large, free-form garden. In this case, the garden is defined by a series of meandering paths that lead the viewer right into and then through the plantings. Perennial flowers can also be mixed in among shrubs, planted around your mailbox, used in woodland or streamside plantings, or even planted in containers.

## How to Select Plants

There are so many varieties of perennials adapted to such a wide range of habitats, that you can be sure to find at least a few that will thrive in your garden. But the fact is, when it comes to deciding which perennials to plant, most of us are not very deliberate about our choices. We either succumb to a luscious photo in a catalog, stumble upon an irresistible beauty at the nursery, or a neighbor sends us home with a whole shopping bag full of cast-offs. If you ever do set out to make an informed, reasoned, and deliberate choice, here are some of the things that you should think about.

**YOUR SITE.** Perennials, like all plants, will live longer and be healthier and more floriferous if they are planted in a location that suits them. Does your garden have sandy soil or is it heavy clay? Is it in the sun or shade? Is the soil moist or droughty? Is the pH high, low, or neutral? Is the site flat, gently sloped, or steep? A good reference book (see "Favorite Books") can help you figure out which plants will probably be happy in the growing conditions that you can provide. Learning about

## Perennial Tips for the Ages

❧ When planting a new perennial garden, prepare the soil well at the outset. That may be your only opportunity to loosen the soil, remove rocks, and add organic matter. Be sure to work rock phosphate or some other source of phosphorus down into the root zone. This nutrient does not move well in the soil and now is the time to put it where it is needed.

❧ If you are establishing a large flower garden, consider starting your own plants from seed. It may take two or three years to get plants of blooming size, but you can get fifty or one hundred plants from a $2.00 packet of seeds. Put your first-year seedlings in a "nursery bed" rather than directly into your flower garden. They will not bloom or have much of a presence until their second year anyway, and a nursery bed will allow you to keep a better eye on their performance.

❧ Most perennials should be divided in early spring when new growth is only a few inches high. If you miss your chance in the spring, wait until fall. Midseason transplanting is risky. Disturbing the roots after the plant has leafed out makes it difficult for the plant to absorb the water it needs to maintain its foliage. Irises are the one major exception to this rule: they should be transplanted in early summer, right after they have bloomed.

❧ Keep newly transplanted perennials well watered for the first few weeks. Water deeply to saturate the entire root ball and establish good contact between the roots and the surrounding soil.

❧ Few gardeners pay attention to the pH level in their perennial garden. Though most perennials prefer a pH of about 6.5, some, including dianthus, salvia, linum, and gypsophila, have a distinct preference for more alkaline soils. Others prefer a more acidic soil. If you have trouble with a particular plant, check its pH requirements and the pH level of the soil in your flower garden. (For more information about pH, see the "Building Healthy Soil" chapter.)

❧ Sick plants attract bugs like a magnet. If your plants look stressed during the growing season, or if you see disease or insect damage, feed your plants with a quick-release organic fertilizer (try a blend of seaweed and fish emulsion).

❧ All plants die eventually, and some will die sooner than others, no matter what you do about it. If a plant performs poorly, try moving it to a different location. If it still is not happy, give it away or send it to the compost pile. Since there are so many outstanding perennial plants to choose from, you should not make do with poor performers.

❧ When designing a perennial garden, think about how you'll get access to your plants to stake, deadhead, or divide them. Flat rocks can be used as stepping stones within the garden. A walkway created at the back of a border will be hidden during the growing season, but will make the bed accessible for spring and fall chores.

---

the plant's native habitat (South Africa versus Labrador) will give you additional insight into what growing conditions the plant prefers.

**HARDINESS.** If a plant is not hardy in your growing zone, it will not survive. (If you don't know which zone you live in, check the USDA Hardiness Zone Map printed on page 242.) Though knowing your zone is very important, altitude, wind exposure, soils, and snow cover can have a dramatic impact on plant hardiness, effectively shifting the hardiness rating for your garden by as much as a full zone. For best results, choose plants that are well within your zone. As you become more experienced, and are exposed to more varieties of plants, you will probably be tempted by those that are at or even just beyond your growing zone. If you can afford to take the gamble (financially and emotionally), it can be very rewarding to discover that you can grow a couple of Zone 5 plants in your Zone 4 garden. Where snow cover is not dependable, a winter mulch of leaves or straw can help marginally hardy plants survive a cold winter. Well-drained soil is also a benefit because it will heave less (and cause less plant damage) than a heavy, wet soil.

Northern gardeners concern themselves with the minimum temperatures that a plant will tolerate, but Southern gardeners must also pay attention to zone ratings. Many popular perennials, including lupines,

---

## SHADE-LOVING PERENNIALS

*Alchemilla mollis* (lady's-mantle)
Astilbe
*Cimicifuga* (bugbane)
*Dicentra eximia* (fringed bleeding heart)
*Dicentra spectabilis* (old-fashioned bleeding heart)
*Digitalis purpurea* (foxglove)
*Helleborus orientalis* (Lenten rose)
Hosta
*Lamium maculatum* (spotted dead nettle)
*Liriope muscari* (blue lilyturf)
*Polemonium caeruleum* (Jacob's ladder)
*Primula* (primroses)
*Pulmonaria saccharata* (lungwort)
*Viola labradorica* (Labrador violet)

## PERENNIALS WITH ATTRACTIVE FOLIAGE

Alchemilla mollis (lady's-mantle)
Artemisia ludoviciana (wormwood)
Astilbe
Baptisia australis (false indigo)
Bergenia cordifolia (heart-leaved bergenia)
Cimicifuga simplex (bugbane)
Heuchera micrantha (alumroot or coral bells)
Hosta
Iberis (candytuft)
Lamium maculatum (spotted dead nettle)
Paeonia lactiflora (peony)
Pulmonaria saccharata (lungwort)
Ruta graveolens (rue)
Sedum x 'Vera Jameson'
Stachys byzantina (lamb's-ears)

## Favorite Books

### For the Intermediate and Expert

**The Random House Book of Perennials** by Roger Phillips and Martyn Rix (Random House, 1992). Outstanding photographs make this a favorite visual reference. The two-volume set is divided into Early Perennials and Late Perennials. Covers a total of 1,250 plants and has the same number of color photographs. Published in Britain, this book's only weakness is its omission of hardiness zones. Lists minimum temperature, but only in degrees celsius. 2 volumes; each is 252 pages, paperback, $27.50.

**Perennials for American Gardens** by Ruth Rogers Claussen and Nicholas H. Ekstrom (Random House, 1989). A comprehensive reference book written specifically for American gardeners. Short on color (only 360 images), but has thorough descriptions of flower color, height, bloom time, habitat, sun/shade, zone, and culture. Includes 400 genera and 300 species, as well as recommended cultivars and hybrids. 640 pages, hardcover, $50.00.

**The Undaunted Gardener** by Lauren Springer (Fulcrum, 1994). Subtitled "Planting for Weather-Resilient Beauty," this is a cover-to-cover read. Excellent sections on making the most of foliage; integrating annuals, coping with shade, planting for winter interest, and much more. Though the author hails from the East Coast, she has done most of her gardening in the West, and this book is geared to gardeners in arid conditions. 244 pages, hardcover, $32.95.

**The Perennial Gardener** by Frederick McGourty (Houghton Mifflin, 1989). One of our country's most distinguished horticulturalists, McGourty has spent over 30 years designing, planting, and writing about gardens. In this book he shares well-earned, practical advice about all facets of perennial gardening in an engaging, down-to-earth style. A delightful read. 250 pages, paperback, $16.95.

peonies, and garden phlox, must be exposed to a period of subfreezing temperatures to produce a good display of flowers. Many other perennials will simply not tolerate long periods of heat and humidity. For a list of recommended perennials for Southern gardens, see page 142.

**COLOR.** In working with color, aim for a balance of integration and contrast. Too much of the same color can be monotonous, yet a cacophony of different colors can be jarring rather than pleasing to the eye. You may want to organize your garden around one color; or choose a theme such as pastels, cool colors, or hot colors. You can also experiment with different color themes in different parts of your garden — hot colors by the front door and cool colors in a quieter part of the yard. And remember that few perennials are in bloom for more than a couple of weeks each year. Most of the time, plants are green, and it is their leaf form and foliage texture that are the "color" in your garden. (See the "Garden Design" chapter for more information about color, color harmonies, and designing with foliage.)

**BLOOM TIME.** Depending on the species or variety of plant, a perennial may be in bloom for two weeks a year or for as long as three months. If your objective is all-season color, choose several plants from each bloom season (see sidebar on facing page). When selecting plants for a spring garden, you will want to concentrate on those that bloom during April and May. After that peak, the garden may lack color for the rest of the season, but you will have achieved a spectacular spring display. For best effect, group at least two or three different varieties of plants together that will bloom at the same time. Remember that specified bloom time is only an average. In California, April may be the peak bloom time for bearded iris, yet in Vermont, the same plant will not bloom until early June. Recording the bloom times of various perennials in your garden will become an invaluable reference. No book, no matter how good, will be as accurate as your own observations about when plants bloom and how they perform in your own garden.

**SEEDLING, POTTED, OR FIELD-GROWN.** When purchasing perennials, try to get the largest, most mature plant that you can afford. The bigger the plant, the more

## Matching Bloom Time to Height

Bloom times will not be accurate for every part of the country, but this chart is a good place to start. Be aware that some species may vary in height depending on the variety (for example, there is a 6"-high creeping cranesbill and tall varieties that are 36").

### SPRING-BLOOMING PLANTS

| | Short 2–8" | Medium 10–18" | Tall 24–48" |
|---|:---:|:---:|:---:|
| Aquilegia x hybrida (columbine) | | ✓ | |
| Dicentra spectabilis (old-fashioned bleeding heart) | | ✓ | |
| Doronicum cordatum (leopard's-bane) | | ✓ | |
| Euphorbia epithymoides (cushion spurge) | | ✓ | |
| Iberis saxatilis (candytuft) | ✓ | | |
| Narcissus (daffodil) | ✓ | | |
| Phlox subulata (creeping phlox) | ✓ | | |
| Polemonium caeruleum (Jacob's ladder) | ✓ | | |
| Primula (primrose) | ✓ | | |
| Pulmonaria (lungwort) | ✓ | | |
| Tulipa (tulips) | | ✓ | |
| Paeonia (peony) | | | ✓ |
| Papaver (poppy) | | | ✓ |
| Veronica | | ✓ | |

### EARLY SUMMER-BLOOMING PLANTS

| | Short 2–8" | Medium 10–18" | Tall 24–48" |
|---|:---:|:---:|:---:|
| Alchemilla mollis (lady's-mantle) | | ✓ | |
| Astilbe | | | ✓ |
| Baptisia australis (false indigo) | | | ✓ |
| Campanula (bellflower) | | ✓ | |
| Dianthus barbatus (sweet William) | | ✓ | |
| Dianthus (pinks) | | ✓ | |
| Digitalis purpurea (foxglove) | | | ✓ |
| Geranium sanguineum (cranesbill) | ✓ | | |
| Heuchera micrantha (coral bells) | ✓ | | |
| Iris | | ✓ | |
| Lupinus polyphyllus (lupine) | | | ✓ |

### MIDSUMMER-BLOOMING PLANTS

| | Short 2–8" | Medium 10–18" | Tall 24–48" |
|---|:---:|:---:|:---:|
| Achillea millefolium (yarrow) | | | ✓ |
| Coreopsis grandiflora (coreopsis) | | ✓ | |
| Delphinium | | | ✓ |
| Echinacea purpurea (purple coneflower) | | | ✓ |
| Echinops (globe thistle) | | | ✓ |
| Liatris (gayfeather) | | | ✓ |
| Lilium (hybrid lilies) | | | ✓ |
| Macleaya cordata (plume poppy) | | | ✓ |
| Monarda didyma (bee balm) | | | ✓ |
| Phlox paniculata (garden phlox) | | | ✓ |
| Physostegia virginiana (obedient plant) | | | ✓ |
| Rudbeckia fulgida (orange coneflower) | | | ✓ |

### LATE SUMMER AND FALL-BLOOMING PLANTS

| | Short 2–8" | Medium 10–18" | Tall 24–48" |
|---|:---:|:---:|:---:|
| Aconitum (monkshood) | | | ✓ |
| Aster | | | ✓ |
| Chrysanthemum x morifolium | | ✓ | |
| Cimicifuga (bugbane) | | | ✓ |
| Filipendula rubra (queen-of-the-prairie) | | | ✓ |
| Gaillardia x grandiflora (blanket flower) | | ✓ | |
| Heliopsis (oxeye) | | | ✓ |
| Sedum spectabile (stonecrop) | | ✓ | |
| Solidago x hybrida (goldenrod) | | | ✓ |

quickly it will fill out and the sooner it will begin blooming. If you are on a tight budget, or if you need a large number of plants, consider starting your own plants from seed. (See the chapter on "Starting Plants from Seed.") You could solicit divisions or cuttings from friends. Some nurseries also offer smaller, less mature plants at a reduced price. Typically plants are available in pot sizes ranging from 3-inch diameter to 12-inch diameter. The larger the pot, the bigger and more mature the plant (and the higher the price). Pot-grown perennials can be planted from spring through fall, and will suffer minimal transplant shock.

Some mail-order companies ship their plants bareroot (without soil). Bareroot perennials are usually available only in early spring when the plants are still dormant. The roots must be kept moist, and the plant should be put into the garden as soon as possible (within a couple of days). Once the plant is in the ground and has emerged from its dormant state, it will take hold relatively fast. Some local nurseries still offer field-grown perennials. These plants are dug up when you come for them and

## MOISTURE-LOVING PERENNIALS

*Aruncus dioicus* (goat's beard)
*Bergenia* (bergenias)
*Chelone* (turtlehead)
*Cimicifuga* (bugbane)
*Eupatorium fistulosum* (Joe-Pye weed)
*Filipendula rubra* (queen-of-the-prairie)
*Iris*
*Lobelia cardinalis* (cardinal flower)
*Primula japonica* (primrose)
*Trollius europaeus* (globeflower)

# What Is a Cottage Garden?

"A cottage garden is a delightful mix of color, size, and fragrance. Annuals, biennials, and herbs mix freely with perennials, while vines roam over adjacent fences and trellises, and roses and other fragrant shrubs mingle with abandon. The cottage garden exemplifies freedom and joy. It's the perfect place for perennials and annuals that self-sow."

—from *Rodale's Illustrated Encyclopedia of Perennials* by Ellen Phillips and C. Colston Burrell (Rodale, 1993)

## Old-Fashioned Cottage Garden Flowers

*Aconitum* (monkshood)
*Alcea rosea* (hollyhock)
*Aquilegia x hybrida* (columbine)
*Campanula* (bellflower)
*Centranthus reber* (valerian)
*Chrysanthemum parthenium* (matricaria or feverfew)
*Delphinium x elatum* (hybrid delphinium)
*Dianthus barbatus* (sweet William)
*Dicentra spectabilis* (common bleeding heart)
*Digitalis purpurea* (foxglove)
*Hemerocallis* (daylily)
*Monarda didyma* (bee balm)
*Myosotis* (forget-me-not)
*Paeonia* (peony)
*Phlox paniculata* (garden phlox)
*Primula* (primrose)
*Stachys byzantina* (lamb's-ears)
*Viola* (violet)

## EASY AND DEPENDABLE PERENNIALS (LONG-LIVED AND NON-INVASIVE)

*Achillea* (yarrow)
*Aconitum* (monkshood)
*Aruncus* (goats beard)
*Asclepias* (butterfly weed)
Astilbe
*Baptisia* (false indigo)
*Dicentra* (bleeding heart)
*Dictamnus* (gas plant)
*Echinacea purpurea* (purple coneflower)
*Geranium sanguinium* (cranesbill)
*Helleborus orientalis* (Lenten rose)
*Hemerocallis* (daylily)
Hosta
Iris
*Paeonia* (peony)
*Papaver* (poppy)
*Rudbeckia fulgida* (orange coneflower)
Sedum

## Arranging Your Plants

The appearance of a perennial garden depends as much upon the shapes of your plants and how they are arranged, as upon their colors.

**HEIGHT.** You'll want to place the tallest plants in the back of the border, or in the center of an island bed, then work down in height, ending with the shortest plants around the edges of an island bed or the front of a border. Books and labels usually list the average mature height for a plant in bloom. Remember that many plants hold their flowers well above the foliage. This means that when the plant is out of bloom, it may be much shorter than the specified height. Heights are also an average. When grown in poor, dry soil, a plant may be only half as tall as the same plant grown in rich, moist soil. Be prepared to move your plants around once you see how tall (or short) they really grow. Even the most experienced gardeners rearrange their plants (usually more than once!).

**WIDTH.** A plant's width, or spread, is just as important as its height. Width figures given in books or on labels are also an average. The actual width of a plant will vary depending on soils, geographical location, and

described as "vigorous." This may be a euphemism for an invasive plant that you'll wish you never set eyes on. Perennials with a reputation for invasiveness include: bamboo, *Macleaya cordata* (plume poppy), *Physostegia virginiana* (obedient plant), *Monarda* (bee balm), *Artemisia ludoviciana* ('Silver King' artemisia), *Lysimachia clethroides* (gooseneck loosestrife), *Tanacetum vulgare* (tansy), *Aegopodium* (goutweed), and *Boltonia asteroides*.

they need to be transplanted immediately (within a few hours) to minimize transplant shock. Field-grown perennials are usually the largest and most mature plants around, but today most nurseries only offer container-grown perennials.

**VIGOR.** Vigor can be good, but it can also create problems. Plants that are too vigorous can invade neighboring plants and gradually take over your entire garden. Determining a plant's propensity for invasiveness can be difficult, because poor growing conditions can render a normally invasive plant relatively tame, whereas in fertile soil, a normally restrained plant may exhibit invasive tendencies. Look closely at plant descriptions and be wary of those

the age of the plant. Be careful about locating slow-growers very close to rapid spreaders. The former may all but disappear by the end of the first growing season.

**SPACING.** Patience is a virtue, but when most people plant a perennial garden, their goal is to create as full an effect as possible, as soon as possible. The challenge is to plant thickly, but not break the bank, or create a crowded, unhealthy situation two or three years down the line. When planting a drift of the same kind of plants, you can put them closer together to create a massed look more quickly. Another trick is to place short-lived plants between slower-growing, long-lived plants. Most peonies, for example, have an ultimate spread of three feet, but it may take seven years for them to reach this size. While you're waiting, you could interplant with Shasta daisies, a fast-growing, short-lived plant that will provide a full look and plenty of flowers while the peonies get themselves established. Remember, too, that some gardeners like the look of individual plants set off by air and open ground. This is especially true in the collector's garden, where there are many different species and varieties to appreciate as individuals.

**DRIFTS VERSUS SPECIMENS.** A garden planted with groupings of five or more plants of the same variety will display drifts of repeating colors and textures — a sophisticated and designerly look. In this type of garden, plants are used primarily as design elements that add up to a

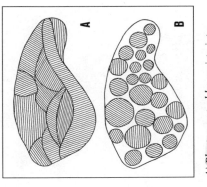

*A) Plants grouped by variety into drifts of color and foliage texture; B) plants positioned individually based on height, color, and texture.*

# Other Good Books

## THE REFERENCE SHELF

**Rodale's Flower Garden Problem Solver** *by Jeff and Liz Ball* (Rodale, 1990). An A–Z listing of both annuals and perennials that identifies specific care requirements and common pest and disease problems on a plant-by-plant basis. Recommended solutions are both preventative and corrective, and are always organic. An essential reference for gardeners of all abilities. 422 pages, paperback, $14.95.

**Herbaceous Perennial Plants** *by Allan Armitage* (Varsity, 1989). This well-respected expert has grown perennials in Montreal and Michigan, as well as in the South, where he is a professor at the University of Georgia. His book

provides detailed, first-hand information on over 3,000 perennials. Includes zone, site-specific needs, height, place of origin, and recommended cultivars. A few color photos, but this is primarily a reference book for the dedicated gardener. 646 pages, hardcover, $37.95.

**Gardening with Perennials Month by Month** *by Joseph Hudak* (Timber, 1993). The author, an American landscape architect and long-time Harvard instructor, has organized this book alphabetically by month of bloom time. It documents 700 species and thousands of noteworthy cultivars. Covers hardy and tender perennials, bulbs, ornamental grasses, and ferns. Small color photos are grouped separately from descriptive copy. Another

reference book suited to the serious gardener. First published in 1976. 327 pages, hardcover, $59.95.

## SPECIALTY GARDENS

For books on specific types of plants (hostas, peonies, etc.), and site-specific types of gardening (shade, rock, bog, etc.), request a copy of the following catalog:
Capability's Books
2379 Highway 46
Deer Park, WI 54007-7506
800-247-8154
http://www.gardens.com (on the GardenEscape site)

## BRITISH FAVORITES

**Hardy Perennials** *by Graham Rice* (Timber, 1995). A cover-to-cover read for the intermediate to advanced gardener. This well-known British author provides an

idiosyncratic review of 20 plant families from primroses to penstemons, chrysanthemums to ornamental grasses. Part history, part personal experience, with details on the merits of various recommended cultivars. 198 pages, paperback, $17.95.

**The Gardener's Companion** *by Christopher Brickell* (Crown, 1995). A very readable, anecdotal tour of 300 favorite garden plants, based on the author's 40 years of experience as Director General of the Royal Horticultural Society in London. Plants are organized by season. A treasure-trove of information for the avid gardener. 240 pages, hardcover, $30.00.

pleasing and integrated visual effect. At the opposite end of the spectrum is the collector's garden, filled with onezies and twozies of all different kinds of plants. These are the gardens of people who simply love plants and want to have one of everything. The look of this type of garden may

# Garden Gear

## Flower supports

Flower supports keep your flowers looking their best. Made of 9-gauge, galvanized steel wire with a green epoxy coating, they are almost invisible in your garden. The rings should be positioned in spring when plants are small. The linking stakes, zig-zag supports, and single stem supports can be positioned during the growing season to support floppy foliage or heavy blooms.

#24-318 Single Stem Supports, set of 5 (36" H) $10.95

#14-320 Grow-Through Supports, set of 3 (26" H x 18" W) $24.95

#14-435 Jumbo Grow-Through Grid, set of 2 (34" H x 22" W) $19.95

#24-273 Double Support Rings, set of 3 (30" H x 14" W) $19.95

#14-277 Mini Support Rings, set of 5 (22" H x 7" W) $9.95

#24-211 Linking Stakes, set of 12 (36" H x 10" W) $29.95

#14-244 Mini Linking Stakes, set of 12 (22" H x 7" W) $16.95

#30-092 Giant Linking Stakes, set of 12 (40" H x 15" W) $25.95

#14-279 In-Line Zig-Zag Supports, set of 5 (36" H x 21" W) $18.95

#14-120 Linking Half-Round Zig-Zag Supports, set of 4 (30" H x 16" W) $24.95

**Organic Flower Fertilizer** keeps perennials in peak condition all season long. Rich in phosphorus (5-7-4) to promote strong root growth and more abundant and longer-lasting blooms. Slow-release all-organic nutrients include peanut and whey meals, sulphate of potash/magnesia, and Chilean nitrate. 5 lbs. Covers 200 square feet.

#07-316 Flower Fertilizer, 5 lbs. $5.95

Plant markers help you keep track of the plants in your garden. On the writing surface you can record variety name, source, and planting date. These permanent markers are neat-looking and last for years. The **Standard** and **Large Markers** have two galvanized wire legs and etched zinc nameplates. The

Our super-sharp **Dutch Edging Tool** makes it easy to maintain a clean, neat edge around your perennial gardens. It is made of solid steel for strength, and slices with ease through even the toughest sod. 12"-wide T-grip handle. Blade is 8½" x 3½". Overall length is 35".

#04-215 Edging Tool $34.95

For transplanting perennials, it is hard to beat this professional **Transplanting Spade**. Narrower than a regular spade, it can be easily maneuvered in a tightly planted bed without damaging neighboring plants. The extra-long, 14" blade also lets you dig deep enough to get the entire root system. Made of tempered steel with a turned foot rest. Handle is ash with a poly D-grip. 5¾" wide, 48" overall.

#04-240 Transplanting Spade $34.95

An **Electric Engraver** has a hardened carbide point that will permanently etch plant information on any of the above markers. 6" long with a 63" cord.

#14-327 Engraving Tool $29.95

**Hi-Rise Marker** has one steel leg and a flip-up nameplate so you can record information on the back as well.

#14-310 Standard Zinc Markers, set of 25 (10" H) $10.95

#14-306 Large Zinc Markers, set of 25 (11½" H) $10.95

#14-401 Hi-Rise Marker, set of 10 (26" H) $14.95

#14-323 Marking Pen $3.50

be a jumble of colors and textures, and maintenance is usually more challenging, but these gardens are about plants first, and design second.

## Maintaining a Perennial Garden

Though most flowering perennials are dependable, easy-care performers, all perennial gardens require some maintenance. Here are the eight most important steps to ensure a healthy and floriferous garden:

**FERTILIZING.** Most perennials are not heavy feeders and they will be happy with one spring application of a low-nitrogen, high-phosphorus fertilizer (5-10-5). For established plantings, scratch in a good handful of fertilizer around each plant. Annual or biennial applications of aged manure or finished compost will restore trace elements and improve the texture of the soil.

**WATERING.** A perennial garden does not require as much water as a vegetable garden. Depending on where you live, if you select plants suited to your site, and mulch them well, you may not need to water at all. If you live where summers are very dry and you do need to water, try to water deeply and avoid getting water on the foliage (soaker hoses and drip irrigation systems are great for perennial gardens). You can also save water, and labor, if you select plants suited to your climate, and group plants together that have similar water requirements. (See suggestions in the "Water-Efficient Gardening" chapter.)

**MULCHING.** By early summer, a densely planted perennial garden will shade out most weeds. But a new garden, a spring garden, or a garden that is more sparsely planted, will benefit from some kind of mulch. The mulch will keep weeds to a minimum and help retain moisture in the soil. In a perennial garden, the aesthetics of the mulch are as important as the function. Your garden will look best with a finely textured material such as shredded leaves, dry grass clippings, peanut shells, cocoa hulls, or shredded bark. Big chunks of bark, newspaper, or straw will overpower your plants.

**NEAT EDGES.** A neat, cleanly defined edge between your lawn and flower bed will give your garden a professional look. You can achieve this in one of two ways: get a nice sharp edging tool and recut the edge several times during the growing season; or install some permanent edg-

## DROUGHT-TOLERANT PERENNIALS

*Achillea*
*Anthemis tinctoria* (golden marguerite)
*Asclepias tuberosa* (butterfly weed)
*Aurinia saxatilis* (basket-of-gold)
*Calamintha nepeta* (catmint)
*Coreopsis verticillata* (threadleaf coreopsis)
*Echinacea purpurea* (purple coneflower)
*Echinops ritro* (globe thistle)
*Euphorbia polychroma* (cushion spurge)
*Gypsophila paniculata* (baby's-breath)
*Helianthus angustifolius* (sunflower)
*Lavandula angustifolia* (lavender)
*Limonium latifolium* (sea lavender)
*Perovskia atriplicifolia* (Russian sage)
*Rudbeckia fulgida* (orange coneflower)
*Santolina chamaecyparissus* (lavender cotton)
*Sedum* (stonecrop)
*Stachys byzantina* (lamb's-ears)
*Thymus* (thyme)
*Pulsatilla vulgaris* (pasque flower)

> **"** Mixing flower colors from different parts of the spectrum, such as yellows and pinks, frequently causes squabbles. Oranges and pinks always bring about pitched battles while the gardener looks on helplessly. Counseling doesn't work under such circumstances, though buffering the contending parties with plenty of silver foliage, white or blue flowers, or green foliage can turn adversity into diversity."
>
> —from *The Perennial Gardener* by Frederick McGourty (Houghton Mifflin, 1989)

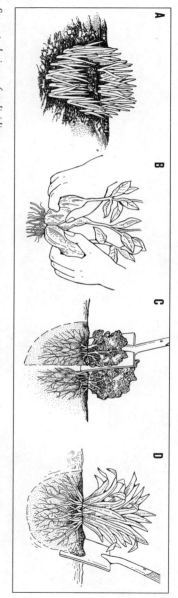

**A**

**B**

**C**

**D**

*Some techniques for dividing perennials: A) remove old growth at center and replant area with new growth from edges; B) remove plant and tease apart bulbous growth; C) use a sharp spade to slice away part of the plant; D) remove entire plant, divide, and replant.*

ing. A defined edge will also help keep grass and weeds from growing into the bed.

**PINCHING.** Some kinds of perennials, including asters, chrysanthemums, phlox, and salvias, benefit from being pinched back. Pinching creates a bushier plant that produces more blooms and is less likely to flop over. Pinch back the growing tips — using thumb and forefinger — once or twice during late spring. However, only some kinds of perennials should be pinched. If in doubt, pinch a little here and there, and see what happens.

**DEADHEADING.** Some plants drop their spent flowers as soon as they wither. Others hold onto them for months, or even right through the winter. Removing spent flowers will keep your plants looking their best. It also prevents plants from expending their energy on seed production, and it often stimulates reblooming. After bloom, some plants should be shorn rather than deadheaded. This is true for creeping phlox, *nepeta*, hardy geraniums, daisies, pinks, and lavender.

**STAKING.** Many tall or weak-stemmed plants need support when they reach blooming size. Delphiniums and hybrid lilies are two prime candidates. But other, shorter plants can also benefit from some kind of support. Supports should be as invisible as possible. For individual stems, you can use bamboo canes. For entire plants you can use wire support rings. For loose and airy plants, try using a few thin branches. For best results, put the supports into position in early spring. That way the plants will hide the supports as they grow.

**DIVIDING.** If your perennials are happy, most of them will need to be divided every few years. They may become too large for the space; the center or oldest part of the plant may die out leaving a bare middle; or the growth may become so dense that the plant is no longer blooming well. The easiest way to divide a plant is to use a shovel to remove the entire plant from the garden and place the root ball on a tarp. Then you can either pry the plant into pieces using two forks, tease the pieces of the plant apart into different sections, or use a shovel or knife to cut the plant into several pieces (see illustration above). Plants should not be divided when they are in bloom or in full growth. In all but a few cases, this is a job for early spring or late fall.

## PLANTS THAT SHOULD NOT BE DIVIDED

*Aconitum* (monkshood)
*Asclepias* (butterfly weed)
*Baptisia* (false indigo)
*Dianthus* (pinks)
*Dicentra* (bleeding heart)
*Dictamnus* (gas plant)
*Gypsophila* (baby's-breath)
*Iberis* (candytuft)
*Limum* (blue flax)
*Lupinus* (lupine)
*Papaver* (poppy)
*Platycodon* (balloon flower)

# Resources

There are thousands of good nurseries growing high-quality perennials. We have listed some of the largest ones here, and have tried to include a few from each region. This is not an exhaustive list and is not intended as an endorsement. There are many excellent growers whose names do not appear here. Most catalogs are available free or for a small refundable charge.

**Andre Viette Farm and Nursery**
Rt. 1, Box 16
Fishersville, VA 22939
703-943-2315
*Large selection.*

**Bluestone Perennials**
7203 Middle Ridge Road
Madison, OH 44057
800-852-5243
*More than 400 varieties of hardy perennials.*

**Borbeleta Gardens**
15980 Canby Avenue
Rt. 5
Faribault, MN 55021
*Specialize in daylilies, iris, and lilies.*

**Busse Gardens**
5873 Oliver Avenue
Cokato, MN 55321-9426
800-544-3192
*Cold-hardy and unusual perennials.*

**Fieldstone Gardens**
620 Quaker Lane
Vassalboro, ME 04989-9713
207-923-3836
*Perennials and rock garden plants.*

**High Country Garden**
2902 Rufina St.
Santa Fe, NM 87505-2929
800-925-9387
*Drought-tolerant perennials and native plants.*

**Holbrook Farm and Nursery**
P.O. Box 368
115 Lance Road
Fletcher, NC 28732
704-891-7790
*Large selection, including native plants.*

**Klehm Nursery**
P.O. Box 197
Rt. 5, Penny Road
South Barrington, IL 60010
*Peonies, Siberian iris, daylilies, and more.*

**Kurt Bluemel**
2740 Green Lane
Baldwin, MD 21013
410-557-7229
*Ornamental grasses, ferns, water plants.*

**Milaeger's Gardens**
4838 Douglas Avenue
Racine, WI 53402-2498
800-669-9956
*Large selection including hostas and daylilies.*

**Niche Gardens**
1111 Dawson Road
Chapel Hill, NC 27516
919-967-0078
*Varieties suited for the southeastern U.S.*

**Roslyn Nursery**
211 Burrs Lane
Dix Hills, NY 11746
516-643-9347
*Plants for shady and woodland gardens.*

**Siskiyou Rare Plant Nursery**
2825 Cummings Road
Medford, OR 97501
503-772-6846
*Specializing in alpine and rock garden plants.*

**Wayside Gardens**
One Garden Lane
Hodges, SC 29695
800-845-1124
*A comprehensive selection.*

**Weiss Brothers Nursery**
11690 Colfax Highway
Grass Valley, CA 95945
916-272-7657
*Large selection.*

**White Flower Farm**
P.O. Box 50, Rte. 63
Litchfield, CT 06759-0050
800-503-9624
*Comprehensive selection, seductively presented.*

For a list of perennial nurseries on the Web, visit Gardening by Mail at http://pathfinder.com/vg, or Cindi's Catalog of Gardening Catalogs at http://www.cog.brown.edu:80/gardening/

## SOCIETIES

**The Hardy Plant Society**
440 Louella Ave.
Wayne, PA 19087

**Perennial Plant Association**
Attn: Dr. Steven M. Still
3383 Schirtzinger Rd.
Hilliard, OH 43026
614-771-8431
sstill@magnus.acs.ohio-state.edu
http://garden.cas.psu.edu/ppa.html

There are dozens of organizations that focus on particular types of perennial plants (The American Dianthus Society, American Peony Society, The Society for Siberian Irises, etc.). For a current listing of addresses, membership fees, and other information, consult Barbara Barton's *Gardening by Mail* (Houghton Mifflin, 1994) or the following web site: http://www.altgarden.com/society.html

## MAGAZINES

*Perennial Plants: The Quarterly Journal of the Perennial Plant Association*
Geared primarily to nursery people, but always something of interest for the avid gardener. For membership and subscription information, contact: Dr. Steven M. Still, 3383 Schirtzinger Road, Hilliard, OH 43026; 614-771-8431; e-mail to: sstill@magnus.acs.ohio-state.edu
For subscription information contact Dr. David J. Beattie, RD1, Box 178B, Spring Mills, PA 16875; 814-364-1272.

The web site is: http://garden.cas.psu.edu/ppa.html

*The American Cottage Gardener*
A beautifully produced, literary quarterly for intermediate to advanced gardeners. For subscription information, write: The American Cottage Gardener, 131 E. Michigan Street, Marquette, MI 49855

*Horticulture*
A well-written monthly that focuses much of its attention on perennial plants. For subscription information, write: 98 N. Washington, Boston, MA 02114.

*Fine Gardening*
In-depth articles with excellent hands-on information. A decided focus on perennials. For subscription information, write: P.O. Box 5506, Newtown, CT 06470.

*Rock Garden Quarterly*
For subscription information, write: The North American Rock Garden Society, P.O. Box 67, Milford, NY 10546; 914-762-2948

# growing
# roses

*Pompon
rose form*

America's most popular flower is also one of the very oldest flowers in cultivation. Some of the same roses grown today are mentioned in texts dating as far back as 470 BC. Roses may move us with their perfect beauty and seductive fragrance, but this flower's appeal is about something more powerful. Roses provide a link with history — both collective and personal. We may be drawn to roses through research into herbal remedies from the 1500s; through Shakespeare's sonnets or Romantic poetry from the 19th century; by trying to reestablish a period garden for a historic home; or by a personal memory of a flower fondly remembered from our childhood.

There are over 2,000 different rose varieties to lure us with their history and fragrance. This is because the rose, like the orchid, crossbreeds readily — a trait exploited first by nature, and then by horticulturalists. Today, we can choose from old-fashioned favorites, as well as modern varieties that are the result of intensive breeding programs throughout the world. The rose is a flower with a rich past, and an exciting future.

## A Rose is a Rose

Finding your way through the rose's large extended family can be both confusing and intimidating. Damasks, musks, gallicas, centifolias, hybrid perpetuals, Bourbons, hybrid teas, ramblers, and climbers — even the most distinguished rosarians have a difficult time determining which rose is which. Tracing the history of a particular rose can be a fascinating adventure, but it is hardly an exact science. The old roses have cross-bred so many times, and so many varieties have been lost to time, that it is often impossible to uncover the exact parentage. If you are one of the many who become possessed by roses, you may eventually find it important to know the difference between a gallica and a Bourbon. But until that point, our advice is not to worry about it. The important thing is to select a rose that you find beautiful, and that suits your garden.

Roses are usually grouped into one of two broad categories: old roses and modern roses. Old roses are those varieties discovered or developed prior to the introduction of the hybrid tea rose in 1867. But like everything else in the world of roses, when it comes to determining how a particular rose should be classified, it's not always crystal clear. It

## Guest Expert
# David King

Sometimes, in order to see ahead, it helps to look back. Last spring I was exploring the back roads of my small Maine town when I came across an unoccupied old farmhouse. Long-term neglect was evident: peeling paint, broken shutters, any effort at gardening long since abandoned. Soaring up out of the mass of overgrowth, however, was a stunning red rose in full bloom. Small semi-double flowers with bright yellow stamens in clusters of three or four, were blooming all along the 6- to 8-foot arching canes. Hardy, disease resistant, defiant in the face of neglect.

These are the characteristics that rose growers and breeders are striving for today. While demand remains strong for the magnificent flower form of the Hybrid Tea, emerging appreciation for old garden shrubs will set the course for new introductions. Well-behaved shrub form, resistance to disease, winter hardiness, and fragrance will be the key criteria for the next generation of roses.

Expect to see the increasing availability of roses hybridized by the late Dr. Griffith Buck of Iowa State University. Among the nearly 100 hardy shrubs he developed, 'Carefree Beauty', 'Amiga Mia', 'Earthsong', and 'Hawkeye Belle' have gained attention recently. Agriculture Canada has also brought us high-performance roses, such as 'William Baffin' and 'Henry Kelsey', which are cold-hardy and tolerant of poor conditions yet bloom repeatedly into the late fall. 'Lambert Closse', 'Louise Jolliet', and 'Simon Fraser' are three of the newest introductions.

*David King is president and owner of Royall River Roses in Scarborough, Maine, a mail-order business specializing in hardy roses. He is an ARS-certified consulting rosarian, with customers around the country.*

# The Basic Rose Classification System

## OLD GARDEN ROSES
## (15 classes)

❧ **Species.** The wild rose, source of all other rose varieties. Simple, very fragrant flowers once a year in spring. Carefree, disease-resistant, and hardy.

❧ **Gallicas.** Probably the oldest cultivated rose in existence in the West. Low, suckering shrubs produce large, fragrant flowers, borne singly or in clusters.

❧ **Damasks.** Closely related to gallicas but larger and taller. Most fragrant of the old garden roses, with semi-double or double blooms. 'Autumn Damask' is the only repeat bloomer.

❧ **Albas.** Believed to be crosses between damask or gallica roses and *R. canina.* Upright, tall and vigorous, with tough leaves and mostly fully double blooms.

*Rosette*

❧ **Centifolias.** Known as cabbage roses for their globe-like flowers. May be a cross between 'Autumn Damask' and an alba. Taller than gallicas, with drooping leaves, prickly stems, and fragrant, nodding flowers.

❧ **Moss roses.** A genetic "sport" from centifolias or damasks. Drooping foliage and sepals, hips, and flower stalks have a mossy, pine-scented covering.

❧ **Chinas.** First discovered in China, and brought to Europe in the 18th century. The ever-blooming ancestors of all modern, repeat-blooming roses. Some are low-growing; some have tall canes and can be treated as climbers. Small flowers are borne on short stems and have a distinct, light fragrance.

❧ **Teas.** Very fragrant forms of the China class, with dainty leaves and stems.

❧ **Noisettes.** The original Noisettes were a cross between a China rose and a European rose. Not very hardy.

❧ **Bourbons.** The original Bourbon was an accidental hybrid of Chinas and 'Autumn Damask'. A repeat bloomer with large, fragrant flowers.

❧ **Hybrid Chinas.** First generation of crosses between Chinas and other rose varieties, developed for larger flowers.

❧ **Hybrid Bourbons.** First generation of crosses between the original Bourbons and gallicas or damask hybrids. Various flower colors and growth habits.

❧ **Hybrid Noisettes.** First generation of crosses between Noisettes and Bourbons, Chinas, and tea roses. Larger flowers.

❧ **Portlands.** Popular in the early 19th century because of their repeat-blooming flowers.

❧ **Hybrid perpetuals.** Hybrids of Portland roses, hybrid Chinas, gallicas, and Bourbons. Very popular in the 19th century. Very hardy, ranging from sprawling to upright in habit, with fragrant, many-petaled flowers on short stems.

❧ **Grandifloras.** Originally crosses between hybrid teas and floribundas, with clustered flowers like the floribundas but larger, and with the long stems of hybrid teas. Tall, often over 6 feet, with masses of color.

❧ **Miniatures.** Except for the miniature cascading and climbing roses,

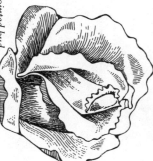

*Pointed bud*

these grow to just 10 to 18 inches. Very hardy, and most grow on their own rootstocks.

❧ **Climbing roses.** Climbers have tall canes that, with support, can be trained to grow upright. Some are ever-blooming; others bloom once at the beginning of the season. **Ramblers** are climbing roses with very pliable canes.

❧ **Shrub roses.** A catch-all category including robust, spreading roses that bloom fairly constantly, some with single flowers, others double.

❧ **Hybrid musks.** Shrub roses distantly related to the musk rose. Can tolerate poor soil and shade. Some can be trained as climbers.

❧ **Eglantine hybrids.** Large, arching shrubs that can reach 10 to 12 feet. Fragrant blooms borne either singly or in clusters and bright red hips in autumn.

❧ **Rugosa hybrids.** Hybrids of hybrid teas and *R. rugosa.* Some of the hardiest roses, these are very easy-care, disease-resistant roses.

## MODERN ROSES
## (10 classes)

❧ **Hybrid teas.** Very popular modern roses with large flowers on long stems. Hybrid teas bloom often, in a wide range of colors; many are fragrant.

❧ **Polyanthas.** Low-growing shrubs with large clusters of small flowers. They grow to about 2 feet, are extremely hardy, and bloom continuously, though with little fragrance.

❧ **Floribundas.** Originally crosses between polyanthas and hybrid teas. Floribundas are hardy, large, shrubby bushes that bloom continuously all summer.

—from *Easy-Care Roses*
(Brooklyn Botanic Garden, 1995)

is generally agreed that "old roses" include species or wild roses; albas; Bourbons; moss roses; China roses; Noisettes; Portland roses; rugosa roses; Scotch roses; centifolias; hybrid pimpinellifolias; damasks; gallicas; hybrid perpetuals; tea roses; and musk roses. Those classified as modern rose varieties are hybrid teas; floribundas; polyanthas; grandifloras; miniatures and dwarfs; modern shrub and landscape roses; climbers and ramblers; and rugosa hybrids.

Why choose an old-fashioned rose over a modern hybrid? Many of the old rose varieties offer more fragrance, more complex and interesting blooms, greater disease resistance, easier care, and more interesting forms. But modern roses can offer all-season blooms, and a much broader range of colors and flower forms. Some are also far more cold-hardy and disease-resistant than any of the old-fashioned varieties.

There are thousands of beautiful roses, far more than any of us will ever have the opportunity to see, much less grow. When choosing a rose for your garden, here are five considerations that should make the selection process easier.

**GROWTH HABIT.** Though roses are usually planted for their flowers, it is important to know what the plant as well as the flowers will look like, in order to determine where it will fit in your garden.

• Hybrid teas and floribundas usually grow no more than 2 to 3 feet high. Their form is coarse, and hardly very appealing, but they do have the ability to produce an abundance of flowers throughout the growing season. The hybrid tea has large, single blooms on long, stiff stems, whereas the floribunda has slightly smaller clusters of blooms on stems that are not as stiff. Miniature roses have tiny flowers, and may be only 10 to 36 inches in height. Dwarf roses grow up to 2 feet high, and their flowers are produced in clusters. Shrub roses, including both the old-fashioned and the modern types, and ground-cover or landscape roses, are generally large and leafy.

• Climbers and ramblers grow from 7 feet to 30 feet in length, and most of them benefit from some support. Standards are roses that are trained into a tree-like form with a single stem and a rounded bush or weeping display of flowers on top.

*Rounded bloom (above) and flat or open bloom (below).*

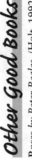

## Other Good Books

**Roses** *by Peter Beales* (Holt, 1992). One of the most authoritative books on roses. It combines the author's previous two books into one comprehensive volume. Detailed descriptions of 2,000 roses, with over 1,000 color photographs. 472 pages, hardcover, $60.00.

**The Random House Book of Roses** *by Roger Phillips and Martyn Rix* (Random House, 1988). A comprehensive, full-color dictionary, covering more than 1,400 varieties. British. 224 pages, paperback, $25.00.

**Landscaping with Antique Roses** *by Liz Druitt and G. Michael Shoup* (Taylor, 1992). The hows and whys of integrating roses into an overall landscape. Recommendations for the use of over 80 old garden roses. 227 pages, hardcover, $34.95.

**The Encyclopedia of Roses** *by Judith C. McKeon* (Rodale, 1995). Based on American rose growing experience, this book profiles 175 roses both old and new. Emphasis on their use in the landscape. Organic methods. 192 pages, hardcover, $29.95.

**Rosa Rugosa** *by Suzanne Verrier* (Capability's, 1991). Northern gardeners with a special interest in ultra-cold-hardy roses will appreciate this well-written and appealing book. The author also has a companion volume called *Rosa Gallica*. 90 pages, paperback, $22.95.

**Easy-Care Roses** (Brooklyn Botanic Garden, 1995). An information-packed handbook providing solid how-tos and recommended varieties by growing zone. 112 pages, paperback, $6.95.

**Climbing Roses** *by Stephen Scanniello and Tanya Bayard* (Macmillan, 1994). Captivating descriptions of over 65 varieties, including history, cultural requirements, and suggestions for use in your landscape. 262 pages, hardcover, $30.00.

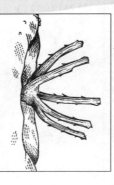

Illustrations by Don Fox, from *The NAtural Rose Gardener*

**HARDINESS.** Northern gardeners need to know the specifics about a rose's hardiness, in other words, exactly what zone it is hardy to. Southern gardeners must also watch to see what zones are recommended for each particular variety, as some roses perform very poorly in hot and/or humid weather. Read the catalogs carefully and, if possible, purchase your roses from a local or regional grower. They will be able to advise you from experience about how a particular variety will perform in your area.

**BLOOM TIME.** Many roses, especially the old-fashioned varieties, have just one flush of blooms per year. Will you be satisfied with a cloud of heavenly pink blossoms for three weeks in June, or do you need your rose to bloom all summer long? This consideration may narrow your choices very quickly.

**DISEASE RESISTANCE.** Hybrid teas are notoriously disease-prone, and seem to lure every insect pest from miles around. They can be difficult to grow without an arsenal of chemical dusts and sprays.

Selecting a disease-resistant rose is the single most effective way to avoid problems and the need for chemicals. You might start by considering some of the old rose varieties, many of which have natural disease resistance. You can also look to many of the modern roses, which are now being bred for improved disease resistance.

**STEM LENGTH.** This may seem like an odd consideration, but it's important if you are growing roses for cutting. The traditional florist rose is a hybrid tea, and it is the only type of rose that flowers on a long, stiff stem. All other roses have shorter, weaker stems, which gives them a more casual — some believe more beautiful — presence in a vase.

## Caring for Your Roses

Roses are rather particular, and you should be aware of the growing conditions and maintenance activities that make them happy.

**SITE.** For most abundant blooms and greatest vigor, roses need to receive 6 to 8 hours of direct sunlight each day. In hot climates, they will

When pruning hybrid tea roses, you should start by removing any damaged canes. Then remove any suckers coming up from below the bud union. (This is the swollen area on the main stem just above the soil line, where the named variety was grafted to a hardier, but less desirable root stock.)

Select the three to six healthiest canes that are evenly spaced around the plant. Remove all other canes.

rule, it's best to prune these roses in the spring, three to four weeks before the last frost.

All other varieties of roses should be thinned out to remove any old, damaged, or diseased canes, but their height should be reduced only if it is necessary for the plant's position in the landscape. These roses should be pruned to follow their natural tendency — arching, vase, or mounded. Be aware that spring pruning may remove the current season's buds, so any major reshaping is best done in midsummer, before the plant sets buds for the next season. Climbers should be trained to run as horizontally as possible to promote leaves and flowers along the entire length of the canes.

Reduce the height of the remaining canes by one-third to one-half. These final cuts should be angled cuts, cutting about 1/4 inch above an outward-facing bud. This will help develop an open, spreading habit. Grandifloras and miniatures should be treated similarly, though they should not be thinned as severely, and their height should be reduced by only 25 percent. As a general

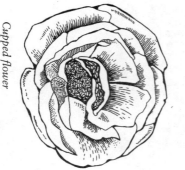

*Cupped flower*

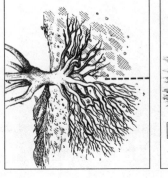

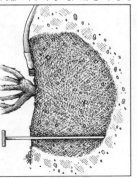

Don Fox, from *The Natural Rose Gardener* by Lance Walheim

*(Top) Good soil that is well mulched will encourage strong root growth; (Above) In poor soil, make a large, enriched root zone and be sure to water thoroughly.*

appreciate receiving protection from the most intense afternoon sun. In cool climates, a fence or a warm south- or west-facing wall can add enough extra warmth to boost flower production and reduce winter damage.

**SOILS.** Roses need good drainage and a rich, moisture-retentive soil, with a pH between 6.5 and 7. If your soil is heavy and wet, you may want to consider planting your roses in raised beds. Compost should be added to create a loose texture with a high organic content. For help correcting a pH imbalance, see "Building Healthy Soil."

**WATER.** Roses require more water than most other landscape plantings, especially during the first year as the plant is getting its roots established. The best way to water your roses is with drip irrigation. It concentrates the water at the root zone where it is needed, and keeps the foliage dry to minimize disease problems. A good, thick layer of organic mulch will help conserve moisture, reduce weeds, and encourage healthy root growth. As the mulch breaks down, it will increase the organic content of the soil.

**FERTILIZER.** Roses are heavy feeders, and will benefit from a steady supply of nitrogen, phosphorus, and potassium. You can provide these nutrients with either liquid or granular fertilizers, at a ratio of approxi-

## Web Sites

**The Rose Gardener's Usenet**
rec.garden.roses
*Visit this site to ask questions about roses. For a compilation of FAQs from this site, visit:* **The Rose Page**
http://www.rnc.edu/~nettles/rofaq/rofaq-top.html

**Yesterday's Rose**
http://www.halcyon.com/cirsium/rosegal/welcome.htm
*Information on old-fashioned, time-tested rose varieties. Includes care and culture, lots of links to other rose sites, extensive book reviews, and a rose finder service.*

**The American Rose Society Home Page**
http://ars.org
*Includes separate sections on different types of roses, with a glossary and links to suppliers. "Ask the Experts" has articles on various topics. Local rose societies are listed by region.*

**Chris & Cheryl Netter's Rose Garden**
http://www.h2net.net/p/cnetter/rose_tour/index.html
*Rose gardening information and links maintained by an avid rosarian in Colorado.*

**All America Rose Selections**
http://www.rose.org/
*Information about the AARS selections and where to find them. Rose gardening tips.*

**Baldo Villegas's Rose Page**
http://www.cris.com/~bugman/
*A rosarian from Sacramento, CA (whose garden contains over 600 roses!) You'll find information on rose societies, nurseries, and growing roses in Sacramento. Good diagnostic pest page.*

**The Canadian Rose Society**
http://www.ccn.cs.dal.ca/~aq448/CdnRoseSoc.html
*Hardy rose information and links.*

**CybeRose Garden**
http://www.geocities.com/RainForest/1978
*Photographs of roses and information about the author's rose breeding program.*

**The Rose Forum at Gardenweb**
http://www.gardenweb.com/forums/roses
*Post your own question and/or view answers to other questions of interest.*

**Heritage Rose Group**
http://www.ostawizn.com/hrg/hrghome.html
*Membership organization dedicated to the old roses. Lots of rose links.*

**Joe & Mindy's Rose Page**
http://www.nhn.ou.edu/~howard/roses.html
*Links and a list of recommended varieties.*

**The Olympia Rose Society**
http://www.cco.net/olyrose
*Maintained by the Washington State Rose Society. Information about selection, planting, and culture.*

**Roseraie at Bayfields**
http://www.midcoast.com/roseraie
*This nursery in Maine offers an online catalog, as well as general information about growing roses in cold climates.*

**The Virtual Rose**
http://www.divanet.com/vvrose/
*A short list of links to web pages maintained by rose enthusiasts.*

**The Heritage Rose Foundation**
http://www.h2net/p/cnetter/heritage/herit.htm

**Felco Pruners** have become the standard by which all other pruners are measured. The No. 2 model has been a favorite since 1940. It features a cushioned shock absorber to prevent wrist fatigue, and a non-corroding spring mechanism. Precision-ground, hardened steel blades with scissor-action provide smooth, clean cuts. All parts are replaceable.
#04-230 Felco No. 2 Pruner $44.95

Good rose **gloves** need to be supple enough to handle delicate blossoms, yet tough enough to protect your hands and arms from thorns. These are made of goatskin, and have up-to-the-elbow gauntlets. Available in women's sizes S, M, L, or XL.
#10-102 Rose Gloves $39.95

**A long-reach pruner** lets you cut roses without getting scratched. This one has razor-sharp steel blades that grip and hold the stem after it is cut. Contoured grips and lightweight aluminum shaft, 19" overall.
#14-115 Long Reach Cut N' Hold Pruner $27.50

**ROOTS Plus for Roses** is a 5-9-5 liquid fertilizer with added organic ingredients to help build the rich soil roses love. Use every 45 days for best results.
#07-286 ROOTS Plus for Roses, 32 oz $10.95

**Greensand** is an all-organic booster that supplies marine potash, silica, iron oxide, magnesia, lime, phosphoric acid, and 22 trace minerals. Prolongs bloom and loosens clay soils.
#07-207 Greensand, 5 lbs $4.95

**Rose Defense** is made from the oil of the neem seed. It wards off most pests, and helps protect plants from rust and powdery mildew. 16 oz. makes 16 gallons of spray.
#30-103 Rose Defense $16.95

Climbing roses need sturdy support. These **arbors** are made in England from powder-coated steel tubing. They have a flat black finish.
#30-222 Wall Arch (attaches to the side of a building) 7' H x 4' W x 18" D $99.95
#30-195 Rose Arch (gothic spire on top) 9'4" H x 41" W x 18" D $169.95

mately 5-8-5. In most cases, regular applications of compost, rotted manure, fish emulsion, and seaweed extracts will provide roses with all the nutrients they need. These organic amendments also help to moderate pH imbalances and stimulate beneficial soil life. Other organic amendments favored by rose growers include greensand, black rock phosphate, and alfalfa meal.

**PRUNING.** Dead, weak, and sickly stems can lead to disease problems. Pruning these away will increase air circulation to the center of the plant and minimize fungus problems. Pruning also stimulates new growth, and allows you to shape the plant in a pleasing manner. Spent flowers should be removed during the growing season to encourage reblooming. Use a scissor-action pruner for the cleanest cuts.

**WINTER PROTECTION.** If possible, select rose varieties that are hardy for your growing zone; ones that can survive the winter with no special protection. In cold climates, hybrid teas and floribundas, as well as some of the smaller shrub roses, will benefit from a little extra insulation. Once you have had several weeks of below-freezing temperatures, cover the

*Remove spent flowers throughout the growing season to encourage reblooming.*

Don Fox, from *The Natural Rose Gardener*

base of the rose with 12 inches of soil or mulch, and then cover the canes with straw, leaves, pine boughs, or even foam insulation. Climbers can be wrapped right on their supports, or you can lay them on the ground and cover the canes with straw or brush. In severely cold climates, hybrid teas are sometimes partially dug up, laid down onto the soil, and the entire plant is then covered with more soil or mulch.

**PESTS AND DISEASES.** Prevention is the best way to avoid pest and disease problems. Start with disease-resistant varieties, keep plants in healthy condition (well fertilized and well watered), maintain good air circulation, keep foliage dry, and remove any diseased foliage or spent flowers.

For persistent pest problems, you can use botanical insecticides such as sabadilla, neem, rotenone, and pyrethrins. These are broad-spectrum controls, meaning they kill many types of pests, both good and bad. Though they are organic, these controls are potent and should be used sparingly. For caterpillars and Japanese beetle grubs, use Bt (*Bacillus thuringiensis*) or milky spore (*Bacillus popilliae*). Insecticidal soaps are effective against scale, spider mites, and aphids. Horticultural oil can be used to smother insects and their eggs. For more information on the agents see the chapter, "Pest and Disease Control."

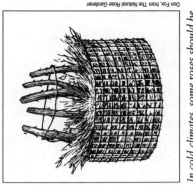

*In cold climates, some roses should be mulched with a thick layer of leaves or straw. Do not mulch until the ground begins to freeze.*

# Resources

## ORGANIZATIONS FOR ROSE GARDENERS

**The Heritage Rose Foundation**
1512 Gorman Street
Raleigh, NC 27606
919-834-2591
*Quarterly publication is The Heritage Rose Foundation Newsletter. Membership and newsletter dues are $10/year.*

**The Combined Rose List**
c/o Peter Schneider
P.O. Box 677
Mantua, OH 44255
*Annually updated list of old garden roses and where to find them. $18.00 includes shipping.*

**The American Rose Society**
P.O. Box 30,000
Shreveport, LA 71130-0030
318-939-5402
fax: 318-938-5405
*Publication is The American Rose Magazine. The Society also offers a hardcover listing of all registered roses, which is updated every few years. Membership, which includes a subscription to the magazine, is $32/year.*

**The Texas Rose Rustlers**
5020 Fairvent
Pasadena, TX 77505
*Quarterly publication is The Old Texas Rose. Membership is $7/year.*

**The Canadian Rose Society**
10 Fairfax Crescent
Scarborough, Ontario
M1L 1Z8
416-757-8809
*Membership is $18/year.*

## ROSE SUPPLIERS

**Antique Rose Emporium**
Route 5, Box 143
Brenham, TX 77833
800-441-0002

**Pickering Nurseries**
670 Kingston Road
Pickering, Ontario L1V 1A6
Canada
905-839-2111

**Heritage Rose Gardens**
16831 Mitchell Creek Drive
Fort Bragg, CA 95437
707-964-3748

**Heritage Rosarium**
211 Haviland Mill Road
Brookeville, MD 20833
301-774-2806

**High Country Rosarium**
1717 Downing at Park Avenue
Denver, CO 80218
303-832-4026

**Historical Roses**
1657 West Jackson Street
Painesville, OH 44077
216-357-7270

**Hortico**
723 Robson Road, RR 1
Waterdown, Ontario
L0R 2H1
Canada
416-689-6984

**Jackson & Perkins**
2518 South Pacific Highway
P.O. Box 1028
Medford, OR 97501
800-292-4769

**Lowe's Own Root Roses**
6 Sheffield Road
Nashua, NH 03062
603-888-2214

**Morden Nurseries, Ltd**
P.O. Box 1270
Morden, Manitoba 40G 1J0
204-822-3322

**Park Seed Company**
Cokesbury Road
Greenwood, SC 29647-0001
800-223-8555

**Royall River Roses**
70 New Gloucester Road
North Yarmouth, ME 04097
207-829-5830

**Roses of Yesterday & Today**
802 Brown's Valley Road
Watsonville, CA 95076

# annual flowers

A s popular as they are, annual flowers suffer from an identity crisis. Most gardeners love them for their beauty, yet relegate them to edgings along a driveway or foundation plantings next to the house. Others see annuals simply as a way to add quick color to a newly planted landscape, perhaps while perennials (in other words, the *real* garden plants) are getting established.

While it is true that most annuals are easy to grow and will bloom their heads off all season long with relatively little care, they deserve (and are starting to get) a closer look. From fast-growing flowering vines that can cover a trellis or screen to plants that are perfect for hanging baskets, window boxes, cutting gardens, and many other uses, annuals are a diverse group, and offer much more than simply "instant color" around the house. In this chapter we'll introduce you to many old favorites, plus a few varieties that may be unfamiliar, but well worth adding to your garden.

## What Are Annuals?

First, let's define what we mean by "annuals." Strictly speaking, an annual plant is one that completes its growing cycle (grows from seed, flowers, and produces seed) in the course of a single growing season. In other words, annuals pack a lot of living into a short span of time.

But beyond this simple definition, there is an even wider range of plants that we treat as annuals. Some, such as impatiens, heliotrope, and tuberous begonias, are actually tender or "half-hardy" perennials that grow poorly in cool weather and can't survive even a light frost. On the other hand, some annuals, such as pansies and ornamental cabbage, are extremely cold-hardy and can withstand freezing temperatures quite well.

One of the best things about annuals is their incredible diversity and versatility. Using them allows you to compose really exciting combinations of color, form, and texture that will last all season long. Colors range from bright midsummer favorites such as marigolds and Mexican sunflowers, to the subtler pastel shades of impatiens or lavatera.

## *Guest Expert*
## Kelly Sweeney

Annuals are holding their heads high in the garden these days. They are gaining momentum as an important plant group for any garden. This recognition is well deserved. Annuals are very easy to grow, and their many forms and heights are suitable for all types of gardening, from container to bedding to topiary.

With interest high in annuals, more and more varieties are being found, tried, and made available commercially. In the pursuit of the unusual, a trend seems to be emerging; the word "annuals" is undergoing a transformation in definition, from a plant group that goes from seed to seed in one growing season, to a plant group that is grown in one's yard for just one growing season. In other words, anything can be grown and treated as an annual!

This new interpretation is opening doors to a new look in annual gardens. Here at Basin Harbor Club in northwestern Vermont, we are using all sorts of plant groups, especially tender perennials, and even tropicals. In the tender perennial category we are growing many wonderful varieties of salvia, from *Salvia patens* to *Salvia greggii* to 'Indigo spires'. Or why not try *Monarda punctata*, otherwise known as horsemint? In the tropical group we are using *Mandevilla* vines on fences and *Pilea* (a creeping ground cover) in the shade, and spider plants make great bedding plants. All of these, along with many other wonderful plants-with-potential, can be found through nurseries, garden centers, and mail-order catalogs.

*Kelly Sweeney is head gardener at the Basin Harbor Club in Vergennes, Vermont.*

## *Favorite Books*

**Annuals for Connoisseurs: Classics and Novelties from Abelmoschus to Zinnia** by *Wayne Winterrowd* (Prentice Hall, 1992). Winterrowd considers annuals an "unexplored dominion," and his book does a terrific job of reintroducing them to gardeners. Over 70 plant portraits include many old favorites such as foxgloves and sunflowers, as well as lesser-known annuals. Well-written, with beautiful color photographs. Highly recommended. 224 pages, paperback, $16.00.

**Annuals and Bulbs** by *Rob Proctor and Nancy J. Ondra* (Rodale Press, 1995). Part of Rodale's Successful Organic Gardening series, this volume offers easy-to-use growing information. Bulbs are in a separate section which covers hardy bulbs as well as "annuals" like canna and gladiolus. 160 pages, paperback, $14.95.

**Annuals** by *Peter Loewer* (Meredith Books, 1994). Another excellent volume in the Better Homes and Gardens Step-by-Step Successful Gardening series. Lots of good advice on designing an annual garden, plus step-by-step photos and growing information. The color-coded encyclopedia of annuals is concise and useful. 132 pages, hardcover, $16.95.

## Shade-Tolerant Annuals

| COMMON NAME | Botanical Name | Height | Hardiness* |
|---|---|---|---|
| Ageratum | Ageratum houstonianum | 4–8" | half-hardy |
| Balsam | Impatiens balsamina | 1–3' | tender |
| Begonia, tuberous | Begonia x tuberhybrida | 8–10" | tender |
| Browallia | Browallia speciosa | 10–15" | hardy |
| Coleus | Coleus x hybridus | 10–24" | tender |
| Flowering tobacco | Nicotiana alata | to 5' | half-hardy |
| Forget-me-not | Myosotis sylvatica | 8–24" | hardy |
| Impatiens | Impatiens wallerana | 6–18" | tender |
| Lobelia | Lobelia erinus | 3–5" | half-hardy |
| Monkey flower | Mimulus spp. | 6–8" | half-hardy |
| Pansy | Viola spp. | 4–8" | hardy |
| Sweet alyssum | Lobularia maritima | 3–5" | hardy |
| Wishbone flower | Torenia spp. | 8–12" | half-hardy |

* Hardy means the plant will tolerate some frost; half-hardy means it will tolerate cool weather and may survive a light frost; tender means the plant is cold-sensitive and will not survive temperatures below 32°F.

You can also select annuals for your garden based on characteristics other than flower color. There are annuals that are tall, medium, short, or climbing; ones that prefer either full sun or partial shade; and those with special virtues, such as delightful fragrance (stock, mignonette, nicotiana) or attractive foliage (caladium, coleus, dusty miller).

## Perennials Grown as Annuals

A tender perennial is one that won't survive the winter in your climate without some sort of protection or special care. Many gardeners simply treat these plants as annuals, enjoying them for one season and letting them die in the fall. Other people move plants inside at the onset of cold weather: treating them as houseplants over the winter; taking cuttings and starting new plants (see box on facing page); or simply digging up and storing part of the plant (usually the roots or bulblike structures) indoors for replanting the following year.

Examples of perennials that are commonly grown as annuals include the more tender flowering sages (*Salvia coccinea, S. patens, S. splendens*, etc.), verbenas, and hyssop (*Agastache* spp.). Geraniums and scented geraniums (*Pelargonium* spp.) can be grown outdoors either in beds or pots during the summer, then brought indoors at the end of the season: to bloom in pots, to store in darkness for replanting, or to use as cuttings for new plants. Petunias, nicotiana, and sweet-alyssum (*Lobularia maritima*) are other plants that can be overwintered in pots and replanted the following year.

If you have a sunspace or attached greenhouse that receives plenty of winter sunlight and doesn't get too cold at night, you might try growing some of the interesting "annuals" that in their native habitats are actually perennial shrubs and trees. Fuchsias are typically seen growing as annuals in hanging baskets in northern climates, but if given some year-round protection the numerous species and hybrids grow rapidly, reaching anywhere from 18 inches to 12 feet or more, and producing their beautiful pendulous blossoms in shades of red, purple, and white nearly all winter long. Brugmansia, or angel's-trumpet, is another plant that can grow quite tall, to 15 feet, in greenhouse cultivation. Its

## How to Start Plants from Cuttings

Late summer or early fall is an ideal time to take cuttings from annuals such as geraniums, coleus, and impatiens, potting them up for winter bloom indoors or to hold them over for the following spring. The following steps will help ensure success.

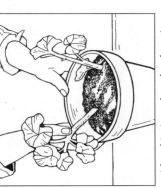

**1.** Clip off any flowers or flower buds on the plant. This is done to focus the plant's energy into developing new roots on the stem cutting.

**2.** Select healthy stem cuttings (preferably healthy growing tips or side shoots) that are 2 to 6 inches long. Strip off any bottom leaves where

the stem will be inserted in the rooting medium (either potting soil or water). Dip the cut end of the stem into a rooting hormone powder to encourage rapid root growth.

**3.** Insert the cutting in potting soil (*not* a soilless seed-starting mix) and

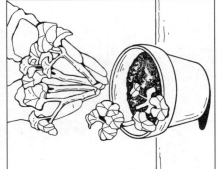

water the container. Cover the flat or pot with a clear plastic bag to create a moist, humid atmosphere. Don't let the plant leaves touch the side of the bag, since this will cause rot.

**4.** New roots should develop in one to three weeks. To test, gently tug on the cutting. Pot up the new plants in 4- to 6-inch containers and keep out of direct sunlight for three days.

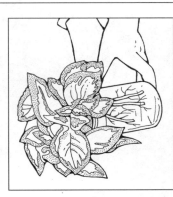

After this time, place the plants in a sunny location.

**5.** An alternative method of rooting plants such as begonias, coleus, or geraniums is to place the stem cuttings in a glass of water to develop

roots. Change the water every few days until plants develop roots, and add a little soil to the jar after new roots appear. Plant rooted cuttings in 4- to 6-inch containers filled with potting soil.

**6.** Once the new plant is well established, pinch off the stem tip to encourage fuller growth and more abundant flowers.

trumpet-shaped flowers are very fragrant and beautiful, but don't grow it in the house if you have small children, since the plants are extremely poisonous.

Flowering plants that grow from tender bulbs, such as dahlias, gladioluses, and cannas, are often planted as annual flowers in cutting gardens or mixed ornamental borders. They, too, are tender perennials, and won't survive the winter outdoors in most of North America. Exceptions include some of the hardier species forms and hybrids, such as the hardy glad (*Gladiolus byzantina*), which is hardy to Zone 5, and the Colville glad (*Gladiolus x colvillei*), hardy to Zone 7. However, it's easy to dig up these bulbs at the end of the growing season and store them indoors for replanting the following year (see the "Bulbs" chapter).

## Starting Annuals from Seed

Seeing all the annuals offered for sale at nurseries and garden centers in the spring, you might wonder who would go to all the trouble of starting their own annuals from seed. There is an economic advantage, of course. A $2.00 packet of seeds might grow four large flats of alyssum plants, which would be a savings of roughly $70.00 over buying the plants from a nursery.

An equally compelling reason for starting your own plants from seed is that even the best garden centers don't carry the full selection of worthy garden annuals. Most sell the popular bedding plants — marigolds, geraniums, petunias, pansies, impatiens, and the like — but when was the last time you saw old-fashioned annuals for sale there, such as love-lies-bleeding (*Amaranthus caudatus*), four o'clocks (*Mirabilis jalapa*), or lavatera (*Lavatera trimestris*)?

Part of the reason for this absence stems from economics (supply and demand) and part is due to the nature of the plants themselves. Garden centers like to sell six-packs of plants that are already in bloom; that way customers know what they're getting, and know that the plants will probably continue blooming after they get them home and in the ground. Instant gratification.

Yet many fine annuals won't start blooming in nursery six-packs. They're either too tall, don't like to be transplanted, or just won't flower until they have been in the ground for a couple of weeks. If you want to experiment with the whole palette of annuals, eventually you will want to grow some of your own plants from seed. The mail-order companies listed on p. 168 are good sources for seeds and information.

Many annuals are easy to seed directly into garden soil. Others are best started indoors under lights in late winter or early spring. Consult seed catalogs, seed packets, or the book *From Seed to Bloom* (see page 35) for information on specific plants. Generally speaking, annuals fall into three main categories, which determine when and where you should sow their seeds. For all categories, a good rule of thumb is to plant seeds at a depth of two or three times their diameter.

## Heat- and Drought-Tolerant Annuals

| COMMON NAME | Botanical Name | Height | Hardiness |
|---|---|---|---|
| Calliopsis | *Coreopsis tinctoria* | 8–36" | half-hardy |
| Cape marigold | *Dimorphotheca pluvialis* | 4–16" | half-hardy |
| Celosia, cockscomb | *Celosia argentea* | 1–4' | half-hardy |
| Globe amaranth | *Gomphrena globosa* | 9–30" | half-hardy |
| Madagascar periwinkle | *Catharanthus roseus* | 4–12" | half-hardy |
| Mexican sunflower | *Tithonia rotundifolia* | 4–5' | tender |
| Moss rose | *Portulaca grandiflora* | 4–6" | tender |
| Spider flower | *Cleome hasslerana* | to 4' | half-hardy |
| Spurge | *Euphorbia* spp. | 2–3' | tender |
| Statice | *Limonium sinuatum* | 1–3' | half-hardy |
| Stock | *Matthiola incana* | 1–2' | half-hardy |
| Strawflower | *Helichrysum bracteatum* | 1–3' | hardy |
| Sunflower | *Helianthus* spp. | 1–15' | tender |

**HARDY ANNUALS.** Can be direct-sown in the garden as early in the spring as the soil can be worked. For an earlier start, sow them indoors in flats 8 to 10 weeks before the last spring frost date, and transplant them to the garden about a month later, after hardening them off.

Some hardy annuals can also be direct-seeded in the fall, and these plants will flower much earlier than plants seeded in the spring. When fall seeding, plant the seeds a bit deeper than you would in the spring, and spread some mulch over the seedbed after the ground has frozen.

Examples of hardy annuals include bachelor's-buttons, calendula, spider flower (*Cleome hasslerana*), pinks (*Dianthus* spp.), larkspur, linaria, Shirley poppies (*Papaver rhoeas*), nigella (love-in-a-mist), scabiosa (pincushion flower), snapdragons, lavatera, annual baby's-breath (*Gypsophila elegans*), heliotrope, stocks, and sweet peas.

**HALF-HARDY ANNUALS.** Can be direct-sown outdoors after the threat of hard frost (temperatures below 25°F) is past. Indoors, start seeds in flats 6 to 8 weeks before the last spring frost date, and harden off the plants before transplanting them to the garden. Once they have hardened off, half-hardy annuals can withstand a light frost.

Examples include statice, nicotiana, painted-tongue (*Salpiglossis sinuata*), China aster (*Callistephus chinensis*), and various types of salvias and chrysanthemums.

**TENDER ANNUALS.** Seed can be sown directly in the garden only after all danger of frost is past. For an earlier start, sow seed indoors 4 to 6 weeks before the last spring frost date for your area. Examples include marigolds, morning glories, zinnias, sunflowers and tithonia (Mexican sunflower), cosmos, amaranth, ageratum, celosia, and gomphrena (globe amaranth).

# Other Good Books

**Annuals: A Gardener's Guide**
*ed. Rob Proctor* (Brooklyn Botanic Garden, 1992).
This book contains chapters from different authors on the many uses of annuals, including as container plants, cut flowers, and bird or butterfly plants. There's an emphasis on the old-fashioned beauty and appeal of annual flowers. 96 pages, paperback, $7.95.

**The Harrowsmith Annual Garden** *by Jennifer Bennett and Turid Forsyth* (Camden House, 1990).
Excellent information and color photos; plants are divided into nine separate chapters based on characteristics important to gardeners: height, climbing habit, sun/shade, scented flowers, and types for cutting. Recommended especially for Northern gardeners. 176 pages, paperback, $19.95.

**The 100 Best Annuals: A Practical Encyclopedia** *by Elvin McDonald* (Random House, 1995).
Extremely slim on text, this book is valuable for its inspirational color photos. 112 pages, paperback, $14.00.

Some annuals are so good at fulfilling their mission in life — flowering and setting seeds — that they will self-sow readily under the right conditions and produce brand-new plants the following year. Common annuals that can self-sow vigorously include ageratum, petunia, foxglove, annual larkspur, forget-me-not, calendula, and wild or striped mallow (*Malva sylvestris*).

## Soil Preparation and Planting

Before transplanting annuals to the garden, or direct-sowing seeds there, it's a good idea to prepare the soil. In general, annuals prefer well-drained soil with a pH between 6.3 and 6.7. Digging in a good quantity of peat moss or compost will help to build up the soil's organic matter and allow the plants' roots to spread quickly and get off to a good start.

Set out young plants at the recommended spacing, to prevent them from crowding each other once they have grown and matured. If you've purchased plants in flats from a garden center, the plants will likely be somewhat potbound when you remove them from their cells or containers. Before placing them in the planting hole, gently break apart the root mass; this encourages roots to spread quickly into the surrounding soil. Fertilize at planting time with an organic or slow-release fertilizer (see "Garden Gear," page 170).

You need to pay attention to whether a particular plant is hardy, half-hardy, or tender before deciding when to purchase and transplant it. Some nurseries sell plants with labels that identify hardiness; when in doubt, put your annuals out after all danger of frost has passed. Another crucial factor, of course, is whether a particular plant prefers sun or partial shade. For a list of some shade-tolerant annuals, see the table on page 162.

If you need to hold plants in flats for more than a couple of days at home, be sure to water them and keep them in a partly shady, protected spot like a porch or under a tree. Don't leave them in a garage or other structure where you store cars or gasoline-powered machines, since ethylene gas can cause flower damage and leaf drop. The best advice is to transplant annuals to the garden as soon as possible after bringing them home.

## Growing and Care of Annuals

Once they start blooming, most annuals will flower all season long, until cold temperatures or frost put an end to their display. However, to keep them flowering and looking good, you will need to perform some simple but easy maintenance.

Deadheading is the most important task, and it involves pinching off old flowers just as they begin to fade. The reason for doing this is simple. Annuals live to flower quickly, produce seed, and die. So long as you keep deadheading blossoms, the plants will continue to produce flowers; once you stop, the plants will reduce or stop flowering, and put their energy into maturing seeds. Some people find deadheading an annoying task, but good gardeners understand its importance and enjoy

taking a walk every day or two through the garden. Pinching off spent blooms is quick and easy, and it ensures season-long bloom.

If you've fertilized at planting time as recommended with an organic or slow-release fertilizer, you shouldn't have to fertilize annuals again during the season. With annuals, the flowers are the thing, and overfertilizing can lead to lush foliage growth, which is really beside the point. The primary exception is container-grown plants, which usually need to be fertilized every couple of weeks to maintain a colorful show.

Annuals have small, shallow root systems and so require a regular supply of water. Avoid overhead watering if possible, which can stain some types of flowers (such as petunias), and make them look unattractive. It also can contribute to a buildup of botrytis fungus, which can affect plants such as zinnias, geraniums, and marigolds. Use a soaker hose or other drip irrigation system, or direct your watering can right at soil level.

## Designing with Annuals

Since they only stay in the garden for one season, annuals offer maximum flexibility. If you don't like the effect you've created one year, you can simply chalk it up to experience and try again next year, without having to move plants around as you would with perennial plants.

The most popular and widely grown annuals are used as bedding plants — combinations of brightly colored flowers and foliage plants in a bed that is accessible from all sides for visibility and ease of maintenance. Such formal plantings can be especially effective if you plant a solid block of color, putting in plants of the same variety and color. Separated by neat strips of lawn, such single-color plantings lend a nice formal effect to the garden. An even more impressive sight is a massed single-color planting divided down the center by a band composed of a flower that has a different, but complementary, color or growing habit. For instance, a dark, vivid color, like the bluish purple flowers of border lobelia (*Lobelia erinus*) might combine well with the white flower mounds of sweet alyssum (*Lobularia maritima*). Both plants are tender perennials grown as annuals, and both are similar in growing habit — low, mounding, and normally used for edging beds.

Annuals work equally well in less formal designs, and they fill an important role by giving you a brilliant palette of color with which to work. They can be inserted into

| **Favorite Cottage Garden Annuals** | |
|---|---|
| **COMMON NAME** | **Botanical Name** |
| Bachelor's-button | *Centaurea cyanus* |
| Bishop's weed; false Queen Anne's lace | *Ammi majus* |
| Cosmos | *Cosmos bipinnatus* |
| Four-o'clock | *Mirabilis jalapa* |
| Godetia | *Clarkia amoena* |
| Larkspur | *Consolida ambigua* |
| Love-in-a-mist | *Nigella damascena* |
| Love-lies-bleeding; tassel flower | *Amaranthus caudatus* |
| Nasturtium | *Tropaeolum majus* |
| Pot-marigold | *Calendula officinalis* |
| Shirley poppy | *Papaver rhoeas* |
| Snapdragon | *Antirrhinum majus* |
| Spider flower | *Cleome hasslerana* |

# Suppliers

## MAIL-ORDER SEED COMPANIES

**Abundant Life Seed Foundation**
P.O. Box 772
Port Townsend, WA 98368
360-385-5660

**W. Atlee Burpee & Co.**
300 Park Ave.
Warminster, PA 18974
215-674-4900
*Large selection.*

**Butchart Gardens Ltd.**
Box 4010, Station A
Victoria, BC, Canada
V8X 3X4
604-652-4422
*Catalog $1.*

**Comstock, Ferre & Co.**
P.O. Box 125
Wethersfield, CT 06109
203-529-3319 *Catalog $3.*

**The Cook's Garden**
P.O. Box 535
Londonderry, VT 05148
800-457-9703
*Nice selection of cutting garden flowers; catalog $1.*

**William Dam Seeds**
P.O. Box 8400
Dundas, ON, Canada
L9H 6M1
800-247-5864
*Catalog $2.*

**DeGiorgi Seed Co.**
6011 "N" St.
Omaha, NE 68117-1634
800-858-2580
*Catalog $2.*

**Ferry-Morse Seeds**
P.O. Box 488
Fulton, KY 42041-0488
800-283-3400

**Flowery Branch Seed Co.**
P.O. Box 1330
Flowery Branch, GA 30542
404-536-8380
*Catalog $4.*

**Harris Seeds**
P.O. Box 22960
Rochester, NY 14692-2960
716-442-0100

**Heirloom Garden Seeds**
P.O. Box 138
Guerneville, CA 95446
*Catalog $2.50.*

**Johnny's Selected Seeds**
Foss Hill Rd.
Albion, ME 04910-9731
207-437-9294
*Wide selection; specializes in flowers for cutting.*

**J.W. Jung Seed Co.**
335 South High St.
Randolph, WI 53957-0001
800-684-9310
*Outstanding selection of old-fashioned flowers; catalog $2.*

**Nichols Garden Nursery**
1190 North Pacific Hwy. NE
Albany, OR 97321-4580
541-928-9280

**Geo. W. Park Seed Co.**
Cokesbury Rd.
Greenwood, SC 29647
864-223-7333

**Pinetree Garden Seeds**
Box 300
New Gloucester, ME 04260
207-926-3400
*Interesting varieties sold in small, inexpensive seed packets.*

**Seeds Blüm**
HC 33, Idaho City Stage
Boise, ID 83706
800-528-3658
*Great selection and information; organized by plant height; catalog $3.*

**Seeds of Change**
P.O. Box 15700
Santa Fe, NM 87506-5700
888-762-7333
*Beautiful catalog; terrific variety of sunflowers, marigolds, and more.*

**Select Seeds Antique Flowers**
180 Stickney Hill Rd.
Union, CT 06076-4617
860-684-9310
*Outstanding selection of old-fashioned flowers; catalog $2.*

**Shepherd's Garden Seeds**
30 Irene St.
Torrington, CT 06790
203-482-3638
*Catalog $1.*

**R.H. Shumway Seedsman**
P.O. Box 1
Graniteville, SC 29829
803-663-9771
*Great old-timey catalog.*

**Stokes Seeds**
Box 548
Buffalo, NY 14240-0548
716-695-6980
*Broad selection (over 200 petunias!). Excellent germination information for each variety.*

**Territorial Seed Co.**
Cottage Grove, OR 97424
541-942-9547
*Offers a nice variety of sweet peas and sunflowers, as well as other annuals.*

**Thompson & Morgan Inc.**
Box 1308
Jackson, NJ 08527-0308
800-274-7333
*All the newest varieties and classic favorites direct from England.*

open spots between and around perennials and flowering shrubs. Adding annuals to a perennial border can bolster the effect of the whole, ensuring a continuity of color and interest even when the perennials are not in bloom. They are great for creating rhythmic splashes of color, for linking different parts of the garden together, and for helping to carry a particular color theme through the garden during the entire growing season.

Some of the best annuals for mixed border plantings include tall species such as nicotiana (flowering tobacco), cleome (spider flower), lavatera, Shirley poppies, foxglove, matricaria, or the vibrant orange Mexican sunflower (*Tithonia rotundifolia*). For color at the front of the

## Flowering Annual Vines

| COMMON NAME | Botanical Name | Height | Hardiness |
| --- | --- | --- | --- |
| Black-eyed Susan vine | *Thunbergia alata* | to 8' | tender |
| Canary creeper | *Tropaeolum peregrinum* | 6–15' | tender |
| Cardinal climber | *Ipomoea x multifida* | to 20' | tender |
| Cathedral bells | *Cobaea scandens* | 10–15' | hardy |
| Chilean glory vine | *Eccremocarpus scaber* | 6–12' | tender |
| Glory lily | *Gloriosa superba* | 3–8' | tender |
| Hyacinth bean | *Dolichos lablab* | 10–15' | tender |
| Moonflower | *Ipomoea alba* | 10–20' | tender |
| Morning glory | *Ipomoea* spp. | 10–20' | tender |
| Scarlet runner bean | *Phaseolus coccineus* | 6–18' | tender |
| Sweet pea | *Lathyrus odorata* | 4–6' | hardy |

border, try planting low-growing annuals like impatiens or sweet alyssum.

With all their different heights, colors, and forms, it's entirely possible to plant a spectacular border composed of annuals alone. Since most annuals flower at the same time, and over an extended season, you may want to choose varieties that will complement each other. You can strive to create a particular color scheme (pink, blue, and white; yellow, blue, and orange), or simply go for a full-blown riot of color. One way to create a more interesting and designerly effect is to include annuals that are grown for their attractive foliage, which can act as a foil for the bright blooms of other plants. The silver foliage of dusty miller (*Senecio cineraria*) is an old standby in the annual garden, but there are lots of other, lesser-known foliage plants as well, including cannas, which have tropical-looking, sometimes bronzed leaves; plectranthus, with its soft, silvery leaves; and perilla (*Perilla frutescens*), a beautiful herb whose dark purple, fringed leaves particularly set off white and pink-purple flowers like petunias.

Climbing annuals are another good choice, especially for cottage garden settings and containers (window boxes, hanging baskets, etc.). They have an old-fashioned, informal quality and will create a colorful living tapestry on fences, screens, trellises, or other supports. Plenty of people grow morning glories (*Ipomoea purpurea* and *I. tricolor*) and its close relatives, moonflower (*I. alba*) and cardinal climber (*I. x multifida*). But that scarcely scratches the surface of great climbers. For a list of other wonderful vining annuals, see the table above.

## Growing Annuals in Containers

The perfect choice for growing in containers, annuals work well either alone or in combined plantings. Be imaginative when selecting contain-

# Garden Gear

Gardener's Supply's **Organic Flower Fertilizer** (5-7-4) is made from all natural materials that are easy to use and virtually odorless. High in phosphorus, it promotes abundant, longer-lasting blooms. Excellent for both annuals and perennials.

Apply 5 lbs. per 200 sq. ft.
#07-316 Flower Fertilizer, 5 lbs. $5.95

vide uncompromising support to keep stems straight. 34" legs anchor grids firmly in place. A dark green epoxy coating protects the sturdy, galvanized steel wire. 24" L x 18" W x 34" H.
#30-106 Super Grow-Thru Grids, set of 2 $19.95

These rectangular grids are great for mass plantings and cutting gardens. The large, 5¾" x 4½" openings let many stems grow up through, yet pro-

With this **Annual Vines Seed Collection** from The Cook's Garden, you can enjoy the beauty of fastgrowing flowering vines that will ramble along a fence, up a trellis, or up and over the front porch. Some of these plants are edible, some fragrant, and all of them are beautiful. The collection includes one packet each of hyacinth bean (*Dolichos lablab*); 'Heavenly Blue' morning glory; 'Early Call' morning glory; moonflower (*Ipomoea alba*); 'Mammoth Mix' sweet pea; canary creeper or climbing nasturtium (*Tropaeolum peregrinum*); and cathedral-bells or

cup-and-saucer vine (*Cobaea scandens*).
Seven packets, $11.00. Available from The Cook's Garden (product #720); 800-457-9703.

This expandable **Bamboo Lattice** is great for climbing plants. The natural bamboo canes are attached with metal rivets so the lattice can be stretched to the size you need — from a 4' x 6' trellis to a narrow 2' x 116" fence.
#14-224 Bamboo Lattice $19.95

ers, and if you have the room and the resources, don't just stick to the tried-and-true terra-cotta pots. Windowboxes are designed for annuals, especially ones that cascade over their sides. The same holds true for hanging containers, where trailing varieties such as the old-fashioned nasturtium 'Empress of India' hang down and make a pretty display.

Impatiens are particularly beautiful when planted in a container set in filtered shade. Most commonly you'll see them planted in the round, usually in a large container like a half whiskey barrel. To set your display apart, try experimenting with something a little different. An old soapstone sink would make an excellent bed for impatiens or other colorful annuals, as would a planter you've either bought or made from hypertufa (a kind of artificial stone). Brown fiber pots and planters are widely available, and will last for several seasons. They're also light (at least when empty) and easy to move.

When planting in containers, make sure that you allow for adequate drainage. If the pot or container doesn't have drainage holes, either insert a smaller container that does inside of it, or cover the bot-

tom with a layer of small stones or Styrofoam peanuts (a terrific way to recycle them).

Like other plants grown in containers, annuals will require regular watering and fertilization throughout the growing season. In addition, you'll also have to deadhead spent blossoms. During hot, dry weather, your plants may need watering once or even twice a day. Certain plants like moss rose (*Portulaca grandiflora*) and calliopsis (*Coreopsis tinctoria*) prefer somewhat dry soil and hot, sunny weather. Other annuals recommended for hot, dry conditions can be found in the table on page 165.

Cover pots of tender annuals to protect them from early frosts. Warm fall days often follow the first frosts, so it pays to prolong the season this way. However, once cool weather becomes the norm and frost kills off your plants, remove them from their pots and clean the containers before storage with soap and water or a dilute bleach solution, to get them ready for next year.

## Wintering Annuals Indoors

The end of the growing season doesn't necessarily mean the end of your annuals. Tender perennial plants already growing in containers can be cut back around the end of summer and brought indoors, while bedding plants such as petunias, impatiens, lantana, and geraniums can be potted up and treated to a prolonged season of bloom inside.

Before bringing these plants indoors, check them for insect or disease problems and either treat them or discard if you find any. Cut back the plants by 4 to 6 inches, and place the pots in a room that gets a lot of light. An add-on greenhouse or sunspace is ideal, but so are sunny windows with a west or south exposure. After cutting back the plants, give them a dose of liquid plant food and they should soon start to develop new leaves and flowers.

Keep a close eye on any plants you bring indoors, at least for the first couple of weeks. The shock of being moved inside makes plants very vulnerable until they become acclimated to their new growing conditions. Pamper your plants as much as you can at this time to ease their transition to indoor life.

Some plants can be dug up in the fall, pruned way back, and stored in a cool, dark place until early spring. This includes most of the tender perennials, such as brugmansia, datura, and geraniums. Water plants sparingly during this time.

Another strategy for overwintering plants is to take cuttings in the summer or early fall and start new plants from your old annuals. This technique works particularly well with coleus, plectranthus, and licorice plant (*Helichrysum petiolare*). For instructions see "How to Start Plants from Cuttings" on page 163.

## Web Sites

**Garden Web Annuals Forum**
http://www.gardenweb.com/forums/annuals
*This ongoing forum allows you to post questions concerning any aspect of gardening with annuals, including how to grow certain flowers, recommended varieties, sources for plants, etc. Or, you can respond to any of the questions already posted. Quite an active site, with intelligent, useful responses from many online gardeners.*

**Plant World**
http://www.plantworld.com/library
*An incredibly rich and well-designed garden site in general, the library section of Plant World contains lots of tips and charts on annuals, plus articles from various agricultural extension programs around the country. Extremely useful.*

**White Flower Farm Annuals Index**
http://www.whiteflowerfarm.com/wffweb/library/pandc/annuals
*Concise cultural information on some of the most popular annuals, plus a key word search engine for locating specific references.*

# flowers for cutting

A flower garden in full bloom, with an artful combination of color, form, and texture, is a masterful achievement and a delight to behold. But cut flowers, artistically arranged in a vase, can be an equally thrilling artistic creation. Cut flowers give us a never-ending opportunity to experiment with colors, forms, and textures: the paintbox colors of orange tulips, blue hyacinths, and yellow forsythia branches; the various flower shapes found in a bouquet of cosmos, pinks, cleome, and oriental lilies; and the contrasting textures in an arrangement of foxgloves, ferns, hosta, lilacs, and tulips. When we bring flowers indoors and up close, we also get the chance to better appreciate the beauty of their satiny petals and fanciful blooms.

The experience of arranging cut flowers is, in itself, a joy — an opportunity for us to "paint" with the world's most beautiful palette. Add to this the satisfaction of sharing our floral creations with others, and it is easy to see why the florist business is booming, and cutting gardens are popping up in backyards throughout the country.

## Eclectic Flair

The trend in flower arrangements today is toward an informal, natural look with an eclectic blend of different plant materials. Florists and amateur flower arrangers are combining pussy willows, forsythia branches, evergreen boughs, rhubarb leaves, and Queen Anne's lace with French tulips, delphiniums, peonies, and roses. It seems like the more variety of plant material and the more unusual it is, the better.

As gardeners, most of us have the luxury of choosing from a wide assortment of shrubs, perennials, annuals, bulbs, and wildflowers,

Though it's hard to compete with the simple beauty of a huge bouquet of white peonies, what makes today's eclectic approach to flower arranging so much fun is the opportunity to be really creative with color, texture, and form.

## Guest Expert
## Lynn Byczynski

Growing any flowers is good for the soul, but growing a garden of cutting flowers has an added benefit: You share the beauty and wonder of your garden with family, friends, and co-workers when you bring a bouquet indoors.

The secret to having beautiful flower arrangements from the garden all season long is to plant several no-fail varieties for each month of the season, then supplement with material from whatever perennials, shrubs, grasses, or trees are looking good. Among the best flowers for early summer bouquets are larkspur, veronica, pastel yarrow, *Salvia horminum*, and snapdragons. These provide a good mixture of colors and shapes by themselves, but to create a spectacular design, look around your yard: perhaps you can cut a few branches from the pink Weigela along the driveway, honeysuckle from the fence, and Canterbury-bells from the perennial border. Now that's a bouquet with impact!

For midsummer bouquets, even a small cutting garden can supply armloads of brilliant annuals such as zinnias, sunflowers, salvia 'Victoria', Rudbeckia 'Indian Summer', statice sinuata, and ageratum 'Blue Horizon'. Add a brilliant lily or a few perennials such as platycodon or liatris, along with the greenery of a landscape shrub, and you have created an extravagant arrangement.

For late summer and early fall bouquets, seed zinnias and sunflowers in midsummer (6–8 weeks before your first frost). They'll start blooming right when some of the long-season plants you set out in spring hit their peak, including celosia, cosmos, gomphrena, salvia, and lisianthus. The golds, reds, and purples of fall are a perfect match for grasses and grains. And by month's end, some of your shrubs and trees will add even more fall color to your bouquets.

*Lynn Byczynski is the author of The Flower Farmer, and a market grower who lives in Lawrence, Kansas.*

## Favorite Books

**The Flower Farmer: An Organic Grower's Guide to Raising and Selling Cut Flowers** *by Lynn Byczynski* (Chelsea Green, 1997).

A clear-eyed, enjoyable read for flower-lovers. Though oriented to small-scale cut flower farmers, serious backyard gardeners will find much that is useful in this book — from specific field-growing instructions to bloom times and conditioning requirements. Profiles of successful growers sprinkled throughout the book are terrific, as are the illustrations and color photographs. 224 pages, paperback, $24.95.

**Cutting Gardens** *by Anne Halpin and Betty Mackey* (Simon & Schuster, 1993).

A visually appealing, yet solid work, with lots of great material. Particularly useful features include a plant encyclopedia, a flower color guide, and sample plans for cutting gardens. 144 pages, hardcover, $27.50.

**Flowers Rediscovered** *by Tom Pritchard and Billy Jarecki* (Artisan, 1994).

A gorgeous feast for the eyes, this big color book stands head and shoulders above most books on flower arranging, with their sterile, stiff-looking photos. The authors, who run the Pure Mädderlake flower shop in New York City, take a refreshingly sane and celebratory approach to the subject. Not much text, but the photo captions are lively and informative. 232 pages, paperback, $24.95.

So what sorts of plant materials are fair game for cutting? Basically, any attractive plant that has stems that are long enough to fit the vases or other containers you plan to use. Florists are interested in flowers that have a good "vase life," which means they will look nice in a vase for at least five days. Home gardeners, though, should feel free to disregard this rule. If a flower gives you joy, even if it looks spectacular for only a day or two, that may be reason enough to use it.

Even the smallest flower garden will provide a few flowers for cutting. But if your dream is to have a bountiful supply of interesting blooms to cut and arrange, what you need is quantity, variety, and all-season availability.

## Conditioning and Arranging Flowers

The best time to cut flowers is either early morning or early evening — in other words, not during the heat of the day. The basic rules for conditioning flowers before arranging them are fairly straightforward:

1. Cut flowers at the proper time in their bloom cycle, not past their prime. Different flowers have different requirements, but many should be cut before the flowers open up (such as iris), or when only one flower on a long stem is beginning to open (such as gladiolus). For specific plants, check the A–Z encyclopedia in *The Flower Farmer* by Lynn Byczynski (see the "Favorite Books" section).

2. Get them into water fast. If you're picking a lot of flowers in the garden, take along a bucket that contains a few inches of tepid (not cold) water. After cutting, the stems of flowers can seal up quickly and prevent the uptake of water, so this step is crucial.

3. Place freshly cut flowers in a cool location out of direct sunlight and let them sit in the water for one or two hours before arranging.

4. Use clean containers, washed out with soap and water, rinsed, and then rinsed out again with a mild bleach solution.

5. Use a floral preservative in the vase water to prolong bloom.

6. Before arranging, recut flower stems at a 45-degree angle. Use a sharp knife or flower shears (not scissors) to avoid crushing the stems. Split stems of woody plants (like roses) 2 to 3 inches up from the bottom, and strip off the bark, to permit better water intake.

7. Remove all foliage that will sit below the water line in the vase, to prevent the growth of bacteria.

8. Check the water in arrangements daily and add more as needed, or change if the water doesn't look clean. Woody cuttings will generally take up more water than herbaceous flowers. Recut stems if necessary, removing up to ½ inch from the bottom.

## Quantity

Though you can usually find a wealth of interesting blooms in a perennial border, most gardeners find it unbearable to cut more than one or two blossoms. Each and every flower seems precious, and critical to the garden's overall look. There are two ways to deal with this. The first is to stay inside and let a friend do the cutting. The other is to plant a garden specifically for cut flowers.

In a cutting garden, flowers are grown for harvest. The plants are usually set out in rows or blocks, and are grouped by variety for easier maintenance. Though a cutting garden can be beautiful (think of the fields of lavender in France, the rows of tulips in Holland, or the blocks of color in a seed trial), its purpose is first and foremost utilitarian. In a cutting garden, you want to be able to harvest the best blooms, often before they're fully open, do your deadheading with a hedge shears, and pull out and reseed plants as needed to ensure a long season of choice cutting material.

Where do you put a cutting garden? Some gardeners integrate theirs right into the vegetable garden. Others create a separate plot, sometimes in an out-of-the-way location. Wherever it is sited, good soil, good air circulation, access to water, and a layout that allows for easy maintenance are essential. You should be spending your time cutting and arranging, not weeding, propping, and primping. Dying tulip foliage and headless lily stalks are the hallmark of a great cutting garden.

How big should your cutting garden be? The box on page 176 has a plant list for a 5-foot-by-12-foot cutting garden. This 60-square-foot area will accommodate about 90 plants — a bounty of blooms for cutting, which can be accented by the annuals, perennials, bulbs, shrubs, and wildflowers growing in the rest of your gardens. The biggest mistake people make when planting a cutting garden is to plant too many different varieties, too close together. If you are able to limit yourself to six or seven kinds of flowers, your cutting garden will be far easier to maintain and much more satisfying.

## Variety

The real fun, excitement, and creativity occurs when you have a wide variety of plant material at your disposal. Annual flowers are very popular with flower arrangers because they produce an abundance of blooms, are dependable performers, and reflower quickly after being cut. Good annuals for cutting include snapdragons, zinnias, cosmos, stock, larkspur, and feverfew. (See pages 176–177 for more ideas.) Many perennials are also grown specifically for cutting. Your cutting gardens might include a core of prolific and cuttable perennials such as Shasta daisies, asters, lady's-mantle, roses, rudbeckia, and phlox. Perennials also provide some of the most spectacular flowers for arrangements: peonies, delphinium, iris, columbine, shrub roses, astilbe, and mums.

Spring and summer bulbs are another excellent source of flowers for cutting. Tulips, daffodils, gladioluses, and lilies are dependable bloomers and long-lasting in a vase. Putting fifty or seventy-five tulip bulbs in your cutting garden will give you a wealth of blossoms for spring arrangements.

Savvy flower arrangers always include "filler" plants in their cutting gardens. These airy plants, such as the delicate flowers of baby's-breath, dill, bishop's weed (*Ammi majus*), and matricaria, and foliage plants such as euphorbia, artemisia, and coleus, help weave an arrangement into a cohesive whole. Shrubs, trees, ferns, ornamental grasses, herbs, and even vegetable foliage, though probably not a part of the cutting

## Other Good Books

**Jane Packer's New Flower Arranging** *by Jane Packer and Louise Simpson* (Trafalgar Square, 1996).
Great color photos of natural-looking arrangements. Offers good general information and around thirty specific projects, organized by season. 128 pages, paperback, $17.95.

**Dried Flowers** *by Martha E. Kraska* (Macmillan, 1995).
Part of the Burpee American Gardening Series, this slim volume represents a bargain for people interested in all aspects of cut flowers that are good for drying. Provides instructions on growing, drying, and designing, plus detailed plant portraits. 96 pages, paperback, $9.00.

## Forcing Blossoms of Woody Plants

Most flowering shrubs have a chilling requirement, which you can usually find listed in reference books. Some peaches, for example, need 200 hours at temperatures of 35°F or below before they can be forced to bloom. Although you can probably tell by looking at a branch whether it has buds on the old wood, there is no way to tell whether it has had a long enough dormancy. You can either wait until late winter (four to six weeks before the usual bloom time) to begin forcing, or cut earlier and keep the branches in a freezer to ensure adequate chilling.

"When you are ready to force the blossoms, recut the stems cleanly at a 45-degree angle and slit thick stems about an inch lengthwise. Put the cut branches into warm water with floral preservative, and bring them into a warm, bright room. Exposing them to direct sun will help the flowers develop good color. Mist the branches regularly to keep them from drying out.

"Commercial growers find that they get more blossoms with longer vase life if they warm up the branches in stages, rather than bringing them immediately into springtime temperatures. For example, start the branches in a 50°F greenhouse for two weeks, then move them to a 75°F greenhouse to finish opening."

—from *The Flower Farmer* by Lynn Byczynski (Chelsea Green, 1997)

# An Annual Cutting Garden

This sample garden is designed for the beginning flower grower. About 60 square feet of annuals — a bed 5 feet by 12 feet — will provide enough stems to fill your house with bouquets throughout the summer.

The flowers in this plan are basic, but they all have many qualities to recommend them. All of them bloom prolifically, most providing multiple stems for cutting each week. This selection of flowers also provides a wide variety of colors and shapes. We have also included some foliage and filler plants to integrate your arrangements. Finally, the plan indicates multiples of six plants, because most garden centers sell six-packs of flowers. If you have to buy more, you can always expand the garden by a foot and squeeze them all in. Here are the plants you'll need:

🌿 Larkspur (*Consolida ambigua*). In many areas, larkspur should be direct-seeded in the fall. You can also freeze the seed for two weeks and then direct-seed in the spring, or buy plants. You'll need 18 plants, or enough seeds for a 12-foot row. Use fresh or dried.

🌿 Tricolor sage (*Salvia horminum*). This heavily branching plant sends up spikes of what look like pink or blue leaves. They're actually bracts surrounding the inconspicuous white flowers. Use fresh or dried. You need only three plants.

🌿 Snapdragons (*Antirrhinum majus*). Be sure to get a tall variety like 'Rocket' or 'Liberty'. You'll need six plants.

🌿 Ageratum 'Blue Horizon'. Be sure to get this tall cultivar. Buy six plants.

🌿 Rudbeckia 'Indian Summer' is a huge-flowered black-eyed Susan. The blooms actually look better a few days after they've been in the vase. Get six plants.

🌿 Zinnia. 'State Fair', 'California Giant', or some other cultivar that is 30 inches tall. Direct-seed an 8-foot row or buy 12 plants.

🌿 Cosmos. 'Versailles' or 'Seashells' are good varieties that can be direct-seeded. Grow a 4-foot row or buy six plants.

🌿 Cockscomb (*Celosia cristata*). 'Chief' is a good variety for long stems. Use fresh or dried. Direct-seed a 4-foot row or buy six plants.

🌿 Mealy-cup sage (*Salvia farinacea*). Good varieties for cutting are 'Victoria'

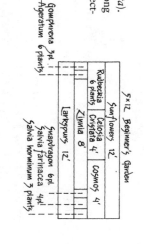

5×12 Beginner's Garden

and 'Blue Bedder'. Lovely blue spikes for fresh or dried use. Buy four plants and cut them hard to encourage branching.

🌿 Matricaria. These 2-foot-high plants produce a succession of tiny, clear white flowers from early July through frost. The ultimate filler flower. Start your own, or buy six plants.

🌿 Bishop's weed (*Ammi majus*). Also known as ammi or false Queen Anne's lace, this flower gives bouquets a light, cottage-garden look. Direct-sow six or eight seeds every few weeks through mid-July.

🌿 Sunflowers (*Helianthus annuus*). Buy seed for a 12-foot row. Grow one of the branching, multicolored varieties such as 'Autumn Beauty' to get the most versatility. Or go for one of the exotic dark-red cultivars like 'Velvet Queen' or 'Prado Red'.

—from *The Flower Farmer* by Lynn Byczynski (Chelsea Green, 1997).

garden, make smashing additions to floral arrangements, and can transform an ordinary bouquet into a work of art.

## All-Season Blooms

Even if you live in one of the coldest parts of the country, you should be able to find interesting flowers and foliage from early March right through November. One of the best ways to plan for a long season of blooms is to keep a flower journal. Having a record of what is in bloom each week can help you identify what kinds of plant material you might want to add next year. It is also invaluable when planning for an upcoming party or wedding. At right is a short list of twenty flowering plants that stretch from early spring to late fall. When looking down the list, you will see that the annual flowers don't kick in until midsummer. This is why bulbs, perennials, shrubs, and wildflowers play such an important role in a garden that provides all-season blooms.

## Web Sites

Ames Lawn and Garden Tools
www.ames.com
A well-organized web site. Ames manufactures non-motorized lawn and garden tools, and their site supplies lots of basic information in easy-to-read chart form on flowers for cutting and bouquets.

## Popular Cut Flowers

| FLOWER | LIFE SPAN | SITE | SOIL | HEIGHT | SPACING | PLANTING | BLOOMS | ZONE |
|---|---|---|---|---|---|---|---|---|
| Baby's Breath | Annual | Full sun | Well-drained, alkaline | 18" | 8" | Spring | Summer | 4–9 |
| Calendula | Annual | Full sun | Well-drained, fertile | 12–30" | 12–15" | Early spring | Spring to early summer | 2–10 |
| China Aster | Annual | Full sun | Well-drained, fertile | 6–30" | 6–12" | Spring | Summer | All |
| Chrysanthemum | Perennial | Full sun | Well-drained, fertile | 18–36" | 12–24" | Spring | Spring to fall | 3–10 |
| Clove Pink | Perennial | Full sun | Well-drained, alkaline | 8–18" | 8–10" | Early spring | Spring to summer | 3–9 |
| Cosmos | Annual | Full sun | Well-drained, fertile | 24–84" | 12" | Late spring | Late spring to early fall | All |
| Daffodil | Perennial | Full sun | Well-drained, fertile | 6–18" | 4–6" | Fall | Spring | 4–10 |
| Dahlia | Annual | Full sun | Well-drained, fertile | 12–20" | 24–30" | Spring | Summer to fall | 4–9 |
| Daisy | Annual | Full sun | Well-drained, fertile | 12–24" | 10–12" | Early spring | Early summer to frost | 4–9 |
| Delphinium | Perennial | Full sun to partial shade | Well-drained, fertile | 48" | 18–24" | Early spring | Spring to early summer | 3–8 |
| Gladiolus | Annual | Full sun | Well-drained, fertile | 24–36" | 3–6" | Early spring to midsummer | Summer to fall | 5–10 |
| Iris | Perennial | Full sun to partial shade | Well-drained, fertile | 15–28" | 12–18" | Early summer to mid-fall | Spring to early summer | 3–9 |
| Larkspur | Annual | Full sun to partial shade | Well-drained, fertile | 14–48" | 10–12" | Early spring to late fall | Spring to early summer | All |
| Marigold | Annual | Full sun to partial shade | Well-drained, fertile | 6–48" | 6–24" | Spring | Early summer to frost | All |
| Phlox | Perennial | Full sun to partial shade | Well-drained, fertile | 24–48" | 18–20" | Early spring | Spring to summer | 3–9 |
| Salvia | Annual | Full sun | Well-drained, fertile | 8–36" | 12" | Late spring | Early summer to frost | All |
| Stock | Annual | Full sun | Well-drained, fertile | 12–30" | 9–12" | Early spring | Spring to summer | All |
| Sweet Pea | Annual | Full sun | Well-drained, fertile | 36–60" | 6" | Early spring | Spring to summer | 2–9 |
| Tulip | Perennial | Full sun | Well-drained | 6–28" | 3–6" | Late fall | Spring | 4–10 |
| Zinnia | Annual | Full sun | Well-drained, fertile | 6–36" | 6–12" | Late spring | Summer to fall | All |

Reprinted with permission of the Ames Lawn and Garden Tools Company, Parkersburg, West Virginia.

flowers for cutting

# Heat Treatment

Some flowers require special conditioning after cutting and before arranging. In general, any plant that exudes a sticky white sap from its stem after cutting needs to have its cut end either seared or scalded to seal the stem end. To do this, either place the stem end in a candle flame or plunge it into boiling water for a few seconds. Do this carefully and quickly to avoid exposing the flowers to prolonged heat.

Some common cutting flowers that require this heat treatment include:

- Canterbury-bells (*Campanula medium*)
- Euphorbia species, including scarlet-plume and poinsettia
- Frangipani (*Plumeria* spp.)
- Hollyhock (*Alcea rosea*)
- Poppies (*Papaver* spp.)

# Floral Design

There are many good books on the art of flower arranging — some instructional, some purely inspirational (see "Other Good Books," page 175). The basic variables include the color, shape, and texture of the flowers used, the setting, lighting, and size of the arrangement, and the characteristics of the container that will hold the bouquet. In the past, floral design instructors have stressed platonic ideals (using S- or Hogarth curves, and the like). At home, the only person you have to please is yourself. So be creative and use what looks good and feels right to you. Most people have an intuitive sense of color and beauty, and flower arranging should above all be a fun, relaxing, even meditative pursuit.

giving precise ratios for height to width, and the like). At home, the only person you have to please is yourself. So be creative and use what looks good and feels right to you. Most people have an intuitive sense of color and beauty, and flower arranging should above all be a fun, relaxing, even meditative pursuit.

# Garden Gear

These rectangular grids are great for mass plantings and cutting gardens. The large, 5³⁄₄" x 4¹⁄₂" openings let many stems grow up through, yet provide uncompromising support to keep stems straight. 34" legs anchor grids firmly in place. A dark green epoxy coating protects the sturdy, galvanized steel wire. 24" L x 18" W x 34" H. #30-106 Super Grow-Thru Grids, set of 2 **$19.95**

**Rogard Professional Floral Preservative** will extend the vase life of your cut flowers, yet not stain your glass vases like some other preservatives. The 12-ounce concentrate makes 16 quarts of clear solution. 12 oz. $5.00. (Available from The Cook's Garden, P.O. Box 535, Londonderry, VT 05148; 800-457-9703.)

**Victorinox Flower Gatherers** are little nippers that allow you to cut and gather flowers with one hand. The cutters have two spring-steel bands that hold the stem without crushing it, for quick and easy harvesting. Wooden handles are comfortable in the hand. 7¹⁄₄" overall length. Made in Switzerland. $16.40. (Available from Johnny's Selected Seeds, Foss Hill Road, Albion, ME 04910; 207-437-9294.)

**Fiskars Flower Scissors** have serrated blades to provide years of sharp performance. Handles are easy to grip, with plenty of room for your fingers. $15.00. (Available from the Cook's Garden, P.O. Box 535, Londonderry, VT 05148; 800-457-9703.)

**Cook's Garden Cutting Flowers Collection** is great for beginners. It is a collection of eight seed packets that pulls together everything you need for a basic, yet exciting cutting garden. Includes one packet each of 'Liberty' snapdragon, 'Victoria Blue' salvia, Cook's Garden aster mix, white annual baby's-breath, 'Scabiosaflora' zinnia mix, lavatera, Cook's Garden cosmos mix, and 'Touch of Red' calendula mix. $14.50. (Available from The Cook's Garden, P.O. Box 535, Londonderry, VT 05148; 800-457-9703.)

PART IV

broader
gardening
horizons

# Container gardening

O f the 60 million gardeners in the United States, about 90 percent grow plants in containers. It may be nothing more than a pot of geraniums, or a couple of window boxes, but it might also be a deck filled with tubs of tomatoes, peppers, lettuce, and annual flowers, or a rooftop garden packed with potted citrus, bougainvillea, and herbs. Growing in containers is a necessity for people without a yard. It's also a smart alternative if you are restricted by too much shade, poor soil, too little time, limited mobility, or a difficult climate. Container gardens can be much more productive than a regular garden. They also allow you to avoid most pest and disease problems. Best of all, growing in containers brings your garden right up close, creating a sense of intimacy that you just don't get in an ordinary backyard garden.

## Types of Containers

Almost anything can serve as a container for growing plants: terracotta, plastic, or pressed-fiber pots, recycled whiskey barrels, 5-gallon food buckets, laundry baskets, bushel baskets, plastic tubs, wooden planter boxes, and yes, even old tires. Select the appropriate container based on the root space required by the type of plants you plan to grow. The general rule is to use the largest container possible, because the more soil you have, the more room there is for root growth, and the longer your plants can go between waterings. Radishes may get by in a 6-inch-deep container, but don't try to grow a tomato plant in a container that holds less than 5 gallons of soil. With experience, you'll get to know the root structure for different kinds of plants and will be able to match the right pots to the right plants.

Whatever types of containers you choose, make sure that they have drainage holes — on the sides rather than the bottom if possible — so excess water can drain away and roots won't get waterlogged.

## Favorite Books

**Container Plants** *by Halina Heitz* (Barrons, 1992).
An excellent book, initially published in Germany, that combines beautiful photography with solid, in-depth information. Specific care instructions for well over 200 different plants, including lots of interesting exotics. The how-to sections are well illustrated, and this book also gets top rating for its section on pest and disease identification. 240 pages, hardcover, $22.95.

**The Complete Container Garden** *by David Joyce* (Reader's Digest, 1996).
A good balance of how-to information and inspiring ideas for creative plant combinations. Includes all the newest plant materials, and covers trough gardens, topiaries, herb jars, window boxes, special decorative pots, wooden planters, and more. 216 pages, hardcover, $30.00.

**Movable Harvests** *by Chuck Crandall and Barbara Crandall* (Chapters, 1995).
One of the few container gardening books that focuses on fruits, berries, and vegetables. Crop by crop instructions, and an extensive section on pest and disease control. Includes recommended varieties of vegetables and fruits. 128 pages, paperback, $19.95.

## Guest Expert

### Jennifer Brennan

*Jennifer Brennan is a master gardener and Horticulture Information Specialist at the Chicago Botanic Garden, where she teaches courses on container gardening and gardening with children, among others.*

Have you ever planted a container in early summer, feeling very proud of the wonderful combination of color, texture, and form, only to be disappointed by midsummer? Ever wonder why you see the same combinations looking exquisite at a botanical garden or other public display? Here are my secrets to successful container gardening.

Plant the container with compatible combinations: all shade-loving plants in shady locations; all moisture-loving plants together; all dry soil plants in well-drained locations.

Avoid water stress with a regular watering schedule, or by adding a water-retaining polymer to the potting medium, which will release moisture when the soil gets dry. These work best when included in the medium prior to planting, but they can be added after the plants are established. Make holes in the soil with a pencil, pour the crystals in, and water.

Fertilization is extremely important. Since the root zone is restricted, and the container is frequently watered, nutrients must be replaced on a regular basis. Use a water soluble fertilizer with a higher ratio of phosphorus for flowering plants, or a balanced ratio of nutrients for foliage plants. Fertilize weekly during the growing season. If following a schedule is difficult, use a slow-release encapsulated fertilizer: when mixed into the soil at planting time, plants flourish throughout the entire growing season.

As plants fill in and crowd out neighbors, deadhead and remove spent parts. Enjoy the evolution as you would the changes in a perennial garden. Container gardens are complete gardens in restricted areas. Meet their needs, and you will enjoy their success.

## ORGANIC BLEND

5 gallons finished compost
1 gallon builder's sand
1 gallon vermiculite or perlite
1 gallon ground sphagnum peat
1 cup granular all-purpose organic fertilizer

## CORNELL MIX

1 bushel vermiculite
1 bushel ground sphagnum moss
8 tablespoons superphosphate
8 tablespoons ground limestone
2 cups steamed bone meal

## LIGHTWEIGHT BLEND for Rooftop Gardens

5 gallons ground sphagnum moss
5 gallons vermiculite or perlite
2 gallons compost
1 cup granular all-purpose organic fertilizer

A 20-gallon pot should have four to six ¾-inch holes; a 30-gallon pot should have at least eight 1-inch holes. You can put stones or bits of crockery in the bottom of the pot, but with a well-aerated soil mix, this is unnecessary and will only steal valuable root space.

## Soil Mixes

Straight garden soil is much too dense for container-grown plants. They need soil that is light and friable, well drained, and moisture-retentive.

A good growing medium for most containerized plants is a soilless blend of peat moss and vermiculite or perlite, which is enriched with finished compost or good garden soil. The ratio of soilless mix to soil may range from 20:80 to 80:20, depending on what you are growing. A greater amount of soilless material will encourage strong root growth, but will require careful attention to water and nutrients. A higher percentage of soil or compost will provide more nutrients and beneficial microorganisms, but it will also be heavier and prone to compaction.

You can now purchase pre-mixed growing mediums specially formulated for container plantings. Or, you can create your own mix, using one of the recipes at left as a guide. Remember that sphagnum peat is naturally acidic. If your custom blend contains a high percentage of peat, you should add ground limestone to neutralize the pH. For best results, all growing mediums should be pre-moistened before they are put into the container.

## Caring for Your Container Plants

The secret to success with potted plants is monitoring them at regular, frequent intervals. Those breathtaking displays of flowering plants that you see at restaurants and inns look fresh and full because someone is attending to them on a daily basis, making sure that they are getting adequate water and fertilizer, that they are not getting too crowded, and that plants get pinched back when blossoms are spent or if the plants start looking scraggly.

**WATERING.** If you have a deck full of patio containers and head off to work in the morning without watering them, you may come home to droopy, if not dead, plants. When plants get too dry, their delicate feeder roots die, and once they get watered again, the plants must concentrate their energy on regrowing damaged roots rather than producing fruit

## Watering Innovations for Containers

**Polymers** are non-toxic "crystals" that absorb up to 400 times their weight in water. When blended into the soil, they retain water and release it gradually, as your plants need it. Polymers can reduce your watering chores by 50 to 70 percent, and their effect lasts up to ten years. They eventually break down into water, $CO_2$ and ammonia. Use coarse crystals for large pots; fine ones for pots smaller than six inches. One teaspoon holds about 2 cups of water. Use about 2 teaspoons per gallon of soil.

**Self-Watering Containers** are a smart way to keep your plants healthy and happy without the daily chore of watering. Typically, these containers have an inner pot that holds the plant and soil, and an outer pot or bottom reservoir that holds extra water. A wick joins the two and pulls water up into the root ball as it's needed. Most reservoirs are large enough to supply water for several days — sometimes a week or more — depending on the weather. Liquid fertilizer can be added to the reservoir to ensure an adequate supply of nutrients. These containers can usually be used both indoors and out. (See the product section for some choices.)

**Drip Irrigation Systems** take the work and worry out of watering your container plants. You can get a simple, easy-to-install system with 50 feet of feeder tube and a dozen emitters for less than $25. Add a timer and your plants will be content even if you can't be there to give them daily attention. (See the products section for details.)

---

or flowers. If you don't use self-watering planters or have a drip irrigation system, you'll probably need to check on your plants daily, and maybe even twice a day if the weather is really hot. If you have more than a few planters, and especially if you travel, a drip irrigation system is the only way to go (see "Watering Innovations" sidebar).

Two cautions about over-watering. In early spring, when the soil is cold and your plants are still small, you should water sparingly. Too much water will stunt root growth. As the season progresses, water thoroughly enough to saturate the entire root ball, but not so much that water runs out the bottom of the container. Overwatering will wash nutrients out of the soil, and will also force air out of the soil, which can create compaction problems. Here are several other watering tips:

• If you are planting in a wooden box or other porous container, consider lining it with perforated black plastic. This will help retain moisture and will reduce soil loss.

• Do not water your plants with softened water. The dissolved salts are toxic to plants. If your water is fluoridated, fill a watering can and let it sit for a few hours before watering your plants. Rainwater is best. To collect a bountiful supply, direct the downspout from your roof into a rainbarrel. (See "Garden Gear" on page 186.)

• Grouping pots together reduces moisture loss by allowing the plants to shade each other and block the wind.

**FERTILIZING.** After drought, starvation is the second biggest problem for container-grown plants. Soilless growing mediums provide few if any nutrients, so your plants will depend on you for their food. The easiest way to ensure that your plants get the nutrients they need is to mix a small amount of granular organic fertilizer into the growing medium at planting time, then water your plants weekly with a one-third-strength fertilizer solution. Once the season is under way, try top-dressing your containers with finished compost. If your plants are looking stressed, or if you have cut them back midseason, spray the foliage with liquid seaweed or fish emulsion for a quick pick-me-up.

**MAINTENANCE.** The soil in your planting containers should be replaced at least every two years. "Sick soil" is soil that has become compacted, has a buildup of fertilizer salts, or disease pathogens, or for some other reason

---

## Web Sites

Container Gardening
http://www.geocities.com/RainForest/1329/containers.htm
*Fact sheet on container gardening.*

Virginia Extension Service
http:/www.ext.va.edu/pubs/envirohort/general/container.html
*Fact sheet for container gardening.*

# Optimum Container Volume and Depth

| | Ideal Vol. (gallons) | Min. Depth (inches) | | Ideal Vol. (gallons) | Min. Depth (inches) |
|---|---|---|---|---|---|
| Beans/peas | 3–5 | 8 | Mustard greens | 2 | 4–6 |
| Beet/Swiss chard | 2 | 8 | Onion (green and bulb) | 2 | 8 |
| Broccoli, cabbage, cauliflower, Brussels sprouts, collards | 3–5 | 10 | Pepper | 3–5 | 12 |
| | | | Potato | 5 | 12 |
| Cantaloupe | 5 | 12 | Radish | 2 | 4–6 |
| Carrots | 2 | 1–12 | Rutabaga/turnip | 2 | 8 |
| Celery | 2 | 4–6 | Spinach | 2 | 8 |
| Cucumber | 5 | 12 | Squash | 5 | 12 |
| Eggplant | 5 | 12 | Sweet potato | 5 | 12 |
| Lettuce | 2 | 4–6 | Tomato | 5 | 12 |
| | | | Watermelon | 5 | 12 |

—from *Container Vegetables* by Sam Cotner. © 1987 by Gulf Publishing Company. Used with permission. All rights reserved.

is no longer a healthy growing medium. For best results, begin each spring with a fresh blend of soilless and organic material.

During the growing season, make it a weekly habit to remove spent flowers and pinch back leggy stems. Be prepared to replace tired plants with some fresh annuals — especially late-season favorites such as flowering kale and mums.

If you will be overwintering container plants, they should be cut back and put into a cool location. Water sparingly and do not fertilize until spring. Once warm weather arrives, remove plants from their containers, tease away old soil, and repot the plants in a fresh soil blend.

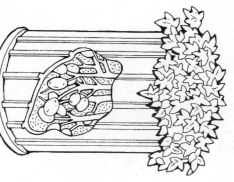

## POTATOES IN A BARREL

Start by drilling eight or more drainage holes around the bottom of the container. Fill with 6" of crushed stone, topped with 6" blend of compost and builder's sand. Put four or five seed potatoes on top, then cover with another 6" of the soil blend. Add more soil whenever the foliage gets at least 6" above the soil surface. Dump the barrel at the end of the season to reveal your harvest!

## Trellises and Supports

Container-grown tomato plants, cucumbers, and other vine crops require some sort of vertical support. Besides playing a practical role, trellises can also be a beautiful vertical accent, especially when covered with morning glories or sweet peas. Try to keep the scale of the trellis in proportion to the pot, and be sure to attach the trellis securely using brackets or wires, to avoid losing a mature tomato plant or flower-covered trellis to an August thunderstorm.

## What to Plant

**COLORFUL ANNUALS.** Composing a visually exciting assortment of flowers and foliage is one of the great pleasures of gardening in containers. You can experiment with all sorts of color combinations, using plants that are already in bloom, rather than having to rely on your imagination. Combine both large and small flowers, with upright forms as well as horizontal and trailing. And don't neglect the importance of foliage. Just as a professional cut flower bouquet always includes plenty of greens, in a container planting foliage helps pull the plants together into a unified whole. Consider going beyond the usual ivies and vinca, to play with the fuzzy leaves of the licorice plant (*Helichrysum petiolare*), the purple-leaved sweet potato vine (*Ipomea batatas* 'Blackie'), and even some small ornamental grasses.

**TENDER EXOTICS.** Containers give you the opportunity to experiment with non-hardy flowering plants such as datura, bougainvillea, passion vine, and hibiscus. These plants can be enjoyed outdoors from spring through fall, and then wintered-over in a cool basement or frost-free garage. Tender perennials can add lots of excitement to your container plantings. Some good candidates include ruffled coleus (*Coleus hybridus*), exotic ivies (*Hedera helix*), scented geraniums (*Pelargonium*), and tropical mints (*Plectranthus*). See the suppliers list for mail-order sources for some of these more unusual plant varieties.

**VEGETABLES.** Many of your favorite vegetables can be grown in containers, including tomatoes, peppers, carrots, beets, lettuce, spinach, squash, cucumbers, and onions. For most of these, you can use the same varieties that you plant in the garden. There are also compact varieties specially bred for container growing. Be aware that in some cases, varieties bred for compactness may not be as flavorful as standard varieties. That's because compact plants have fewer leaves, and sugar production occurs in the leaves.

Salad greens are very easy to grow in containers. Try combining several greens in one pot for a ready-made salad mixture. Simply mix together the seeds of lettuces, chervil, arugula, endive, herbs, radicchio, or other greens and sow them in a wide shallow container. Snip off the leaves when they are young and tender. Since you can expect about four harvests from every planting, reseed a new container every few weeks for a continuous harvest. See the sidebar for other vegetables that are suited for container growing.

**HERBS.** Most herbs thrive in containers because they get better exposure to heat and sun. They grow quickly and can be harvested over many months or even years. Tender perennial herbs, such as rosemary and bay, can be grown outside during the summer and then be moved

## Other Good Books

**The Book of Container Gardening** *by Malcolm Hillier* (DK Publishing, 1991).

Renowned British floral designer Malcolm Hillier presents an inspiring collection of plant combinations that reflect the colors, textures, and plant materials suited to each season. More inspiring than practical. 192 pages, hardcover, $27.50.

**Contained Gardens** *by Susan Berry and Steve Bradley* (Garden Way Publishing, 1995).

Written and first published in England, this book has lots of ideas for creative plant combinations and unusual containers. Presentation and content make it more suitable for the experienced gardener. 160 pages, hardcover, $25.00.

# Suitability of Common Vegetables for Container Gardening

| | Poor | Fair | Good | Excellent |
|---|---|---|---|---|
| Beans | | ✓ | | |
| Beets | | | | ✓ |
| Broccoli | | | ✓ | |
| Brussels Sprouts | | | ✓ | |
| Cabbage | | | ✓ | |
| Cantaloupe | | ✓ | | |
| Carrots | | | | ✓ |
| Cauliflower | | | ✓ | |
| Celery | | | ✓ | |
| Cucumber | | | | ✓ |
| Eggplant | | | ✓ | |
| Kale/Collards | | | ✓ | |
| Lettuce | | | | ✓ |
| Mustard Greens | | | | ✓ |
| Okra | ✓ | | | |
| Onion (green/shallots) | | | | ✓ |

| | Poor | Fair | Good | Excellent |
|---|---|---|---|---|
| Onion (bulb) | ✓ | | | |
| Peas | | ✓ | | |
| Pepper | | | | ✓ |
| Potato | ✓ | | | |
| Pumpkin | ✓ | | | |
| Radish | | | | ✓ |
| Southern Peas | ✓ | | | |
| Spinach | | | ✓ | |
| Squash (summer) | | | ✓ | |
| Squash (winter) | ✓ | | | |
| Sweet Corn | ✓ | | | |
| Sweet Potato | | | ✓ | |
| Swiss Chard | | | ✓ | |
| Tomato | | | | ✓ |
| Turnip/Rutabaga | | | ✓ | |
| Watermelon | | ✓ | | |

# Garden Gear

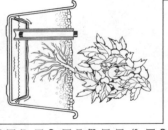

The **Self-Watering Patio Container** is a self-watering patio tub that is large enough to hold a full-size tomato plant, peppers, a salad garden, or most any kind of flowers. The built-in water reservoir holds 4 gallons. A float indicates water level at a glance. Each tub holds 48 quarts of soil. 26 3/8" L x 18 3/4" W x 10 1/2" H. Color is brown.

#03-150 Self-Watering Patio Container $39.95
#06-181 Self-Watering Patio Container, green $39.95

Get the look of antiqued **terra cotta** without the weight or expense. These pots are made from a weather-proof foam resin that is 90 percent lighter than clay. Available in two colors: dark or faded terra cotta.

#30-125 16" Ultra-Light Pot $29.95
#30-126 20" Ultra-Light Pot $29.95

Our **Self-Watering Pots** have the look of terra cotta, but are made of weatherproof plastic, and have an internal water reservoir to keep plants happy for a week at a time.

#30-052 8" Self-Watering Pot $8.95
#14-162 12" Self-Watering Pot $11.95
#30-054 16" Self-Watering Pot $19.95

**Window boxes** dry out so quickly that keeping them watered can become a real chore. These polypropylene window boxes have a 7-quart reservoir that keeps plants watered for several days at a time. Bottom drain prevents overflows. Comes with mounting brackets. 32" L x 9" W x 7 1/2" H. Available in white or terra cotta.

#30-025 Self-Watering Window Box $28.95

**Container plants thrive** in this blend of sphagnum peat, vermiculite, and odor-free composted manure. Retains moisture and provides essential nutrients.

#30-375 Professional Container Mix, 20 quarts $6.95

**HydroSource** crystals are made from a non-toxic polymer that absorbs up to 400 times its weight in water. Mix these crystals into the soil in your containers, and your plants will get the moisture they need, as they need it.

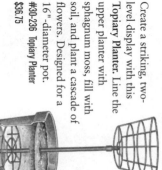

**Gardener's Best All-Purpose Granular Fertilizer** can be mixed right into the growing medium to provide slow-release all-organic nutrients throughout the season.

#07-300 All-Purpose Fertilizer, 5 lbs $5.95

**ROOTS Plus Liquid Fertilizers** provide essential macronutrients as well as the enzymes, vitamins, minerals, humus, and algae found in the richest of soils. Stimulates strong root growth for stress resistance. Liquid concentrate.

#07-276 ROOTS Plus All-Purpose, 32 ounces $10.95

Effective for up to ten years. Fine grind is recommended for pots 12 inches or smaller.

#06-307 HydroSource, 1 lb $9.95
#30-105 HydroSource Fine Grind, 1 lb $9.95

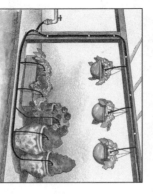

Create a striking, two-level display with this **Topiary Planter.** Line the upper planter with sphagnum moss, fill with soil, and plant a cascade of flowers. Designed for a 16"-diameter pot.

#30-236 Topiary Planter $36.75

Precision-irrigate up to ten plants at once with this simple and inexpensive **Patio Watering System.** It attaches to your outdoor faucet, and includes 60' of micro-tubing, 10 micro-drippers, mounting clips, and detailed instructions. Can be used for window boxes, planters, and hanging baskets.

#30-235 Patio Irrigation System $19.95

## Tips for Gardening in Containers

- Some plants can survive on only 4 hours of sun per day. But most plants, especially annuals, require at least 6 to 8 hours per day.

- Tall plants need heavier soil to keep them from tipping over. Add some builder's sand if overall weight is not an issue.

- For large containers, cover the soil surface with a thin layer of mulch (shredded bark, leaf mold, dry grass clippings, or straw) to help reduce moisture loss.

- Shield plants from midsummer heat by using a lattice, trellis, awning or umbrella, or shade fabric.

- Scrub old pots with a 10 percent bleach solution before re-use. This will kill disease and pests, and will help remove any accumulated fertilizer salts.

- Season new terra-cotta pots by submerging them in water for 15 minutes

before you fill them with soil. This will force air out of the pore spaces and will help keep the soil moist.

- Consider putting casters on wooden planters or putting your large pots on a little dolly before they're filled with soil. A 30-gallon planter can weigh over 200 pounds.

---

indoors to a protected location for the winter. Most herbs prefer a sandy soil, and they should not be fertilized more than a few times during the growing season.

**TREE FRUITS.** Dwarf varieties and genetic miniatures are the best fruit trees for container growing. Dwarfs mature at 4 to 12 feet, while miniatures grow only 3 to 6 feet; both produce full-size fruit and will live fifteen years or more. Fruit trees require a lot of space for their roots, so use large containers and put them on wheels if possible. In cold climates, non-hardy tree fruits, such as 'Meyer' lemon, figs, and apricots, will need to be wintered indoors or in a protected location.

**SMALL FRUITS.** Strawberries, currants, and gooseberries can be grown fairly easily in containers. Raspberries and blackberries are more of a challenge. Blueberries (half-high and low-bush cultivars) do well in containers because it is easier to maintain the acid soil that they love. All of these plants should be well mulched for winter protection.

**EDIBLE FLOWERS.** Having a supply of edible flowers close at hand makes it easy to dress up a salad or serving platter. Not all flowers are edible — some are even poisonous. The tasty ones include squash blossoms, tulips, nasturtiums, roses, pansies, calendulas, carnations, borage, yuccas, daylilies, and violets. As a general rule, you should remove the calyx at the base of the flower and the pistils and stamens before eating, as these parts can be bitter. (See "The Kitchen Garden" for more on edible flowers.)

---

## Resources

### SUPPLIERS

**Glasshouse Works**
Church Street
Stewart, OH 45778-0097
http://www.glasshouseworks.com
*A nursery in Ohio offering thousands of unusual plants that can be grown indoors or in containers. A huge selection of exotic coleus, plectranthus, succulents, passiflora, jasmines, ivies, and much, much more.*

**Simple Gardens**
RR2, Box 292
Richmond, VT 05477
802-434-2624
http://homepages.together.net/~smplgrdn/grow.htm
*A fledgling business with assorted products for container gardening.*

**The Banana Tree**
715 Northampton Street
Easton, PA 18042
610-253-9589
*Primarily a seed source for all sorts of rare and tropical plants. They also offer rhizomes for heliconia and gingers, and small plants of palms, bananas, cycads, and more. Catalog $3.00.*

**Four Winds Growers**
P.O. Box 3538
Fremont, CA 94539
*Citrus plants for container gardening.*

# water gardening

W ater — be it a flowing stream, a spouting fountain, or a quiet reflecting pool — is a natural complement to any garden. A water feature can be as simple as a hollowed-out stone that catches rainwater, or as complex as a half-acre pond, complete with water lilies, ducks, fish, and a fountain. Whatever size or form it takes, water brings an exciting new dimension to the garden, and opens up a whole new world of planting and landscaping possibilities.

## Water Features

Water has been an important feature in formal gardens throughout the world. The grandeur of a French, English, or Moorish garden (and the importance of its owner) could be measured by the height of its foundations and the length of its reflecting pools. Precision, symmetry, and sophistication were the hallmarks of these water gardens. In the Far East, water features were used to symbolize spiritual journeys and sacred landscapes. They helped to create an atmosphere in these gardens conducive to quiet introspection.

Today, water features are being introduced into backyard gardens throughout North America. But instead of formal or ritualized, the trend is toward water features as an integrated part of the landscape: as gardens are miniature ecosystems that invite the gardener who tends them, and others who experience them, into an intimate new relationship with the natural world.

To manage a water garden, it helps if you have experience as a landscape architect, contractor, biologist, and pool service person. But since few of us sport such a resume, our recommendation is to do your homework and take it slow. Unlike regular gardening, where you can blunder your way through almost any experiment and start fresh the following year, a water garden usually involves a fairly substantial investment of time and money. Before the picture books seduce you into a half-acre pond with fountain, island, and large school of koi, here's a brief overview of what's involved.

## Siting and Design

Your water garden should be located where it will receive a minimum of 5 to 6 hours of sun each day. Avoid low spots (unless you are creating a wetland or bog garden), and stay away from areas that may accumulate runoff from other parts of your property. You should also avoid locating your water garden beneath large trees. Leaves, acorns, and other debris will tend to clog the water with organic matter and lead to algae problems.

If you live in a warm climate, where frost heaving is not a problem, you have the option of lining the bottom of your pond with concrete, brick, or even clay. Today, most gardeners and professional landscapers

## Favorite Books

**Waterscaping**
*by Judy Glattstein*
(Storey, 1994).
The best all-around book if you want to create a naturalistic water garden that fits into the landscape and includes a variety of interesting plant materials. Covers bog gardens, wet meadows, marshes, and swamps, as well as more traditional types of ponds. Does not address fish or water lilies. 184 pages, paperback, $18.95.

**Water Gardens**
*by Peter Stadelmann*
(Barron's, 1992).
An information-packed book, originally published in German. Great photographs, excellent how-to illustrations. Covers the entire subject more completely than most books of twice the length. 144 pages, paperback, $13.95.

**Sunset Garden Pools, Fountains, and Waterfalls**
(Sunset, 1996).
This revised version still looks a bit dated, but the information is solid and clearly presented. Good how-to diagrams for different construction options. Very little on plant materials and water quality. A good overview for beginners. 96 pages, paperback, $9.95.

## Guest Expert
### Pete Orelup

It's hard to explain the special qualities of a water garden to those who have not been fortunate enough to experience one firsthand. I need say very little, though, when I first guide people through the gate and into my garden. Visitors immediately connect with the coolness of the water, the sound of the waterfall and wind through the cattails, and the slow graceful movements of the fish. If they were hurried, they slow to a stroll as they inevitably follow the path around the pond. If we were preoccupied with conversation, it soon ends as they turn their full attention to the garden. I've learned to say little and let the eloquence of the stream, rocks, irises, and lilies be heard without interference.

For those who have not had the pleasure, I can only suggest that a stroll through a water garden is worth the while. To those gardeners who then may contemplate a water garden of their own, be prepared to let your garden speak for itself.

*Pete Orelup is a water gardening enthusiast and the creator of Pete's Pond Page, http://reality.sgi.com/employees/peteo*

## A Bog Garden

A bog is a unique ecosystem characterized by water-logged, oxygen-poor, low-pH soil conditions. There are many interesting plants that are uniquely adapted to a bog, including carnivorous plants and many kinds of orchids. Creating bog-like conditions on a small scale is not particularly difficult. You can even make a bog garden in a container. For a good explanation of building a bog garden see pages 109–110 of *Waterscaping* by Judy Glattstein.

Note: In England and Canada, "bog gardening" often refers to growing moisture-tolerant plants. If you are aiming to create a garden for specialty bog plants, be careful that these different definitions don't get you off track.

create ponds by using a preformed liner made from fiberglass or plastic, or a flexible, cut-to-fit liner made from PVC or butyl rubber. The preformed liners are quicker to install, but the flexible liners allow for much greater creativity.

It is important that your site is level (easier said than done), and that you have relatively easy access to power and fresh water. Ideally, a naturalistic water garden has sloped sides with planting terraces that step down toward the deepest area of the pond. This allows you to plant a diversity of plant material and create lots of appealing habitats. In northern areas, a depth of 24 to 36 inches is usually necessary to ensure that the pond will not freeze solid during the winter. (Hardy water lilies and fish will not survive if they are frozen.)

### Water Lilies and Lotuses

The botanical stars of the water garden are water lilies and lotuses. Both require full sun.

**HARDY WATER LILIES** float right on the surface of the water, and will usually bloom from late spring to frost. They should be planted in sturdy containers (like 3-gallon plastic pots) that can be submerged 10 to 18 inches deep. Hardy water

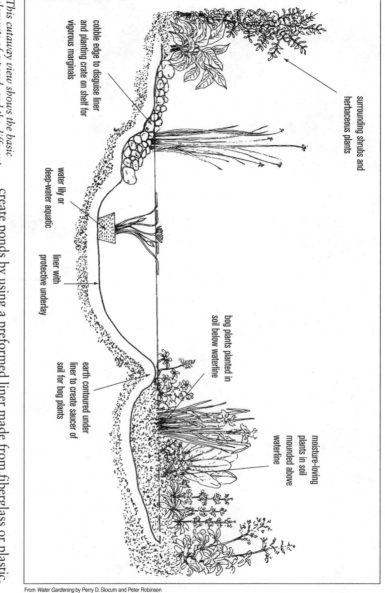

*This cutaway view shows the basic elements of a pond, and the different types of plants that can occupy various niches.*

From *Water Gardening* by Perry D. Slocum and Peter Robinson lilies will winter-over in ponds as far north as Zone 4, as long as their roots are submerged deep enough that they don't freeze solid. Otherwise, the pots should be removed from the water in late fall, and stored in a protected area over the winter. Hardy water lilies should be fertilized monthly, and divided every 3 years. There are hundreds of varieties to choose from, including some that are suitable for container growing.

**TROPICAL WATER LILIES** look very similar to the hardy varieties, but the blooms are larger and more dramatic. These plants are hardy only to Zone 10, and will not flower unless they are grown in full sun and are exposed to several weeks of temperatures over 80°F. (Don't bother trying them in northern New England or the Pacific Northwest.) Their flowers are held slightly above the water surface. Some tropical water lilies are day-bloomers and some are night-bloomers. Because their roots are very delicate and can be easily damaged, most water gardeners treat tropical lilies as annuals.

**LOTUSES** raise their leaves and flowers 4 to 8 feet above the water. The blossoms can be 10 to 12 inches across, and they leave behind a large and distinctive seedpod. Both the American lotus and the sacred lotus are hardy to Zone 4 or 5 if their roots are not allowed to freeze solid. Their roots are slow to get started, and, like tropical water lilies, they won't bloom without full sun and several weeks of 80°F temperatures. Once they get established, lotuses are vigorous growers and demand a lot of room. Under good conditions, one plant can spread 25 to 45 feet in a season. For this reason, lotuses are often grown in containers. Some dwarf cultivars are also available.

Note: most water lilies do not like moving water. If you want to grow lilies, you may either need to create a special area just for them, or forgo having a fountain or waterfall.

## Other Water Plants

If water lilies are the stars of a water garden, the supporting cast includes floating plants, submerged plants, and edge plants. Floating plants, such as water hyacinth, water lettuce, and duckweed, shade the water and absorb dissolved nutrients. By doing so, they help to suppress algae and keep the pond clean.

## Other Good Books

**The Pond Doctor** *by Helen Nash* (Sterling, 1995).
An accessible, yet very thorough guide to planning and maintaining a healthy water garden. Covers plant, fish, and water quality problems; filtration systems; insect life; and more. 160 pages, paperback, $17.95.

**Water Features for Small Gardens** *by Francesca Greenoak* (Trafalgar Square, 1996).
Lots of inspirational ideas for fountains, sculptures, basins and tubs, canals, splash fountains, and more, including very simple projects that could be created over a weekend. 96 pages, hardcover, $22.95.

## A Patio Water Garden

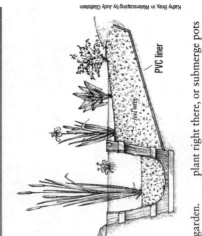

Kathy Bray, in Waterscaping by Judy Glattstein

PVC liner

potting soil

Not everyone has the time, space, or money to dive into the world of water gardening. One way to get your feet wet is to try growing a few plants in a tub of water on the deck. You can use an ordinary whiskey barrel lined with plastic, or purchase a poly tub that is specially designed for a water garden. Even a 2- to 3-foot-diameter container can usually support a miniature water lily or lotus; a submerged plant; some floating plants such as water hyacinth or duckweed; a grass-like plant such as an iris or dwarf cattail; and a few guppies, mosquito fish, or goldfish to eat up any insect larvae. You can put soil into the bottom of the container and plant right there, or submerge pots filled with the different kinds of water plants.

For excellent information about creating water gardens in containers, see pages 127–146 of *Waterscaping* by Judy Glattstein. Also visit the web site sponsored by Jeff Cook, called the Half Barrel Pond Page. You'll find it at: http://www.primenet.com/~jvc/hbpond.html

# Other Good Books

**Earth Ponds** *by Tim Matson* (Countryman, 1991). Oriented to rural property owners. Covers siting, excavation, maintenance and restoration, as well as algae and weed control, and landscaping. 150 pages, paperback, $18.00.

**Water Gardening in Containers** *by Helen Nash and C. Greg Speichert* (Sterling, 1996). An inspirational guide to container selection, recommended plants, and special care. 128 pages, hardcover, $24.95.

Submerged plants, usually called *oxygenators*, spend their entire lives growing beneath the surface of the water. Though they have roots to keep them anchored, these plants obtain their nutrients from the water directly through their stems and leaves. By consuming these dissolved nutrients, oxygenating plants help keep your water garden from becoming a slimy green ooze. They also provide a spawning area and hiding place for fish and other water creatures. Common oxygenating plants include anacharis, arrowhead, eelgrass, and water milfoil. A general guideline is to plant one bunch of anacharis for every one or two square feet of pond surface. Because many of these plants can be invasive, you may want to consider growing them in containers.

There are two types of plants that grow at the edges of a pond. The first are water-loving plants that should be planted on a "shelf," 5 to 10 inches below the surface of the water. These plants include stream- and pond-side favorites such as sweet flag, water plantain, marsh-marigold, pickerel rush, various sedges, cattails, and arrowhead. These water-loving plants provide important shelter for fish, frogs, and other pond life. The next zone is for plants that require moist soil but will not tolerate permanently wet conditions. Appropriate plants for this area include filipendula, Japanese and Siberian iris, trollius, liatris, and ajuga. These plants provide color and texture, and help to visually integrate the water garden with the rest of the landscape.

### Fish and Other Water-Loving Creatures

Fish are a fun addition to the water garden. They also play an important role in keeping the mosquito

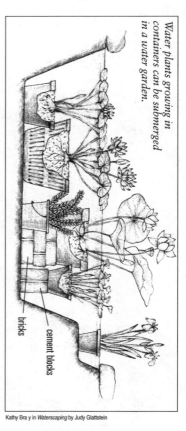

Water plants growing in containers can be submerged in a water garden.

bricks

cement blocks

Kathy Bra y in *Waterscaping* by Judy Glattstein

## Water Gardening Tips

- To maintain a healthy pond, foliage from water plants should cover about one-half of the surface of the water. This will allow adequate sunlight to reach the submerged plants, yet will help keep algae growth in check. Use water lilies, water hyacinths, parrot's feather, water lettuce, duckweed, or others.

- A 50-square-foot surface area seems to be an ideal size for a water garden. This is approximately an 8-foot-diameter circle.

- A little algae in your water garden is fine, but it should be considered a problem if you can't see your hand at a depth of 12 inches. Floating algae should always be removed (it makes excellent compost or mulch material).

- It takes at least 4 to 6 weeks for the ecology of a new water garden to stabilize. During this initial period, the pond water may become murky. You can use a filter to clean the water, but this is usually unnecessary. Once the plants get established, the water will gradually become clearer.

- Native fish, such as guppies and mosquito fish, can tolerate water with a low oxygen content. Goldfish and koi require a much higher oxygen level.

- To minimize algae growth, remove dead and dying foliage and use a long-handled net to filter out any debris that may fall into the water.

population in check, and their wastes are a good source of nutrients for water plants. The challenge is to keep the fish population under control. Too many fish means too many nutrients, and that leads to big algae blooms. The surface area of your pond will determine the number of fish that can be accommodated. A general rule is 1 fish per 3 square feet of surface area. If you will be using an active filtration system and air pump, the number can be much higher.

Most native fish (like guppies and mosquito fish) as well as some types of goldfish, can overwinter in the pond if the water doesn't freeze completely to the bottom. Remember to keep a hole open in the ice to allow oxygen exchange (an electric de-icer can work quite well). If your pond is likely to freeze solid, your fish will need to be overwintered in an indoor aquarium.

Koi, which are a type of carp, are the large, colorful fish that are so popular in Japan. Koi require highly oxygenated water, which means your pond will need to have a well-functioning filter and air pump. Like other kinds of pets, koi require daily feeding and an attentive owner. Unfortunately, these non-native fish have a nasty habit of eating water plants (especially expensive water lilies). Though they are unquestionably beautiful and exciting to watch, it may be wise to speak with someone who keeps koi before you decide to add them to your water garden.

## A Stream Garden

"There is much to be said for having a stream in the garden. If you already have a garden pool, a properly laid out stream can effectively take over the function of a filter. . . . The stream, acting as a biological filter, keeps the water clear and helps maintain the biological balance in the pool, while simultaneously adding oxygen to the pool water. A stream also functions very well without a garden pool. As a rule, a stream running through the garden should resemble a babbling meadow brook; that is, it should flow gently and slowly."

A babbling brook, splashing over rocks and spilling into pools, may be the most exciting of all water features. The sound and movement soothe the senses, and the streambank provides opportunities for many interesting plantings. A site-built stream, even if only eight or ten feet long, can be surprisingly effective. But making it look natural requires careful planning and well-placed rocks, pools, and plantings. *Water Gardens*, by Peter Stadelmann, has an excellent chapter on creating a stream garden.

—from *Water Gardens*
by Peter Stadelmann (Barron's, 1992)

## Web Sites

**Pete's Pond Page**
http://reality.sgi.com/employees/pete0
*Lots of photos of Pete's backyard pond and stream, tracking its evolution over the past 5 years. Construction and maintenance techniques.*

**Jeff Cook's**
**Half Barrel Pond Page**
http://www.primenet.com/~jvc/hbpond.html
*Practical information about setting up a containerized water garden.*

**USENET.REC.PONDS**
*An active newsgroup for people interested in ponds and water gardening.*

**Austin Pond Society**
http://www.ccsi.com/~sgray/austin.pond.society/apshome.html
*Online tours and links to pond clubs.*

**Northern Pond**
http://www.cyberus.ca/~north
*Has an extensive alphabetical list of links to other sites of*

*interest to water gardeners. Art gallery too!*

**Lily Blooms**
http://www.jbic.com/lilyblooms/index.htm
*A retail store and catalog in Ohio. Lots of information, links, and products.*

**Keith's KOI Information Page**
http://www.bayareatech.com/koi
*Lots of links to other web sites offering information and products of interest to koi enthusiasts.*

**The Very Small Pond**
http://wkweb4.cableinet.co.uk/JohnRogers/pond.htm
*Friendly tips that make water gardening sound fun and not the least bit intimidating.*

**The Bloomin Bog**
http://www.icis.on.ca/homepages/personal/rwebb
*A retail store in London, Ontario with a wide range of water gardening supplies.*

Once your new pond has settled in and the water quality has stabilized, frogs, toads, and other amphibians will begin to appear as if by magic. You may even see some snails and clams. Water insects, such as water striders, dragonflies, and mayflies, will also be drawn to your water garden. Each of these creatures will settle into its preferred habitat, helping to complete the ecosystem.

## Maintaining Water Quality

If you have the right mix of water plants, are careful to remove dead or dying plant matter, and don't mind that the water in your pond isn't crystal clear, you probably won't need to install an active filtration system. If, however, your pond is stocked with fish — especially koi — you may need a filtration system to clean and oxygenate the water. (A small waterfall, fed by a recirculating pump, can sometimes be an adequate substitute.) By limiting the number of fish in your pond, you may be able to avoid installing a filtration system, which can be expensive, especially when added after the fact.

Understanding the science behind water quality can be very helpful as you work to balance the aquatic ecosystem you create. (For a good overview see Helen Nash's book *The Pond Doctor*, listed on page 191.) But equally important, be attentive to what's going on in that ecosystem. Water gardening is a dance with nature, and in this dance, nature always leads.

# Other Good Books

**Gardening with Water** *by James Van Sweden* (Random House, 1995). This award-winning landscape designer focuses on naturalistic ponds. Includes garden designs and plant recommendations. 192 pages, hardcover, $40.00.

**Water Gardening: Water Lilies and Lotuses** *by Perry D. Slocum and Peter Robinson* (Timber, 1996). An instant classic from two of the world's most distinguished water gardeners (one British and one American). Comprehensive coverage of all kinds of plant material (with over 100 pages devoted exclusively to water lilies and lotuses). Thin on design, construction, and maintenance. 322 pages, hardcover, $59.95.

# Resources

## SUPPLIERS

There are many fine nurseries offering water lilies and other water plants by mail. Many also carry other water gardening supplies, including pre-formed pools, filtration systems, and even fish. Here are just a few of the larger ones. For others, check out one of the periodicals listed below, or some of the water gardening web sites.

Waterford Gardens
74 East Allendale Rd.
Saddle River, NJ 07458
201-327-0721

Slocum Water Gardens
1101 Cypress Gardens Blvd.
Winter Haven, FL 33884
813-293-7151

Lilypons Water Gardens
6800 Lilypons Rd.
Buckeystown, MD 21717
800-999-5459

Wm. Tricker, Inc.
7125 Tanglewood Drive
Independence, OH 44131
216-524-3491

Perry's Water Gardens
191 Leatherman Gap Rd.
Franklin, NC 28734
704-524-3264

Van Ness Water Gardens
2460 North Euclid Ave.
Upland, CA 91784
909-982-2425
http://www.vnwg.com

## MAGAZINES

*Pondkeeper Magazine*
The National Pond Society
1000 Whitetail Court
Duncanville, PA 16635
800-742-4701

*Pondscapes Magazine*
P.O. Box 449
Acworth, GA 30101
800-742-4701
404-975-0277

*Water Gardening*
49 Boone Village
Zionsville, IN 46077
317-769-3278

*The Aquatic Gardener*
The Aquatic Gardeners Association
83 Cathcart St.
London, Ontario, Canada
N6C 3L9

## ORGANIZATIONS

International Water Lily Society
P.O. Box 2309
Columbia, MD 21045
410-730-8396
http://www.h2oily.com/

Associated Koi Clubs of America
http://www.koiusa.com/

National Pond Society
P.O. Box 449
Acworth, GA 30101
770-975-7095
http://www.pondscapes.com

Internet Pond Society
http://w3.one.net/~rzutt/
*A new, interactive, volunteer-run site that includes FAQs from the Usenet REC.PONDS site.*

## Garden Gear

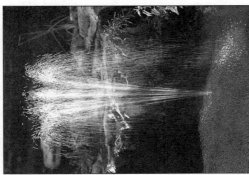

pre-formed poly shell. This one is made of polyethylene, and measures 26" W x 46" L x 12" D. It holds 30 gallons of water.
#30-189  Serenity Pond  $60.00

A good way to experiment with water gardening is to start with a patio water garden. The eight-sided **Cedar Pond** is 32" across and 14" high. It holds 30 gallons of water. Another option is a

Every garden, even if it's on a tiny balcony in the city, has room for a water feature. This **Stone Bowl** holds a cup or two of rainwater. A celtic cross, carved into the inside the bowl, adds a touch of mystery. 12" L x 9¾" W.
#30-165  Celtic Knot Stone Bowl  $44.95

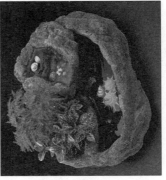

You can enjoy the sound of moving water indoors or out with a **Tabletop Water Garden**. Fill the bottom pool with about 2 quarts of water, add a few plants, and plug it in. Water is circulated over a tiny waterfall, creating a soothing sound.
#23-026  Tabletop Water Garden  $149.00

The easiest way to construct an in-ground water garden is to use a

36-inch-diameter molded polyethylene **Kettle Pond**. It has shelves inside to support potted water plants, and it holds 35 gallons of water.

If you have a half whiskey barrel, you can create a patio water garden with either the **American Village Fountain**, or the **Bamboo Fountain**. The first one looks like an old-fashioned hand-crank pump, and the second is a traditional Japanese style. Both kits include a poly liner for the barrel, an electric pump, and all necessary hoses.
#30-190  Cedar Deck Pond  $160.00
#30-305  Kettle Pond  $120.00
#30-238  American Village Fountain  $165.00
#30-237  Bamboo Fountain  $165.00

ity, and is suitable for containers or small ponds. The **Multi-Fountain** has four spouts that produce a flowery spray up to 4 feet high. For a large pond, the **Floating Fountain** will create a variety of different spray patterns, including a 12-foot-high column. It will aerate a pond up to one-quarter acre in area. No electric power at your pond site? A **Solar Panel** produces standard AC current to power a pump or fountain.
#30-297  Column Fountain  $44.95
#30-298  Multi-Fountain  $59.95
#30-300  Floating Fountain  $1495.00
#30-299  Solar Panel  $299.99

Fountains add excitement and also aerate the water to help keep it clean. The **Column Fountain** adjusts from a gurgling bubbler to a 2-foot-high column. It runs on just 4 watts of electric-

Help keep your water garden clear with **Bacta-Pur**. It contains water-cleaning microorganisms that help prevent algae growth and break down oxygen-robbing sediments. 2 ounces per week treats 100 gallons of water.
#06-950  Bacta-Pur, 1 qt.  $19.95

**Mosquito Rings** contain a natural bacterium that kills mosquito larvae. Each ring treats an area up to 100 square feet and lasts 30 days.
#05-390  Mosquito Rings, six  $11.95

# gardening indoors

PASSPORT TO GARDENING
GARDENING INDOORS

M ost avid gardeners don't check their love of plants at the door. We keep ferns in the bathroom, begonias in the study, a dwarf citrus in the bedroom, pots of rosemary in the kitchen, and seedlings in the basement. Today there are so many interesting plants that can be grown indoors that there's simply no reason for a gardener not to be surrounded by plants all year-round.

Indoor gardening had its first heyday during Victorian times. As plants such as abutilons, palms, and hibiscus were discovered by botanists in remote parts of the world, those who could afford to scrambled to fill their parlors and conservatories with these exotic beauties. There was another indoor plant revival during the 1970s, though it was largely confined to foliage plants such as spider plants, Swedish ivy, and ferns. Today, commercial greenhouses offer an eye-popping selection of plants to choose from, including orchids, bougainvillea, scented geraniums, exotic begonias, pentas, and gardenias. All these beauties are within your reach. The trick is learning how to keep them happy indoors.

## Understanding Indoor Plants

The more you know about your indoor plants and where they come from, the better you will be able to please them. Understanding a plant's native habitat can help you decide what potting soil to use, how often to water, what window the plant should be in, and whether or not it needs extra humidity. But even if you don't have specific cultural information about each and every one of your houseplants, you can feel your way to success with some general guidelines.

**SOIL.** If possible, your potting soil should be tailored to the particular type of plant you are growing. Cactus, succulents, and rosemary, for example, prefer a coarse, well-drained soil that is about one-third sand. Seedlings should be grown in a light, moisture-retentive, soilless mix. African violets and ferns prefer soil with a high humus content, which can be achieved by adding leaf mold or shredded bark. Many kinds of orchids are happiest growing in nothing but fir bark or sphagnum moss. (See page 199 for some common soil blends.)

## Guest Expert

### Tovah Martin

Why does everyone line up their houseplants in soldier-straight rows on the windowsill? Why are houseplants displayed in leprechaun-colored plastic pots? The garden that grows on the inside of the window-panes should be just as carefully designed as the landscape in your backyard. It's so easy to cluster potted houseplants in groupings that enhance the color of each bloomer. It's so easy to place plants so tall topiaries stand closer to the panes and cascading sprawlers are showering over the window ledge. Think of the indoor garden as a design challenge, just as you approach the garden outdoors in a creative fashion. Be daring, match colors, play with forms and textures. Train plants with an eye attuned to achieving a pleasing overall picture. Display those plants in containers that are as natural and pleasing as the plants themselves. Rustic baskets, twig trellises, metal trellises, terra cotta pots, and colorfully glazed containers can all enhance the scene. Choose plants that match the decor of your room; select plants that carry out a theme. With a little creativity and imagination, your windowsill can become a garden in miniature.

*Tovah Martin is a staff horticulturist at White Flower Farm. She is also the garden editor for Victoria magazine and The Litchfield County Times. She is the author of several gardening books including Tasha Tudor's Garden, Well-Clad Windowsills, and Windowboxes, a book in the Taylor's Weekend Gardener Series. The windows of her home in Roxbury, Connecticut are dense with a garden of houseplants.*

## Favorite Books

**The Houseplant Encyclopedia** by *Ingrid Jantra and Ursula Kruger* (Firefly, 1997). A hefty, full-color reference book, originally published in Germany. Over 100 pages of general how-to information, followed by an alphabetical listing of indoor plants with excellent color photographs and detailed cultural information. Besides ivies and begonias, this book includes lots of unusual plants ignored by other books. 384 pages, hardcover, $40.00.

**Well-Clad Windowsills** *by Tovah Martin* (Macmillan, 1994). A connoisseur's guide to flowering plants for indoor growing. Plants are grouped by the window exposure they prefer (east, west, north, south). Includes abutilons, bougainvilleas, pentas, jasmines, rex begonias, camellias, ferns, and more than a dozen others. Easy, engaging reading, with valuable advice based on several generations of experience with indoor plants. 212 pages, hardcover, $27.50.

**Grow It Indoors** *by Richard W. Langer* (Stackpole, 1995). Interesting reading, with more background information about indoor plants than any other book reviewed. The black and white illustrations will not help you identify plants, but they do an excellent job of showing cultural techniques. The fun and engaging tone is accessible to beginners, but the depth of information will also satisfy more experienced growers. 363 pages, paperback, $16.95.

## QUICK REFERENCE WATERING GUIDE

### Water needed more often if:

The plant container is made of unglazed clay.

The plant is large but the pot is small.

The plant has filled the pot with tightly packed roots.

The plant is in an active growth period.

The temperature is high.

The humidity is low.

The plant has large, thin leaves.

### Water needed less often if:

The container is glazed clay or plastic.

The plant is small and the pot large.

The plant has not filled the pot with roots.

The plant has just been repotted.

The plant is in a rest period.

The temperature is low.

The humidity is high.

The plant has succulent leaves or stems.

—from *Success with Houseplants* (Reader's Digest, 1981)

## Giving the Right Amount of Water

### Watering plentifully

Refresh a plant that needs watering plentifully when the surface of the potting mixture begins to feel dry to the touch.

Flood the surface with water until the entire mixture is saturated and water flows through the drainage hole.

As soon as excess water has drained from the mixture, remove the plant and empty the saucer before replacing it.

### Watering moderately

Refresh a plant that needs watering moderately when the top half inch of the mixture feels dry to your finger.

Pour water onto the surface until the entire mixture is thoroughly moistened but not saturated.

It is time to stop adding water when a few drops appear from the hole in the bottom of the pot.

### Watering sparingly

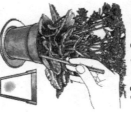

Refresh a plant that needs watering sparingly when two-thirds of the mixture has dried out. Test with a stake.

Just cover the surface with water, so that it percolates down through the mixture, but does not appear in the saucer.

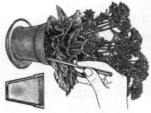

Test with the stake again — the entire mixture must be barely moist, so if there are still dry patches water a little more.

—from *Success with Houseplants* (Reader's Digest, 1981)

Many types of potting mixes are composed of peat moss, vermiculite, and perlite. These soilless mixes absorb moisture very well and resist compaction, but they tend to dry out very quickly. Since they do not contain any nutrients, you must provide your plants with a consistent supply of fertilizer. One advantage to a soilless mix is that it is sterile, so there is no chance of introducing pest or disease problems.

Many gardeners combine a soilless mix with some organic components such as leaf mold, finished compost, composted peat, or sterilized garden soil. A growing medium that contains some organic matter will usually not dry out as fast as a soilless mix. You will also be introducing beneficial microorganisms and nutrients.

The most critical consideration when you're purchasing or blending your own potting soil is to ensure that the mix is light enough to provide adequate pore space for air, water, and healthy root growth. Month after month of overhead watering, without the benefit of earthworms and weather to aerate the soil, usually results in an unhealthy, compacted root ball. To ensure that your plants have the oxygen they need for healthy root growth, your potting soil should contain plenty of perlite, vermiculite, or sharp sand. This will allow water to drain freely, and ensure that the soil is at least 10 to 20 percent air.

**TEMPERATURE.** In their natural habitat, most plants experience a day-to-night temperature fluctuation of at least 10°F. In your home, they will benefit from having this same temperature differential. Most plants also expect a resting period each year; in fact, some flowering plants actually require a period of dormancy before they will set bud and flower. During the late fall and early winter, when the intensity and duration of natural light is lowest, it's wise to cut back on water and fertilizer. Once the day length begins to increase, you can declare it to be spring, and step up the water and fertilizer. Your plants will respond with healthy new growth.

**HUMIDITY.** Most plants are happiest when the relative humidity is 50 percent or higher, though they can usually survive at 30 to 40 percent. If the air is much drier than that, they are unable to absorb enough water through their roots to keep up with the water lost through their leaves. Unfortunately, indoor air, especially in the winter, is often as low as 10 to 20 percent humidity. Misting your plants is beneficial, but it only helps for an hour or so. A better solution is to use a cool vapor humidifier (which you will benefit from as well). You can also cluster your plants together so that, as they release moisture into the air, they'll humidify their neighbors. Another effective technique is to arrange your plants on a gravel-

## SOIL BLENDS FOR INDOOR PLANTS

### Soilless Mix
1 quart ground sphagnum moss
1 quart horticultural vermiculite
1 quart perlite
3 tablespoons dolomitic lime
1 cup horticultural charcoal

### Soil-Based Mix
*(from Logee's Greenhouse, Danielson, Conn.)*
1 part loam
1 part perlite or vermiculite
1 part milled sphagnum moss
1 part sand
1 cup bone meal per bushel
10 tablespoons ground limestone per bushel

### Humus-Rich Mix
1 part sand
1 part milled sphagnum moss
1 part rich garden soil
1 part leaf mold

### Orchid Mix
1 quart whole sphagnum moss
1 quart coarse perlite
1 tablespoon dolomitic lime
1 cup horticultural charcoal

## Other Good Books

**Success with Houseplants** (Reader's Digest, 1981).
Good section on lighting and general plant care. Lots of color photos. A good reference for beginner to intermediate gardeners. 480 pages, hardcover, $26.00.

**Gardening in Your Apartment** by *Gilly Love* (Lorenz, 1996).
A book of pure inspiration for gardeners with limited space. 144 pages, hardcover, $27.50.

**The Heathy Indoor Plant** by *Charles C. Powell and Rosemarie Rossetti* (Rosewell, 1992).
Written for interior plantscapers, this book goes into far more detail than most indoor gardeners need. But the serious enthusiast will be delighted to find a wealth of in-depth information about lighting, soil mixes, and more. 297 pages, paperback, $27.00.

## Web Sites

**Houseplants at the Gardening Launch Pad**
http://www.tpoint.net/neighbor.HsP.html
Alphabetical listing by Latin name.

**Time-Life Pavilion**
http://pathfinder.com/vg/TimeLife/Houseplants/directoryflowering.html
Characteristics and needs of 130 flowering houseplants. Links to other information and sources.

**Horticulture Solutions Series from Illinois Cooperative Extension Service**
http://www.ag.uiuc.edu/~robsond/solutions/horticulture/house.html
Cultural information for common houseplants.

**Houseplant Survivor's Guide**
http://www.ext.vt.edu:4040/eis/owa/docdb.getcat?cat=ir-ih-ig
Monthly houseplant tips from Virginia Cooperative Extension Service.

**The Sunroom**
http://www.prairienet.org/garden-gate/sunroom.htm
Fact sheets, tips, and discussion lists about indoor gardening.

---

# How to Revive a Parched Houseplant

The leaves of this plant are wilting and falling, obviously because water is not getting through to them.

It may be that the dried-out root ball has shrunk away from the side of the pot so that water runs down the gap.

Or the potting mixture may have become compacted and insufficiently porous, so that water cannot penetrate.

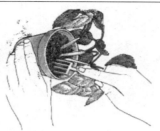

To revive the plant begin by breaking up the surface of the mixture with a pointed tool, taking care not to harm roots.

Then immerse the pot in a bucket of water, until bubbles stop rising from the mixture. Meanwhile, spray leaves.

Let excess water drain away. If the problem recurs after a week, assume the mixture is wrong, and repot the plant.

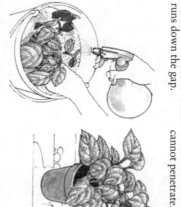

— from *Success with Houseplants* (Reader's Digest, 1981)

filled tray that contains about ¼ inch of water. As the water evaporates, it will humidify the air around your plants. Just be careful that the pots don't sit directly in the water.

**WATER.** More houseplants die from overwatering than from anything else. The best advice is to resist the temptation to water on a regular schedule. Your plants will require frequent watering if the weather has been sunny and warm, and they may not need a drop if the weather has been cool and cloudy. Make a habit of checking the soil of at least a few indicator plants, and water only if it feels dry to a depth of ½ to 1 inch.

When you do water, drench the root ball until you can see some water seep out the bottom of the pot. This will ensure that the entire root ball gets moistened. Small pots will benefit from being soaked in water for about an hour, once a month. Whenever possible, try to water your plants with room temperature water to avoid shocking the roots.

And never use water that has been chemically softened. It contains salts that are harmful to plants. If your water is very hard, consider installing a demineralizing attachment to filter out impurities, such as lime and chlorine.

**NUTRIENTS.** Indoor plants are usually not too fussy about fertilizers. The most important thing is to not overdo it. Follow the instructions on the package, and err on the weak side. Always water your plants

## Levels of Light Intensity in a Room

Different levels of light in a typical room, in the northern hemisphere, on a summer day when direct sunlight is not obscured by clouds. In lower latitudes the light would be brighter, but would extend less far into the room. Obviously, the amount of light entering a room will be affected by local factors such as the number and size of the windows, and the presence of nearby buildings and trees.

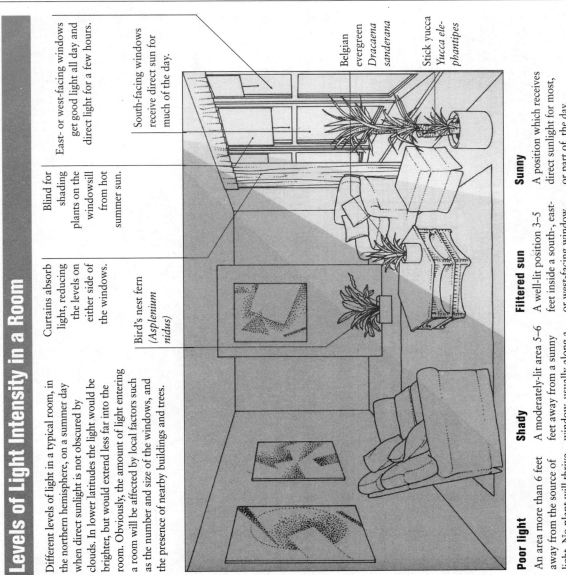

East- or west-facing windows get good light all day and direct light for a few hours.

South-facing windows receive direct sun for much of the day.

Blind for shading plants on the windowsill from hot summer sun.

Curtains absorb light, reducing the levels on either side of the windows.

Bird's nest fern (*Asplenium nidus*)

Belgian evergreen *Dracaena sanderana*

Stick yucca *Yucca elephantipes*

**Poor light**

An area more than 6 feet away from the source of light. No plant will thrive here, even though the area seems bright to the human eye.

**Shady**

A moderately-lit area 5–6 feet away from a sunny window, usually along a side wall, or near a well-lit north-facing window.

**Filtered sun**

A well-lit position 3–5 feet inside a south-, east- or west-facing window, or one receiving direct sunlight filtered by a tree or curtain.

**Sunny**

A position which receives direct sunlight for most, or part of, the day. The strength of the sunlight will depend on your latitude.

—from *The Indoor Garden Book* by John Brookes (DK Publishing, 1994)

# Garden Gear

**Professional Container Mix** is a specially formulated blend of sphagnum moss and vermiculite designed to retain moisture and keep soil loose and aerated. Odor-free composted manure and other nutrients. Highly recommended for use in self-watering containers and for large potted plants, indoors or out.
#03-375 Professional Container Mix, 20 quarts $6.95

A steel **Plant Terrace** gives you plenty of room to display a large collection of potted plants. The stands can be used separately, or can be combined as needed. Made of sturdy steel and wire with a green vinyl finish. Quarter Terrace is 23" W; Straight Terrace is 39" W; Both are 27" H.
#30-034 Quarter Round Terrace $49.95
#30-033 Straight Terrace $89.95

**Copper Humidity Trays** protect your windowsills. Filled with a little water, they will also help humidify your plants. Solid copper with rolled edges. The 1-inch-high sides hold water and pebbles. Both sizes are 5 inches wide.
#30-058 20" Copper Tray $29.95
#30-059 29" Copper Tray $39.95

**ROOTS Plus for Houseplants** is a kelp-based, 2-4-4 formulation, with liquid humus, balanced nutrients, and trace minerals to help your plants overcome the stress of dry air and irregular watering.
#30-028 ROOTS Plus for Houseplants, 8 oz $4.95

**Hydrosource** is a non-toxic, water-absorbing polymer that can be mixed into potting soil to help retain water. Effective for 10 years or more. Use 1 teaspoon per quart of soil.
#30-105 Fine Grind Hydrosource, 1 lb $9.95

**An Indoor Watering Hose** saves on trips to the faucet and reduces spills. It attaches to any standard faucet and comes with 50' of hose.
#23-041 Aqua-Matic Indoor Hose $21.95

**A Soil Moisture Meter** can help you avoid problems with overwatering. Just press the meter into the soil and it tells you if you need to water. 11" overall.
#06-110 Soil Moisture Meter $14.95

**Self-Watering Planters** are durable polypropylene pots that look like terra cotta. An integrated reservoir at the bottom provides water for up to a month. Available from Gardener's Supply in 8", 10", 12", 14", and 16" diameter. Prices are $8.95–$19.95

thoroughly before applying any sort of fertilizer. A standard 10-10-10 formulation is fine for most indoor plants. Supplementing with an organic amendment such as liquid seaweed or fish emulsion, or a bios-timulant, will provide some of the trace nutrients lacking in an inorganic plant fertilizer. A top dressing of compost or worm castings is another effective way to add organic nutrients. Be aware that some plants are particularly sensitive to pH level, and that this sensitivity can be either exacerbated, or corrected, with the right fertilizer.

**LIGHT.** Plants differ greatly in their need for light. Some will be happy with the diffused light from a north window. Others will languish if they don't receive 12 hours of bright light all year-round. Knowing the light requirements for each of your plants will allow you to determine where they will be happiest. Here are some general guidelines for matching plants to various locations in your home.

• Most flowering plants, and some other sun-lovers, need to be within 3 feet of a sunny, south-facing window.

• Plants that prefer bright, indirect light, can be located 3 to 5 feet away from a south-facing window, or within 3 feet of an east- or west-facing window.

• Plants that thrive in diffused light can be placed 6 to 8 feet away from a south-facing window, or within a foot of a north-facing window. In that location they'll receive about 25 percent of the light they would get if they were in front of the sunny, south-facing window.

• During the winter months, you may need to move all of your plants closer to the window in order to compensate for the decrease in light.

• Most plants perform best when they receive 12 to 16 hours of light per day. If you want to keep your plants happy during the short days of winter, you may need to provide supplemental lighting.

## A Few Words of Comfort

Plants have a lifespan, just as people do. If you have a struggling houseplant that has been around for a few years, it may be tired, and all the TLC in the world may not be able to revive it. Consider starting over with a new plant. Remember that unhealthy plants attract insects like a magnet, and when the infestation spreads to your other plants, you may regret your earlier large-heartedness. Gift plants, such as cinerarias, poinsettias, chrysanthemums, azaleas, and cyclamen, are specifically grown and sold as temporary indoor decorations, to be discarded after they have finished flowering. Some of these plants can be nursed along to flower again, but it is usually difficult to provide the conditions they need for another lush display of blooms.

## Resources

**Indoor Gardening Society of America**
944 South Monroe Road
Tallmadge, OH 44278

### SUPPLIERS

**The Banana Tree**
715 Northampton Street
Easton, PA 18042
610-253-9589
*Seeds for unusual plants from around the world. Catalog $3.00.*

**Davidson-Wilson Greenhouses**
RR 2 Box 168
Crawfordsville, IN 47933-9426
765-364-0556
http://www.gardenscape.com/davidson-wilson.html
*Common and exotic geraniums, tropicals, and novelty plants.*

**Glasshouse Works**
Church Street
Stewart, OH 45778-0097
800-837-2142
http://www.glasshouseworks.com
*An awesome selection of exotic plants. Over 100 varieties of ivies, 80 varieties of coleus. Also passiflora, plectranthus, jasmine, kalanchoe, and much more. Catalog $2.00.*

**Logee's Greenhouses**
141 North Street
Danielson, CT 06239
860-774-8038
http://www.logees.com
*A venerable family business offering a broad selection of unusual and tropical plants for windowsills, patios, or greenhouses. Catalog $3.00 (refundable with order).*

# growing under lights

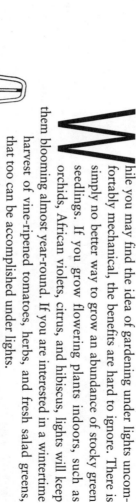

GROWING UNDER LIGHTS

W hile you may find the idea of gardening under lights uncomfortably mechanical, the benefits are hard to ignore. There is simply no better way to grow an abundance of stocky green seedlings. If you grow flowering plants indoors, such as orchids, African violets, citrus, and hibiscus, lights will keep them blooming almost year-round. If you are interested in a wintertime harvest of vine-ripened tomatoes, herbs, and fresh salad greens, that too can be accomplished under lights.

By learning how plants use light, and about the many bulb and fixture options now on the market, you can select an indoor lighting system that is perfectly suited to your home and the types of plants you want to grow. Not all plants require the same color, intensity, and duration of light. To be successful gardening under artificial lights, you should understand the needs of your plants, and then provide them with the right quality of light.

## The Right Color Light

Sunlight contains the complete spectrum of light including all colors of the rainbow — red, through yellow, to blue and violet. Plants utilize the full spectrum of light for photosynthesis, though red and blue light seem to be most critical. Red light stimulates vegetative growth and flowering, but if a plant gets too much red light, it will become tall and spindly. Blue light regulates plant growth, which makes it ideal for growing foliage plants and short, stocky seedlings.

Some plants perform best when given more of a certain color light. An African violet, for example, will thrive under blue light, but if it doesn't also receive an abundance of red light, it will probably never flower. If you learn what color light your plants need, you can then select the right type of bulbs to meet that need.

## The Right Intensity of Light

The intensity of light that a plant receives indoors is determined by the wattage of the bulb and by how close the plant is to the light source. Just as plants differ in their need for certain colors of light, they also differ in their need for light intensity. Typically, those plants that are native to

*Guest Expert*

## Rick Ceballos

I n photosynthesis, the raw materials of carbon dioxide and water, in the presence of light, combine to form energy-rich carbohydrates to fuel plant growth. Of all these components, light is the most limiting factor.

Plants such as spinach and lettuce will do well under relatively low-intensity lighting, such as is produced by standard fluorescent bulbs. Tomatoes, cucumbers, and most tropical flowering plants require a higher intensity of light to properly flower and fruit. For these plants, fluorescent bulbs are fine during the early vegetative stages, but high-intensity lighting such as that produced by metal halide or sodium vapor lights is needed to produce full-grown, well-fruited plants.

Plants utilize only the visible part of the light spectrum. The blue-violet range has the most influence on vegetative growth, while the yellow-orange range affects fruiting and flowering. When growing plants under artificial lights, the spectral characteristics of the light is a vital factor. This is especially true when using fluorescent and incandescent lights, which have a relatively low light intensity. Recent research has shown that high light levels will offset imbalances in the spectral makeup of the lighting. This suggests that high intensity discharge (HID) lights such as halide or sodium, can produce favorable results through the output of high light levels alone.

*Rick Ceballos is a Gardener's Supply Greenhouse Technician.*

*Favorite Books*

Several light gardening books were published during the 1960s and 1970s, but they are dated and most are out-of-print. Besides the book listed below, we have been unable to find any recent publications that focus on this topic. A good indoor gardening book (see pages 197 and 199) will often include some information about growing plants under lights. Books about hydroponic gardening often include a detailed section about gardening under lights.

**The Healthy Indoor Plant** *by Charles Powell and Rosemarie Rossetti* (Rosewell, 1992). Though this book is written for interior plantscaping professionals, it is the only one we could find that includes solid information about gardening under lights. It covers how to measure light intensity, adjust for seasonal fluctuations in natural light, and manage photoperiods, the advantages and disadvantages of various types of lights, and much more. Not a book for the average gardener. 274 pages, paperback, $27.00.

> " If you were to measure light intensity at various spots outdoors as well as in an indoor garden, you would clearly see the tremendous variability of this environmental element. Light intensities vary markedly in any interiorscape. Furthermore, plants in even the most highly lighted indoor garden generally must adjust to much lower levels of light intensity than do those plants growing outdoors, in shaded sites. Management of light, then, often becomes an all-consuming factor in the mind of a good indoor gardener."
>
> by Charles C. Powell and Rosemarie Rossetti
>
> —from *The Healthy Indoor Plant* (Rosewell, 1992)

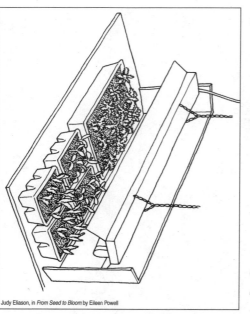

Judy Eliason, in *From Seed to Bloom* by Eileen Powell

*Fluorescent lights should be positioned no more than 4–6 inches away from young seedlings. For best results, the height of the fixture should be adjusted weekly.*

tropical jungles or shady forests do not require as much light as plants that evolved in dry, sunny climates such as the Mediterranean or southern Mexico.

Most common flowering houseplants, such as African violets and begonias, are usually quite happy being 10 to 12 inches away from a light source. Non-flowering foliage plants, such as ivy or philodendron, can be placed as much as 36 inches away from a light source. But most flowering plants, such as orchids, gardenias, and citrus, as well as most vegetable plants, require a much higher light intensity to flower and produce fruit. This need for intense light holds true even when the plants are seedlings (which is why vegetable and flower seedlings have a tendency to get so tall and spindly if they don't have adequate light). If you are trying to grow light-hungry plants indoors, you must be able to meet their need for plenty of bright light.

## The Right Duration of Light

No matter what types of plants you are growing indoors, you must be sure to always give them time to sleep. When it's dark, plants respire, which is an important part of their growth process. The balance of rest time to active growth time affects many biological processes, including growth rate, and the setting of buds and fruit.

Like people, plants differ in the amount of rest they require. Botanists usually divide plants into one of three categories relating to their preferred day length: short-day, long-day, or day-neutral. Short-day plants, such as chrysanthemums, kalanchoe, azaleas, and begonias, will thrive on less than 12 hours of light per day. In fact, these plants must usually go through a series of even shorter days (less than 12 hours) before they will set buds and flower.

Long-day plants require at least 14 to 18 hours of light each day. Once you understand that most vegetables and garden flowers are long-day plants, it's easy to see why the seedlings of these plants get pale and leggy when they receive less than 16 hours of light each day. Day-neutral plants, which include non-flowering foliage plants, as well as geraniums, coleus, and African violets, are usually satisfied with 8 to 12 hours of light all year-round.

Using automatic timers is the best way to ensure that your plants receive the right duration of light each day. If you start by grouping your plants according to what day length they prefer, and what color and intensity of light they need, your indoor gardening adventures will be easier, and much more rewarding.

## Types of Bulbs for Indoor Growing

There have been some significant innovations in lighting technology over the past ten years, and this has opened up many new opportunities for indoor gardeners. Today you can choose between incandescent, fluorescent, and high-intensity discharge (HID) bulbs, each of which has its own benefits. Your choice should be determined by the type of plants you want to grow, and where you plan to locate your indoor garden.

**INCANDESCENT BULBS** are the type of light bulbs used in most homes. They are a good source of red light, but a poor source of blue. These bulbs also produce a great deal of heat in relation to the amount of light they give off. If you position your plants too close to an incandescent bulb, the foliage can be easily burned. Though **halogen** light bulbs produce a more balanced spectrum of light, they generate even more heat than incandescent bulbs.

**FLUORESCENT BULBS** produce two to three times more light than incandescent bulbs for the same amount of energy. They are the most inexpensive lights for indoor gardening. The color of light produced by fluorescent bulbs is determined by the type of phosphor coating on the inside of the bulb. Most stores and office buildings use **cool white** fluorescent bulbs, which are a good source of blue and yellow-green light, but are a poor source of red light. **Warm white** fluorescent bulbs emit plenty of orange and red light, but less light in the blue and green spectrum. If you are growing seedlings under 2-bulb fluorescent fixtures, you can usually achieve a good color balance by combining one cool white and one warm white bulb.

The newest and most popular bulbs for indoor gardening are **full-spectrum lights**. These bulbs duplicate 90 to 94 percent of the natural solar spectrum, which keeps almost any kind of plant happy — especially seedlings.

## Suppliers

Many of the hydroponics suppliers listed on page 226 also offer a selection of HID lighting.

**Hydrofarm Gardening Products**
3135 Kerner Blvd.
San Rafael, CA 94901
1-800-634-9999

**Diamond Lights**
628 Lindaro Street
San Rafael, CA 94901
1-800-331-3994

## Tips for Growing Under Lights

→ You may notice that the light from a fluorescent bulb is more intense at the center of the bulb than it is at the ends. For this reason, you should rotate your plants on a weekly or monthly basis.

→ Painting your growing trays white, or using foil-covered reflectors, can also increase the amount of light your plants receive.

→ When the ends of a fluorescent tube darken, it means that the light

is aging. Light output from an old bulb can be less than half that of a new bulb.

→ Be sure to clean your fluorescent bulbs monthly. An accumulation of dust and dirt can dramatically reduce the amount of light your plants receive.

→ If you place your hand where the light hits the foliage, you should not feel any warmth. If you do, the light is too close.

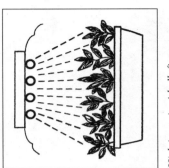

*High intensity 4-bulb fixtures put out twice the light. They are ideal for flowering plants or indoor herbs.*

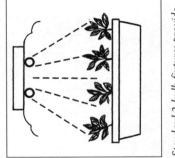

*Standard 2-bulb fixtures provide good light distribution for seedlings, houseplants, or an indoor bed of lettuce.*

From Gardener's Supply Company

Unlike traditional grow lights, which emit a purplish or pinkish glow, full-spectrum bulbs emit a pleasant white light that does not distort foliage or flower colors. Their usable life is usually about twice as long as standard bulbs, and they are available as either fluorescent or incandescent bulbs.

**HIGH-INTENSITY DISCHARGE LAMPS** (HIDs) are used by commercial growers and serious horticulturalists. They generally emit twice the amount of light (lumens) as an incandescent or fluorescent bulb for the same amount of energy. Because they are so energy-efficient, HIDs are used to light shopping malls, baseball fields, streets, and gymnasiums. The special fixtures and bulbs used in HID lighting are considerably more expensive than those needed for incandescent or fluorescent lights. They also tend to be high-wattage bulbs, so you need to consider the load on your electrical system. Some of these lights burn so brightly that they must be located in a special room and eye protection must be worn when working around them.

Metal halide, high-pressure sodium, and mercury vapor lights are three different types of HIDs. **Metal halide lights** emit an intense, bluish-white light that is excellent for growing plants. The foliage stays green and vigorous, and plants are usually stocky and strong. At present, metal halide lights are the number one choice for serious indoor gardeners.

## Light Intensities of Common Sites

| | Footcandles Commonly Measured* |
| --- | --- |
| **OUTDOORS** | |
| Sunny spot in summer | 10,000 to 15,000 |
| Open shade in summer | 4,000 to 8,000 |
| Sunny spot in winter | 7,000 to 10,000 |
| **INDOORS** | |
| South-facing window, full summer sun | 8,000 to 10,000 |
| South-facing window, curtain filtered sun | 1,000 to 3,000 |
| Bright, indirect window light | 600 to 1,000 |
| North-facing windows, sunny summer day | 2,000 to 4,000 |
| North facing windows, sunny winter day | 500 to 1,000 |
| Fluorescent fixture with 2, 40-watt bulbs (6 inches below) | 600 to 800 |
| Fluorescent fixture with 2, 40-watt bulbs (12 inches below) | 300 to 500 |
| Comfortable reading light | 50 to 100 |
| Minimal reading light | 20 to 30 |
| Chapels | 5 to 10 |
| Reception desk | 20 to 50 |

*The footcandle ranges result from measurements for average situations at about 42 degrees North latitude. Window measurements are in the center of unobstructed windows.

—from *The Healthy Indoor Plant* by Charles C. Powell and Rosemarie Rossetti (Rosewell, 1992)

The **Wonderlight** is a wide-spectrum grow light, specially designed for light-hungry flowering plants, including orchids and bougainvilleas. The 160-watt bulb lasts 10,000 hours and is rated at 3,200 lumens. It lights up to a 15-square-foot area.

**#18-017 Wonderlight $49.95**

**Sun-Gro Incandescent Bulbs** can be used in most standard light fixtures. The **Natural Bulbs** replicate 93% of the solar spectrum, making them ideal for foliage plants and seedlings. People also appreciate this balanced light for reading, crafts, or sewing. **Sun-Gro Floral Bulbs** emit extra red-spectrum light to stimulate flowering plants. The 75-watt bulbs are rated for 1,100 hours.

**#03-376 Sun-Gro Natural Light Bulb $9.95**
**#03-377 Sun-Gro Floral Light Bulb $9.95**

## Garden Gear

**Floralight** indoor light gardens are available in 14 different models to suit the needs and space constraints of nearly every indoor gardener. They feature a chromed steel frame, a sliding channel for easy light adjustments, wide-body light fixtures (with the option of 2 or 4 bulbs per fixture), removable waterproof trays, and casters. Prices range from $149 for the tabletop model, to $819 for the 4-tier, high-intensity. Call Gardener's Supply for complete details.

The most popular model is the 3-tier Floralight, which measures 65" H x 51" W, with three growing levels. It uses standard 4-foot fluorescent bulbs.

**#03-292 3-Tier Floralight $459.00**

**SunLite fluorescent bulbs** duplicate 94% of the solar spectrum. Each 40-watt, 4-foot tube is guaranteed for 24,000 hours — 50% longer than a standard fluorescent bulb. The 20-watt, 2-foot tubes are guaranteed for 14,000 hours.

**#03-333A SunLite, two 2-foot tubes $29.95**
**#03-332 SunLite, six 4-foot tubes $74.95**

A **programmable light timer** will turn your light garden on and off automatically. This one has 42 settings and an LCD digital readout. UL-listed.

4½" x 2½".
**#30-420 Digital Programmable Timer $42.95**

---

**Mercury vapor,** or mercury discharge lamps, emit an intense bluish light. These lamps are popular with gardeners because they produce a relatively well-balanced, high-intensity light. Like the other HIDs, a mercury vapor light requires a specialized fixture, and a dedicated location. **High-pressure sodium** bulbs are usually used to promote flowering and fruiting. Their yellow-orange hue makes plants think that fall is coming, which stimulates flower and fruit production. When used exclusively, high-pressure sodium lights produce leggy, weak-stemmed plants. For this reason, they are often used in conjunction with metal halide lights and/or natural sunlight. There are now color-corrected high-pressure sodium lights to provide more of the blue-light spectrum.

Whether you grow under lights for only a few short weeks each spring, or make it a year-round hobby, today's technology makes it easy to ensure that your plants get the quality, intensity, and duration of light they need to stay in peak condition.

# growing
# orchids

The beauty, complexity, and incredible diversity of orchid flowers are unrivalled in the plant world. These exotic beauties comprise the largest family of flowering plants on earth, with over 30,000 different species, and at least 200,000 hybrids. Orchids can be found in the equatorial tropics, the arctic tundra, and everywhere in between. The reason for this diversity lies in the orchid's amazing ability to adapt to its given environment. With so many different orchid varieties that thrive in so many different growing conditions, it is relatively easy to find an orchid that is well suited to the conditions that you can provide — whether it is a kitchen window or a full-size greenhouse. Exploring the diversity of this crowded corner of the plant kingdom has kept many a gardener captivated for a lifetime.

## Orchid Habitat

Most cultivated orchids are native to the tropics. In their natural habitat, they attach themselves to the bark of trees, or the surface of other plants. Their thick, white roots are specially adapted to absorb moisture and dissolved nutrients. Because these tropical orchids usually grow high in the trees, rather than on the forest floor, they are accustomed to good air circulation and plenty of light. They prefer a 12-hour day, all year-round, and require a high intensity of light — about the same as midsummer conditions in temperate regions.

Are orchids difficult to grow? Many of them are. In fact, some are almost impossible to keep alive, much less bring into bloom — even for professional growers. But there are dozens of varieties of orchids, and hundreds of hybrids, that are perfectly happy growing on a sunny windowsill or under lights. For your best crack at success, start by choosing one of the less fussy varieties (see chart on page 215) that is adapted to the type of growing conditions you can provide. Buy the most mature plant you can afford (young plants are much more difficult to please), and, if possible, buy it in bloom, so you'll know what you're striving for.

(see chart on page 215)

## Guest Expert

### Henry Jaworski

Whenever I'm asked to recommend an orchid to a new grower, one of my first questions is, "Where do you live?" No, I'm not after a dinner invitation. The answer helps me decide what to recommend. For instance, if the person lives in the South, I will suggest one of the Phalaenopsis, the so-called Butterfly orchid, which likes a night temperature that rarely drops below 60°F. In this climate Phalaenopsis can be grown outdoors for much of the year, and brought inside to a gauze-covered eastern window once the nights have reached the critical temperature.

For Northerners, my first choice would be one of the Paphiopedilums, the slipper orchids. They can withstand night temperatures five to ten degrees lower than Phals and have a huge variety of flower colors to choose from. They, too, will live outdoors for much of the summer in dappled shade until it is time to go indoors when cold weather bites. Both of these orchid families have simple cultural needs: water at least once a week, with a

light all-purpose fertilizer mixed in every third week. Do not overwater and avoid direct sunlight. Ideally, your hand should barely cast a shadow when light falls on it where the plants will be growing. Treat them with benign neglect and they should survive your ministrations.

Once you have gained confidence with these two families, try Cymbidiums if you live in a cool, moist coastal area, or Oncidiums, which look like a swarm of yellow bees hovering over the pot. I'm also very fond of Cattleyas, which often have strong and interesting scents. They like a night temperature between Phalaenopsis and Paphiopedilum and a bit more light on their thick, hard leaves.

After a year or two of experience you will be hooked enough to try any one of the 20,000 species of orchids.

*Henry Jaworski is the author of Orchids Simplified (Chapters, 1992). He lives in Toronto.*

**Orchids Simplified** *by Henry Jaworski* (Chapters, 1992). An easy-to-read text with a friendly tone. The author conveys the enthusiasm of an avid hobbyist. Excellent cultural information, with useful charts and plenty of how-to photos. Hundreds of color photos showing the beauty and diversity of orchid flowers. Highly recommended. 143 pages, paperback, $19.95.

**Orchid Growing Basics** *by Dr. Gustav Schoser* (Sterling, 1993). Solid information presented in a clear and easy manner. Covers general cultural information for all orchids, as well as very specific growing instructions by variety. Includes recommended varieties and hybrids, with place of origin noted. Highly recommended. 128 pages, paperback, $12.95.

**Home Orchid Growing** *by Rebecca Tyson Northern* (Prentice-Hall, 1992). Intermediate to advanced orchid enthusiasts agree that this is the #1 reference book. First published in 1950, it has been updated several times. Very comprehensive, yet accessible. 384 pages, paperback, $50.00.

**Growing Orchids** *prepared by the American Orchid Society* (AOS, 1993). A bit technical in its delivery. A 30-page introduction to the orchid family is followed by a series of 4- or 5-page sections devoted to each of the 15 most popular genera. Sections are written by expert growers, and cover light, temperature, watering, humidity, fertilizing, and potting. 136 pages, paperback, $8.95.

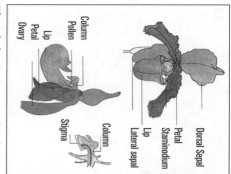

Dorsal Sepal
Petal
Staminodium
Lip
Lateral sepal

Column
Pollen
Lip
Petal
Ovary

Stigma
Column

Regina Brendel, Aarbergen-Panrod, in *Orchid Growing Basics* by Gustav Schoser

*Though the appearance of orchid flowers varies greatly, they all follow a certain basic structure.*

# Understanding How Orchids Grow

Orchids are usually grouped into two broad categories that characterize their growth habits. **Monopodial** orchids have a single, upright stem, with leaves arranged opposite each other along the stem. The flower stem appears from the base of the uppermost leaves. Orchids with this growth habit include the phalaenopsis and vandas. The more common growth habit is **sympodial**. These orchids grow horizontally, sending out new shoots from the old rhizome. Leaves and flower scapes form at the top of the new shoots. Many sympodial orchids form pseudobulbs, which are swollen shoots that store water and nutrients to help the plant survive periods of prolonged drought. Sympodial orchids include (among others) cattleya, cymbidium, oncidium, and dendrobium.

Orchids can also be classified by their native habitat, which gives an indication of the temperature, moisture, and light levels they prefer. Orchids native to the humid tropics, such as phalaenopsis and paphiopedilum, prefer daytime temperatures of 73° to 85°F, with 80 to 90 percent humidity. They are happiest in an east or southeast window where the light is not too intense. Warm-climate orchids, including cymbidiums and dendrobiums, are accustomed to an average temperature of 55° to 70°F, a steady supply of moisture, and good air circulation. They are generally happy in a south-facing window, though they may need a little shading during high summer. Cattleyas and some oncidiums grow where days are dry and relatively cool. They are able to tolerate a long dry season with temperatures of 80° or 90°F, followed by a distinct rainy season. Their need for light is high, so they should be placed in a sunny, south-facing window. High-altitude orchids, such as masdevallia and epidendrum, grow in the cloud forests where average temperatures are 60° to 70°F, and humidity is very high. These orchids prefer filtered light that is not too intense.

# Caring for Orchids

With 30,000 different species of orchids, it is impossible to give general care and cultivation instructions. However, how an orchid looks can provide clues to its preferences for light, water, and growing medium. If the plant has few leaves, or leatherlike leaves (like most cattleyas and oncidiums), that indicates it has a high light requirement. If the leaves are soft and limp (like some phalaenopsis and most paphiopedilum), the plants are probably very light-sensitive, and should not be placed in a sunny south-facing window. If the orchid has fat pseudobulbs, it should be watered sparingly, and should be grown on coarse chunks of bark or lava rock. If the orchid has no pseudobulbs, it may require more frequent watering, or should be grown in a more moisture-retentive growing medium, such as sphagnum moss.

**LIGHT.** As a general rule, orchids are light-hungry plants. For best results, they should get 12 to 14 hours of light each day, year-round. In a tropical environment, the duration and intensity of natural light does not vary as it does in temperate climates. For this reason, you may need to move your orchids around, and supplement with artificial light to keep them happy during the winter months.

South- and east-facing windows are usually the best spot for orchids. West windows can be too hot, and northern ones are usually too dark. If you don't have a good window location for your orchids, they will be perfectly happy growing under artificial lights. Orchids should be positioned no more than 6 to 8 inches away from a set of 4-foot fluorescent bulbs. Opinions vary as to the benefits of cool white, warm white, and grow light bulbs. The new full-spectrum bulbs, such as VitaLite, are probably the best all-around choice. Some orchids with very high light requirements, such as vandas and cymbidiums, may need high-intensity discharge lighting in order to flower. See the chapter on "Growing Under Lights" for more information.

**GROWING MEDIA.** Terrestrial orchids, such as paphiopedilums and some cymbidiums, grow in soil. But most tropical orchids are *epiphytes*, which means that they grow in the air, rather than in soil. Their fleshy roots are covered with a layer of white cells called *velamen*, which acts as a sponge to absorb water. The coating also protects the roots from heat and moisture loss.

An orchid growing medium must provide good air circulation, and permit water to drain very quickly. It must also give the roots something secure to cling to. Depending on the type of orchid, they can be happy growing in peat moss, fir bark, dried fern roots, sphagnum moss, rock wool, perlite, cork nuggets, stones, coconut fiber, lava rock, or a blend that combines several of these materials. Some epiphytic orchids can also be wired onto slabs of tree fern or cork. As a general rule, fir bark nuggets are the most popular growing medium.

**WATERING.** Most orchids can tolerate drought far better than they can tolerate excess moisture. Nothing kills an orchid faster than letting it sit in a water-logged pot. Without adequate air circulation, the plant will suffocate and die. As a very general rule, orchids should be watered once a week. The growing medium should be allowed to dry out between waterings, and excess water should not come in contact with the roots or the growing medium. After being repotted, most orchids will not resume active growth for several months. Water very sparingly during this readjustment period.

Ed Bonoyer for Gardener's Supply Company

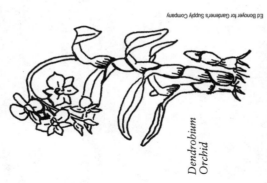

*Dendrobium Orchid*

## PRONUNCIATION BASICS

| | |
|---|---|
| Angraecum | an-GRYE-kum |
| Cattleya | KAT-lee-a |
| Coelogyne | see-LOJ-in-ee |
| Cycnoches | SIK-no-keez |
| Cymbidium | sim-BID-ee-um |
| Dendrobium | den-DROH-bee-um |
| Paphiopedilum | paf-ee-oh-PED-i-lum |
| Phalaenopsis | fal-en-OP-sis |
| Phragmipedium | frag-mi-PEE-dee-um |

—from *Orchids Simplified*
by Henry Jaworski (Chapters, 1992)

## Hints for Repotting

- Repot at the end of flowering, when new roots appear at the base of the latest growth. Do not let the roots get more than half an inch long before you repot. If roots do get too long, the plant will lose its momentum of growth and often won't flower on the new growth.

- Most orchids begin new growth in the spring. Repot between late winter and early summer.

- If a plant has to be repotted out of season because of an accident or damaged roots, drape a tent of clear plastic over the plant and pot to retain humidity.

- Repot only a few plants at a time.

- Don't jump from mix to mix. It takes a year to determine how the roots will react to a new potting mix.

- Repot into a smaller pot if the orchid has lost many roots. This makes watering accurately less problematic.

- Don't disturb an orchid's roots needlessly.

- Don't let a plant jiggle in its new home. Secure it with rhizome clips, an upright stick, or even masking tape, so that the plant does not move in its pot. An insecure plant is shy about throwing roots and takes forever to reestablish itself.

—from *Orchids Simplified*
by Henry Jaworski (Chapters, 1992)

## Orchid Facts

❧ Unlike other plants and animals, orchids can produce hybrids between species, and also between related genera. This permits a mind-boggling number of complex hybrids, and is the reason for the very complex names given to most orchids.

❧ Most orchids bloom once a year, but if they are really happy, they may bloom more often. If you want an orchid that blooms during a particular season, the best bet is to purchase a plant that is in bloom at that time.

❧ When an orchid does flower, it usually remains in bloom for six to ten weeks.

❧ Orchids resent repotting, and usually will not flower for at least a year after they have been disturbed. If possible, purchase your orchids in pots, rather than bareroot.

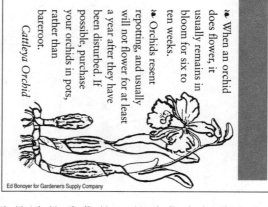

*Cattleya Orchid*

Ed Bonoyer for Gardeners Supply Company

**HUMIDITY.** Most tropical orchids prefer humidity levels of 60 to 80 percent. With the winter-time humidity level in most homes hovering closer to 30 percent, most orchid growers use a humidifier, or set their orchids in gravel-filled trays. Some orchids also benefit from being misted.

**FERTILIZER.** Orchid-growing media provide very few nutrients, so orchids must be fertilized to sustain healthy growth. Use a liquid fertilizer, and dilute it more than you would for other plants. Fertilizer should only be applied when plants are in active growth. This means that most orchids should not be fertilized in midwinter, or right after they have been repotted. Many growers use a 30-10-10 fertilizer, though others prefer 10-10-10 or 10-10-30. Misting your orchids with fish emulsion or seaweed extracts will provide micronutrients.

**POTTING AND REPOTTING.** Orchids are usually happiest in a relatively small pot. Plastic pots are preferred because when it's time to repot, the roots can be more easily detached, or the pots can simply be cut apart. To ensure good drainage, you can fill the bottom inch or two of the pot with Styrofoam "peanuts." Suspend the orchid over the pot, and gradually fill the pot with fir bark chunks or whatever other growing medium you are using. The crown of the plant should be just a bit below the top of the pot. (See page 213 for special tips.)

Some orchids should be re-potted every year. Others may be happy in the same pot for seven or more years. As a general rule, don't repot your orchid unless necessary. Orchids resent being disturbed. Repot if the growing medium has started to break down enough to reduce aeration; if the

## Web Sites

**The Orchid House**
http://retirees.uwaterloo.ca/~jerry/orchids/
*Easy to use. Lots of information, cultural notes, links, FAQs, and music!*

**The Orchid Mall**
http://www.netins.net/showcase/novacon/cyphaven/chorcmall.htm
*Announcements, suppliers, software, societies, reading room, photographs, and places to visit.*

**OrchidWeb**
http://pathfinder.com/vg/Gardens/AOS
*The web site for the American Orchid Society. News, events, judging standards, books, and more.*

**OrchidMania**
http://www.orchids.org
*Lots of links and great information with a socially responsible slant.*

**Orchid Weblophilia**
http://conbio.bio.uci.edu/orchid
*Links, bulletin board, search engine, and more.*

**Linda's Orchid Page**
http://www.lgcy.com/orchids
*An avid orchid enthusiast's award-winning site.*

**Orchid FAQs**
http://www.infomatch.com/~gsinger/orchids/faq/faq14toc.htm
*Contains much of the information from The Orchid House, presented in a more accessible manner. Includes a list of hundreds of orchid suppliers organized by state.*

**The Orchid List Digest**
*A virtual newsletter for the world orchid community. E-mail conversations are compiled daily and are forwarded as a single e-mail document to subscribers. To receive subscription instructions via e-mail, send an e-mail message to MAILSERV@SCIACC.SCU.EDU. In the body of the message put SUBSCRIBE ORCHIDS.*

roots are creeping out well beyond the pot; or if new growth has unbalanced the plant.

**PROPAGATION.** Propagating orchids from seed is quite difficult. Unlike the seeds of other plants, orchid seeds do not contain nutritional storage tissues. To grow, the seed must land where it will find a particular kind of fungi that can penetrate its root system and convert nutrients into a usable form. To overcome the odds, an orchid seed capsule typically disburses millions of microscopic seeds, which can be carried hundreds of miles from the mother plant.

To propagate orchids from seed, you must work in sterile conditions. The seeds must be grown in a gelatinous substance that contains nutrients and growth hormones. You must also be very patient. It takes months for the first leaves to develop, and, even then, they will only be visible with a magnifying glass. Roots appear even later. It will be at least three, and possibly as many as eight years before you see a bloom.

It is far easier to propagate orchids by division. But remember that dividing a plant means forsaking blooms for at least a year. Also, the larger the orchid plant, the more flowers it will produce. Small divisions take many years to mature. For detailed instructions on dividing orchids, consult the book *Home Orchid Growing* by Rebecca Tyson Northern (see "Favorite Books" page 211).

## EASY ORCHID VARIETIES FOR BEGINNERS

**Cattleya.** High light; 55° to 90°F; 40 to 80% humidity; alternate wet and dry; coarse fir bark.
**Phalaenopsis.** Bright light; 65° to 85°F; 40 to 70% humidity; do not allow to dry out; medium fir bark.
**Paphiopedilum.** Bright light; 50° to 80°F depending on variety; 40 to 60% humidity; continuous moisture; bark or fluffy moss mix.

*Ed Bonaver for Gardener's Supply Company*

*Phalaenopsis Orchid*

# *Resources*

## PRODUCTS

There are many suppliers who offer specialized orchid products such as pots, moss, coconut fiber, bark, fertilizers, baskets, wire clips and hangers, labels, shade fabric, etc. Here are a few of them:

**Elmore Orchids**
324 Watt Road
Knoxville, TN 37922
423-966-5294

**M & M Orchid Supply**
P.O. Box 306
Whippany, NJ 07981
201-515-5209

**Orchids by Hausermann, Inc.**
2N 134 Addison Road
Villa Park, IL 60181
630-543-6855

**Teas Nursery Catalog**
P.O. Box 1603
Bellaire, TX 77402-1603

**Tropical Plant Products**
1715 Silver Star Road
P.O. Box 547754
Orlando, FL 32854
407-293-2451
*Wholesale; orders under $150 charged 10% handling fee.*

## ORCHID NURSERIES

Dozens of orchid growers advertise in the American Orchid Society Bulletin (at right). Some of the web sites listed on page 214 also offer orchid plants. A couple contacts to get you started:

**E.F.G. Orchids, Inc.**
2N 150 Addison Rd.
Villa Park, IL 60181
630-543-5628

**J & L Orchids**
20 Sherwood Road
Easton, CT 06612
203-261-3772

**Odom's Orchids, Inc.**
1611 South Jenkins Rd.
Fort Pierce, FL 34947
407-467-1386

**RF Orchids**
28100 SW 182nd Ave.
Homestead, FL 33030
305-245-4570

**Seagulls Landing Orchids**
P.O. Box 388
Glen Head, NY 11545
516-367-6336

**Stewart Orchids**
P.O. Box 550
Carpinteria, CA 93014
800-621-2450

**Windsong Orchids**
14N 456 Factly Rd.
Sycamore, IL 60178
847-683-2139

## MAGAZINES

*Orchids*
The American Orchid Society
6000 S. Olive Ave.
West Palm Beach, FL 33405
561-585-8666.
71726-1741@compuserve.com

*A monthly publication received by all members of the American Orchid Society. As described on the Web by orchid enthusiast Aaron Hicks, this is "a first-class journal, bursting with articles on technique, on culture, and on the latest in orchid science and politics." This is indeed, the definitive publication for orchid growers. It is also a great way to locate orchid growers and specialty products. One-year memberships start at $36. To request a copy of their seasonal book list, which offers over 200 titles, call 561-585-2510.*

# greenhouse gardening

greenhouse gardening

GREENHOUSE GARDENING

Most gardeners would love to own a greenhouse. This appeal may be strongest in cold climates, where a greenhouse can extend the gardening season by several months. But being able to grow an endless supply of sturdy little seedlings is a pretty appealing concept no matter where you live. And what gardener isn't intrigued by the idea of having a tropical environment filled with orchids, citrus, and jasmine; or wouldn't relish the opportunity to pick fresh salad greens and vine-ripened tomatoes on a cold winter day. Greenhouse gardening is a rewarding complement to other gardening activities, and for many people, it can become an absorbing hobby in itself — as exciting and fulfilling as any outdoor garden.

In England, most backyard gardeners own some sort of greenhouse. The cool summers and relatively mild winters make greenhouse gardening a practical necessity. But here in the United States, home greenhouses are still relatively uncommon. As America's gardeners become more experienced and knowledgeable, greenhouse gardening has begun to grow in popularity. There are now dozens of affordable, well-constructed greenhouses on the market, as well as a full range of accessories that make greenhouse gardening easier and more successful. Is there a greenhouse in your future? If you're an avid gardener, the answer is probably yes. The question is, which one to choose, and when to get it!

## Why Do You Want a Greenhouse?

This may seem like a simplistic question, but function is really the most important factor in determining the type and size of greenhouse you choose. An attached greenhouse or sunroom is the right choice if you

want a place to read and putter among potted plants. If starting seeds is your primary goal, a freestanding polyethylene-covered hoop house can probably give you everything you're looking for. If your objective is to have a nearly year-round supply of fresh organic greens and herbs, you may want to consider a solar greenhouse that requires little or no supplemental heat. Can you imagine yourself tending an extensive collection of orchids, propagating begonias, and experimenting with oleander and passiflora? If so, you'll want a well-insulated, professional-quality

## Guest Expert
### Miranda Smith

A solar greenhouse, attached to the south side of your home, is the most versatile type. It will pay for itself in reduced heating costs within 5 to 10 years, and you can expect to eat fresh produce through the year. But the system won't run itself: an attached greenhouse demands daily care.

If you aren't daunted by such responsibility but are put off by the cost of a permanent structure, consider using less expensive materials. Clever design and wise material selection can minimize heat loss and avoid disaster in case of a freeze. A frame made of PVC plumbing pipe and covered with a double layer of greenhouse polyethylene can still add heat to your home and give your plants a fine environment. Insulate this greenhouse with a layer of bubble pack plastic on the insides of the gable ends. On the long side, double the plastic and install a small blower to inflate it; the air insulates the greenhouse while allowing in plenty of light. Rather than using water-filled drums for heat storage, you can use rocks. Build frames to hold rock walls and set your growing beds on top of them.

The least expensive option is the seasonal greenhouse. You can build a sturdy free-standing greenhouse from wood, PVC pipe, or metal hoops and glaze it with anything from glass to 6-mil construction-grade polyethylene. With such a greenhouse, you can start plants in March and carry them through November, even in the cold, cloudy Northeast.

*Miranda Smith teaches organic horticulture and farming at the New England Small Farm Institute (NESFI) in Belchertown, Massachusetts. She has written or contributed to 11 gardening books. In recent years Miranda has developed a 100-member CSA farm and has been teaching greenhouse growing, floriculture, and vegetable production to young farmers.*

Note: Greenhouse gardening is quite different in England than it is here in the U.S., and for this reason, our favorite books are all by American authors. There are many British books with good information about propagating, and some of the finer details relating to specialty plants, but they are best for the more experienced greenhouse gardener who knows which advice should be followed and which should not.

**Greenhouse Gardener's Companion** by *Shane Smith* (Fulcrum, 1993). If you only buy one greenhouse book, this is the one to own. With over 20 years of practical experience in home and commercial greenhouses, the author has an easy, common-sense approach. The book covers both food and ornamental crops, with information on how to select and set up a greenhouse; schedules for year-round harvests; watering techniques; heating and cooling; cultural information about more than 300 flowers, fruits, vegetables, and herbs; solutions for pest and disease problems; and much more. 532 pages, paperback, $19.95.

**Greenhouse Gardening** by *Miranda Smith* (Rodale, 1985). This is not a comprehensive book, but it is filled with great tips about growing vegetables in a home greenhouse. The author takes a holistic approach to greenhouse management, believing that a healthy environment produces the best food with the fewest problems. Out of print.

**Planning, Installing and Using Greenhouses** (Ortho Books, 1991). A good basic book, especially for those who are still dreaming or trying to determine which greenhouse is right for their needs. Includes plans for nine different greenhouses. 112 pages, paperback, $9.95.

## Other Good Books

**The New Organic Grower** by Eliot Coleman (Chelsea Green, 1995). Includes an excellent chapter on hoop-house structures. Based on his market gardening experience, the author provides detailed information on crop rotation cycles for optimum health and maximum yields. 340 pages, paperback, $24.95.

**The Complete Book of the Greenhouse** by Ian G. Walls (Sterling, 1996). British orientation, with good information on plant care, especially tomatoes. Good information about calculating heat loss and computing heating requirements. 256 pages, paperback, $19.95

**The Practical Book of Greenhouse Gardening** by Ronald L. Menage (Sterling, 1991). A British bias against plastic glazings, solar heating, foundations, and heat requirements, but otherwise sound information. 168 pages, paperback, $17.95.

**Building and Using Our Sun Heated Greenhouse** by Helen and Scott Nearing (Garden Way Publishing, 1977). Timeless, practical wisdom from two gardening gurus. A favorite with several Gardener's Supply staff members. Out of print, but worth seeking out.

### VIDEO

**How to Grow Plants in a Greenhouse** by Jeff Ball. Part of the "Yardening" series, this video has practical advice on greenhouse technology, plant selection, watering and fertilizing techniques, and pest control tips. 47 minutes, $19.95 (Available from A.C. Burke & Co., 2554 Lincoln Blvd., Suite 1058, Marina Del Rey, CA 90291; 310-574-2770.

greenhouse that can be temperature-controlled year-round, with running water, a power source for supplemental lights, active ventilation, and plenty of room for expansion.

Appearance may also be an important consideration. Will you be happy with a polyethylene hoop house, or is it important that your greenhouse be a more aesthetically pleasing addition to your home and your landscape?

Climate and location are crucial considerations. One reason greenhouses are so popular in England is that their climate is far more moderate than what most of us must cope with here in the U.S. Operating a year-round greenhouse in Vermont or Minnesota usually requires an insulated foundation, double glazing, insulating shades, buried power and water lines, and a serious financial commitment for heating. In the summer, maintaining a plant-friendly environment may require shade cloth, multiple fans, and a misting system. But people who do have a greenhouse, and have tasted the pleasures of being able to fuss around in their own warm, plant-filled jungle, would be quick to argue that the benefits outweigh the challenges.

## What Sort of Greenhouse is Right for You?

**CUSTOM DESIGN OR KIT?** There are now so many companies offering so many different styles and price ranges of greenhouses, that there's little reason to start from scratch designing your own. The exception to this is if you are building a new house, or are concerned about integrating your greenhouse into the architecture of your home. In this case, it may be wise to seek some professional advice.

Greenhouse kits may be as elaborate as a site-built gazebo room with turrets, or as simple as a box of plans with some hardware and a roll of polyethylene. Send for literature on all the greenhouse kits that interest you. Get on the Internet. Ask other gardeners about their experiences. And be sure to find out whether the supplier provides technical support.

**FREESTANDING OR ATTACHED?** Having a greenhouse connected right to your home has many advantages — especially if you want to grow year-round. You can wander in and out to see what's happening at any time, day or night, no matter what the weather. With your plants so close at hand, it's easier to remember about watering and other tasks. Access to water and electricity is also easy. On sunny winter days, an attached greenhouse can add a significant amount of free heat to your home. But attached greenhouses have a few downsides as well. Without proper venting and a way to isolate the greenhouse from the rest of your house, it may make your home too warm in the summer, and can keep your furnace running day and night in the winter.

Freestanding greenhouses are usually less expensive than attached models, and are much easier to set up. They can be placed right on the ground (though if you intend to heat the greenhouse through the winter, you should consider insulating the foundation down to the frost line). If

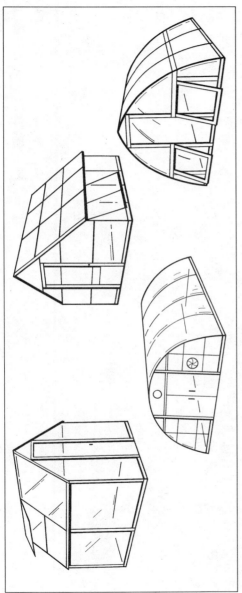

*Four styles of greenhouses (left to right): cape, hoop house, saltbox, gothic arch.*

you will only be using your greenhouse seasonally, a freestanding model will be relatively out of sight during the "down-times" of midwinter and midsummer. Putting in access to power and water may be relatively costly, but many greenhouse gardeners get along just fine with an extension cord and a garden hose.

**CLASSIC OR MODERN?** Unless you have a freestanding greenhouse that is located a good distance from your home, you will probably want to ensure that the shape or style of the greenhouse is compatible with your home. Even the most elegant Victorian-style greenhouse will not make an attractive addition to a New England saltbox. Northern gardeners must also consider snow load when choosing a greenhouse. If snow doesn't slide off the roof naturally, you'll have to shovel it off to protect the glazing and allow light to enter the greenhouse. The overall shape of the greenhouse also determines the interior space and how it can work. Make certain that the style you choose provides enough headroom, wall area for displaying plants, a work area, and enough roof area for venting.

**GLASS OR PLASTIC?** Glass is still the traditional choice for greenhouse glazing, but there are now many high-quality horticultural plastics to choose from, including polycarbonate, acrylic, polyethylene, and tedlar. When selecting a glazing material, you need to consider appearance, lifespan, whether you need single- or double-glazing, how weathertight your greenhouse needs to be, and, unfortunately, price.

Traditional multi-pane glass greenhouses are notoriously difficult to seal. Modern attached greenhouses, with large panes of insulated glass, are usually very

## Flowers for the Winter Greenhouse

Stick to the flowering plants on this list if your night greenhouse temperature runs below 45°F in winter.

| | | |
|---|---|---|
| ageratum | freesia | malope | poppy |
| alyssum | geranium | mandevilla | primrose |
| amaryllis | gerbera | flowering maple | ranunculus |
| anemone | hibiscus | marguerite daisy | shrimp plant |
| angel's trumpet | hyacinth | mullein | snapdragon |
| bougainvillea | impatiens | nasturtium | stock |
| calendula | jasmine | nemesia | sweet pea |
| Christmas cactus | kalanchoe | pansy | thunbergia |
| cineraria | flowering kale | petunia | |
| cyclamen | larkspur | pineapple sage | |

# Resources

## MAGAZINES

*Greenhouse Grower Magazine*
37841 Euclid Avenue
Willoughby, OH 44094
216-942-2000

*Hobby Greenhouse Association*
8 Glen Terrace
Bedford, MA 01730
617-275-0377
Quarterly publication.

*Grower Talks Magazine*
P.O. Box 532
Geneva, IL 60134
630-208-9080

## Greenhouse Products

The **Patio Greenhouse** is designed to be attached to a wall, or two can be set up back to back. It has a 4½-foot-high x 3-foot-wide greenhouse with 2 big doors and 3 shelves for plants. Polycarbonate glazing (single pane) with an all-aluminum frame.

34" L x 18" W x 53" H.
**#11-228 Patio Greenhouse $225.00**

The **Garden Starter Greenhouse** is a fully-functional 6' x 8' freestanding greenhouse with a large roof vent and standard-size door. Polycarbonate double-glazing with all-aluminum

framing. Assembles in 4 hours. 8' L x 6' W x 7' 4" H.
**#30-029 Garden Starter Greenhouse $995.00**

The **American Harvest Greenhouse** is a full-size greenhouse with polycarbonate and cedar double-glazing, aluminum framing, and a wood base wall. Roomy interior with over 8½' of headroom. Four side-wall vents and one roof vent. Many sizes available.
Call Gardener's Supply for prices.

The **Northern Light Greenhouse** has a unique solar shape to capture maximum sunlight, and an insulated north wall to retain heat. High-tech, horticulturally superior double-glazing and all-aluminum framing. Spacious interior. Automatic venting. Many sizes available.
Call Gardener's Supply for prices.

## Gardening in a Greenhouse

Owning a greenhouse can give you the opportunity to grow plants from all over the world. But before you stock up on potted citrus, orchids, cacti, scented geraniums, and bromeliads, you need to stop and think about what sort of growing environment you will actually be able to provide. A common mistake made by beginning greenhouse gardeners is to fill the greenhouse with any plant that piques their interest. An

weathertight. If you live where the ground freezes, a glass greenhouse needs to sit on a permanent foundation, or frost heaves could break the glass. Glass lasts almost indefinitely, and its light transmission is very high.

That said, plastic glazings offer some distinct advantages over glass. They are far more forgiving of temperature fluctuations. They are easier to handle (lighter weight and non-breakable). They diffuse incoming sunlight, which prevents leaf-scorching. Last but not least, they won't be shattered by an errant frisbee or softball.

The **Grow House** is a classic hoophouse style, with strong PVC ribs and standard 2 x 4 framing on gable-end walls. Full size door and big 3"-square vents. Kit includes ribs, glazing, hardware, vents, lumber list, complete instructions. Larger sizes are available.
**#11-301 Standard Grow House, 12' x 12' $299.00**

*The Gardener's Supply*
*Greenhouse Accessories Catalog*
A full range of heaters, shading devices, benching, fans, watering devices, and other products of interest to greenhouse gardeners. Free for the asking. Call 1-800-688-5510.

The first step in successfully managing your greenhouse environment is to train yourself to perceive the environment from a plant's point of view. Light, temperature, relative humidity, carbon dioxide levels and air circulation are the standards by which plants measure a growing day. Outdoor gardeners can take some of these things for granted, but in an artificial environment each element must be controlled and balanced. Remember that a greenhouse is a coherent system of checks and balances. The gardener must assume the role of a conductor, synchronizing each element into a harmonious orchestration."

—from *Greenhouse Gardening* by Miranda Smith (Rodale, 1985)

eclectic assortment of plants such as this may look fine for a few months, but they will soon begin to suffer.

Though most plants will tolerate a temperature range of 55°–85°F, some plants are happier in the 55°–60° range, and some at 80°–85°. Some plants need cold nights, some need warm nights. Some like lots of bright light, some require filtered shade. Some need water twice a day, some only every few days. The challenge for the greenhouse gardener is to decide what sort of greenhouse environment you will be able to provide, to take advantage of the microclimates within the greenhouse, and to choose plants that will thrive in the conditions that can be provided.

If you plan to run your greenhouse year-round, you first need to determine what temperature range you want to maintain — both in winter and in summer. Wintertime temperatures ranging from 40° to 60°F may be ideal for growing salad greens, herbs, camellias, and for overwintering tender exotics. But these temperatures are too cold for producing healthy tomatoes, gardenias, and tuberous begonias. During the summer months, bright sun and daytime temperatures of 85°–90°F may be fine for potted tomatoes, bananas, figs, and geraniums, but alpine plants, African violets, and many types of orchids will not tolerate the heat.

Within any greenhouse, there are also certain areas that are hotter or cooler, brighter or shadier. By taking advantage of these natural microclimates, you can provide optimum growing conditions for a wider range of plants. Shade cloth, lathe, small fans, propagation chambers, heat mats, and other devices can also be used to help create and manage these microclimates. Your climate, the type of greenhouse you have, and the amount of time and money you are willing to invest in heating and cooling, will determine what sorts of plants you'll be able to grow successfully.

## Web Sites

**The Gardener's Source List**
http://w3.aces.uiuc.edu/horticulture/Sources/grnhse.htm
*A list of sources for greenhouses and greenhouse growing supplies.*

**Sherry's Greenhouse**
http://www.teleport.com/~earth/
*Lots of greenhouse gardening information including personal tips. Good question and answer section with meaty replies and useful referrals.*

**Scott's Indiana Greenhouse**
http://www.teleport.com/~earth/ScottHgse.html
*Tips from an avid home greenhouse owner and do-it-yourselfer. Good information about selecting and installing plumbing and electrical equipment for the greenhouse.*

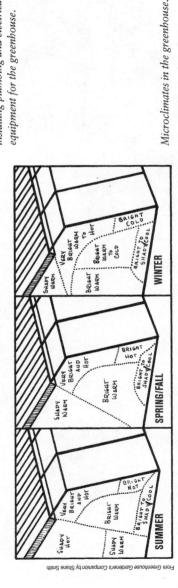

*Microclimates in the greenhouse.*

From Greenhouse Gardener's Companion by Shane Smith

# hydroponic gardening

magine tending a garden that relies on timers, pumps, chemical nutrient solutions, and high-intensity lights. Why would someone choose to garden this way? For one thing, hydroponic gardening gives you complete control over a plant's growing environment. Plants that receive all the light, water, and nutrients they could want respond with vigorous growth; yields are maximized, and the harvest can continue year-round. Hydroponic gardens are also clean, efficient, and relatively low-maintenance. Pest and disease problems are largely eliminated. Weeds are nonexistent. And, last but not least, a hydroponic garden can be located just about anywhere: in a city apartment; on a patio; in a greenhouse; even in outer space!

There has been a big boom in hydroponic gardening over the past fifteen years, fueled by commercial vegetable growers, urban gardeners, and, at least in part, by a subculture of marijuana growers. Whether or not you support the latter activity, the surge of interest in hydroponic gardening has brought many new and exciting products to market. Gardeners can now choose from a wide range of growing systems and lighting options. This chapter will provide only a brief overview of hydroponic gardening. For more information, and to get a sense of the growing interest in this high-tech approach to horticulture, start by logging onto one of the many Internet sites listed in this chapter.

## Hydroponics from a Plant's Perspective

Plants require four basic things: air, water, light, and nutrients. The objective with hydroponic gardening is to determine exactly what a plant needs for optimum performance, and then provide precisely those conditions. In a hydroponic garden, plant roots get all the air they need, and there is little or no competition from other plants. Hydroponically grown plants also receive a continuous supply of

## Guest Expert
## Tom Alexander

*Tom Alexander is publisher of Growing Edge magazine, available at P.O. Box 1027, Corvallis, OR 97339; phone: 541-757-8477. The web site is at <http://www.growingedge.com >*

The current worldwide boom in growing crops hydroponically is mainly because plants grow faster and growers harvest larger volumes of produce in the same amount of space as soil growers. Some growers, using a stepped, inverted, V-shaped growing system, can harvest four or five times the produce in the same square footage as a soil grower. Plants also grow faster because nutrients are readily available and they don't have to make an elaborate search for food.

The recent interest in hydroponics coincides with an increase in the demand for nutritious, wholesome, and fresh food. Health-conscious consumers want fresh food year-round and hydroponic growers are supplying that demand. Growers are raising many kinds of gourmet lettuce and other leafy greens to supply the burgeoning restaurant trade for fresh salad ingredients year-round. Hydroponically raised produce is reliable and fast-growing, providing the grower with a quicker cash flow. In Australia, growers have leased the rooftops of skyscrapers to produce salad greens and culinary herbs for the restaurants down below.

Home gardeners are using hydroponics in conjuction with a high-intensity lighting system to grow fresh, nutritious produce for salads in the winter. Because hydroponics produces more vegetables and fruit in less time, interest will continue to grow.

# Web Sites

**InterUrban WaterFarms**
http://www.wiasub.net/IUWF
FAQ's, links, a reading room, and general information.

**Aquaponics**
http://www.intercom.net/biz/aquaedu/hatech/index.html
Information on hydroponics as well as aquaculture and aquaponics (integrated fish and plant systems).

**The GrowRoom**
http://www.growroom.com
Lots of links to other hydroponic gardening sites; question/answer exchange. International.

**Get Set to Garden!**
http://www.gardeningbc.com
An index of, and links to, hydroponics suppliers on the Internet. Great search engine.

**Homegrown Hydroponics**
http://www.hydroponics.com
Information on every aspect of hydroponics. Canadian store with 22 locations.

**Mayhill Press**
http://www.mayhillpress.com
Good start-up information. Self-promoted hydroponics book.

**Raymond Bridwell**
http://home.earthlink.net/~bridwell/hydroponic1.html
The home page for an avid hydroponic gardener who has also written books on hydroponics. Great links.

---

water and are fed a carefully balanced diet of nutrients. Light is regulated as to intensity and duration. With such perfect growing conditions, hydroponic plants are able to produce an abundance of fruit and flowers.

# The Growing Chamber

In most hydroponic systems, plant roots are periodically bathed in a watery nutrient solution, which then quickly drains away, leaving the roots moist, but not wet. The objective is to keep the pore spaces in the soilless growing medium filled with moist air, not water. Depending on the type of medium used, and the environmental conditions, the nutrient solution can be pumped into the growing medium as infrequently as twice a day, or as frequently as every hour. Typical growing media include perlite, crushed stone, rockwool, sand, lava stone, and clay pellets.

Some types of plants, including lettuce, can be grown right in water, if it is adequately oxygenated. A more common method is the nutrient film technique (NFT). In this method, seedlings are started in rockwool cubes, which then sit in a gutter-like channel that is periodically flooded with nutrient solution. Yet another option is aeroponics, in which plants are suspended in the air, and their roots are continuously misted with an air/nutrient solution. All of these systems can be fully automated with timers and pumps.

---

## Garden Gear

The **Baby Bloomer** is a perfectly sized system for growing your own indoor salad bar. It comes with an expanded shale growing medium (reusable indefinitely), a 30" L x 10" W x 12" H growing tray, ten 5½" pots that fit

inside the tray, a pump and fittings, nutrient mix, a pH test kit, seeds, and user-friendly instructions. Approximately $159.95. Available from Worm's Way (see suppliers list on page 226).

The **NFT Gulley System** hails from Australia and New Zealand, where it has been used for over 10 years. An ebb and flow system, it comes with all necessary hardware to set up a 4' x 4' NFT system. You get a 30-gallon reservoir, gulley support stands, 25 reuseable grow cups, perlite growing media, submersible pump, and all required plumbing. Approximately $329.00. Available from Worm's Way (see suppliers list).

**Ebb and flow system**

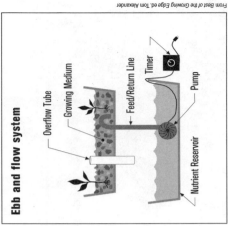

Overflow Tube
Growing Medium
Feed/Return Line
Timer
Pump
Nutrient Reservoir

**NFT pipe system**

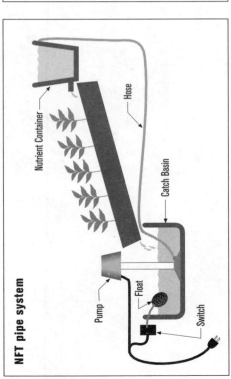

Nutrient Container
Hose
Catch Basin
Pump
Float
Switch

There are many ready-made hydroponic units on the market. To learn about some of the options, check the "Garden Gear" section and the suppliers list, and visit a few of the many web sites. Several of the recommended books also have instructions for building your own customized hydroponic system.

## The Nutrient Solution

Though it is possible to formulate your own nutrient solution, most hydroponic gardeners use a commercial mix. The nutrient solution should be replaced once a month, and the growing medium should be flushed with clear water about once a month. To avoid trace element deficiencies, plant foliage can be misted with seaweed or fish emulsion. The pH level of the nutrient solution should be monitored with a simple litmus test. If the pH level is too acid or too alkaline, nutrients will become bound up and unavailable to your plants.

## Lighting Your Hydroponic Garden

If you are lucky enough to have a sunny, south-facing window, you may be able to grow salad greens and herbs without supplemental lighting. But if you want to grow tomatoes, peppers, beans, flowers, and other light-hungry plants, you will need to use artificial lights. The intensity of light coming through a window, even a south-facing window, is just not adequate to stimulate fruit production. During the fall and winter months, artificial lights are necessary to ensure that your plants receive the 12 to 18 hours of light they require each day. Flowering and fruiting plants also need to be given the right color of artificial light to stimulate flower production.

Many hydroponics suppliers offer hobby-scale systems that are paired with a light fixture. If you know what sort of plants you want to grow, these suppliers can usually recommend a light system that is well-suited to those plants. For more information about lighting see "Growing Under Lights."

"Ebb and flow" and "NFT" (nutrient film technique) are two of the most effective and popular hydroponic systems.

## Resources

Hydroponic Society of America
P.O. Box 3075
San Ramon, CA 94583
510-743-9605
http://www.intercom.net/user/aquaedu/hsa/index.html
*Membership is $40 per year.*

### PUBLICATIONS

*The Growing Edge Magazine*
New Moon Publishing
215 S.W. 2nd
Corvallis, OR 97333
541-757-0027; 800-888-6785
http://www.teleport.com/~tomalex/GE.html
*A quarterly magazine for hobby and commercial growers interested or involved in high-tech horticulture (including hydroponics). Free sample available for $2.00 s/h.*

*Practical Hydroponics & Greenhouses Magazine*
P.O. Box 225 Narrabeen, NSW
Australia 2101
612-9905-9933
http://www.world.net/hydroponics
*A bimonthly magazine from Australia (a hotbed of hydroponics enthusiasm!). U.S. subscription is $55/year.*

# Other Good Books

**Hydroponics for Everyone** by Dr. Struan Sutherland and Jennifer Sutherland (Hyland House, 1987). From Australia, this book provides a good overview of all the different methods of hydroponic growing. A somewhat rambling format, but it covers lots of different crops, from asparagus to potatoes. 142 pages, paperback, $22.95.

**Hydroponic Tomatoes** by Howard M. Resh, Ph.D. (Woodbridge, 1993). A very thorough and easy-to-follow guide for the serious hobby grower. 142 pages, paperback, $9.95.

# Suppliers

**Albuquerque Hydroponics & Lighting**
1001 San Mateo S.E.
Albuquerque, NM 87108
800-753-4617
http://www.ahl-hydroponics.com
*A variety of different hydroponics systems, lights, and more.*

**Crop King Home Page**
http://www.CropKing.com/index.html
*Hydroponic information and products for both commercial and hobby gardeners.*

**General Hydroponics**
P.O. Box 1576
Sebastopol, CA 95473-1576
800-37-HYDRO
http://www.genhydro.com

**Hamilton Technology Corp.**
14902 S. Figueroa St.
Gardena, CA 90248
800-458-7474
*Manufacturer and retailer of many different hydroponic growing systems, growing mediums, nutrient mixes, and more.*

**Harvest Moon Hydroponics**
http://www.hmoonhydro.com/
*Retail establishment with several U.S. locations and on-line ordering.*

**Homegrown Hydroponics**
416-242-4769
http://www.hydroponics.com
*Offers lights and various hydroponics systems.*

**Hydrofarm Gardening Products**
3135 Kerner Blvd.
San Rafael, CA 94901
800-634-9999
http://www.hydrofarm.com
*Several U.S. locations and on-line ordering for hydroponic gardens and light systems.*

**Pacific Northwest Garden Supply**
10330 152nd St., #10
Surrey, BC PNW
604-581-6467
http://www.pacific-hydro.com
*A broad selection of hydroponic supplies.*

**Worm's Way**
7850 North Highway 37
Bloomington, IN 47404
800-274-9676
http://www.wormsway.com
*On-line ordering from a large network of stores in Ontario.*
*Free catalog and on-line ordering.*

# The Plants

Though it is possible to plant seeds directly into some hydroponic growing mediums, most gardeners start their seedlings in rockwool cubes, peat pellets, or a standard soilless growing medium, and then transfer them into the hydroponic growing unit when they have three or four leaves. If you are transplanting seedlings or plants that have been growing in a medium that contains any soil or organic matter, all the soil must be carefully removed from the roots before the plants are set into the hydroponic unit. Cut back on or eliminate nutrients until the plants become well established in their new environment.

Your choice of plants should be based on the temperature and amount of light that you can provide. Some plants will thrive in a cool greenhouse (50°–70°F) but others prefer a temperature range of 60°–85°F. If you'll be growing indoors, temperatures are usually even more narrowly confined to the comfort zone of 65°–70°F.

In general, the easiest and most reliable vegetables for hydroponic production are tomatoes, European cucumbers, peppers, and lettuce. Most herbs also grow well in a hydroponic garden. But half the fun of hydroponic gardening is experimentation and innovation. As a hobby hydroponic gardener, you should try growing the crops you are most interested in. Plant a few things as a gamble. Plant some flowers. You may not get the optimum yields required by commercial growers, but your own pleasure and satisfaction are more appropriate measures of success.

PART V

# gardening in harmony with nature

PASSPORT TO GARDEN
THE EDIBLE LAWN-SCAPE

WILDFLOWERS AND NATIVE PLANTS

BACKYARD BIODIVERSITY

PASSPORT TO GARDENING
NATURAL LAWN

# backyard biodiversity

Almost every garden reflects a creative tension between the natural and the human world, an "interface" (to use a modern computer term) between our built environment and the wild and sometimes inscrutable designs of nature. In recent years, there has been a shift away from carefully manicured lawns and gardens and toward more natural-looking, informal landscapes, ones that make greater use of native plants that require little maintenance.

In this chapter we'll suggest some ways to turn more of your property into a natural landscape, one that is beautiful, requires less effort to maintain, and provides a haven for many species of birds, insects, and animals.

## Beyond the Lawn

The typical turfgrass lawn can be a beautiful and integral part of the home landscape. Yet our American fascination with lawns and lawn care comes at a steep cost. Over 25 million acres of America — an area roughly the size of Pennsylvania — is now devoted to lawn grass. This carpet of green has replaced the natural habitats of our native plants, songbirds, and many kinds of small animals. The summer air is filled with pollution and noise from the gasoline-powered mowers and string trimmers that are required to maintain it. And mowing and other lawn-care tasks eat up millions of hours each year that could be spent more productively or enjoyably.

It wasn't always this way, of course. Early settlers once maintained a small clearing around their houses with the help of an occasional

**Noah's Garden: Restoring the Ecology of Our Own Back Yards** by *Sara Stein* (Houghton Mifflin, 1993).

An influential and beautifully written book. The author's essay-like chapters describe the process of "unbecoming a gardener," explaining how she transformed her suburban lawns and gardens into a more diverse and natural place. Highly recommended. 304 pages, paperback, $10.95.

**Natural Landscaping: Gardening with Nature to Create a Backyard Paradise** by *Sally Roth* (Rodale, 1997).

Lots of practical, easy-to-find information on plants, wildlife, and garden design techniques, such as channeling water and building a "100-year" stone wall. Includes lots of sample garden designs. No index. 256 pages, hardcover, $29.95.

## Guest Expert

### Ken Druse

*Ken Druse is a garden designer, photographer and author whose books include* The Natural Garden, The Natural Habitat Garden, *and* The Natural Shade Garden, *all published by Clarkson N. Potter.*

I love plants, but I have to admit a partiality to natives. In my new garden, I have plantings of exotics and North American natives, but also a large area of indigenous plants. In fact, ones from within a 10-mile radius of the property. When you include such truly local plants, non-opportunistic animals such as rare birds and butterflies — not raccoons or deer — begin to show up. I have heard tales of indigenous berry plantings attracting bird species back to an area where they had not been seen for fifty years. This is because many animals have developed a symbiotic relationship with certain plants. Sure, buddleia will attract butterflies, but the plants that they evolved with over thousands of years will serve them even better. A good example is the monarch butterfly and its plant partner, milkweed (*Asclepias syriaca*).

Monarch butterfly larvae taste bad to birds — and the birds know to avoid them. The larvae get their bitter taste, and actual toxicity, from the milkweed plant, to which they have an immunity. But as milkweed habitat is pushed back by development, the monarch larvae turn to other food sources. Birds learn quickly that the striped yellow and black caterpillars are now edible, and they begin to reduce the butterfly population.

In a habitat-style planting, the whole food chain is welcome: not just flowers for birds and butterflies, but also decaying tree stumps that teem with life — microorganisms or fluted fungi. Rather than carrying off a dead tree or mopping up puddles, the natural gardener views these "imperfections" of site as potential habitat, and rejoices at the creatures who come to bathe, drink, feed, or breed because of them. These spots are where the action is. In fact, *Don't fight the site* is the natural habitat gardener's guiding principle.

# Converting a Suburban Landscape

From Gardener's Supply Company

**BEFORE**

LAWN
LAWN
LAWN

## South Burlington, Vermont

This is a typical ¼-acre suburban lot on a shaded street. By planting a diversity of trees and perennials, the owners now maintain less than ⅛ acre of lawn. The area is small enough that they can use a reel mower to maintain it.

*¼ acre of lawn and young birch trees*

"mowing" from sheep, cattle, or a scythe. Their home landscapes were diverse, featuring gardens, fruit trees, and native shrubs and trees, which in turn were surrounded by pastures and cropland. When the first reel-type mower was introduced in 1830, manicured lawns quickly became the vogue at estates and parks. Yet the popularity of lawns didn't really explode until after World War II, when new suburban neighborhoods were developed with rolling carpets of turf that extended from one yard to the next.

Obviously we can't go back to the haphazard landscape of the early European settlers. But we *can* reduce the size of our lawns and make our yards more natural and ecologically sustainable by incorporating a diversity of plant materials into the landscape: stately trees, native shrubs, evergreen ground covers, ornamental grasses, and perennials. With thoughtful plant selection and placement, it's easy to design a low-maintenance yard that still gives the appearance of neatness and care. What's more, by incorporating certain plants into the landscape,

### The Patio Porch

Unlike most decks that are landscaped with traditional shrubbery, the Schules' porch is surrounded by birdhouses, birdbaths, blueberries, blueberries, and raspberries — all attractants for feathered friends.

### Fencing

A split-rail fence is used to define the more formal landscape from the Schules' forest property on the left. Besides providing a backdrop for the perennials, the fence also helps keep the neighborhood kids in check.

### Shade-Loving Low-Maintenance Ground Covers

Large beds of ferns, pachysandra, and vinca border the forest and fenceline.

### Perennial Bed for Seasonal Color

This sunny street-side perennial bed contains daffodils, tulips, crocuses, daylilies, chrysanthemums, and asters. Like all perennial beds on the property, this garden is mulched with leaf compost to help retain moisture, squelch weeds, and keep it looking attractive.

### The Compost Pile

A small grass path leads to the compost pile, which is hidden behind clumps of hemlock and serviceberry trees. Consisting of mostly leaves and vegetable scraps, the finished compost is used on the perennial beds.

### Naturalized Garden

Shade-tolerant plants like Solomon's-seal, ferns, bloodroot, and astilbe fill out the area under white birches (normally a difficult place to maneuver a lawn mower).

FOREST
ASSORTED TREES
BIRCH
LAWN
HEMLOCK

## Converting a Country Landscape

### Knoxville, Tennessee

The residence is in a rural area, and the 7-acre property is a combination of open land and forest. The owners have gradually reduced their lawn area from 5 acres to ¼ acre. The remaining lawn areas are edged with landscape timbers and are kept neatly manicured. Visitors have remarked that this makes the property look like an estate.

**Butterfly Shrubs**
The back lawn area is being replaced with grouped plantings of coneflower, butterfly bush, and chaste tree, which attract a variety of butterflies.

**Brick Patio and Kitchen Herb Garden**
The Caldwells use weed matting under all of the garden paths, raised beds, and even the brick patio to prevent weed growth.

**Perennial Ground Covers**
Former lawn areas have been replaced with vinca and liriope (lilyturf) for zero maintenance.

**Natural Trees**
White pine trees (not shown) have been planted to create a buffer zone between the house and neighbors and to help decrease the amount of area that needs to be maintained.

**Vegetable Garden**
Watering is important in hot Tennessee summers. This garden has an underground irrigation system that waters plants at the root zone, eliminating the need for sprinklers and hand-watering.

**Shade Garden**
Hostas, astilbe, and other shade lovers carpet the ground beneath a grove of fast-growing birch trees.

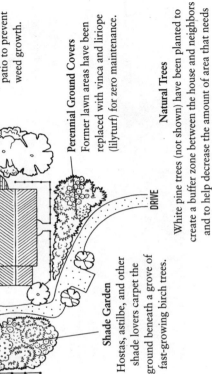

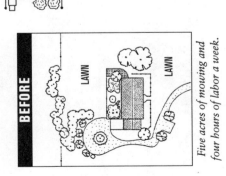

**BEFORE**

*Five acres of mowing and four hours of labor a week.*

From Gardener's Supply Company

we can restore the wildlife habitat that is so critical for songbirds, butterflies, and other welcome visitors from nature.

## Where to Begin

Start by taking a good look at your lawn. The most obvious place to begin turning your lawn into a natural landscape is in those areas where grass doesn't thrive in the first place: shaded areas under trees, wet sections of the yard, and rocky outcroppings. Also, don't forget the steep bank where you risk your life mowing every weekend. These places are all perfect candidates for alternative plantings.

Next, take time to do some research and develop a plan of what you'd like to see growing in these "problem" areas. Start small and replant step by step. The following key principles are important to

## Ground Covers for Natural Gardens

**SHADE LOVERS**

| | BOTANICAL NAME |
|---|---|
| Pachysandra; Japanese spurge | *Pachysandra terminalis* |
| Sweet woodruff | *Galium odoratum* |
| Bloodroot | *Sanguinaria canadensis* |
| Ajuga; bugleweed | *Ajuga* spp. |
| Ferns | |
| Maidenhair fern | *Adiantum pedatum* |
| Christmas fern | *Polystichum acrostichoides* |
| Ostrich fern | *Matteuccia pensylvatica* |
| Cinnamon fern | *Osmunda cinnamomea* |
| Vinca; periwinkle | *Vinca minor* |
| Solomon's-seal | *Polygonatum biflorum* |
| Astilbe | *Astilbe* spp. |
| Bleeding-heart | *Dicentra* spp. |

**SUN LOVERS**

| | BOTANICAL NAME |
|---|---|
| Daylilies | *Hemerocallis* spp. |
| Creeping thyme | *Thymus praecox* ssp. *arcticus* |
| Creeping juniper | *Juniperus horizontalis* |
| Rockcress | *Arabis* spp. |
| Ornamental grasses | various spp. |
| Lady's-mantle | *Alchemilla* spp. |
| Liriope; lilyturf | *Liriope* spp. |

remember as you go about creating an attractive and low-maintenance yard:

- Go for a natural look rather than a formal one. For instance, use curves instead of arrow-straight lines or rigidly defined beds or borders.

- Select a limited number of plant varieties and bunch them together in drifts.

- Plant evergreen ground covers for year-round color.

- If you live in a dry climate, select drought-tolerant native plants; in any climate, conserve water by mulching the soil or installing a drip irrigation system (see the chapter on "Water-Efficient Gardening").

- Incorporate paved surfaces (flagstones, gravel paths, etc.) and fences to separate natural plantings from more formal gardens and lawns near the house.

**THE NATURAL LOOK.** A formal yard has lots of open space, with plants strategically placed on the edges of the lawn. The natural landscape, however, incorporates more native plants — trees, shrubs, ornamental grasses, and flowering perennials — that are grouped together in free-flowing swaths around the property. The plants used in a biodiverse backyard are often ones that are native to your area. Native plants generally require less fertilizer and water than some of the introduced species that are commonly used in home landscaping.

You can incorporate these native plants into your current landscape, create special areas that focus on native plants (like a cactus garden or a bird or butterfly sanctuary), or you can simply allow sections of your yard to "go wild." Many nurseries and garden centers now carry a good selection of hardy native plants (for a partial list, see the suppliers listed in the chapter on "Wildflowers and Native Plants").

Whatever you do, though, please do not remove plants from the wild to transplant into your garden. Many wild plant species are rare or endangered and could be irretrievably lost if they do not survive the move to your yard.

**PLANTING IN DRIFTS.** Traditional gardens tend to incorporate a large number of different plant varieties, but keeping all those competing

plants in their place can be very labor-intensive. To avoid this predicament, limit the number of plant varieties, and group the plants together, giving them enough elbow room so that they will grow for many years without crowding each other out. You'll find that, in time, the shrubs and perennials will merge into one large planting that helps suppress weeds and that creates a safe haven for birds, toads, and other small creatures.

**GROUND COVERS.** Although it takes a little patience and effort to establish ground covers, their year-round color and interest makes it well worth the wait. These plants form a ground-hugging companion for taller plants and protect the soil from erosion as they spread. Plus, when they're mature, they keep weeds and other unwanted plants from gaining a foothold. Best of all, you don't have to mow them!

## Other Good Books

**Planting Noah's Garden: Further Adventures in Backyard Ecology** by Sara Stein (Houghton Mifflin, 1997). The latest book from gardener-ecologist Stein is part inspirational, describing natural gardens across the U.S., and part practical, with lots of great information on creating your own diverse landscape. 464 pages, hardcover, $35.00.

**Going Native: Biodiversity in Our Own Backyards** ed. Janet Marinelli (Brooklyn Botanic Garden, 1994). Stresses plant diversity, with good lists of native plants for use in different regions, and in country or city gardens. 112 pages, paperback, $6.95.

**The National Wildlife Federation's Guide to Gardening for Wildlife** by Craig Tufts and Peter Loewer (Rodale, 1995). An accessible introduction, featuring color photos and plans of gardens in different states and different natural settings. 192 pages, hardcover, $29.95.

### BACKYARD BIRD BOOKS

**The Bird Garden** by Stephen W. Kress (Dorling Kindersley, 1995). A colorful, easy-to-use book written under the aegis of the Audubon Society. About 300 recommended plants are profiled. 176 pages, hardcover, $24.95.

**Hummingbird Gardens: Attracting Nature's Jewels to Your Backyard** by Nancy L. Newfield and Barbara Nielsen (Chapters, 1996). How-to information on feeders, plant combinations, and garden designs for attracting hummers. Six different regional sections, plus an excellent "master guide" to hummingbirds. 144 pages, paperback, $19.95.

**Impeccable Birdfeeding** by Bill Adler, Jr. (Chicago Review Press, 1992). A book on attracting the "best" birds to your backyard, from the author of the best-selling *Outwitting Squirrels*. 176 pages, paperback, $9.95.

### BUTTERFLY GARDEN BOOKS

**Butterfly Gardening: Creating Summer Magic in Your Garden** by the Xerces Society (Sierra Club Books, 1990). Stunning photographs of a wide range of butterflies accompany articles on butterfly garden design, plant selection, and more. 208 pages, paperback, $20.00.

**Butterfly Gardens: Luring Nature's Loveliest Pollinators to Your Yard** ed. Alcinda Lewis (Brooklyn Botanic Garden, 1995). Separate plant and butterfly encyclopedias and regional species lists. 112 pages, paperback, $7.95.

**The Butterfly Garden: Turning Your Garden, Window Box, or Backyard into a Beautiful Home for Butterflies** by Mathew Tekulsky (Harvard Common Press, 1985). No inspiring color photos, but well-organized information on nectar sources, larval food sources, rearing butterflies, and much more. 160 pages, paperback, $9.95.

### REGIONAL BOOKS

**The Wildlife Garden: Planning Backyard Habitats** by Charlotte Seidenberg (University of Mississippi Press, 1995). Especially relevant for gardeners in the Southeast, but provides excellent hands-on information for anyone. 336 pages, paperback, $15.95.

**Plants for Natural Gardens** by Judith Phillips (Museum of New Mexico Press, 1995). An excellent and thorough look at native and adaptive trees, shrubs, wildflowers, and grasses of the Desert Southwest, particularly the high desert regions where daily and seasonal temperatures fluctuate widely. 160 pages, paperback, $27.50.

**Natural by Design: Beauty and Balance in Southwest Gardens** by Judith Phillips (Museum of New Mexico Press, 1995). Much useful material for gardeners who live in dry and difficult climates. 208 pages, paperback, $35.00.

backyard biodiversity   **233**

# GOOD PLANTS FOR BUTTERFLY GARDENS

## Plants for Immature Butterflies (Caterpillars)

Birch
Dogwood
Poplar, aspen, and cottonwood
Milkweed
Clover
Carrot tops
Fennel
Willow

## Plants for Adult Butterflies

Lilac
Butterfly bush (*Buddleia davidii*)
Asters
Mexican sunflower
Lavender
Butterfly weed (*Asclepias tuberosa*)
Garden sage
Hollyhock
Purple coneflower
Cosmos
Zinnia

# Resources

## SUPPLIERS

**Duncraft, Inc.**
102 Fisherville Rd.
Penacook, NH 03303
603-224-0200
*Wild bird specialists selling bird feeders, bird houses, and special seed mixes to attract certain kinds of birds.*

**Earthly Goods, Ltd.**
903 East 15th St.
New Albany, IN 47150
*Wildflower seeds for natural habitat gardening; bird and bat houses; catalog $2.*

**Hearts and Flowers Butterfly Farm**
P.O. Box 1069
Sunbury, OH 43074
614-965-2133
*Send SASE plus $2 for plant list and information.*

**Kester's Wild Game Food Nurseries**
P.O. Box 516
Omro, WI 54963
414-685-2929
*Plants for wildlife, including aquatic species for ponds; catalog $2.*

**Native Nurseries**
1661 Centerville Rd.
Tallahassee, FL 32308
904-386-2747
*Catalog for Southern naturalists features bird feeders and houses.*

**Wildlife Nurseries**
P.O. Box 2724
Oshkosh, WI 54903
414-231-3780
*Plants and seeds of wildlife plants, including aquatics; catalog $2.*

## ORGANIZATIONS

**American Bat Conservation Society**
P.O. Box 1393
Rockville, MD 20849
301-309-6610

**Bat Conservation International**
P.O. Box 162603
Austin, TX 78716
512-327-9721

**National Audubon Society**
950 Fifth Avenue
New York, NY 10022
*In addition to its regular programs, NAS carries two new videos on butterflies: "Butterflies for Beginners" (60 min., $20.00) and "Butterfly Gardening" (90 min., $25.00). Both are available in book and video stores, or by calling 800-876-0091.*

**North American Butterfly Association (NABA)**
4 Delaware Rd.
Morristown, NJ 07960
*$25 annual membership.*

**National Wildlife Federation**
1400 16th St., NW
Washington, DC 20036
202-293-4800

**Xerces Society**
10 Southwest Ash St.
Portland, OR 97204
*Works to preserve butterflies and their habitats; $25 annual membership.*

## PERIODICALS

**Butterfly Gardener's Quarterly**
P.O. Box 30931
Seattle, WA 98103

---

For shaded areas, try planting periwinkle (*Vinca minor*) under your trees, or incorporate ferns, lily-of-the-valley, and pachysandra in shady corners of the yard. For spring color, plant spring-blooming bulbs, Solomon's-seal, and old-fashioned bleeding-heart (*Dicentra spectabilis*) between the ground cover plants.

For sunny, dry areas, daylilies are one of the easiest, fastest-spreading perennial ground covers you can grow. Creeping thyme (*Thymus praecox* spp. *arcticus*, also sold as *T. serpyllum*), as well as juniper, euonymus, and creeping phlox (*Phlox stolonifera*) also make a nice carpet in sunny spots.

## Inviting Wildlife into the Garden

Backyard biodiversity involves much more than just plants. While trees, shrubs, and perennials may form the basis of the natural landscape, they are only part of a much larger ecosystem, one that includes a whole host of animals that depend on plants for food or habitat. From bees, birds, and butterflies to larger animals like squirrels and chipmunks, the natural landscape — even on a modest backyard scale — can play host to a fascinating diversity of creatures.

Encouraging wildlife to come into your garden, and, once there, to hang around, requires a shift in the way that we perceive our home landscapes. As with those "problem" areas that we identified above (wet, shady, steep, rocky, etc.), there are an abundance of potential habitats in the typical backyard, ones that most of us might overlook without a thought.

Features like brush piles, compost heaps, hedgerows, and stone walls may seem like utilitarian areas of the yard, but they can provide shelter for a range of small animals that need a place to call home. Once you start looking at your yard from a wild perspective (a "bird's-eye view," one might say), you will undoubtedly discover other features that, while they might be relatively unimportant to you, provide wonderful habitat for wildlife. A standing trunk of a dead tree, for instance, might represent home (or the diner) for a surprisingly large range of birds, insects, and mammals. Rather than removing it entirely from the landscape, you might want to leave it right where it is, lopping off any dangerous or unsightly limbs and letting nature take its course with the rest. A dead tree trunk, surrounded by daylilies or lilies-of-the-valley, can even become a beautiful landscape feature, evoking visions of ancient ruins or natural decay, which, after all, is simply another strand in the web of life.

Now look over your landscape through this new, wild perspective, and imagine what you would need to survive there. You'd need food, of course, and a source of water. You'd also need a place to take shelter from weather and hungry predators. These are the same things that the wild visitors to your garden require, and to create a truly diverse landscape, you will have to provide for these needs. There are a couple of ways to do this.

First, of course, is to do some research and identify the "host plants" that are food sources for the particular native creatures you want to attract. One common example is the monarch butterfly, which has a special relationship with the milkweed plant (see the "Guest Expert" box on page 229). Although many animals and insects will feed on a variety of plants, there are often one or two plant species that particularly appeal to them. Incorporating these specific plants into your landscape will

## Bird-Friendly Plants

Trees, shrubs, and flowers provide food and shelter for birds and enhance the landscape. Here is a partial list of plants that are known to attract birds.

| COMMON NAME | BOTANICAL NAME |
| --- | --- |
| Oak | Quercus spp. |
| Wild cherry | Prunus pensylvanica |
| White pine | Pinus strobus |
| Shadbush; serviceberry | Amelanchier spp. |
| Crabapple | Malus spp. |
| Rhododendron | Rhododendron spp. |
| Azalea | Rhododendron spp. |
| Honeysuckle | Lonicera spp. |
| Trumpet vine | Campsis radicans |
| Viburnum | Viburnum spp. |
| Chokecherry | Prunus virginiana |
| Barberry | Berberis spp. |
| Brambles | Rubus spp. |
| Bee-balm; bergamot | Monarda spp. |
| Veronica; speedwell | Veronica spp. |

# Garden Gear

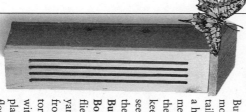

Transform any area of your garden into an exciting gathering spot for birds. The **Misting Birdbath** is hand-wrought from gleaming copper. The fine mist adjusts from 1" to 10" in height. Includes 20' of tubing that attaches to a standard garden hose. 1⅛"-deep bowl. Overall height is 48".
**#30-368 Misting Birdbath $99.95**

Made of clear glass, redwood mill scraps, and enameled copper, this elegant **Hummingbird Feeder** has three feeding stations. A rubber stop-per makes cleaning and filling easy. Measures 12" high and holds 12 oz. The **Hummingbird Nectar** contains 90% less red dye than most other kinds. 2 fl. oz. makes 12 oz. of nectar.
**#19-101 Glass Hummingbird Feeder $29.95**
**#19-102 Hummingbird Nectar, 16 oz. $4.95**
**#19-099 Feeder and Nectar $32.95**

Butterflies such as monarchs, swallow-tails, and fritillaries are a highlight of the sum-mer garden. But as their natural habitats keep shrinking, it seems we see fewer of them each year. The **Butterfly Hibernation Box** will give butter-flies a home in your yard and protect them from cold and preda-tors. Filled loosely with tree bark and placed near your flowerbeds, it simu-

lates the natural crevices where butter-flies seek shelter. Made from weather-resistant Western red cedar, it has a hinged top for easy cleaning. Measures 24½" H x 5" W x 6¾" D.
**#19-150 Butterfly Hibernation Box $29.95**

The purple martin's appetite for insects has made it a favorite with gar-deners. Each bird eats thousands of flying insects every day. It's easy to attract martins to your yard by setting out the right kind of **Martin House.** From the rooftop roost to the self-draining, ventilated floors, this alu-minum house has all the features mar-tins love. The white, baked-enamel finish reflects heat to keep the house cool all summer long. Guard rails pro-tect young birds from falling. All com-part-ments have hinged fronts that open out, with winter door stops to keep out other birds.

The 8-nest house measures 12" x 18" x 15" H; the 12-nest house is 18" x 20" x 16" H. Both models come with a 12' galvanized pole, lan-yard, nylon rope, and instructions. Assembly required.
**#10-298 Martin House, 8-nest $149.00**
**#10-297 Martin House, 12-nest $199.00**

Bats used to have a bad image, but all that is changing. That's because a sin-gle bat can eat up to 500 flying insects in just one hour. With a **bat house,** you can encourage these voracious insect-eaters to patrol your yard all season long. Made in Vermont from unstained Eastern white pine, these bat houses come with a mounting board, hardware, and complete instructions.

For best results, place it in an open area near water.
The **Regular Bat House** accommo-dates up to 30 bats, and is 9" W x 7" D x 17" H.
The **Jumbo Bat House** measures 11½" W x 10½" D x 27" H, and has six roost-ing areas to accommo-date over 100 bats, plus a special "attic" that stores heat and provides an alternate roosting space.
**#10-205 Regular Bat House $29.95**
**#10-192 Jumbo Bat House $39.95**

In order to reproduce, beneficial insects need a source of nectar and pollen. If they don't find it in your field (and they are very particular — just any old flower won't do), they leave and usually do not return.

Peaceful Valley Farm Supply has devel-oped a **Good Bug Blend** of flower seed specifically designed for beneficial insect habitat. It includes plants that are proven hosts to beneficials such as predatory mites and wasps, ladybugs, lacewings, syrphids, tachnids, and predacious beetles.

Since the mix blooms nearly year-round in some areas, the Good Bug Blend should be planted in areas that are somewhat wild, such as field borders, ditchbanks, fence rows, and the like.

Blooms begin 45 to 90 days after planting and will continue for years. Peaceful Valley's mix contains crim-son, rose, and sweet clovers; alfalfa; baby's-breath; California buckwheat; white alyssum, nasturtium; yarrow; and a variety of insectary vegetables and herbs.
**Available from Pleasant Valley Farm Supply, P.O. Box 2209, Grass Valley, CA 95945; 916-272-4769.**

obviously improve your chances of attracting the creatures you would like to see in your garden.

Second, even if you don't have a large yard that can support a wide variety of habitats or food plants, you can still bring wildlife onto your property by providing artificial shelters or food sources. Many homeowners already encourage birds, by erecting houses designed to attract bluebirds or purple martins, or by simply putting out seed and suet in feeders. However, you can also set up hummingbird feeders to provide nectar (or, alternatively, put up hanging baskets of fuchsia or other flowers hummers love). And there are simple, relatively inexpensive shelters you can build or buy to house bats (which are voracious insect-eaters), butterflies, toads, and other creatures. Once you know which kinds of houses certain animals prefer, you can even make them out of recycled materials. For instance, a broken terra-cotta flowerpot isn't good for much, but instead of chucking it in the trash, you might be able to reuse it, turned upside-down, as a perfect home for garden toads.

In addition to food and shelter, the availability of water is crucial for most animals in the natural garden. A pond or a bog is what most people think of first, and these of course will attract a large assortment of creatures, from dragonflies to migrating waterfowl. But for gardeners who don't have such a site, a small pool or fountain may be all that is needed to liven up a natural landscape. Even a half whiskey barrel sunk into the ground can provide the perfect home for minnows, water striders, and a family of frogs.

Specific plants and habitat requirements obviously vary for different birds, insects, and animals, and separate regions of the country have different native species. Before getting too far into backyard biodiversity, you should first decide what kinds of native species you'd like to attract to your garden, then consult field guides or one of the many books listed in this chapter for more information. With only a little research, you should be able to design and create a happy home in your garden for an impressive array of creatures, and they in turn will reward you with their beauty and vitality, turning your garden into a living ecosystem and a mirror of the natural world.

## Web Sites

**The Butterfly Web Site**
http://mgfx.com/butterfly
Includes information on landscaping for butterflies, conservation and ecology. Also lists societies and public butterfly gardens and zoos that have butterfly houses you can visit.

**The Butterfly Zone**
http://www.butterflies.com
A very colorful web site that is a public information source about butterflies and the environment. Features good lists of the plants preferred by many different species of butterflies. There's also an on-line store that sells butterfly gardening supplies (seed mixes, books, etc.).

**National Wildlife Federation**
http://www.nwf.org/nwf/habitats
Explains how and why to create backyard habitats, with questions and answers, links to related web sites, and information on programs for the school and workplace.

**North American Butterfly Association**
http://www.naba.org
Includes a list of publications, addresses of local chapters throughout the U.S., and annual butterfly census information.

# wildflowers and native plants

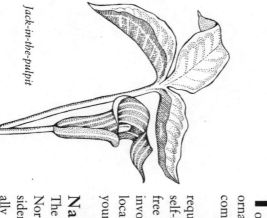

*Jack-in-the-pulpit*

In a world of flashy flowers, where petunias, geraniums, impatiens, and other showy plants seem to rule the roost, wildflowers possess a sweetly simple grace and elegance. Almost any landscape or garden, from wild to formal, benefits from the presence of wildflowers or other native plants. They deserve to be included not only for their ornamental qualities, but for their toughness and ease of maintenance compared to more demanding or finicky modern cultivars.

Once established in their preferred habitat, wildflowers usually require little maintenance or attention. In fact, many types will happily self-seed or spread out on their own, providing you with years of care-free bloom and beauty. This chapter looks at some of the considerations involved in selecting the best wildflowers and native plants for your location, and suggests ways in which you might incorporate them into your yard or garden plantings.

## Native or Not

The first thing to understand is that not all plants that grow wild in North America are necessarily natives. Many plants that we now consider wildflowers have been introduced to these shores, either intentionally or by accident. Some of these garden plants escaped from cultivation and have become widely naturalized over the years, surviving and spreading in the wild. In fact, a few, such as Queen Anne's lace (*Daucus* carota) and purple loosestrife (*Lythrum salicaria*) have proven so successful in their new country that they are now considered weeds, albeit pretty ones.

It is also important to understand the natural growing range of a particular "native" plant. Books on wildflowers often feature maps of North America, with shaded regions indicating where a particular wildflower grows as a native species. Of course, the fact that a plant isn't native to your region doesn't necessarily mean that you can't grow it successfully. For instance, plenty of gardeners outside of California grow its state flower, the California poppy (*Eschscholzia californica*) — usually as

## *Guest Expert*
## C. Colston Burrell

A common vision of a garden of native plants is of an untidy mess, soliciting scorn from the neighbors and tickets from the local weed police. Yet "native" does not have to mean "unruly." Formal design is one way of getting beyond this mistaken notion. Natives look quite good with a frame around them. In fact, this formal framing acts as a cultural cue. It lets less enlightened onlookers know that the assemblage of plants they call weeds (and you call wildflowers) has been intentionally planted and cared for. It is a garden.

Many wildflower gardens are planted by sowing seeds in the fall and then waiting through a long, ungainly adolescence, until the adult meadow or prairie rises like a phoenix from the melting snows. A formal wildflower garden, though, requires an orchestrated planting scheme. Few people would attempt to grow a herbaceous border or cottage garden by scattering seeds on open ground. Instead, they would set out plants, and you can do the same when growing natives.

Remember that a native garden design should follow many of the same tenets common to traditional gardens, such as siting plants to maximize the combined power of their color, form, and texture. Even if your intent is to let the garden evolve with the forces of natural change and succession, your starting point should always be a good design, one that is informed by the nature, love, and intimate knowledge of plants.

*C. Colston Burrell is a garden designer, writer, and photographer. His books include* A Gardener's Encyclopedia of Wildflowers *(Rodale Press, 1997).*

## *Favorite Books*

A Gardener's Encyclopedia of Wildflowers *by C. Colston Burrell* (Rodale, 1997). A comprehensive guide to choosing, growing, and using woodland, meadow, and prairie wildflowers in the home garden. More than 200 plant species profiled. 216 pages, hardcover, $29.95.

The Native Plant Primer: Trees, Shrubs, and Wildflowers for Natural Gardens *by Carole Ottesen* (Harmony, 1995). Excellent color photos of different types of native plants in landscape settings. Lots of useful region-specific lists and species tables. 368 pages, hardcover, $50.00.

Easy-Care Native Plants *by Patricia A. Taylor* (Holt, 1996). Elegant and useful, this book features the history and current use of American native plants; profiles of public and private gardens; and descriptions of more than 500 plants, including trees, shrubs, ferns, and grasses. Highly recommended. 336 pages, hardcover, $35.00.

A Garden of Wildflowers: 101 Native Species and How to Grow Them *by Henry W. Art* (Garden Way Publishing, 1986). An easy-to-use guide to 101 native species. Beautiful plant illustrations and concise growing information. 304 pages, paperback, $18.95.

# BASIC SOIL MOISTURE CATEGORIES

| Soil Type | Description |
| --- | --- |
| Wet | Soggy or marshy most of the year. |
| Wet Mesic | Excessively wet in winter, spring, and after heavy rain, but often dries in summer. |
| Mesic | Medium moist. Water soaks in with no runoff. Average garden soil. |
| Dry Mesic | Well-drained. Water is removed from soil readily, not rapidly. |
| Dry | Excessively well-drained; sandy or gravelly. |

a hardy annual. But in its native range and preferred growing conditions (Zone 8 to 10, well-drained soil, full sun), California poppy self-sows vigorously and is considered a short-lived perennial. Many species exhibit this kind of "home court advantage"; they are adaptable enough to grow well in other regions of the country, but tend to perform best in the climate and growing conditions found in their own native range.

In other words, when you are considering which wildflowers to grow in your garden, remember that species that are native to your part of the country will usually have an advantage over other native plants. Topography, soils, and other factors all come into play, but generally speaking, it is easier to find or create the ideal growing conditions for wildflowers that are already well adapted to your region. Companies that sell wildflower seed recognize this fact, and they typically offer special regional seed mixes for the Northeast, Midwest and Plains states, Southwest, and other areas. Better yet, some companies offer mixes keyed to specific soil or habitat types, such as Short Grass Prairie or Tall Sedge Meadow.

## Site and Soil Considerations

The characteristics of your garden or landscape site will determine to a great extent the specific kinds of wildflowers or native plants that you can grow. Fortunately, there are wildflowers well suited to practically every niche or setting, from the bog-loving marsh marigold (*Caltha palustris*) to the desert marigold (*Baileya multiradiata*).

Before deciding what types of wildflowers to grow, take a walk around your property and observe the different kinds of sites you have.

> I wonder why some wildflowers like human association so much better than others? Is it merely curiosity or just plain friendliness that prompts them to come out of the forest and live by the roadside where they can see and be seen? Sometimes one member of the family, such as the Red Baneberry, will come out to the edge of the road to live, and leave its very close relative, the White Baneberry, which must be much shyer, lingering in the depths of the woods, as if afraid.
>
> "No, I am afraid that, much as we would like to think it is love of human company that brings these flowers into closer companionship with people, we must ascribe it to more practical, if less romantic reasons.
>
> "I think they make their home by the roadside for these reasons. The soil is very likely to be rich; the roadsides are nearly always well-drained; and if through a forest these plants also have the benefit of sunshine part of the day and shade the rest. And it is under these conditions that many delightful species seem to thrive best."
>
> — from *Pioneering with Wildflowers* by George D. Aiken (Alan C. Hood & Co., 1994)

## How to Grow a Wildflower Meadow

The easiest way to establish a large planting of wildflowers, one that will naturalize and provide years of color, is to sow the seeds on well-prepared ground where they will not have to compete with weeds and grasses. The process is similar to that used for seeding a new lawn, and here are the basic steps.

1. Decide when to sow. Wildflower seed can be planted in either spring or fall. In colder climates, fall-seeded wildflowers will remain dormant until the following spring; in warmer areas, plants will usually germinate and become established before winter. For planting dates in specific growing zones, see the Recommended Sowing Dates map on page 242.

2. Select a sunny, well-drained site. Most wildflowers in meadow seed mixes prefer growing in well-drained soils. Also, most meadow wildflowers need a sunny site, one that has at least five to eight hours of sunlight a day.

3. Prepare the ground. Mow down any existing vegetation as close to the ground as possible; remove clippings. Turn over the plot with a rototiller; set the tines at a very shallow depth (maximum 1 inch). If you are replacing part of your lawn or a grassy meadow with wildflowers, you may have to rake out and remove sod after tilling.

4. Eliminate young weeds. **Do not plant wildflower seeds immediately after tilling.** Tilling the soil brings weed seeds to the surface, where they will quickly germinate. Wait two weeks or so after tilling, then go over the ground again with the tiller, to expose the roots of the germinating weeds.

   Many people spray a pre-emergent herbicide like Roundup™ on the ground after tilling, to eliminate the young weeds and prepare the ground for seeding. The manufacturer claims that this product is rel-

atively benign and does not persist in the soil. Organic gardeners will probably want to avoid using chemical herbicides, but get the facts and make up your own mind.

5. Mix the seed. Before seeding, mix the seed in a pail with fine-grade builder's sand, which will help ensure even coverage. Use four parts sand to one part seed.

6. Spread the seed. Broadcast one-half of the seed/sand mix using a hand-held broadcast seeder, or by hand, using an even, sweeping motion. For an illustration of this technique, see the video by the Vermont Wildflower Farm in the "Garden Gear" section.

   Walk across the seedbed at right angles to the path you took before, sowing the other half of the seed. Sow seed rather thickly; this will encourage the wildflowers to choke out any weeds or grasses.

7. **Do not cover. Firm in the seed.** Even if it were practical on a large planting, seed that is buried too deep will never germinate.

   Instead, walk across the seedbed, tamping it down with your foot or the head of a garden rake, to ensure good contact between the seeds and the ground. An even better method is to rent a lawn roller, a large cylinder that you fill with water and then push over the seedbed to firm it down.

8. Water and, if needed, fertilize. Seeds require water to germinate. You should water during dry periods until the plants are about 1 to 2 inches tall. After that point, water only if plants look wilted or stressed.

   Wildflowers normally grow well in average soil and don't require fertilizer. If your soil is nutrient-poor, however, spread a good, all-purpose fertilizer at the same time you plant seeds (see "Garden Gear" section).

9. Control weeds. If your wildflowers germinate well and grow thickly, they should choke out most weeds. When weeds do spring up in the midst of the wildflowers, pull them by hand before they have a chance to flower and disperse their seeds.

10. Mow annually. A few weeks after the flowers have faded in your meadow planting, you can do a high mowing of the field (set the mower to 4 to 6 inches above the ground). This helps control unwanted weeds and grasses, and also helps disperse the mature seeds of your wildflowers.

    *Note:* Wildflower seed mixes commonly include seeds of both annual and perennial plants. This is done so that the annuals will grow quickly and cover the ground, while the perennial plants are still getting established. In the second and succeeding years, you will probably find that your meadow has more perennial species, and few annuals (unless the annuals are native to your region and self-sow vigorously). One method of having annual wildflowers every season is to till and seed a new small portion of meadow each year.

*Evening primrose*

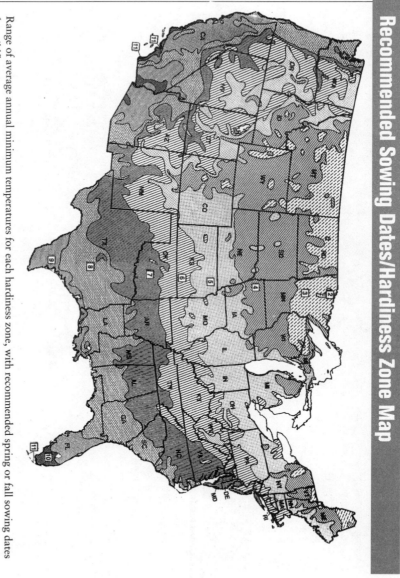

Range of average annual minimum temperatures for each hardiness zone, with recommended spring or fall sowing dates for wildflowers.

**ZONE 1**  below -50°F  Sow seed in early spring when soil can be worked

**ZONE 2**  -50° to -40°  Sow seed in early spring when soil can be worked

**ZONE 3**  -40° to -30°  Spring: April 15–June 15 / Fall: August 15–October 1

**ZONE 4**  -30° to -20°  Spring: April 15–June 15 / Fall: September 1–October 15

**ZONE 5**  -20° to -10°  Spring: April 15–June 15 / Fall: September 1–October 15

**ZONE 6**  -10° to 0°  Spring: March 15–May 15 / Fall: September 15–November 1

**ZONE 7**  0° to 10°  Spring: February 15–April 15 / Fall: September 15–November 15

**ZONE 8**  10° to 20°  Spring: January 15–March 1 / Fall: October 1–December 1

**ZONE 9**  20° to 30°  Spring: January 1–March 1 / Fall: October 1–December 1

**ZONE 10**  30° to 40°  Spring: January 1–March 1 / Fall: October 1–December 1

**ZONE 11**  above 40°  Spring: January 1–March 1 / Fall: October 1–December 1

Reprinted courtesy of Wildseed Farms, Eagle Lake, TX

Try to gauge the sunlight on particular locations: does a spot receive full sun for many hours a day, is it shaded part of the time, or does the sun filter down through leaves to create a dappled light shade? If you're observing from late fall through early spring, when trees and shrubs are leafless, picture how much shade wildflowers will get in the summer if planted in their vicinity. Also consider the soils. Are areas dry and parched, or moist and boggy? Are sites protected or exposed?

*Dutchman's breeches*

The amount and quality of sunlight received each day can be crucial for native plants. Wildflowers common to prairies and large, open meadows normally grow in full sun, and do best when they receive half a day or more of direct sunlight. Plants classified as savanna or open woodland species prefer growing in partial shade, with sunlight reaching the ground between trees. Woodland plants grow in partial to full shade, beneath a more or less solid canopy of trees.

Some flowers that grow in shady woods manage to get the sunlight they need by flowering early in the spring. For instance, trillium and hepatica love growing in humus-rich woodland soil; they bloom quite early, while the spring sun shines through the bare trees. Once the weather warms up and the trees leaf out, these plants enjoy growing in filtered shade. They can't just pick up their roots and move, so they have arranged their flowering schedule accordingly.

The other major factors to consider when looking over your property are the types of soil you have, their acidity or alkalinity as measured by soil pH, and the amount of water they retain at various times of the year. The table on page 240 describes the basic soil moisture categories, and is adapted from the Prairie Moon Nursery catalog (see "Plant and Seed Sources," page 245).

## Other Good Books

**Wildflowers in Your Garden** by Viki Ferreniea (Random House, 1993). Written by the former director of the New England Wild Flower Society, this book discusses the best plants to use in a variety of settings (woodland, rock garden, container garden, sunny border, bog garden, and more). 224 pages, hardcover, $35.00.

**The Wild Gardener: On Flowers and Foliage for the Natural Border** by Peter Loewer (Stackpole, 1991). Loewer's short essays about wild plants are graceful, informative, and perfect for readers who love nature and gardening. 256 pages, hardcover, $19.95.

**Pioneering with Wildflowers** by George D. Aiken (Alan C. Hood & Co., 1994). Originally published in 1933, this garden classic (written by

the former U.S. Senator from Vermont) is still relevant and readable today, particularly for Northeast gardeners. 160 pages, paperback, $12.95.

**Native Perennials: North American Beauties,** ed. *Nancy Beaubaire* (Brooklyn Botanic Garden, 1996). An introduction to native perennials, with plant portraits grouped by bioregion. 112 pages, paperback, $7.95.

**Step-by-Step Wildflowers & Native Plants** by Peter Loewer (Meredith, 1995). Includes step-by-step color photographs, sample garden designs, lots of tips, and profiles of 150 wildflowers. 132 pages, paperback, $12.95.

### REGIONAL BOOKS

**The Wildflower Gardener's Guide** by Henry W. Art (Garden Way Publishing, various dates). A series keyed to regions of North America. Volumes include 1) Northeast, Mid-Atlantic, Great Lakes, and Eastern Canada; 2) Pacific Northwest, Rocky Mountains, and Western Canada; 3) California, Desert Southwest, and Northern Mexico; 4) Midwest, Great Plains, and Canadian Prairies. All paperback, prices vary.

**How to Grow the Wildflowers** by Eric A. Johnson and Scott Millard (Ironwood Press, 1993). Features over 180 plants that are native or adapted to regions of the West. Beautiful photography and good basic growing instructions. 128 pages, paperback, $16.95.

**Gardening with Native Wild Flowers** by Samuel B. Jones, Jr., and Leonard E. Foote (Timber Press, 1990). For gardeners in the East. 196 pages, hardcover, $32.95.

**Plants for Natural Gardens** by Judith Phillips (Museum of New Mexico Press, 1995). For the high desert region of the Southwest; includes good descriptions of native and adaptive trees, shrubs, wildflowers, and grasses. 160 pages, paperback, $27.50.

**Wildflowers of the Northern Great Plains** by F. R. Vance, et al. (University of Minnesota Press, 1984). 352 pages, paperback, $15.95.

| BOTANICAL NAME | COMMON NAME | NOTES |
| --- | --- | --- |
| Amorpha canescens | Leadplant | full sun; dry soil; fernlike leaves; dark blue or purple flowers; 2–3' |
| Anaphalis margaritacea | Pearly everlasting | sun to part shade; white buttonlike flowers; 1–2' |
| Asclepias tuberosa | Butterfly weed | sun to part shade; dry, sandy soil; showy orange flowers; 2–3' |
| Aster laevis | Smooth aster | sun to part shade; rich, well-drained soil; blue flowers in fall; 2–4' |
| Aster novae-angliae | New England aster | sun to part shade; moist, rich soil; blue-purple fall flowers; 4–6' |
| Baptisia australis | Blue wild indigo | sun to part shade; rich, well-drained soil; blue pealike flowers; 2–4' |
| Echinacea purpurea | Purple coneflower | sun to part shade, well-drained soil; pink-purple flowers; 2–4' |
| Epilobium angustifolium | Fireweed | full sun; moist soil; tall, rose-pink flower stalks; spreads easily; 2–6' |
| Eupatorium purpureum | Joe-Pye weed | part shade; wet to moist, rich soil; pink-purple flower clusters; 4–6' |
| Gaillardia aristata | Blanketflower | full sun; well-drained soil; yellow/red flowers; 2–4' |
| Liatris pycnostachya | Gayfeather, blazing star | sun to part shade; moist, rich soil; lavender flower spikes; 2–4' |
| Lobelia siphilitica | Great blue lobelia | sun to part shade; moist, well-drained soil; light blue flowers, 1–3' |
| Monarda fistulosa | Wild bergamot | sun to part shade; moist to dry soil; lavender flowers; 2–4' |
| Monarda punctata | Horsemint, spotted bee balm | sun to part shade; well-drained soil; spotted flowers, pink bracts; 1–2' |
| Oenothera hookeri | Giant evening primrose | full sun; biennial; large yellow flowers open in the evening; 3–5' |
| Rudbeckia hirta | Black-eyed Susan | full sun; tolerates dry soil; orange-yellow flowers, dark centers; 1–3' |
| Solidago spp. | Goldenrod | sun to part shade; drought-tolerant; yellow flowers; several spp.; 1–4' |
| Thermopsis montana | False lupine | sun to part shade; moist, rich soil; bright yellow flowers; 2–3' |
| Vernonia noveboracensis | New York ironweed | sun to part shade; moist, rich soil; shaggy purple flowers; 4–6' |
| Veronicastrum virginicum | Culver's root | sun to part shade; moist, rich soil; white flower spikes; 3–6' |

Many wildflowers will tolerate drought conditions or relatively poor soils. Yet even these tough customers, such as black-eyed Susan (*Rudbeckia hirta*), will grow taller and more vigorously if planted in richer soil. In fact, you might decide to plant black-eyed Susan on a well-drained, but not overly rich soil, simply to curb its enthusiastic nature.

Finally, when reading up on wildflowers and the conditions they like, remember that the same plant often prefers different growing conditions in different regions of the country. For instance, many species that grow well in full sun in the North perform best in partial shade when planted in areas that have longer, hotter summers.

## Sources of Native Plants

Collecting native plants from the wild is at best unethical and often illegal in the case of rare or threatened species like lady's-slippers and pitcher plants. What's more, wild plants frequently do not survive the move from their natural habitat to the confines of the home garden. In

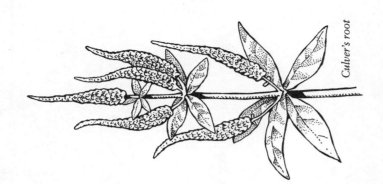

*Culver's root*

other words, you should never dig up a plant in the wild for your garden. Fortunately, there are many reputable nurseries that raise wildflower plants from seed. See the Plant and Seed Sources list below, or order the publication, "Sources of Propagated Native Plants and Wildflowers," available for $3.50 from the New England Wild Flower Society (see Native Plant Societies, page 248). Mail-order nurseries ship plants when they are dormant, usually in early spring or in the fall. Either season is fine for transplanting most wildflowers, although certain species reportedly do better when they are planted in the fall, such as birdsfoot violet (*Viola pedata*) and violet wood sorrel (*Oxalis violacea*).

Collecting seeds of wildflowers is appropriate, so long as you harvest seeds judiciously, taking only a small sample so that plant colonies will be able to reproduce themselves. But many nurseries sell wildflower seeds, so you're frequently better off ordering from them. Growing plants from seed is certainly more economical than buying mature plants. However, the main disadvantage is that many native plants require a long time to mature or even to germinate from seed. Also, the seeds of many species need some sort of pretreatment before they can be

## *Suppliers*

### PLANT AND SEED SOURCES

**Appalachian Wildflower Nursery**
Rte. 1, Box 275A
Reedsville, PA 17084
717-667-6998
*Perennials and rock garden plants; catalog $2.00.*

**Brookside Wildflowers**
Rte. 3, Box 740
Boone, NC 28607
704-963-5548
*Nursery-propagated wildflowers; catalog $2.00.*

**Clyde Robin Seed Co.**
3670 Enterprise Ave.
Hayward, CA 94545
510-785-0425
*Wildflower mixes for various regions; catalog $2.00.*

**Colorado Alpines, Inc.**
P.O. Box 2708
Avon, CO 81620
303-949-6464
*Alpine and rock garden plants; catalog $2.00.*

**Desert Moon Nursery**
P.O. Box 600
Veguita, NM 87062
505-864-0614
*Southwestern native plants; catalog $1.00.*

**Holland Wildflower Farm**
290 O'Neal Lane
Elkins, AR 72727
501-643-2622
*Prairie wildflowers, plants and seeds; long SASE for catalog.*

**Moon Mountain Wildflowers**
P.O. Box 725
Carpinteria, CA 93014
805-684-2565
*Annual and perennial wildflowers; catalog $2.00.*

**Native Gardens**
5737 Fisher Lane
Greenback, TN 37742
615-856-3350
*Native plants and seeds; catalog $2.00.*

**Native Seeds, Inc.**
14590 Triadelphia Mill Rd.
Dayton, MD 21036
301-596-9818
*Wildflower seeds and seed mixes.*

**Niche Gardens**
1111 Dawson Rd.
Chapel Hill, NC 27516
919-967-0078
*Southeastern wildflowers and native plants; catalog $3.00.*

**Prairie Moon Nursery**
Rte. 3, Box 163
Winona, MN 55987
507-452-1362
*Wildflower seeds, plants, and seed mixes; catalog $2.00.*

**Prairie Nursery**
P.O. Box 306
Westfield, WI 53964
608-296-3679
*Wildflowers and native grasses (both seeds and plants); catalog $3.00.*

**Southwestern Native Seeds**
P.O. Box 50503
Tucson, AZ 85703
*Seeds for Western and Southwestern natives; catalog $1.00.*

**Sunlight Gardens**
174 Golden Lane
Andersonville, TN 37705
423-494-8237
*Eastern wildflower plants; catalog $3.00.*

**Vermont Wildflower Farm**
Route 7, P.O. Box 5
Charlotte, VT 05445
802-425-3500 (retail store and garden).
800-424-1165 (catalog requests and orders).
*Wildflower seeds and seed mixes; catalog $3.00.*

**Wildseed Farms**
P.O. Box 308
Eagle Lake, TX 77434
800-848-0078
*Wildflower seeds and seed mixes; catalog $2.00.*

planted. Most often this involves *stratification* — placing seeds for one to two months (or longer) in refrigerated storage in a soilless growing medium, which signals the seed to break its dormancy. For details on starting wildflower plants from seed, consult *Step-by-Step Wildflowers & Native Plants* (see "Other Good Books," page 243).

Unless you are patient and adept at growing plants from seed, it's probably best to start your wildflower garden by purchasing a few plants from a reputable nursery. The main exception is growing a wildflower lawn or meadow, in which case you can sow mixed seeds directly on top of the ground in either the fall or spring. For specifics on site preparation and seeding, see "How to Grow a Wildflower Meadow," on page 241.

## Plants with Aggressive Tendencies

As survival species, ones that exist happily in the wild without human care, wildflowers tend to be very efficient at reproducing themselves

## Native Plants for Shade and Woodlands

| BOTANICAL NAME | COMMON NAME | NOTES |
| --- | --- | --- |
| Adiantum pedatum | No. maidenhair fern | wet to moist, rich soil; 3–4' |
| Aquilegia canadensis | Eastern columbine | part shade; rich soil; red and yellow flowers, 8–24" |
| Aralia racemosa | Spikenard | wet to moist soil; green flowers; 3–6' |
| Arisaema triphyllum | Jack-in-the-pulpit | moist, rich soil; green or black-striped hooded spathe; 1–3' |
| Asarum canadense | Wild ginger | moist soil; heart-shaped leaves; dark red flowers; aromatic; 4–8" |
| Aster divaricatus | White wood aster | moist soil; white flower with yellow eye; blooms fall; to 3' |
| Cimicifuga racemosa | Black cohosh, snakeroot | part shade; moist, well-drained rich soil; creamy white flowers; 3–8' |
| Dicentra cucullaria | Dutchman's breeches | sun to shade; moist to wet soil; white flowers in spring; 6–12" |
| Dodecatheon media | Eastern shooting star | sun to shade; moist, rich soil; white or pink flowers; 8–24" |
| Erythronium americanum | Eastern trout lily | sun to shade; rich soil; yellow flowers; mottled leaves; 3–10" |
| Gaultheria procumbens | Wintergreen | part to full shade; rich, acid soil; white flowers, red berries; 2–4" |
| Hepatica acutiloba | Sharp-lobed hepatica | moist, calcium-rich soil; blue or white flowers in spring; 4–9" |
| Hydrastis canadensis | Goldenseal | part shade; moist, rich soil; showy crimson fruits; to 12" |
| Impatiens capensis; I. pallida | Jewelweed | wet to moist soil; yellow or orange flowers; 3–5' |
| Matteuccia struthiopteris | Ostrich fern | wet to moist soil; 3–4' |
| Mitchella repens | Partridgeberry | moist, rich, acid soil; white or pink flowers, red berries; groundcover |
| Polygonatum biflorum | Solomon's seal | sun to shade; yellow-green tubular flowers; blue-black berries; 1–4' |
| Sanguinaria canadensis | Bloodroot | sun to shade; white daisylike spring flowers; 2–6" |
| Smilacina racemosa | False Solomon's seal | full shade; moist, rich soil; white flowers; edible red berries; 1–3' |
| Trillium spp. | Trillium | moist, rich soil; maroon- and white-flowered species; 1' |
| Zizia aurea | Golden Alexander | full sun to part shade; moist soil; yellow flowers in spring; 1–3' |

## Garden Gear

Produced by the folks at The Vermont Wildflower Farm, this 30-minute videotape, **"How to Create Your Own Wildflower Meadow,"** offers clear advice on how to choose a meadow site, how to clear the ground, how to sow seed, and more. Wildflower Video, VHS format, 30 min., $9.95. Available from The Vermont Wildflower Farm (product #V00016); to order, phone 800-424-1165.

The experts at The Vermont Wildflower Farm recommend this special **Wildflower Booster** (5-10-5), which contains a blend of slow-release fertilizers and organic bonemeal for fast, strong growth of your wildflowers. To apply, just sprinkle on the beds at the same time you scatter your seed. It's great for established wildflower plantings, too. Wildflower Booster, 24 oz, $4.99 or 3 packages for $12.99. Available from The Vermont Wildflower Farm (product #V00139); to order, phone 800-424-1165.

Save time, money, and frustration by broadcasting your seeds and fertilizers evenly and accurately. The **EZ Hand Spreader** is ideal for sowing your wildflower seeds in the spring or fall. Five

selector settings are built into the handle to adjust the flow of material. Spread pattern is 8 feet. Constructed of heavy-duty plastic; comes fully assembled, with a five-year warranty. EZ Hand Spreader, $11.95. Available from Wildseed Farms (product #4016); to order, phone 800-848-0078.

through seed dispersal and other means. In many situations, this is a desirable trait. After all, it's satisfying to see plants so happy with their site that they increase the size of their colony and naturalize in the landscape.

Other native plants, however, take this growing exuberance to extremes, and can spread across a landscape like an army on the march. That doesn't necessarily mean you shouldn't plant these wildflowers, but it does pay to know which ones are likely to be most aggressive, so that you can select plants that will be well suited to their location.

The most aggressive plants are those that are both rhizomatous (spreading underground by means of roots or rhizomes) and prolific seed producers. Nature abhors a vacuum, and such plants are well equipped to fill in the gaps on disturbed or barren ground. These plants include fireweed (*Epilobium angustifolium*), prairie sage (*Artemisia ludoviciana*), and sawtooth sunflower (*Helianthus grosseseratus*). Fortunately, all of these plants are attractive, or you probably wouldn't be

# Resources

growing them in the first place. Still, you can get too much of a good thing. The best advice is to put in only a few plants of these aggressive species, and give them a year or two to see how rapidly they spread. Then, if necessary, control their growth. Fireweed, for instance, colonizes burned-over clearings in the wild (hence the name), but it will present less of a problem if it is forced to compete with other plants in a meadow or field.

## Wildflowers in the Formal Garden

There's no need to relegate wildflowers to the landscape outside the garden. While it would be a mistake to introduce highly aggressive plants into a formal bed or border, many other wildflowers are well-mannered and perfectly at home in the garden proper.

A little garden of wildflowers, one that is set off unto itself, can be a lot of fun to grow. It's also a great way to get to know the habits and ornamental qualities of various native plants that you might like to try in your other beds and borders.

Rock gardens are the perfect spot for low-growing wildflowers. Alpine plants and those native to the arid West or Southwest tend to be the best rock garden specimens. For best results, they need plenty of sun,

## NATIVE PLANT SOCIETIES

In addition to the following organizations, many states and provinces have their own active native plant societies. Botanical gardens are another good place to get information on wildflowers common to a particular region. For a state-by-state listing of native plant organizations and gardens, check out the web site of the National Wildflower Research Center (see page 247).

**Canadian Wildflower Society**
Unit 12A, Box 228
Markham, ON L3R 1N1
Canada
416-294-9075
*A group dedicated to growing and preserving the wild flora of North America. Annual membership is $30.00 and includes access to a seed exchange and a subscription to their quarterly magazine.*

**National Wildflower Research Center**
4201 La Crosse Blvd.
Austin, TX 78739
512-292-4100
*A nonprofit organization with more than 20,000 members, committed to the preservation and reestablishment of North American wildflowers, grasses, trees, shrubs, and vines in planned landscapes. NWRC has demonstration gardens at its Visitors Center and headquarters in Austin, as well as one of the largest collections of information on North American native plants. Annual membership for individuals is $25.00.*

**New England Wild Flower Society**
180 Hemenway Rd.
Framingham, MA 01701
508-877-7630
*Founded in 1900, the NEWFS is the nation's oldest native plant conservation group. The society maintains the 45-acre Garden in the Woods, which displays more than 1,600 varieties of native plants, including 200 rare or endangered species. Members enjoy free admission to the garden, and can participate in trips, tours, and a seed exchange program. NEWFS also sells a national directory of responsible nurseries that propagate wildflowers. Annual membership for individuals is $35.00.*

**North American Rock Garden Society**
P.O. Box 67
Millwood, NY 10546
*Founded in 1934, NARGS has 4,500 members who are interested in alpine, saxatile, and low-growing perennials. The organization is also dedicated to the study and cultivation of wildflowers that grow among rocks. There are local chapters, and members have access to a seed exchange, a library, and slides and videos. Annual membership is $25.00.*

**Theodore Payne Foundation for Wildflowers and Native Plants**
10459 Tuxford St.
Sun Valley, CA 91352
818-768-1802
*This nonprofit foundation has 21 acres of gardens, featuring some 800 species of California wildflowers and native plants. The garden site is open to the public Tuesday through Saturday from March through May. They also sell seeds by mail and plants at the nursery, which is open Tuesday through Saturday year-round. Send $3 for catalog.*

> When Mother Nature sets out to make a rock garden she spends the first million years in a thorough preparation of the soil, pulverizing and disintegrating the limestone or slate ledges and cliffs, and hollowing out little pockets or seams where this material, mixed with the leafmold of untold centuries, may collect. Then, too, she provides for thorough drainage, and also for plenty of moisture from water trickling down the cliffs in springtime. And when, after numberless aeons have passed, she gets ready to plant this rock garden, she selects the choicest, loveliest flowers of the woods to put there.
>
> "Not many acid-loving plants are found in Nature's rock garden and the soil is most likely to be nearly neutral as regards acidity. Of course, human beings, always anxious to improve on Nature, may fill certain pockets with acid soil where a Moccasin Flower or Arbutus may grow, but why not plant these in their own natural location under the spreading pines and use the plants for the rock garden that Nature has provided?
>
> "Nature usually has her rock garden in partial shade. So why not follow her few simple rules — partial shade, trickling water in springtime, perfect drainage and pockets filled with pulverized stone and leafmold."
>
> —from *Pioneering with Wildflowers* by George D. Aiken
> (Alan C. Hood & Co., 1994)

good air circulation, and sharply drained soil. Two good examples are the spring-blooming pasqueflower (*Anemone patens*), with its pretty pastel blue blossoms and fuzzy white seedheads, and the poppy mallow (*Callirhoe triangulata*), a low, spreading relative of the hollyhock that has deep magenta flowers.

As mentioned previously, the California poppy (*Eschscholzia californica*) is a popular annual in many parts of the country, with golden orange flowers blooming all season long. Many of the perennial wildflowers have long stems and showy blossoms that add interest to both borders and indoor arrangements. Some common examples are the purple coneflower (*Echinacea purpurea, E. pallida*, and other species), foxglove beardtongue (*Penstemon digitalis*), and the false dragonhead or obedient plant (*Physiostega virginiana*).

Integrating wildflowers with other cultivated varieties in the context of a formal garden can often prove challenging. It's an aesthetic issue, really: the casual nature of most wild plants doesn't always marry well with more prim and proper garden flowers. When you're including wild or native plants in the formal garden, try to select ones that will not only complement the rest of the bed in terms of height, bloom time, and color, but that will also be compatible partners for the more refined cultivars and won't crowd them out over time.

# natural lawn

In the United States, over 56 million homeowners regularly tend a lawn. That makes lawn care by far the biggest "gardening" activity in the nation. Some people love to get out the mower every weekend and go to work. Others consider lawn care at best a nuisance, and at worst a colossal waste of time that could be better spent on other activities.

This chapter outlines some of the key principles involved in growing a natural, low-maintenance lawn — one that you can feel good about growing and that won't take over your life. And in the chapter on "Backyard Biodiversity," we show you how to redefine your backyard, reduce the size of your lawn, and become a grower, not a mower.

## The Lawn and the Short of It

Regardless of whether you consider lawn care wholesome exercise or a weekly curse, having a healthy lawn as part of your home landscape does confer some significant benefits — both environmental and aesthetic. For one thing, a healthy, thriving lawn acts like a miniature forest. It helps to modify the climate around your home, keeping air temperatures much cooler in the summertime. Grass, like other plants, draws carbon dioxide from the atmosphere and gives off oxygen. And, of course, lawns are the ideal outdoor carpet for recreation or home entertaining.

However, there is a downside to our American love affair with turf-grass lawns, one that involves the huge lawn care industry and its reliance on chemicals to achieve "the perfect lawn." Americans spend $956 million on synthetic lawn fertilizers each year, and an incredible $1.5 billion on pesticides and weed killers. These chemicals, even when used correctly, can migrate from areas that are "targeted" for application and enter into our lakes, rivers, and groundwater. What's more, dosing your lawn with chemicals can kill or adversely affect beneficial soil life and insects, pets and wildlife, and even human beings who are sensitive to toxins.

## Guest Expert
## Warren Schultz

Until surprisingly recently, most of our lawn grasses were selected from pastures and prairies. Turf experts searched the wild for "sports" — single plants of a species that showed better texture, improved vigor, or other outstanding qualities. They dug up these talented plants and grew them out for seed. The millions of pounds of 'Manhattan' ryegrass sold since 1967 originated from a single plant dug out of Central Park in New York City. 'Merion' Kentucky bluegrass, which turned the turf world on its ear with excellent disease resistance and hardiness, came from a single plant discovered growing on a golf course in Ardmore, Pennsylvania. That's the way all new grass cultivars were developed until the late 1960s.

Now breeders are using hybridization, cloning, and selection to produce grasses our parents could only dream about. And they are looking for grasses that will perform well on lawns, not just on golf courses. Traditionally, most turf grass was bred to thrive under intense management, high fertility, low cutting heights, and frequent irrigation — the sort of conditions that prevail on a golf course. When those grasses were sown in the home lawn, the homeowner had to follow a high-maintenance program to keep them healthy and looking good. The emphasis has changed. The new byword is *low* maintenance.

*Warren Schultz is the author of* The Chemical-Free Lawn *(Rodale, 1989) and other gardening books and articles. He is the former editor of* National Gardening *and* Garden Design *magazines.*

## Favorite Books

**The Chemical-Free Lawn** *by Warren Schultz* (Rodale, 1989). Still one of the best books available on earth-friendly home lawn care, covering everything from using a spreader to non-chemical strategies for controlling weeds, pests, and diseases. 208 pages, paperback, $14.95.

**Redesigning the American Lawn: A Search for Environmental Harmony** *by F. Herbert Bormann, Diana Balmori, and Gordon T. Geballe* (Yale University Press, 1993). A thought-provoking and very readable little book that examines the American love affair with lawns; the lawn industry; the environmental costs of all our spraying, mowing, and watering; and practical suggestions for a "new American lawn." Highly recommended for all ecologically minded gardeners. 176 pages, paperback, $11.00.

**The Wild Lawn Handbook: Alternatives to the Traditional Front Lawn** *by Stevie Daniels* (Macmillan, 1995). Lots of useful material on planting the alternative lawn: ground covers, moss lawns, fire-resistant landscaping, and more. 224 pages, hardcover, $20.00.

# Types of Grasses for Your Region

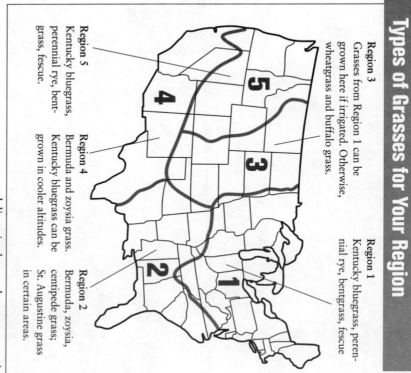

**Region 1**
Kentucky bluegrass, perennial rye, bentgrass, fescue

**Region 2**
Bermuda, zoysia, centipede grass; St. Augustine grass in certain areas.

**Region 3**
Grasses from Region 1 can be grown here if irrigated. Otherwise, wheatgrass and buffalo grass.

**Region 4**
Bermuda and zoysia grass. Kentucky bluegrass can be grown in cooler altitudes.

**Region 5**
Kentucky bluegrass, perennial rye, bentgrass, fescue.

The good news is, you don't need to depend upon these chemicals (and worry about your kids and your pets) to have a healthy, good-looking lawn. Will it be the much-vaunted "perfect lawn" — that putting green you see in chemical company ads? Probably not. But how many of us host the Masters Tournament in our backyard? For homeowners, the goal should be, not the "perfect" lawn, but the "good-enough" lawn. In other words, learn to relax your standards a little and begin working with nature. You may have a few dandelions pop up here and there in the spring, but instead of reaching for the spray bottle of herbicide, buy a dandelion fork to dig up the roots. Or pick the leaves and cook them up as a tasty "spring tonic"; eating your weeds can be the sweetest revenge. Some people even *like* having a few dandelions in the yard, not to mention other non-grassy "weeds" like clover, oxalis, violets, and carpet bugleweed (*Ajuga reptans*). As long as these plants don't get out of hand, they can even enhance a lawn, providing pretty flowers or interesting leaf texture to what would otherwise be a monocultural carpet of green.

## Start with the Right Kind of Grass

The simplest, yet most common problem with lawns occurs when the type of grass grown does not suit the site. There are a dozen or more different types of lawn grasses, and to choose the best type, you need to consider several factors: your climate, your soil, the amount of sun your lawn receives, and the amount of foot traffic the grass will have to tolerate. (See sidebar on page 254.)

**CLIMATE.** Although Kentucky bluegrass is the most commonly used grass seed for American lawns, it is not always the best choice. Many grass varieties will not tolerate extreme cold or heat, or extremely dry or wet weather. Check the map above or consult a local landscaping service or garden center for recommended varieties in your area.

**SUN OR SHADE?** Is your lawn in the shade or the sun? Most grass varieties (fescues, Kentucky bluegrass, perennial rye) require full sun to remain lush and green — although some tolerate more shade than others. If your yard receives less than four hours of full sun each day, or if it's partially shaded all day long, you should select grass varieties that are especially suited to the shade (see listing on page 254). Remember that your landscape will change over time: trees grow to shade existing lawns; old plantings die, exposing lawns to more sunlight. You may need to reseed your lawn with the proper grass variety, one that will thrive under the new growing conditions.

**RECREATIONAL LAWNS.** If you and your family use your lawn as a playground or sports area, you'll need to plant a hardy grass. Varieties such as tall fescue or Bermuda grass stand up well under heavy foot traffic, and some, like 'Rebel' tall fescue, will tolerate shade as well. You'll need to water grass during the summer months, to keep it looking healthy and to overcome the stress of being trampled.

**DIFFICULT SITES.** Steep slopes, deep shade, rocky areas, and footpaths are difficult to maintain. On these kinds of sites, consider replacing turf with bark or gravel footpaths, perennial ground covers, or shrubs. In areas with mild winters, you can grow many interesting hardy ornamental grasses, such as blue fescue (*Festuca ovina* var. *glauca*), Japanese blood grass (*Imperata cylindrica* var. *rubra*), or golden hakonechloa (*Hakonechloa macra* 'Aureola'). For more information on ground covers and other alternatives to turf lawns, see the chapter on "Backyard Biodiversity."

## Start from the Ground Up

Let's take a close look at your lawn. With a trowel or small shovel, cut out a small piece of sod at least 4 inches deep. Is the soil crumbly and soft? Does it contain a dense patch of healthy grass blades, a vigorous root system, and maybe a worm or two? These are the characteristics of healthy turf.

Few people, however, start out with an ideal lawn. You may find that your sod piece is dry and compacted. The grass roots may appear weak and shallow, and weeds may grow thickly in places. If you see a dense accumulation of dead roots and stems and partially decayed organic matter at the base of the grass, that's called "thatch." Thatch accumulates when organic matter at the soil surface isn't incorporated into the soil quickly enough by earthworms and microscopic soil life. A buildup of thatch can lead to dead patches in the soil and a spongy feeling when you walk across the lawn. All of the above conditions can be changed by taking a natural approach to lawn care.

## I'M GROWING WHERE THE WEATHER SUITS MY MOWS

**Cool-Climate Grasses**
tall fescue
red fescue
Kentucky bluegrass
perennial ryegrass
meadow fescue
colonial bentgrass
creeping bentgrass
fine fescue

**Warm-Climate Grasses**
Bermuda grass
St. Augustine grass
Bahia grass
Carpet grass
Zoysia grass
Centipede grass

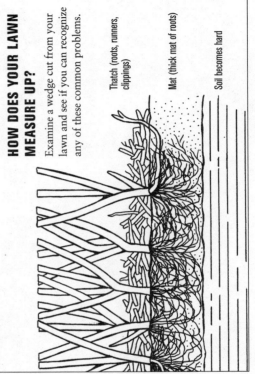

## HOW DOES YOUR LAWN MEASURE UP?

Examine a wedge cut from your lawn and see if you can recognize any of these common problems.

Thatch (roots, runners, clippings)

Mat (thick mat of roots)

Soil becomes hard

The key to natural lawn care is providing a healthy soil environment. You can improve your soil in just one growing season by paying attention to three simple soil requirements.

**1. Soil Acidity.** Grasses prefer a well-drained soil with a slightly acid to neutral pH (6.5 to 7.0). A simple soil test will tell you if your soil needs an application of lime to make it more neutral, or sulfur to make it more acidic. Send soil samples to your local Agricultural Extension Service office or purchase a pH meter and test it yourself. Ideally you should apply lime or sulfur in the fall to allow these elements time to dissolve and disperse.

**2. Feed the Soil to Feed Your Plants.** Grass, like all plants, requires organic matter in the soil to promote strong and vigorous root growth. If your soil is low in organic matter, apply a ¼-inch layer of compost or good topsoil and rake it into the turf. This addition of organic matter will stimulate biological activity and improve the health of your soil.

**3. Aerating the Soil.** Grass roots and soil microorganisms benefit from loose, airy soils. If

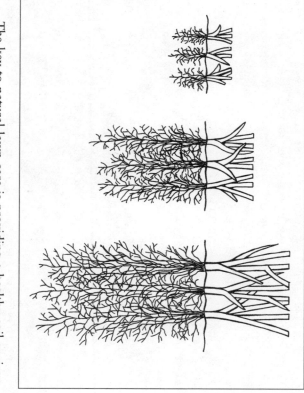

## Characteristics of Grass Varieties

| GRASS | SHADE | SUN | DURABLE |
|---|---|---|---|
| Tall fescue | | ✓ | ✓ |
| Tall fescue, 'Rebel' | ✓ | ✓ | ✓ |
| Perennial rye, 'Manhattan' | | ✓ | ✓ |
| Meadow fescue | | ✓ | |
| Kentucky bluegrass | | ✓ | ✓ |
| Kentucky bluegrass, 'Park' | | ✓ | ✓ |
| Red fescue | ✓ | ✓ | ✓ |
| Red fescue, 'Ruby' | ✓ | ✓ | ✓ |
| Colonial bentgrass* | | ✓ | |
| Creeping bentgrass* | ✓ | ✓ | |
| Manila grass (*Zoysia matrella*) | | ✓ | ✓ |
| Bermuda grass | | ✓ | ✓ |
| St. Augustine grass | ✓ | ✓ | |
| Carpet grass | ✓ | ✓ | |
| Centipede grass | | ✓ | |
| Buffalo grass | | ✓ | ✓ |
| Chewings fescue | ✓ | | |

*Bentgrass is a high-maintenance grass.

your lawn has become compacted from a heavy lawn tractor, or if there's a thick, spongy layer of thatch on top of the lawn, spring is the season in which to aerate. Either rent a "power rake" lawn aerator, or purchase a dethatching rake yourself (see "Garden Gear," page 258). This is also a good time to apply fertilizer or lime, while the soil is exposed. Remove and compost the old thatch and dead grass.

## Fertilizing

There are two different fertilizing schedules for American lawns — one for cool-climate grasses and the other for warm-climate grasses. Before you fertilize, it's important to understand what type of grass you're growing, because they can have very different growing cycles.

Cool-climate grasses (Kentucky bluegrass, perennial rye, bentgrass, and fescues) grow best in northern climates. They are the first to green up in early spring and stay green longer into the fall. When summer temperatures rise above 80°F they go dormant, and on really scorching days the blades will turn brown. The best time to fertilize these varieties is in the fall, because they need all the food they can get after being dormant all summer. The next best time to fertilize is late spring, when the grasses' winter food supply is all used up. Avoid fertilizing a cool-

(see "Garden Gear," page 258)

---

### Turfgrass Tips

≈ **Mowing.** Set your mower high and remove only one-third of the grass blade's length. Frequent, short mowing stresses plants and encourages weeds such as crabgrass. Don't mow with a dull blade, and do leave short clippings on the lawn to decompose and feed the soil.

≈ **Fertilizing.** Grass clippings alone can supply up to 40 percent of a lawn's annual fertilizer needs. For the remainder, apply a slow-release organic fertilizer at the correct sea-

son for your growing region. Top-dress the lawn with compost and rake it in at the same time you remove thatch and dead grass.

≈ **Watering.** During dry periods, either make a commitment to watering your lawn deeply and regularly, or, better yet, conserve water and let the grass enter its natural period of dormancy. It will bounce back with the return of cool temperatures and/or rainfall.

---

## Other Good Books

**Building a Healthy Lawn: A Safe and Natural Approach** by Stuart Franklin (Garden Way Publishing, 1988).
A basic guide to lawn care, written by a professional landscaper. Stresses natural controls for weeds, insects, and disease, but also includes a thoughtful, measured discussion of the use of lawn chemicals. 176 pages, paperback, $12.95.

**Lawns and Ground Covers** (Sunset, 1989).
Features growing and watering information for 18 types of turfgrass and 125 ground covers. Good color photos

and plant information. Gives both chemical and nonchemical controls for most lawn pests and diseases. 160 pages, paperback, $13.99.

**Ground Covers** ed. by Jennifer Bennett (Firefly Books, 1996). This little handbook includes an alphabetical section on ground covers, and a chapter on wildflower meadows. 96 pages, paperback, $10.95.

### GREAT GRASS GUIDES

**The Encyclopedia of Ornamental Grasses** by John Greenlee (Rodale, 1992).

Features color photographs of a wide range of grasses and grasslike plants. Individual plant entries include growing information and landscape uses. Good general text and sample garden designs. 192 pages, hardcover, $29.95.

**Step-by-Step Ornamental Grasses** by Peter Loewer (Meredith, 1995).
An easy-to-use guide to selecting, growing, and landscaping with ornamental grasses. Features sample garden plans, seasonal tasks, and an encyclopedia of 115

grasses. 132 pages, paperback, $12.95.

**Grasses: An Identification Guide** by Lauren Brown (Houghton Mifflin, 1992).
A great field guide that identifies the major grasses, sedges, and rushes by their basic visual appearance. Graceful drawings by the author accompany the entries, which include many interesting facts as well as botanical information. Very useful, particularly for the Northeast. 256 pages, paperback, $10.95.

> "Whoever can make two ears of corn or two blades of grass to grow upon a spot of ground where only one grew before, deserves better of mankind, and does more essential service to his country, than the whole race of politicians put together."
>
> Jonathan Swift, *Gulliver's Travels*

climate lawn when it is dormant during the heat of summer.

Warm-climate grasses (such as Bermuda, zoysia, and St. Augustine) thrive in areas with hot summers and mild winters. They stay green during the hot months but go dormant and turn brown during the winter (without regular watering, they'll also turn brown during the summer). Warm-climate grasses have a different fertilizing schedule. Unlike cool-climate grasses, which are dormant during midsummer, they grow prolifically during the summer months, in preparation for winter. To encourage this growth, fertilize in small doses from early spring through late summer. Do not fertilize in the fall or winter when the grass is dormant, since this encourages weeds, not grass, to grow.

Turfgrasses have a reputation for being "heavy feeders," requiring lots of fertilizer. But that's true only of lawns that have poor soil with little organic matter, earthworms, or other soil life. Chemical fertilizers feed the grass, but they do nothing to enrich the soil and promote healthy soil life. They provide only a quick hit of nutrients and then leach out of the soil. Chemicals also tend to stimulate rapid plant growth that is vulnerable to insects and disease. For the optimum long-term health of your lawn, use organic fertilizers. Organic fertilizers release their nutrients slowly over time, supplying continuous nutrition and improving the life of the soil. They also contain important trace elements, which your lawn needs in minute quantities but which aren't found in most synthetic fertilizers.

Finally, don't forget about an abundant, and free, source of nutrients — grass clippings. By leaving clippings on the lawn after mowing, you're adding nutrients (especially nitrogen) to the soil and stimulating biological activity. Research has shown that leaving short clippings (½ inch or finer) on your lawn can supply up to 40 percent of its annual fertilizer needs. If you find that your clippings are thick, wet, and smothering the lawn, by all means rake them up and compost them for later application. But high, frequent mowing will help ensure that short clippings easily work their way down into the soil, where they can do some good.

## Mowing

One of the most common mistakes people make is to cut their lawns

## What's So Great About Zoysia?

You've probably seen zoysia advertised as the "miracle grass," and, for some regions of the country, this fine-textured, low-maintenance grass does perform extremely well. Native to southern Asia, some kinds of zoysia grass are winter-hardy, especially the popular species known as Japanese lawn grass (*Z. japonica*). Zoysia is a slow starter, taking up to two years to establish itself. But once it does, zoysia resists heat, drought, insects, disease, weeds, and foot traffic.

Zoysia turns straw-colored after the first frost, and in cooler climates it can remain dormant from fall through mid-spring. It may be best suited to a low-maintenance area, one that serves as a functional and not a formal part of the lawn.

Other types of zoysia include Manila grass (*Z. matrella*), which is hardy and tolerates shade, and Mascarene grass (*Z. tenuifolia*), which is the least winter-hardy of the three zoysias and is really appropriate only for the mildest winter regions.

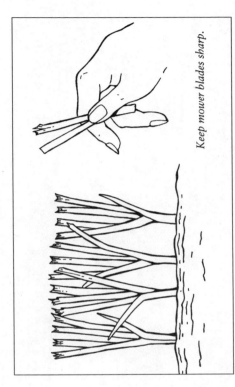

*Keep mower blades sharp.*

too short. Grass roots tend to grow about as deep as the blades grow tall, so a lawn that's clipped to a height of 1 inch will have only about 1 inch of root growth for the uptake of water and nutrients. In addition, the more leafy material that's removed, the more the grass is stimulated to replace it by using up food reserves stored in the roots. Cutting off too much of the grass blade at one time can deplete these food reserves faster than they can be replenished, resulting in a weak root system and a lawn that is more susceptible to diseases and weeds.

So mow high and a little at a time, cutting off no more than one-third of the grass blade. Warm-weather grasses should be mowed to a height of 2 inches; mow cool-weather grasses to a height of 2 to 3 inches. Do your mowing only when the grass is actively growing, not when it's dormant. It does no good to mow a cool-climate grass on a hot day in July. The grass will not produce new growth, and it may turn brown from the evaporation of moisture from the freshly cut blades. A dull blade injures your lawn by tearing blades of grass, and pulling out tender new growth.

Above all, remember to keep your mower blade sharp. A dull blade injures your lawn by tearing blades of grass, and pulling out tender new growth.

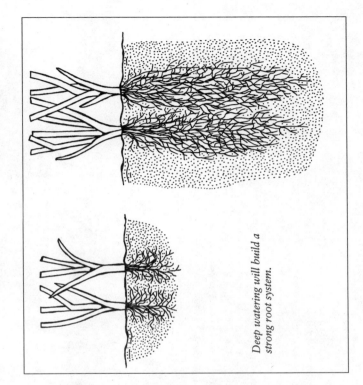

*Deep watering will build a strong root system.*

## Watering

Watering recommendations often call for 1 inch of water every week during the mowing season. However, the actual amount of water your lawn requires depends upon many factors, such as weather conditions, grass variety, and soil type. Sandy soils, for instance, drain quickly, while clay soils retain moisture longer. (For more information about soils and water retention see the chapter on "Water-Efficient Gardening.")

The most important rule in watering is to either water deeply or not water at all. Frequent shallow watering promotes a shallow root system and weak growth. However, watering to a depth of 6 to 8 inches encourages deep rooting and a more

# Garden Gear

Gardener's Supply's **100% Organic Lawn Fertilizer** (7-3-4) contains only naturally occurring minerals (including Chilean nitrate) and recycled agricultural products, such as whey meal and leather meal. It produces no dust or odor. Apply 12½ pounds per 2,500 square feet.

The specially blended **Fall Lawn Fertilizer** (4-6-6) provides extra phosphorus and potassium for healthy root growth in the fall and quick green-up the following spring. Apply 25 pounds per 2,500 square feet.

#07-301 GSC Lawn Fertilizer, 5-lb. bag $5.95
#07-305 GSC Lawn Fertilizer, 25-lb. pail $24.95
#07-314 GSC Fall Lawn Fertilizer, 25-lb. pail $24.95

**ROOTS Plus for Grass** is a 12-2-3 fertilizer that contains organic elements and enough nonorganic nutrients to ensure vigorous green-up and plant growth. This product is particularly good when used as a "bridging" fertilizer for gardeners switching from chemical to organic lawn care. One gallon treats 16,000 square feet. Accurate application is easy with the optional **ROOTS Hose-End Sprayer**.

#07-292 ROOTS Plus for Grass, 1 gal. $34.95
#07-284 ROOTS Plus for Grass, 32 oz. $10.95
#07-274 ROOTS Sprayer $5.95

This easy-to-use **Liquid Lawn Dethatcher** creates a favorable environment for microbial activity, and encourages the natural decomposition of lawn thatch. Spray on your lawn through the pre-calibrated hose-end sprayer (included). No adverse effect on living grass or earthworms. One quart covers 5,000 square feet.

#13-182 Liquid Lawn Dethatcher $14.95

Here's an easy and inexpensive way to open up hard, compacted soils and help reduce thatch in your lawn. Strap on these **Lawn Aerator Sandals** and take a walk around your yard. The 1½-inch-long steel spikes open air passages to allow water, air, and nutrients to penetrate down to the root zone where they're needed. The sandals strap on to adult shoes from size 6 to 10.

#13-231 Lawn Aerator Sandals $17.50

Does your lower back hurt after an afternoon of raking? **The Power Rake** lets you get the job done without stooping or lifting. Push it forward, and the curved tines glide smoothly over leaves and debris. Pull it back and the upper basket collects the leaves right at your feet. The 24-inch-wide head clears a broad swath, and the narrowly spaced teeth collect even the smallest debris (like pine needles). Also good for dethatching lawns, leveling raised beds, and moving gravel. Made from rough, high-density polyethylene, with a 5-foot handle.

#04-125 Power Rake $32.00

**Milky Spore** is a naturally occurring, microscopic bacterium (*Bacillus popilliae*) that kills grubs (including Japanese beetle larvae) before they can grow into ravenous adults and destroy your lawn's root system.

Simply broadcast the powder in a grid pattern on your lawn, and the spores will gradually spread out and attack grubs for up to 20 years. Safe to use around people and pets, and will not harm beneficial soil organisms. For best results, apply when the soil is warm. One 10-ounce can covers 2,500 square feet.

#05-153 Milky Spore Powder $29.95

These special seed mixes combine slow-growing dwarf grasses with fragrant herbs and flowers to "spice up" your lawn, giving it a wonderful new look and texture. They require less water and fertilizer than an all-grass lawn, and need to be mowed just once every two to four weeks.

The **Floral Mix** fills your lawn with baby blue eyes, pink English daisies, sweet alyssum, and yarrow. After mowing, most of the flowers rebloom within five days. The **Herbal Mix** blends grasses and herbs such as chamomile, sweet alyssum, yarrow, and strawberry clover for a novel texture and a sweet fragrance when you mow. One pound of Herbal Mix covers 700 sq. feet; one pound of Flower Mix covers 1,000 sq. feet. Recommended for gardeners in Zones 4-8.

#16-280A Floral Lawn Seed Mix, 1 lb. $29.95
#16-280B Herbal Lawn Seed Mix, 1 lb. $29.95

vigorous lawn. In general, you'll probably need to run your sprinkler for two to four hours each week. To conserve water, try to water early in the morning, not in the middle of a hot, sunny day.

If you are not willing or able to water the lawn (and in dry years and arid regions many communities institute watering bans), simply don't water at all. The grass will stop growing and go dormant, resuming its growth when the weather cools and/or the rains return. It is important, though, to decide at the beginning of the summer whether you will water or not: to vacillate between watering and not watering only stresses the lawn.

## Weed Control

The best way to control weeds is to maintain a healthy lawn. In fact, weeds are often indicators of infertile soil or unhealthy grass. Moss indicates a shady, acid, and infertile soil. Nutsedge indicates that the soil is too wet and poorly drained. Crabgrass indicates that the turf is sparse and unhealthy and that you may be mowing the grass too short. Dandelions prefer an acid soil and may also indicate a potassium deficiency. By simply improving the health of your soil, weed growth should be minimal.

Mowing high also helps to reduce weed problems. Most weed seeds need light to germinate, and taller grass will shade them out.

If you have a small backyard and just a few weeds, you can hand-pull them and then fill in with a fast-growing variety of grass seed. Stubborn dandelions and thistles, which have deep tap roots, can be removed using a dandelion fork.

If your lawn is sparse and very weedy (at least 50 percent weeds), you may need to start all over again. Rototill a small section at a time (preferably in the spring when the weeds are not yet growing) and then reseed the area. This is the perfect time to add organic matter, lime (if needed), and the proper variety of grass seed for your climate and site.

## Insects

A healthy, properly maintained lawn will be able to resist most insect problems. Grubs and chinch bugs are the most common insect pests on lawns. Grubs are the larval stage of several different types of beetles, the most familiar being the Japanese beetle. They feed on the roots of grass and can sometimes kill entire sections of lawn. To control moderate populations of grubs, apply beneficial nematodes in early spring or fall.

You can spray the biological control milky spore (*Bacillus popillae*) on the affected area of lawn, or apply Neemachtin™, a natural insecticide derived from the seeds of the neem tree, which works by interrupting the molting process of the developing grubs. For more information about these agents see the chapter on "Pest and Disease Control."

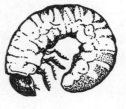

## Web Sites

**Ampac Seed Company**
http://www.ampacseed.com
*A supplier of turfgrass and forage grass seed, Ampac's web site contains information on controlling common turfgrass diseases, as well as links to other material.*

**The Lawn Institute**
http://www.lawninstitute.com/
*The national turfgrass authority since 1955. The institute's site includes information about its on-line newsletter, free bulletins on lawn care issues, and links to other lawn-related sites.*

**Ornamental Grasses**
http://ourworld.compuserve.com/homepages/RUDA/
*Includes an A–Z list of appropriate ornamental grasses for sun, light shade, Xeriscape gardens, water gardens, and other settings. Also lists over 300 hostas.*

## Mower Garden Gear

Chinch bugs appear during the summer months. They suck the grass blades to withdraw moisture and then inject a toxic saliva that can kill the grass. Severe infestations can be controlled by spraying a quart of premixed insecticidal soap with a tablespoon of isopropyl (rubbing) alcohol. Spray the lawn every three to four days for two weeks.

If you must apply an all-purpose insecticide to your lawn, remember that many of these products are toxic to earthworms and other ben-

tempered steel blades cut a full 20-inch swath, and ball bearings keep the blades spinning smoothly. Cutting height adjusts from 1 to 3 inches. Comfortable padded grip and 10-inch radial tread tires. Optional Grass Catcher has a galvanized steel base, and holds one full bushel.

#13-189  Classic Reel Mower $175.00
#13-257  Grass Catcher $27.50

The **Mole Mover** uses harmless underground vibrations to drive moles and voles from your yard and keep them from coming back. Its unique design intensifies these vibrations to ensure

maximum effectiveness. Depending on your soil type and obstructions like buildings and driveways, the Mole Mover will protect an area up to 1/4 acre in size. Volume, duration of vibrations, and interval of vibrations are adjustable.

#30-134 Adjustable Mole Mover $125.00

Imagine how great it would be to start your mower with a flick of a switch and mow your entire yard without the ear-splitting roar and nasty fumes of a gasoline engine. This **Rechargeable Mower** has a powerful electric motor that starts instantly and runs up to 90 minutes on an overnight charge. Its tempered steel blades cut a clean 18-inch swath, and you can choose from five different cutting heights. A patented system chops grass clippings into an ultrafine mulch that eliminates the need for raking or bagging. Designed for easy cleanup and built to last, it recharges from a standard 110-volt outlet. Two-year warranty. Made in USA.

#13-225  Rechargeable Electric Mower $425.00

Keep your lawn looking great and get some pleasant exercise, too. Like old-fashioned reel mowers, the **Classic Reel Mower** cuts your grass cleanly and runs without noise or fumes. But unlike older models, it won't bind as easily in tall or wet grass, because the traditional drag roller in back has been replaced by two smooth-rolling wheels. The 5 hear-

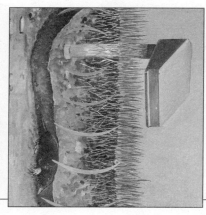

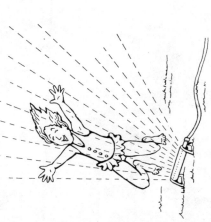

efical soil life that act as predators against the "bad bugs." In other words, by using a powerful insecticide, you may actually be increasing your insect problems rather than solving them.

## Diseases

Lawn diseases can be difficult to recognize, because the symptoms often resemble nutrient deficiencies and insect damage. If you think your lawn has a fungal disease, contact your local nursery or extension agent for a diagnosis. You can avoid most fungal diseases by following proper lawn maintenance practices:

• Do not overwater.
• Do not water in the late evening. Water in the morning, so that excess moisture will evaporate in the sun.
• Plant a mixture of grasses rather than one variety to reduce disease spread.
• Remove accumulating thatch.
• Mow high. Close mowing encourages succulent leaf growth that is more susceptible to fungal disease.

## Going Organic

If your lawn has grown accustomed to a chemical diet, you'll need to allow some time for it to make the transition back to natural care and feeding. Your soil probably won't contain much organic matter, and it may also be devoid of biological activity.

You can wean your lawn off of chemicals with extra applications of a low-nitrogen fertilizer. Then make one spring application of a slow-release organic fertilizer (see "Garden Gear," page 258). The organic nutrients are released slowly, over the entire growing season, which helps rejuvenate a worn-out lawn.

You'll also want to do some careful monitoring of weeds, diseases, and insect pests because pest/predator imbalances may exist coming off of a chemical lawn-care program. But, once established, your natural lawn will reward you with green, lush grass that will enhance your yard year after year.

A child said *What is the grass?* fetching it to me with full hands,
How could I answer the child? I do not know what it is any more than he.

I guess it must be the flag of my disposition, out of hopeful green stuff woven.

Or I guess it is the handkerchief of the Lord,
A scented gift and remembrancer designedly dropt,
Bearing the owner's name someway in the corners, that we may see and remark, and say *Whose?*

Or I guess the grass is itself a child, the produced babe of the vegetation.

Or I guess it is a uniform hieroglyphic,
And it means, Sprouting alike in broad zones and narrow zones,
Growing among black folks as among white,
Kanuck, Tuckahoe, Congressman, Cuff, I give them the same, I receive them the same.

And now it seems to me the beautiful uncut hair of graves."

Walt Whitman, "Song of Myself," 6

# the edible landscape

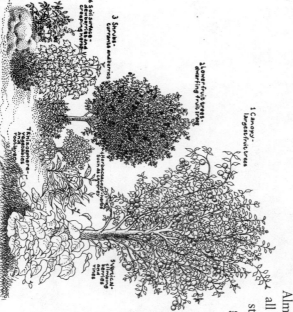

*The seven levels of an edible forest garden are: 1) the canopy of standard fruit trees; 2) the understory of dwarf fruit trees; 3) shrubs; 4) the herbaceous layer; 5) the vertical layer of climbing plants; 6) the ground layer; and 7) the rhizosphere, or below-ground layer.*

From Forest Gardening by Robert Hart © 1996 Green Books

The idea of an edible landscape stretches all the way back to the Garden of Eden. In Genesis 1:29, God says to Adam, "Behold, I have given you every seed-bearing plant that is upon all the earth, and every tree that has seed-bearing fruit; they shall be yours for food." And while even Paradise needed some tending by the first gardeners, Adam and Eve, in return it produced abundantly and provided for all their needs.

Almost no one today is so self-sufficient that they grow all of their food at home, yet the edible landscape is still a popular concept. After all, why just stick to growing ornamentals in your garden, when you can incorporate many types of interesting plants that are both decorative and useful: herbs, edible flowers, small fruits and nuts, and perennial vegetables. Whether you have a small patio or a large estate to work with, you can take advantage of the many virtues of edible plants, and recreate a little bit of Paradise right in your own backyard.

## Consider a Plant's Whole Personality

An edible landscape doesn't ignore the ornamental qualities of plants — far from it. But it doesn't begin and end with their outer beauty, either. Many plants have other useful qualities to recommend them, ones that make them especially valuable for use in the home landscape. Most directly, of course, they might be a food source, providing us with fruits, nuts, leaves, seeds, or edible flowers. But they may also have other virtues: providing food and habitat for birds, wildlife, and beneficial insects; or improving the soil by mining certain nutrients and making them available to other plants; and so forth.

In one sense, the goals and challenges of making an edible landscape are the same as with any landscape design: to create an aesthetically pleasing whole from a combination of plants that complement each other in terms of their growing habit, season of bloom or interest, and cultural requirements. Including useful plants in the landscape means exploring and exploiting their full potential, rather than sticking

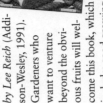
## Guest Expert
## Robert Hart

*Robert Hart has popularized the principles of agroforestry and edible landscaping in books such as Forest Gardening (Chelsea Green, 1996). He lives in Shropshire, England.*

An old orchard makes a very good nucleus for a forest garden, unless the trees are severely diseased. My forest garden was planted in a 25-year-old orchard of apples and pears, some of which were in pretty poor condition. But the aromatic herbs that have been planted beneath them seem to have rejuvenated them.

These old trees constitute the "canopy" of the forest architecture. If one is starting a forest garden from scratch, the best way to form a canopy is by planting standard apples, plums, or pears at the recommended spacing: 20 feet each way. Then fruit or nut trees on dwarfing rootstocks can be planted halfway between the standards, to form the "low-tree layer," and fruit bushes between all the trees to form the "shrub layer." Herbs and perennial vegetables constitute the "herbaceous layer," and spreading plants like dewberries and other *Rubus* species, as well as creeping herbs such as sorrel and lady's-mantle, will form the "ground-cover layer." For root vegetables, a low mound can be raised, so that they will not be swamped by the herbs. As for the climbers that constitute the "vertical layer": grapevines, nasturtiums, and runner beans can be trained up the trees, while raspberries and other cane fruits can be trained over a trellis fence, forming a boundary to the garden.

to the tried-and-true criteria of height, spread, bloom time, and flower color. In time, each type of plant comes to have its own unique "personality," a combination of its growing needs and its endearing qualities that distinguishes it from all other species, adding a deeper meaning and interest to your gardening efforts.

## What Is an Edible Plant?

Remember the old TV commercial for Grape Nuts cereal that featured wild plant authority Euell Gibbons? He looked into the camera and asked, "Ever eat a pine tree? Many parts are edible." That comment has long since become a cliche, and yet it rings true for a wide range of plants, not just pine trees.

One estimate puts the number of edible plants in the world at between 30,000 and 80,000 species. According to Kenny Ausubel, the author of *Seeds of Change* (HarperCollins, 1987), humans rely on only about 150 of these plants for food, and only 20 species account for 90 percent of our food supply. Of these 20 plants, three grains — wheat, corn, and rice — account for fully half our food production.

What does this have to do with the backyard gardener? Well, it means that many plants that we don't commonly consider food sources can add a new spark and flavor to your seasonal eating when grown in the edible landscape. Say you have a shallow pond or marshy wetland

## Wet-Tolerant Edible Landscape Plants

| Botanical Name | Common Name | Plant Type | Growing Zones | Edible Uses |
|---|---|---|---|---|
| Amelanchier canadensis | Shadblow, serviceberry | Shrub | 3–7 | fruit; jam |
| Angelica atropurpurea | Angelica | Herb | 3–6 | stems candied or cooked vegetable |
| Carya laciniata | Shellbark hickory | Tree | 5–8 | nuts |
| Impatiens capensis | Jewelweed, touch-me-not | Herb | 3–8 | young stems cooked; leaves a topical remedy for poison ivy |
| Lilium canadense | Canada lily | Flower | 4–6 | bulbs boiled or roasted |
| Lilium superbum | Turk's-cap lily | Flower | 4–8 | bulbs boiled or roasted |
| Lindera benzoin | Spicebush | Shrub | 5–9 | leaves and twigs for tea; berries for seasoning |
| Matteuccia pensylvanica | Ostrich fern | Fern/ground cover | 2–8 | young shoots ("fiddleheads") steamed |
| Rosa carolina | Carolina rose | Shrub | 4–9 | fruits (hips), flower petals |
| Sambucus canadensis | Elderberry | Shrub | 3–9 | fruit and flowerheads for juice, wine, jelly; other parts poisonous |
| Sorbus americana | American mountain-ash | Tree | 2–7 | fruit cooked and sweetened for jam |
| Vaccinium corymbosum | Highbush blueberry | Shrub | 3–8 | fruit; jam, pies, etc. |
| Viola spp. | Violets | Flower/ground cover | 3–8 | leaves cooked as greens or dried for tea; flowers for salad use or candied |

## Disease-Resistant Fruits and Nuts

| Common Name | Botanical Name | Growing Habit |
| --- | --- | --- |
| **FRUITS** | | |
| Actinidia (kiwi, silvervine) | *Actinidia* spp. | Vine |
| Beach plum | *Prunus maritima* | Shrub |
| Blueberry | *Vaccinium* spp. | Shrub |
| Elder | *Sambucus* spp. | Shrub/Tree |
| Elaeagnus (Russian olive, autumn olive, gumi) | *Elaeagnus* spp. | Shrub/Tree |
| Fig | *Ficus carica* | Shrub |
| Hawthorn | *Crataegus* spp. | Shrub/Tree |
| Jostaberry | *Ribes nidigrolaria* | Shrub |
| Juneberry (shadbush, serviceberry, saskatoon) | *Amelanchier* spp. | Shrub/Tree |
| Medlar | *Mespilus germanica* | Tree |
| Mountain-ash (rowan, service tree) | *Sorbus* spp. | Tree |
| Mulberry | *Morus* spp. | Tree |
| Oregon grape-holly | *Mahonia* spp. | Evergreen shrub |
| Quince | *Cydonia oblonga* | Shrub/Tree |
| **NUTS** | | |
| Black walnut | *Juglans nigra* | Tree |
| Chestnut | *Castanea* spp. | Tree |
| Hazelnut | *Corylus* spp. | Shrub/Tree |

on your property. Finding plants that will thrive in such a "problem" site can prove challenging. But consider the possibilities that open up once you start looking at edible landscape plants. You might decide to plant cattails (*Typha* spp.), which are not only an ideal wetland plant, but whose young stalks can be steamed and eaten in the spring (a delicacy known as "Cossack asparagus"), and whose pollen, sprouts, and rhizomatous roots are also edible and nutritious. The cattail is just one example of a versatile wetland species; other plants that tolerate wet soils are listed in the table on "Wet-Tolerant Edible Landscape Plants." (See also the books recommended in the "Right Plant, Right Place" section of the "General Resources" chapter.)

The point is, almost any site can be transformed into an edible landscape. In a typical vegetable garden, most crops are treated as annuals and most also require a lot of sun every day in order to flourish. The edible landscape, however, can include a more diverse group of plants, ones that are adapted to a variety of soils and growing conditions, and that often live for many years, requiring very little maintenance or attention.

## Ornamental Edibles

As suggested earlier, growing edible plants in the landscape doesn't mean you need to sacrifice the beauty or design advantages of ornamental plants. After all, edible plants are like any others, and many of them have striking flowers or foliage that fit well into an existing landscape.

It's a good idea to start off small, incorporating a few edible annuals or perennials into your existing garden beds. Then, as you discover more plants you'd like to try, consider creating a small garden space that's devoted exclusively to edible perennials. Finally, as you become more ambitious and knowledgeable, you may decide to transform part of your yard or landscape into a "forest garden" — a multileveled planting where trees, shrubs, perennials, vines, and other types of plants harmonize in a naturalistic way.

**BRING EDIBLES INTO YOUR ORNAMENTAL BEDS.** As a first step, try mixing a few edible perennials into your existing flower beds or borders.

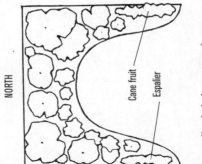

NORTH

*A woodland glade pattern features tall trees planted around the outside of the garden, with shorter plants and sun-loving plants grouped in the middle.*

Cane fruit

Espalier

# Resources

Remember, they don't have to be wild, exotic, or even unusual plants to make an impact. Rhubarb, with its large, palmate leaves and red stalks, makes an attractive specimen in a mixed-bed planting. An asparagus patch may be interesting during the spring harvest, but the tall, lacy plants look great later in the season and can serve as an effective foil for other flowers grown nearby, such as garden phlox and Russian sage.

Many annual vegetables also deserve a chance to strut their stuff outside the vegetable garden. Swiss chard makes a nice display, and it tolerates both partial shade and cool temperatures. Colorful varieties of chard such as 'Rhubarb' and 'Rainbow' are extremely valuable for landscape use in beds. Lettuce and kale leaves, with their different colors and textures, also work well in combination with flowers. 'Lacinato' is a highly ornamental variety of kale, with straplike, blistered leaves that are dark blue-green, almost black, in color. The variegated green-and-white leaves of 'Alaska' nasturtiums precede and then set off its cheerful orange, red, and yellow flowers; what's more, both the leaves and flowers are edible, with a sharp, peppery flavor that's great for salads or garnishing. Finally, attractive garden herbs and edible flowers such as opal basil or calendula definitely deserve a place in the flower bed.

## MAIL-ORDER PLANT SOURCES

**Bear Creek Nursery**
P.O. Box 411
Northport, WA 99157
*Wide variety of fruit trees and shrubs; offers scionwood and budwood for home grafters, and does custom grafting.*

**Edible Landscaping Nursery**
P.O. Box 77
Afton, VA 22920
804-361-9134
*Ships container plants year-round; good variety.*

**Northwoods Nursery**
27635 S. Oglesby Rd.
Canby, OR 97013
503-266-5432
*Edible and ornamental plants.*

**Oikos Tree Crops**
P.O. Box 19425
Kalamazoo, MI 49019
616-624-6233
*Edible native fruits and nut trees.*

**Raintree Nursery**
391 Butts Rd.
Morton, WA 98356
360-496-6400
*Edible and ornamental plants, including some hard to find elsewhere.*

**St. Lawrence Nurseries**
325 State Hwy. 345
Potsdam, NY 13676
315-265-6739
http://www.sln.potsdam.ny.us
*Extremely cold-hardy edible landscape plants; many unique varieties.*

**Tripple Brook Farm**
37 Middle Rd.
Southampton, MA 01073
413-527-4626
*Small nursery carrying a wide range of useful plants, from herbs to trees.*

## ORGANIZATIONS

**Home Orchard Society**
P.O. Box 230192
Tigard, OR 97281-0192
503-835-5040
*A nonprofit educational organization formed to assist both new and experienced fruit growers. Membership is $15 per year and includes a subscription to the quarterly journal Pome News.*

**The International Ribes Association (TIRA)**
c/o Jeanne Nickless
P.O. Box 428
Boonville, CA 95415
707-895-2811
*Dedicated to furthering the cultivation and knowledge of currants, gooseberries, and jostaberries. Membership is $20 per year and includes a subscription to the "Ribes Reporter" newsletter.*

**North American Fruit Explorers (NAFEX)**
c/o Jill Vorbeck
1716 Apples Rd.
Chapin, IL 62628
*NAFEX has over 3,000 members who are committed to discovering and growing superior varieties of fruits and nuts. Membership is $8 per year, or $15 for two years. Members receive a subscription to the quarterly journal Pomona, as well as access to the extensive NAFEX library.*

**Northern Nut Growers Association**
c/o Kenneth Bauman
9870 S. Palmer Rd.
New Carlisle, OH 45344
513-878-2610
*Annual membership dues are $15.*

**California Rare Fruit Growers**
The Fullerton Arboretum—CSUF
P.O. Box 6850
Fullerton, CA 92834-6850
http://www.crfg.org

**EDIBLE SHRUBS AND TREES FOR LANDSCAPE USE.** The next logical step in edible landscaping is to consider planting some fruits, nuts, or other woody plants in your yard or landscape. The easiest and best candidates for adding to existing beds and borders include diminutive fruits such as alpine strawberries (*Fragaria vesca*) and lowbush blueberries (*Vaccinium angustifolium*), both of which are noninvasive and grow to form a neat, attractive edging or "minihedge" for other plants.

Larger shrubs and trees usually need their own space and can be planted either in small groups, such as highbush blueberries, or in larger groups to form a hedgerow or windbreak. When selecting shrubs and trees, consider their ornamental qualities (flowers, foliage, fruits, scent, shape, etc.), just as you would with any other landscape plant. Do a little research in the nursery catalogs or books on edible landscaping that are listed in this chapter, and don't feel you have to stick to the most obvious fruits. For instance, the Russian olive (*Elaeagnus angustifolia*) has beautiful silvery leaves and is often grown as an ornamental tree or (when planted 3 to 5 feet apart) a bushy hedge. Yet its sweet, mealy fruits are quite edible for humans, and birds and other wildlife absolutely love them. The hardy hybrid nuts known as hazelberts (*Corylus* spp.) also form an attractive edible hedge, growing 6 to 12 feet tall. The nut clusters have fringed husks that are highly ornamental, and in the fall the leaves make a brilliant display of red, yellow, orange, and green. The number of excellent shrubs and small trees for edible landscape use is truly impressive; for a few more plant recommendations, see the tables in this chapter.

## Thinking Like a Forest

One of the most exciting movements in the gardening world these days is that of "forest gardening," a design technique that in a way goes edible landscaping one better. Its goal is to create productive landscapes (even on a backyard scale) that mimic the kind of diversity, stability, and resilience found in nature.

Forest gardening isn't about growing plants in the middle of the woods. Instead, the idea is to design landscapes where plants can grow *like* a forest. Everyone is familiar with the example of the tropical rain forests, where tall trees act as the "canopy" layer and other plants and animals live on different levels or stories — some high in the treetops, others down on the forest floor. Forest gardening takes this natural concept of multileveled "niches" and applies it to growing edible and ornamental plants together, intensively, on even a small piece of land. In other words, almost anyone can use the forest garden model to create a highly productive and diverse edible landscape — even in a small backyard.

Robert Hart, the pioneer of forest gardening in Britain, has identified seven different levels of plants that combine to form the whole edible landscape or ecosystem. In temperate climates like Europe and most of North America, the "canopy" layer of a typical edible forest garden would normally consist of standard-sized fruit or nut trees (see

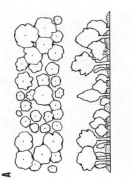

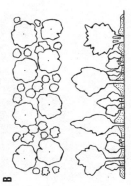

*Two basic forest garden designs. A) Areas of closed canopy alternate with areas of open canopy. B) Trees are more evenly spread out, creating a generally broken canopy.*

A

B

# Other Good Books

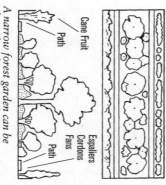

Cane Fruit
Path
Espaliers
Cordons
Fans
Path

*A narrow forest garden can be planted with a spine of trees down the center, paths on either side, and vertical plants along the edges.*

**Forest Gardening** (video). This inspiring video profiles three fascinating gardens in Britain, and in the process illustrates many of the key principles of forest gardening. It features pioneering author Robert Hart and his forest garden in Shropshire; Ken Fern, who grows 1,500 useful plants on a windswept site in Cornwall; and Mike and Julia Guerra, who have a tiny, but highly productive backyard food garden. 45 minutes, $24.95. To order, call 800-639-4099.

**The Practical Garden of Eden** by Fred Hagy (Overlook Press, 1990). Colorful drawings accent the design and plant information in this book. Especially useful are the plant information sheets, which include data on the landscaping value and season of interest for a wide range of plants. 288 pages, hardcover, $35.00.

**How to Make a Forest Garden** by Patrick Whitefield (Permanent Publications, 1996). A practical guide to forest gardening for backyard growers. Seasonal growing information is geared toward Great Britain, not the U.S., but the book still contains much useful information. 184 pages, paperback, $24.95. Available from the Rodale Institute, 611 Siegfriedale Road, Kurztown, PA 19530; 800-832-6285.

illustration on page 262). The seven layers of a forest garden include the following:

1. **Canopy:** standard or semidwarf fruit trees.
2. **Understory (low-tree layer):** fruit and nut trees on dwarfing rootstocks; bamboo.
3. **Shrub layer:** woody plants such as currants or shrub roses.
4. **Herbaceous layer:** herbs and perennial vegetables.
5. **Vertical layer:** climbing plants and vines.
6. **Ground layer:** creeping plants less than 6 inches tall.
7. **Rhizosphere (root layer):** plants that grow primarily below ground.

Not every forest garden has to have all of these distinct layers, but the whole point of planting in this way is to maximize productivity and diversity. If you are dealing with an especially small or limited growing space, you can still put these general principles to good use. Instead of growing full-sized trees as the "canopy" of your forest garden, plant trees on dwarfing rootstocks and scale down your other "understory" plants accordingly. Dwarfs will not live as long as standard-sized trees, but they will start producing fruit much sooner. (See the "Fruits" chapter. For some sample designs of typical forest gardens, see the overhead plan drawings in this chapter, which come from Patrick Whitefield's book, *How to Make a Forest Garden* (Permanent Publications, 1996).

Obviously, an edible forest garden will vary greatly by region, climate, site specifics, and the personal tastes of the gardener. The complex interactions of the plants that grow in each garden are unique. However, there are a few useful ground rules that apply to almost any forest garden, and these are discussed below. For more information on edible landscaping in general, or forest gardening in particular, consult the books and other resources mentioned in this chapter.

## Designing a Forest Garden

Careful advance planning and plant selection is probably the most crucial step in successfully creating an edible forest garden. Trees and shrubs form the backbone of the garden and determine to a great extent what types of other plants will fit in around them. Because you don't want to be moving trees and shrubs around after planting, site them first, setting them at the recommended spacing from one another. Then you can plant the understory, herbaceous, and other levels of plants underneath them.

Obviously, trees will not be full-sized specimens when you plant them, so until they grow to their mature height and spread, you will be able to temporarily plant sun-loving perennials or annuals between the young trees and shrubs. Just as a forest matures with a changing succession of plants, so too will your forest garden. Eventually, as the trees and shrubs grow larger, you will need to grow herbaceous perennials and groundcover plants that are more tolerant of shade.

**THE EDGE EFFECT.** When planning a forest garden, it is important to allow yourself access to all the plants for mulching, harvesting, and other chores. Siting paths through the garden that are wide enough for a wheelbarrow or garden cart not only provides this access, but also lets in more sunlight to those plants grown on the edges of the paths.

This "edge effect" is an important concept in designing the edible forest garden. Typically, the edge zones where woods meet meadows play host to a greater number and diversity of species than either a deep forest or a large, open field or prairie. You can use these areas on the

# Garden Gear

The **Ratchet Lopper** has a built-in ratchet mechanism that makes it easy to cut through thick hardwood branches, even with very little hand strength. Just give the handles a gentle squeeze, and release. With each squeeze, the ratchet moves up another notch, until the blade has cut completely through the wood. Will slice through hardwood limbs up to 1¾" thick.

The **Ratchet Pruner** lets you trim branches up to ¾" thick with ease, delivering a clean cut.

#04-308  Ratchet Lopper  $34.95
#30-171  Ratchet Pruner  $26.00

Bonide's **Fruit Tree Spray** controls many common fruit and berry pests and diseases in one easy step. The carefully balanced mix of pyrethrin, rotenone, sulfur, and copper controls aphids, cherry fruit flys, and more, while simultaneously warding off diseases like anthracnose, cedar rust, blossom blight, and brown rot. One pound covers approximately 1,000 square feet.

#12-220  Fruit Tree Spray  $8.95

This soft, no-tangle **Bird Netting** will protect your fruit trees and berry bushes from bird damage. The mesh is fine enough to keep birds off, yet it

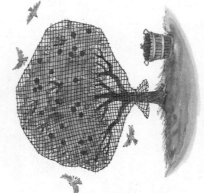

allows good air circulation. It's tough enough to last several seasons, and the green color blends with your garden. Use ¼" mesh for placing directly on plants like strawberries, raspberries, and corn. Use ½" mesh for trees, bushes, and grapes, or for covering netting structures. (For correct size, multiply the height of the tree or bush by 2 and order the closest size.) Use the **Bird Net Clips** to keep your netting securely in place.

#05-315  ¼" Mesh Netting, 4½ x 40'  $8.95
#05-316  ¼" Mesh Netting, 9' x 15'  $7.95

#05-317  ¼" Mesh Netting, 14' x 25'  $16.95
#05-318  ½" Mesh Netting, 14' x 14'  $8.95
#05-319  ½" Mesh Netting, 28' x 28'  $29.95
#05-329  ½" Mesh Netting, 45' x 45'  $84.95
#05-328  Bird Net Clips, pack of 35  $1.95

**Weed Mat** is a three-layer fabric that makes it easy to prevent weed growth around shrubs, trees, and other areas of your yard. It lets air, water, and nutrients through, while blocking weeds and conserving soil moisture. The all-purpose **Weed Mat** is available in a 50' length for rows and borders, or a 9' x 9' square that's perfect for landscaping and perennial beds. **Weed Mat Extra** contains an additional layer of polyester fibers, to resist tears and suppress even the toughest weeds. Both grades are guaranteed to block weeds for five years. For best results, cover these fabrics with a 2" layer of organic mulch.

#04-211  Weed Mat, 3' x 50'  $16.95
#04-214  Weed Mat, 9' x 9'  $9.95
#04-218  Weed Mat Extra, 3' x 100'  $34.95
#04-903  Weed Mat Extra, 3' x 250'  $79.95
#04-219  Weed Mat Extra, 4½' x 250'  $99.95
#09-213  Earth Staples, pack of 15  $2.95

# Web sites

**Edible Landscaping Nursery**
http://www.eat-it.com
*Edible Landscaping is a nursery that operates this site, which features an on-line catalog of fruit and nut plants, from akebia to strawberries. There's also a photo gallery and a recipe exchange, with suggestions on how to prepare less common fruits like pawpaws.*

**Edible Landscaping Database**
http://www.efn.org/~bsharvy/edible.html
*An on-line database (also available as a hypercard stack for Macintosh) with information on 80 different edible perennial plants suited to the U.S. Also a list of related sites.*

**Permaculture Magazine**
http://www.gaia.org/permaculture/
*Permaculture news from in and around Britain. Design information for edible landscapes. Earth Repair catalog. Provided by the Gaia Trust in Denmark.*

**Midnet Organic Permaculture Links**
http://www.midinet.com/midinet/organic/permlink.htm
*Links to worldwide permaculture sites.*

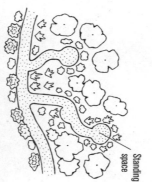

Standing space

*A keyhole path, which ends in a cul-de-sac, allows light and access to the interior of a forest garden.*

edges of paths to plant perennial vegetables, herbs, and flowers that require more sunlight than is found in the middle of the forest garden.

Another way to create paths and to provide a lot of "edge" in a forest garden is to design and cut in "keyholes," narrow paths that penetrate the garden and end in a cul-de-sac, around which sun-loving plants like rhubarb or Jerusalem artichoke will do well (see illustration).

**PLANTING A FOREST GARDEN.** Weed competition and how to prevent it is probably the most important thing to consider when planting an edible forest garden.

One easy method for controlling weeds around young plants is to use *sheet composting*. This is also a good way to begin establishing understory plants beneath existing trees or shrubs. The technique involves laying down pieces of cardboard or multiple layers of newspaper that have been soaked in water. Start by placing a layer of this material around trees and shrubs, mulching right around the plants to a distance at least 2 feet away from the stem. Make sure the edges of the mulch overlap to prevent weed growth.

Next, cover the paper or cardboard completely with a layer of compost, well-rotted manure, or some other organic material. This will hold down the paper or cardboard and prevent it from drying out or blowing away. Finally, cover the organic matter with a layer of straw and water the whole area.

Sheet composting is an effective way to smother existing weeds and to keep new weeds from getting a foothold around newly planted trees and shrubs. The paper or cardboard breaks down within a year or so, helped along by the action of earthworms and other soil life. Plus, after you have sheet-composted under the trees and shrubs, you can cut holes in the paper or cardboard and plant herbs or flowers between the taller plants. Any weeds that pop up through the planting holes are easy to see and pull out.

**MAINTAINING A FOREST GARDEN.** One of the best features about a forest garden is that, like the forest ecosystem it imitates, it demands very little attention once it is planted and has become well established. As trees and shrubs mature, less and less effort is needed to maintain what has become, in essence, a largely self-regulating edible landscape.

Rather than having to do all of the tilling, raking, seeding, transplanting, and other tasks associated with an annual vegetable garden, a forest gardener need only perform regular maintenance — simple tasks that can become an extension of daily walks through the garden. A little judicious pruning or weeding keeps the plants in bounds and in balance with one another.

Mulching deeply around plants with organic matter is critically important to the health of the forest garden. Mulch enriches the soil, regulates seasonal temperatures, protects plant roots, conserves soil moisture, and suppresses weeds.

Harvesting is probably the most time-consuming task in the edible forest garden. Fortunately, picking fresh food for the table is the one chore that almost no one minds doing.

PART VI

gardening
beyond
your own
backyard

# community gardening

M ost of the chapters in this book tell you, the individual gardener, how to get started on specific kinds of gardening projects. But while gardening is a very personal activity, it also has communal and political dimensions that can provide another level of personal satisfaction and spiritual meaning. In this chapter we want to give you a glimpse of how a variety of activities — urban community gardening, market gardening, gardening with children, gardening with prison inmates, CSA farms (community-supported agriculture), easy-care design for the elderly and people with disabilities — can enrich and nourish the lives of individuals, neighborhoods, and communities. Gardening can be a root of social transformation.

## Urban Community Gardening

Gardens are blooming in cities across America. In a sense, this has always been the case. Immigrants from other countries, and rural folk moving in from the American hinterlands, often brought their agricultural customs with them to the urban environment. These gardens usually had a practical focus, supplying food for struggling families. But they have also provided people with an important connection to the land, to tradition, to memories, and to family. Today, the spirit of urban gardening remains strong and the practice is spreading.

Urban gardens take many forms and fulfill a number of purposes. Some occupy previously vacant lots, some are in parks, some are squatted on undeveloped land — and some, of course, are in people's yards. Many of these gardens arose through the stubborn persistence of individuals or groups of neighbors, while others have been sponsored by community organizations. Some are for personal use; some serve soup kitchens, food assistance pantries, or shelters; some are market gardens

## H. Patricia Hynes

Late 20th-century cities need local community gardens even more than they need grand central parks. The give-and-take of working in gardens attaches people to a particular place through physical and social engagement. Community gardens create relationships between city dwellers and the soil, and instill an ethic of urban environmentalism that neither parks nor wilderness — which release and free us from the industrial city — can do.

Economists are fidgeting to put a value on the kind of beauty and conviviality that begins with a simple corner-lot sitting garden and becomes an entire block of window boxes, streetside trees, and home improvements. They point to the enhanced property value of houses located near parks and gardens, and the fresh incentive for businesses to locate or remain in neighborhoods with gardens. But there is also an elusive, transcendent, and non-financial value in those "flowers that feed the soul." I would suggest that community gardeners, as they turn dirt back into soil, may again create vibrant city life *through plant life* in late 20th-century America.

*H. Patricia Hynes is Professor of Environmental Health at the Boston University School of Public Health, where she works on issues of the urban environment, environmental justice, and feminism. This excerpt is from her book,* A Patch of Eden: America's Inner-City Gardeners *(Chelsea Green, 1996) which won the 1997 National Arbor Day Foundation Book Award.*

**Accessible Gardening: Tips & Techniques for Seniors and the Disabled** *by Joann Woy* (Stackpole, 1997).

The most comprehensive book we've found in this genre. How to design and plan an easy-care garden to overcome the limitations of age and/or physical condition. Especially good chapters on garden layout, watering, tools (with specific product recommendations), and horticultural therapy. Suggestions about plants for accessible landscaping. Extensive appendices of suppliers, resources, and accessible public gardens. 224 pages, paperback, $16.95.

**Sunflower Houses: Garden Discoveries for Children of All Ages** *by Sharon Lovejoy* (Interweave Press, 1991).

A wonderful, creative, charmingly illustrated book of games, poems, puzzles, and pleasures. Gems include a floral clock, flowers and veggies that kids especially love, zucchini fish in a bottle, secret messages, faerie tea parties, flower dolls, sunflower houses, and lots more. 144 pages, paperback, $16.95. See also Lovejoy's companion volume, **Hollyhock Days: Garden Adventures for the Young at Heart** (Interweave Press, 1994), which has more stories and lore and not quite as many hands-on projects, but is equally delightful. 96 pages, paperback, $16.95.

**A Patch of Eden: America's Inner-City Gardeners** *by H. Patricia Hynes* (Chelsea Green, 1996).

Moving and inspirational case studies of urban gardening projects in New York, Chicago, Philadelphia, and San Francisco that have contributed to neighborhood and personal revitalization. Describes pitfalls, problems, and politics. 216 pages, paperback, $18.95.

**The New Organic Grower: A Master's Manual of Tools and Techniques for the Home and Market Gardener** *by Eliot Coleman*, 2nd edition (Chelsea Green, 1995).

Probably the best all-around introduction to the philosophy and practice of small-scale organic farming. Comprehensive, readable, and detailed.

Excellent discussions of crop rotation, tools, season extension, growing forage crops for composting, a "plant-positive" approach to insect control, and vegetables. 352 pages, paperback, $24.95.

**Backyard Market Gardening: The Entrepreneur's Guide to Selling What You Grow** *by Andrew W. Lee* (Good Earth Publications, 1993).

An optimistic and encouraging do-it-yourself manual, based on personal experience. Strong emphasis on market-

ing, with descriptions of 11 different strategies, and a good chapter on developing a successful business plan. Lots of good tips, interesting profiles, and vignettes. 352 pages, paperback, $24.95. Available from the publisher, P.O. Box 160, RR2 Box 1875, Columbus, NC 28722.

---

that provide produce, herbs, and flowers for local restaurants; and some exist simply to freshen the city air and beautify neighborhoods. Many community gardens are tended by elderly and retired people, children, and even recent prison inmates (see the excerpt "Jail, Gardening, and Self-Worth," page 276). All of these gardens share two common threads: they help city people intimately connected to nature, and they link people together into grassroots networks that build and strengthen the bonds of community.

Unfortunately, many urban gardens are under seige and their existence is constantly being threatened. Land is an enormously valuable commodity in cities, and it is often a difficult challenge to justify using otherwise undeveloped land "just to grow things." Urban gardeners are battling at a great disadvantage to preserve their important and precious enclaves, all too often competing with housing advocates or others who want to supply the community with necessary services. In Milwaukee, gardeners are fighting plans by the county to sell their land to raise funds for the strapped public treasury. In New York City, the Giuliani administration has decided that several hundred garden plots, many of them at least ten years old and some of them profiled in *A Patch of Eden* by H. Patricia Hynes (see "Favorite Books"), must be razed to make way for affordable housing in some of the city's poorest areas: Harlem, the South Bronx, Coney Island, and parts of Brooklyn. In Burlington,

## The Philosophy of Community-Supported Agriculture

The result of this cooperation between farmer and consumer in the CSA model is that everyone has the satisfaction of becoming part of the solution. They no longer have to remain part of the problem. It brings the community back to farming, and the farmer back to the community. The public needs to know where their food comes from and the amount of work, knowledge, and capital investment it takes to be a farmer today. The farmers need to know that someone cares, and is willing to support them.

"We can begin by developing, testing, and demonstrating models of community-supported food production that are environmentally sensitive, economically sensible and socially just. Each of us can take a small step to create these systems. Combining our efforts will achieve gigantic results. These models will be the first giant step in ending America's hunger for safe, flavorful food. With these models we can fulfill our yearning to be connected to the land that grows our food and to the farmers who steward the land."

—from *Backyard Market Gardening* by Andrew W. Lee
(Good Earth Publications, 1993)

Vermont, gardeners are fighting two large housing projects proposed for community gardening sites that have multi-year waiting lists.

Municipal leaders in Philadelphia are pursuing a more enlightened strategy. There the Philadelphia Green Program is successfully lobbying community development corporations to include community garden plots in new housing units being built on vacant land. This model offers the hope that crucial public needs — gardening and housing — will not be pitted against each other, but mutually accommodated at the ground level of sensible, human-scale public policy.

## Market Gardening and Community-Supported Agriculture

Many of us lament the fact that we live in a culture where the vast majority of people have no idea where their food comes from. There are many reasons to be concerned about this situation, from the small to the big: poor nutrition, exposure to dangerous chemicals, energy consumption, agricultural pollution, exploited farm workers, erosion of irreplaceable topsoil, depletion of aquifers, climate change, the political and economic power of huge corporations, planetary ecological imbalance, spiritual hollowness. All of this is summed up in one of the buzzwords of the 1990s, "sustainability" — the idea that humanity needs to figure out how to live on Earth in harmony with global ecosystems, using only the resources we really need and giving back as much as we can.

There are two very positive movements afoot that are turning the tide toward greater sustainability: market gardening and Community-Supported Agriculture, or CSA. You can act on the idea "Think Globally, Act Locally" by patronizing local market gardens and supporting networks of local and regional agricultural producers, thus expressing your commitment to sustainable living. At the same time, you will be reconnecting with the people who produce your food (CSAs are often billed as "farming with a human face") and ensuring that you and your family receive fresher, healthier, and better-tasting food than can be found in most supermarkets and "food warehouses."

We often choose to become gardeners out of a desire to be closer to our food, to have a direct hand in creating a beautiful and harmonious ambience at home, and to nurture ourselves through integral connection to the earth. Buying plants and vegetables from local farmers is taking the next step. Supporting local growers enables people in your community to make a living through sustainable enterprise, it strengthens the market for local and/or organic produce, it helps to preserve open land, and it builds regional economic networks that can be genuinely responsive to personal and community needs. Make a point of shopping at farm stands and farmer's markets, or buying locally grown produce at your supermarket.

The concept of Community-Supported Agriculture is another promising development. CSAs can operate in a variety of ways, but the basic idea is that an agricultural producer and a group of consumers join together to support each others' primary interest (i.e. growing food, and eating it). Participants usually subscribe in advance to purchase a weekly share of a farm's harvest, which might include flowers in addition to vegetables, or the opportunity to buy organic meat, milk, eggs, fruits and berries, or winter storage crops. The farmers get some money up front, which smoothes out their finances until the harvest season kicks into high gear, and the subscribers agree to take what the farm provides them week-by-week as the harvest progresses. In many CSAs members are asked or required to put in some time working on the farm, or helping with organizational details. A CSA is a community: The risks, joys, benefits, and disappointments of farming are shared among all the participants.

The CSA movement has accelerated tremendously in the past decade: there are currently about 1,000 CSAs throughout the country. It seems like an idea whose time has come — and it promises to help sustain locally based food production and distribution systems in our highly concentrated, industrialized society.

Perhaps you've been bitten by the gardening bug so fiercely that you dream about seriously growing food and flowers for sale. Or maybe you're ready to extend your concern about the environment or an unsafe

---

## Jail, Gardening, and Self-Worth

In 1982 Cathrine Sneed, a counselor at the San Francisco County Jail in San Bruno, set out to teach inmates how to grow vegetables and flowers in a novel eight-acre classroom called the Horticulture Project . . . Today she is special assistant to the sheriff and director of the Garden Project, a half-acre organic market garden and community service program which she founded in 1991 for 'graduates' of the Horticulture Project.

"Many students have said that Cathrine Sneed changed their lives. As she sees it, she taught them how to garden, the garden gave them something good — a feeling of faith in themselves — that they had never had, and then *they changed* their lives. 'I have seen this program make people have hope who have had no hope, when they grow food at San Bruno for people who have no food, when they plant and tend trees on city streets in the Mission district that have no trees, when they grow flowers at Hunter's Point where there were no flowers.' It is not herself and not her staff, Sneed insists, 'it's working with those green things' that gives these women and men a sense of life that most have never felt anywhere else."

— from *A Patch of Eden* by H. Patricia Hynes (Chelsea Green, 1996)

food supply into a personal commitment to creating a more sustainable lifestyle. The books we have recommended in this chapter offer inspiration and models of how to engage in these activities. Support your local farmer's market, look for the CSA farm in your community — or better yet, start one yourself!

## Gardens for All: Kids, the Elderly, the Disabled

Anyone can garden. And everyone is entitled to experience the pleasures and rewards of cultivating the earth. In recent years efforts have been made to ensure that gardening is indeed accessible to people who might otherwise be left out of the gardening mainstream. For many of these people, the therapeutic aspects of growing plants are just as important

## Resources

**CSA of North America**
c/o WTIG
818 Connecticut Ave. NW
Suite 800
Washington, DC 20006

**Community Farms/CSA Project**
c/o Bio-Dynamic Association
P.O. Box 550
Kimberton, PA 19442
215-935-7797

**New England Small Farm Institute**
Box 937
Belchertown, MA 01007
413-323-4531

**Sustainable Agriculture Network**
SANlink, c/o AFSIC
Room 304
National Agricultural Library
10301 Baltimore Blvd.
Beltsville, MD 20705-2351
301-504-6425
*A cooperative effort of universities, government, business and nonprofit organizations, dedicated to*

*information exchange; numerous publications.*

**Appropriate Technology Transfer for Rural Areas (ATTRA)**
P.O. Box 3657
Fayetteville, AR 72702
800-346-9140
*Provides technical information on sustainable agriculture, and resource lists.*

**The Intervale Foundation**
128 Intervale Rd.
Burlington, VT 05401
802-660-3508
*The Intervale Foundation is a nonprofit organization attempting to reclaim a former agricultural area in Burlington, with the goal of growing 10% of the city's fresh food.*

**The Urban Agriculture Network**
1711 Lamont St. NW
Washington, DC 20010
72144.3446@compuserve.com

**American Community Gardening Association**
100 N. 20th Street, 5th Floor
Philadelphia, PA 19103-1495
215-988-8785

**National Gardening Association**
180 Flynn Ave.
Burlington, VT 05401
800-538-7476
*NGA offers many programs and resources for teachers and community gardeners, including the GrowLab Indoor Garden-Based Science program for grades K–8; Growing Ideas: A Journal of Garden-Based Learning for teachers; a professional development program for educators using plants to enrich instruction; and the Youth Garden Grant Program, which makes annual awards for youth garden initiatives.*

**Minnesota Green**
Center for Northern Gardening
1755 Prior Ave. North
Falcon Heights, MN 55113-5549
800-676-6747

**Cabrini Greens**
c/o Jack Davis, Edwin C. Sigel, LTD.
3400 Dundee Rd., Suite 180
Northbrook, IL 60062
*A market gardening, education, and job training*

*program at a Chicago housing project.*

**The Garden Project**
35 South Park
San Francisco, CA 94107
*A film about the Garden Project at the San Francisco County Jail, "Growing Season," is available from Bullfrog Films, P.O. Box 149, Oley, PA 19547, 800-543-3764; 25 minutes, $95 purchase/$40 rent, plus $5 s/h.*

**The Greening of Harlem Coalition**
c/o Bernadette Cozart
Harlem Hospital KP 17103
506 Lenox Ave.
New York, NY 10037

**Penn State Urban Gardening Program**
4601 Market St., Third Floor
Philadelphia, PA 19139
215-560-4167

**American Horticultural Therapy Association**
362A Christopher Ave.
Gaithersburg, MD 20879
800-634-1603
ahta@ahta.org
http://www.ahta.org

**Northeast Organic Farmers Association (NOFA)**
411 Sheldon Rd.
Barre, MA 01005
Journal: *The Natural Farmer*

# Other Good Books

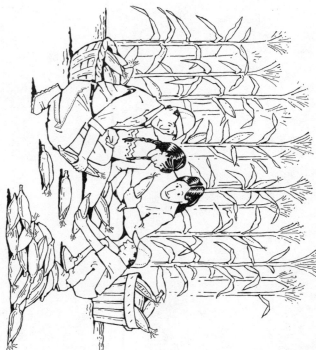

### ACCESSIBLE GARDENING

Accessible Gardening for People with Physical Disabilities by Janeen R. Adil (Woodbine House, 1994).
A thorough how-to manual about easy-care gardening to minimize physical strain. Good specific product and plant recommendations. Special chapters on vertical gardening, and on gardening with kids, especially kids with disabilities. 316 pages, paperback, $16.95.

### GARDENING WITH CHILDREN

Let's Grow!: 72 Gardening Adventures with Children by Linda Tilgner (Garden Way Publishing, 1988).
A complete guide to gardening with kids. More hands-on projects than you can shake a cornstalk at. Project lists are organized by age and season. Chapters on wildflowers and wild vegetables, kids and houseplants. Superb black-and-white photographs. 216 pages, paperback, $10.95.

Kids Garden: The Anytime, Anyplace Guide to Sowing and Growing Fun by Avery Hart and Paul Mantell (Williamson, 1996).
Written for kids (and their families); project-oriented. Adults might find the relentlessly cheery tone and cartoonish drawings a bit tiresome, but kids will love this book. Especially appropriate for ages 7 to 15. 160 pages, paperback, $12.95.

### MARKET GARDENING AND COMMUNITY-SUPPORTED AGRICULTURE

Farms of Tomorrow Revisited: Community Supported Farms/Farm Supported Communities by Trauger M. Groh and Steven S.H. McFadden (Bio-Dynamic Farming and Gardening Association, 1997).
An introduction to the principles of biodynamic farming and community-supported agriculture. Includes profiles of 9 CSAs, with details about these farms, how they work, and the mechanics of community land trusts. Suffers a bit from a dogmatic tone and uneven writing. 240 pages, paperback, $15.95.

Rebirth of the Small Family Farm by Bob and Bonnie Gregson (IMF Associates, 1996).
A "handbook for starting a successful organic farm based on the CSA concept." How a middle-aged couple with little gardening experience left the corporate world for the CSA, and are loving it. Inspirational, with a good view of the process, although a bit narrow-minded about their approach being the best. 64 pages, paperback, $9.95 (available from IMF Associates, P.O. Box 2542, Vashon Island, WA 98070).

as producing food, and particularly powerful.

Many devoted gardeners trace their love of gardening back to childhood experiences. It seems as if everyone has a story to tell about hiding under an arch of forsythia, the thrill of planting seeds and seeing them sprout, or memories of Grandma's flower garden, triggered suddenly by a fragrance or a glimpse out of the corner of an eye. The plain and simple truth is, that kids are born gardeners. They love the outdoors, they love playing in the dirt, they love planting things, and they love watching things grow. What could be more natural?

In the garden children learn many valuable lessons about the workings of nature, respect for life, personal responsibility, cooperation, and self-esteem. It's especially nice to give young kids their own gardening plot where they can have free reign to putter with a minimum of guidance (or interference) from you. This arrangement allows children to entertain themselves while the adults garden in earnest, and it reduces the stress you are bound to feel about the kids mucking around and destroying or disrupting things in the "real" garden. Best of all, they get to experience the thrill of harvesting the flowers and vegetables they planted and tended themselves.

Many of us who are physically fit may not realize that the joys of gardening can be fully shared by people whose physical condition is limited due to age or disability. Books and resources are available that explain how to design yards and growing spaces that minimize the labor of gardening for elderly people and people with physical limitations; and tools and techniques have been developed that reduce bodily strain. Check out our recommended books lists. The psychological and emotional benefits of growing plants can provide a tremendous sense of satisfaction, accomplishment, and connection to the earth for people who are often otherwise prevented from fully participating in many activities.

## Web Sites

### KinderGarden
http://aggie-horticulture.tamu.edu/kinder/index.html
*Part of the excellent Texas A&M University web site, this piece focuses on "human issues in horticulture," with information, resources, and web links about urban gardening, horticultural therapy, school gardens, and community gardens.*

### Kids & Classrooms
http://www2.garden.org/nga/EDU/Home.html
*This page is the National Gardening Association's forum for teachers, educators, and community partners "interested in using plants and gardens to enrich learning."*

### Urban Agriculture Notes
http://www.cityfarmer.org
*Maintained by City Farmer, Canada's Office of Urban Agriculture, founded in 1978. Lots of interesting articles on a wide range of urban gardening topics, with an international focus.*

### American Community Gardening Association
http://lag.arizona.edu/~bradley/acga/acga.htm
*Membership information, publications, FAQs, and an online publication about how to start a community garden.*

### Pat's Horticultural Therapy Page
http://http.tamu.edu:8000/~pnw3384/
*A guide to positive interactions between people and plants.*

### American Horticultural Therapy Association
http://www.ahta.org
*Offering professional registration, conferences, education, and links to other horticultural therapy sites.*

### Keith's Tomato Home Page
http://www4.ncsu.edu/eos/users/k/kdmuelle/public/hp.html
*Besides tons of information about tomatoes, Keith has assembled a terrific bunch of links to sites pertaining to horticultural therapy, community gardening, children and gardening, urban gardening, and more!*

# garden touring

PASSPORT TO GARDENING
GARDEN TOURING

W hether it's a trip next door to see how the neighbor's tomatoes are coming along, or a two-week tour of the great gardens of Europe, gardeners never seem to tire of visiting other people's gardens. Being able to wander among beautiful flowers and pleasing vistas is satisfying enough in itself, but the observant gardener can also discover a wealth of new ideas and inspiration.

What sorts of things can you discover? You might be inspired by seeing a plant that you have in your own garden, used in a new setting or combination — such as red monarda growing alongside deep blue delphiniums, or lamb's-ears used as edging for a crushed stone walkway. You may discover a solution to a challenge that has baffled you for years — a free-standing picket fence defining a small herb garden, or evergreen shrubs anchoring the back of a perennial border. You may be inspired by a gardening style and plant materials that are dramatically different from those in your own garden: a rooftop garden with everything growing in containers; a desert garden that is more stone than plants; a wildflower garden with birdbaths and frog ponds. What may be most enjoyable of all is the simple joy of experiencing the very personal vision of another fellow gardener.

## Close to Home

Finding beauty and inspiration does not require a trip to Europe. In fact, once you start poking around, you will probably be surprised by how

---

## *Guest Expert*

### Gordon Hayward

When you visit a garden for the first time, be non-judgmental. Rather than thinking "I like this . . . I don't like that," think "What can I learn from this garden?" No matter the size or style, every garden has lessons to teach us about design, composition, and sensibility.

First, look at the house and imagine it as your own. How has the designer linked the house to the front, side, and back gardens with paths? What do you think is the overarching idea of this garden? As you walk around, be aware of how each area makes you feel: serene, excited, curious, nervous, comfortable. Has the designer achieved graceful transitions from one area to the next? Are gardens in proportion to each other?

Next, notice the sensory elements of this garden experience: straight or curved bed edges; paths; sculpture; water features; sound and fragrance; openness and enclosures; light and shade; moisture; stillness and wind.

Then look closely at the plants. Is a given area planted intensely? in masses? with considerable detail? Try to determine the purpose of plant combinations: for foliage and texture contrast? for color contrast? for simplicity or complexity? Try to pick up cues from the ground: are mulch and compost used? What is the nature of the soil? And how are other materials, such as stone, furniture, containers, or trellises, related to the plantings?

Finally, ask yourself what this garden is used for, and if those objectives have been achieved. Do the plants, paths, structures, ornaments, forms, and colors work together to create coherent spaces?

*Gordon Hayward is a professional garden designer, writer, and English garden tour leader. He is the author of Garden Paths (Camden House, 1993), Designing Your Own Landscape (Whetstone Press, 1989), and more than 40 articles in publications such as Horticulture and Fine Gardening.*

---

## *Favorite Books*

### THE ARMCHAIR TRAVELER

**Sissinghurst: Portrait of a Garden**
*by Jane Brown* (Weidenfeld & Nicolson, 1994). The story of how two passionate gardeners transformed the ruins of a sixteenth-century castle into a private home and garden that is now the most popular public garden in England. Beautiful photographs complement the moving account of Vita Sackville-West and her husband Harold Nicolson's thirty years of gardening at Sissinghurst. 136 pages, paperback, $19.95.

**Monet's Garden: Through the Seasons at Giverny**
*by Vivian Russell* (Stewart Taboori & Chang, 1995). A photographic tour of the most visited garden in France. Luscious, full-color images, descriptive text, planting details, and a history of the restoration work. 168 pages, hardcover, $32.50.

**Traditional English Gardens**
*by Arabella Lennox-Boyd* (Weidenfeld & Nicolson, 1996). 160 pages, paperback, $17.95.

**Gardens of Colonial Williamsburg**
*by M. Kent Brinkley, Gordon W. Chappell, David Doody, Kent Brinkley* (Colonial Williamsburg Foundation, 1996). 176 pages, hardcover, $29.95.

# Other Good Books

## GUIDES TO GARDENS IN THE UNITED STATES

**The Garden Tourist: A Guide to Garden Tours, Garden Days, Shows and Special Events** *by Lois G. Rosenfeld* (Garden Tourist Press, 1997). An indispensible guide to over 1,500 happenings throughout the U.S. and Canada of interest to gardeners. Updated annually, the book is organized by state (and province), and then chronologically by event. It includes a description of the event, location, dates, times, and phone numbers. 222 pages, paperback, $15.95.

## REGIONAL GUIDES

**American Gardens: A Traveler's Guide** *ed. Claire E. Sawyers* (Brooklyn Botanic Garden, 1989). Order from: Brooklyn Botanic Garden, 1000 Washington Avenue, Brooklyn, NY 11225 ($5.95 plus $3.75 postage & handling).

**Beautiful Gardens: Guide to Over 80 Botanical Gardens, Arboretums and More in Southern California and the Southwest** *by Eric A. Johnson and Scott Millard* (Ironwood Press, 1991). Paperback, $12.95. Order from: Ironwood Press, 2968 West Ina Road, #285, Tucson, AZ 85741.

**The Complete Guide to North American Gardens: The Northeast,** and **The Complete Guide to North American Gardens: The West Coast** *by William C. Mulligan* (Little, Brown, 1991). paperback, $15.95 each.

**Glorious Gardens to Visit: 58 Gardens Within 3 Hours of New York City** (Clarkson N. Potter, 1989) and **Glorious Gardens to Visit in Northern California: 65 Gardens Within 3 Hours of San Francisco** *by Priscilla Dunhill and Sue Freedman* (Clarkson N. Potter, 1993). 228 pages, paperback, $12.95 each.

**California Public Gardens: A Visitor's Guide** *by Eric Sigg* (John Muir Publications, 1991). 304 pages, paperback, $16.95.

**Guide to Mid-Atlantic Gardens** *by Jack Dempsey* (Carolina Connections, 1995). 216 pages, paperback, $15.95 (plus $3.95 postage). To order call: 800-553-5424.

**Green Byways: Garden Discoveries in the Great Lakes States** *by Sharon Lappin Lumsden* (Lime Tree Publications, 1993). 320 pages, paperback, $19.95. Order from: Lime Tree Publications, 507 S. Garfield Ave., Champaign, IL 61821, or call 217-355-5424.

**Gardens of the Hudson River Valley** *by Ogden Tanner and Ted Spiegel* (Abrams, 1996). paperback, $19.95.

**The Northwest Gardener's Resource Directory** *by Stephanie Feeney* (Cedarcroft Press, 1997). Order from: Cedarcroft Press, 59 Strawberry Pt., Bellingham, WA 98226 ($22.95 plus $2.50 postage & handling).

**French Gardens: A Guide** *by Barbara Abbs* (Sagapress, 1995). 180 pages, paperback, $15.00.

**Gardens of the National Trust** *by Stephen Lacey* (Abrams, 1996). Too heavy to tote around, but terrific for planning your itinerary. Color photographs and descriptions of 130 of the Trust's gardens. Hours and directions. 320 pages, hardcover, $45.00.

## GUIDES TO GARDENS ABROAD

**The 1997 Gardener's Guide to Britain** *by Patrick Taylor* (Timber Press, 1997). Organized by region (with a good map), this guide describes almost 500 places of interest to gardeners. All are open to the public. Includes nurseries and notable garden shops as well. Engaging, personal commentary with good color photographs (though not of every site). 320 pages, paperback, $19.95.

**1997 Good Gardens Guide** *by Peter King* (Trafalgar Square, 1997). No color photos, but this book provides basic descriptions and important details on 1,000 gardens in the British Isles as well as several in France, Belgium, and the Netherlands, paperback, $22.95.

**Gardens in Normandy** *by Marie-François Valery* (Abbeville, 1995), 216 pages, hardcover, $50.00.

**The Garden Scheme** or **The Yellow Book.** This is the all-important home town guide that lists private gardens and the dates they are open each year. Available from the British Tourist Office or by calling: 011-44-81-697-1899.

**Australia's Open Garden Scheme.** A down-under version of the original Garden Scheme. Available by calling: 011-61-54-28-4557 or Fax: 011-61-54-28-4558.

## VIRTUAL GARDEN TOURS

**The Great Gardens of England** (Hidcote Manor, Sissinghurst, Mortisfield Abbey); **English Cottage and Country Gardens** (eight English gardens at their peak); **Britain: The Garden Kingdom** (eight superior British gardens). Each video is approximately 1 hour long. Available for $19.95 ea. from Capability's Books, 2379 Highway 46, Deer Park, WI 54007-7506. 1-800-247-8154.

**Gardens of the World** (Rose Gardens; Tulips and Spring; Formal Gardens; Flower Gardens; Country Gardens; Public Gardens/Trees; Tropical Gardens; Japanese Gardens). A series of eight videos hosted by Audrey Hepburn. Available for $19.95 ea. from Capability's Books.

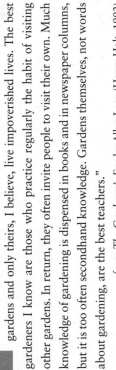

> "Those gardeners who are content to take pleasure from their own gardens and only theirs, I believe, live impoverished lives. The best gardeners I know are those who practice regularly the habit of visiting other gardens. In return, they often invite people to visit their own. Much knowledge of gardening is dispensed in books and in newspaper columns, but it is too often secondhand knowledge. Gardens themselves, not words about gardening, are the best teachers."
>
> —from *The Gardener's Eye* by Allen Lacy (Henry Holt, 1992)

much hidden beauty and gardening talent exists right in your own area. Consider joining a local garden club, participating in a house and garden tour, or just being bold enough to stop and introduce yourself to someone whose garden you have admired. Besides discovering new gardens, you will undoubtedly meet some new neighbors who share your gardening enthusiasm.

Within your state, there are probably several universities or colleges that maintain a public arboretum and greenhouse, and certainly some historical sites and other public attractions that incorporate gardens. Traveling out of state? You can easily build a whole vacation around visits to spectacular gardens (assuming your companions are willing!). If you can do a little advance planning, even a business trip can sometimes accommodate an arboretum visit or gardening-related event. Check out *The Garden Tourist* by Lois G. Rosenfeld, and some of the

## *Resources*

### TOUR GUIDES

The following list is not an endorsement of any of the tour operators. It is provided as a jumping-off point for interested travelers. We recommend that you send for information, ask around, or use the Internet for references.

**The American Horticultural Society**
800-777-7931

**Coopersmith's England**
415-669-1914

**Expo Garden Tours**
*Tours throughout the U.S. and abroad.*
203-938-0410 or
800-448-2685

**Ellen Henke**
*Tours throughout the U.S. and abroad.*
800-488-3377 or
fax: 919-933-1600

**High Land Flings**
*Tours of the Hudson River Valley.*
800-453-6665

**Horticulture** Magazine
212-514-8921 or
800-221-1944

**Ingatours**
*Tours abroad.*
800-786-5311

**Learned Journeys**
*Tours for various botanic gardens and societies.*
805-682-6191

**Limewalk Tours**
*Tours abroad.*
802-864-5720 or
800-426-5720

**Lord Addison Travel, Ltd.**
*Tours to Britain.*
603-924-8407 or
800-326-0170

**Lucas & Randall**
*European tours.*
916-922-7927 or
800-505-2505

**Spectrum Tours**
*Tours for non-profit groups.*
805-969-9665

**T.O.C. Travel**
*First-class tours abroad.*
916-922-7927 or
800-505-2505

**Leonard Haertter Travel Co.**
7922 Bonhomme Avenue
St. Louis, MO 63105
314-721-6200 or
800-942-6666

**Reeve Garden Holidays, Inc.**
*Tours worldwide.*
603-643-5002

> It is agreeable to waddle about in one's own paradise, knowing that thousands of others have better gardens with better thises and thats, and better grown too, and no weeds at all. To know this and grin as complacently as a terrier who just got into the deviled eggs, and to reflect that there is no garden in England or France I envy, and not one I'd swap for mine: this is the aim of gardening — not to make us complacent idiots, exactly, but to make us content and calm for a time, with sufficient energy (even after wars with bindweed) to feel an awestruck thanks to God that such happiness can exist. For a few days, of course."
>
> —from *One Man's Garden* by Henry Mitchell (Houghton Mifflin, 1992)

web sites listed below, for a month-by-month listing of gardening events by state or province, with prices, addresses, and phone numbers.

## Farther Away

If you're lucky enough to be planning a garden tour abroad, you might want to consider participating in a charter tour (some tour operators are listed on page 283). A chartered trip makes logistics easy, and most guides are quite knowledgeable. Chartered tours are also a wonderful way to meet fellow gardening enthusiasts. If you go on your own, there are some excellent books that provide descriptions, hours, and directions (see our recommendations, page 282). When traveling abroad, it's critical to plan ahead, for many of the public gardens, especially in England, get very busy. You may want to include one of the big horticultural events like the Chelsea Flower Show in England, the Journees des Plantes in Paris, or the spring bulb show at the Keukenhof Gardens in Holland.

The World-Wide Web is a great resource for travelers. There are web sites that list public gardens and events from New York to New Zealand. Many of the most noteworthy gardens maintain their own web sites, which often feature photographs and detailed information about plant collections, display gardens, and best times for visiting. Chat forums (on the Inter-

## Web sites

**Botanique**
http://www.botanique.com
*State by state list of botanical and public gardens in the U.S. and Canada. Calendar of events. Links.*

**The Gardening Launch Pad**
http://www.tpoint.net/neighbor/
*The Gardening Launch Pad has links to an extensive list of arboretums and botanical gardens in the U.S. and around the world.*

**The Garden Gate**
http://www.prairienet.org/ag/garden/downpath.htm
*A list of web sites for botanical gardens, greenhouses, and private gardens around the world.*

**GardenNet's Guide to Gardens of the USA**
http://trine.com/GardenNet/GardensOnline/gardenlh.htm
*A listing of over 200 gardening events throughout the year. Listings are by month with descriptions of the events, locations, phone numbers, fees, etc.*

**GardenWeb**
http://www.gardenweb.com/
*Web tours of several gardens around the world.*

**Gardens in Canada**
http://www.icangarden.com/gardens.htm
*A listing, by province, of public gardens in Canada.*

**American Association of Botanical Gardens and Arboreta**
http://cissus.mobot.org/AABGA/aabga1.html
*The web site for the American Association of Botanical Gardens and Arboreta.*

**Internet Directory of Botany, Arboreta, and Botanical Gardens**
http://www.helsinki.fi/kmus/botgard.html
*Links to botanical gardens and arboretum sites around the world. Alphabetically listed by country.*

> After spending some time this winter reading about and looking at pictures of the world's great gardens (this, along with paging through catalogs, being the gardener's proper winter work), I was surprised at just how much they had to teach me — about what I'd already done (often thoughtlessly), and what I still need to do (for I am still in the middle of making this garden, as probably I will always be). Not in the specifics — the linked, yew-walled rooms at Sissinghurst, the stonework in the Boboli, the prospects at Stourhead — but in the aims and senses of these places, in the spirit that informs them, we can find things that, writ small, belong in our garden. . . . Approached in the right spirit (and not slavishly), our conversations with the classic garden writers and designers have something to teach us about discerning the genius of our own little places, and about how we might begin to devise some styles of gardening that will suit them, ourselves, and this country."
>
> —from *Second Nature* by Michael Pollan (Atlantic Monthly Press, 1991)

net) are another opportunity to confer with gardeners from around the world who can share experiences about gardens, events, tour operators, restaurants, and so on.

What will you need to bring along? The essentials include water-resistant shoes, a sun hat, a notebook for sketching or jotting down specific plant varieties, and maybe a camera. But what may be even more important is the companionship of a fellow gardening enthusiast. It's much more fun to tour a garden when there is someone along who can respond to your oohs and ahhhs!

# thinking regionally

W here do you live? Northern New England? Arizona? West of the Cascade Mountains? Central Wisconsin? New Orleans? Maybe you've heard the saying "All politics is local." Well, it's even truer of gardening. Wherever you live in the United States or Canada, there are regional peculiarities of climate, weather, and soil that determine how you garden and what you can grow. Furthermore, every individual garden site has unique features that can help or hinder your success. The key is to understand the broad characteristics of your region, and to become intimately familiar with your own site. Our objective is to introduce you to the incredible variety of growing conditions on this continent, and to steer you toward resources that will help you become as successful and satisfied a gardener as possible — wherever you live.

## Keys to Successful Gardening in Your Region

All successful gardening begins with close attention to the basics: good site selection and design; building healthy soil; using proper tools; choosing appropriate plants; efficient watering; keeping ahead of weeds and insect and animal pests; etc. But because growing conditions vary so widely, these basics must be adapted to the particulars of your own garden site. Here are some of the factors to consider.

**HARDINESS ZONES: PROCEED WITH CAUTION!** You have probably seen a U.S. Department of Agriculture (USDA) Hardiness Zone map (see page 242). Most gardening reference books have one. The boundaries of these zones are based on long-term observations of the average lowest winter temperature range. Those lows in turn determine which plants are reliably winter-hardy in that growing zone, and which are likely to be killed over the course of an average winter.

Zone maps should be used as an approximation, not as gospel truth, since hardiness is influenced by many different factors. To start with, weather is anything but predictable. Topographical features such as mountains and lakes, or the location of your site relative to a ridge or basin, affect localized climates, sometimes significantly. Low temperatures will cause more damage if they persist over three days rather than for one night. Several hard freezes in a year will cause more damage to plants than one or two. Good snow cover will protect plants from cold, but thin snow cover in another year makes them that much more susceptible to freezing. A good summer growing season can enable your plants to withstand cold temperatures, but a lousy season can make them more vulnerable. So use hardiness zones as a general gauge of what you can grow in your region, but rely on the advice of local growers, regional gardening books, and your own observations for more detailed information.

**WARM, SHORT, WET, DRY.** Temperature, moisture, and sunlight conditions combine in any number of ways throughout North America. The planting and harvesting schedule in Maine is obviously very different from what it is in Houston. Indeed, the whole rhythm of gardening is different. But there may also be significant differences between coastal and inland areas of Maine or Texas. Even within the same hardiness zone, some areas are consistently wetter or drier, warmer or cooler.

Each region of the continent has a unique set of general climatic characteristics. For example, the coastal Northwest typically has moderate winter temperatures, a rainy spring, and long summer dry spells. The lower Midwest and upper South have similar temperature conditions, but completely different moisture patterns. The plains and prairies of the upper Midwest are often subject to extremes of temperature and rainfall. In northern New England frosts often come late in the spring and early in the fall, and some years there is not much hot weather during the summer. Over time you become familiar with the patterns in your own region. But if you are just beginning to garden, if you have recently relocated, or if you need some reassurance or inspiration borne of frustration, consult some of the regional gardening books we have recommended here.

**MICROCLIMATES.** Amount of sun, harshness of wind, minimum temperatures, timing of first and last frosts, not to mention soil conditions, can all vary within a town or neighborhood. Indeed, your own yard or garden may contain a few different highly specific microclimates. Northern and southern exposure; hedges; tree lines, or other windbreaks; slopes and depressions; ponds and brooks; structures that absorb and radiate heat, or ones that create shade — all of these natural or artificial features can create microclimates where growing conditions may be different enough to support different communities of plants. By locating these microclimates and taking advantage of their diversity, you can position plants that prefer certain conditions in the place that suits them best. It is worthwhile to study these features and conditions, so you can enhance and diversify your gardening experience, pleasure, and expertise.

Once you understand how microclimates work, you may even decide to create your own. A rockery in a sheltered, sunny spot near the house might allow a Zone 4 gardener to grow a few plants that normally are hardy only to Zone 5 or 6. Adding a small pond might buffer a harsh spring climate and make an ideal place for planting early-flowering fruit tress, such as pears, peaches, or cherries.

**KEEP A JOURNAL.** Without a doubt, the best way to learn about your site and become a more successful gardener is to keep a journal. This point cannot be stressed too strongly: good records are the basis for gardening wisdom. Information from this year's garden will be incredibly valuable next year. And when you have accumulated 5 or 10 years' worth of information, you will have a priceless reference. Write down as much as you possibly can: daily high and low temperatures, frost dates, rainfall, arrival of the birds and frogs, the first spring flowers, budding of the trees, full moons, droughts and storms. Make a garden plan every year and keep track of

# Favorite Regional Books

When reading these reviews of our recommended regional gardening books, please keep in mind that the collections of essays tend to be sketchier than the thematic books on specific cultural information and detailed how-to suggestions.

## NORTH

### Cold-Climate Gardening: How to Extend Your Growing Season by at Least 30 Days *by Lewis Hill* (Garden Way Publishing, 1990 [rev. ed.]). A classic by a professional Vermont nurseryman with a good sense of humor. Everything you need to know about growing vegetables, fruits, berries, trees, and flowers in the North. Very accessible. Discussions consistently related to the regional climate, especially northern New England. Chapter on extending the season is excellent. 320 pages, paperback, $14.95.

**The New Northern Gardener** *by Jennifer Bennett* (Firefly Books, 1996 [rev. ed.]). A beautiful comprehensive book with fantastic photographs and lots of charts, tables, and tips. Deals with a greater variety of specific topics than Hill, *Cold Climate Gardening*, such as herbs and pests; however, this book is not as easy to use. 256 pages, paperback, $24.95.

**Flowers for Northern Gardens** *by Leon C. Snyder* (University of Minnesota Press, 1983). An excellent botanical handbook covering 800 species and 1,100 named cultivars. Organized alphabetically by genera, with an index of common names. More than 250 photographs; fine descriptions and cultural information. Best for intermediate to advanced gardeners. (Also appropriate for the Upper Midwest.) 396 pages, paperback, $19.95.

## MIDWEST AND PLAINS

### Gardening: Plains and Upper Midwest *by Roger Vick* (Fulcrum, 1991). Straightforward and comprehensive on the basics. Not organic; he has no problem with chemicals, although he favors integrated pest management. Good on ornamentals and trees, shrubs, and ground covers; pretty good on vegetables. Has a helpful month-by-month planner, lengthy discussions of greenhouses, pests, and diseases, and a useful glossary. (Also suitable for the North.) 384 pages, paperback, $16.95.

**Gardening in the Upper Midwest**, 2nd edition, *by Leon C. Snyder* (University of Minnesota Press, 1985). An authoritative book by the head of the University of Minnesota department of Horticultural Science and Landscape Architecture and director of its arboretum. Includes the basics of soil

science and botany. More than half the book is on trees, shrubs, lawns, and ornamentals; especially good on fruits. *Not* organic. (Also suitable for the North.) 310 pages, paperback, $17.95.

**Perennials for the Lower Midwest** *by Ezra Haggard* (Indiana University Press, 1996). An excellent encyclopedia; not comprehensive but extensive (excludes roses and delphiniums.) Entries chosen based on appeal, suitability to the climate, long-standing foliage, extended bloom period, adaptability to soils, and easy care. Nice photos; excellent descriptive notes, design ideas, and cultural suggestions. 224 pages, paperback, $19.95.

---

your seeding, transplant, and harvest dates; your crop rotations, pest problems, treatments and soil amendments; your successes and failures. "Inch by inch, row by row, gonna make this garden grow"; year by year, your garden knowledge and wisdom will grow, and you and your plants will be happier for the effort.

**USE LOCAL RESOURCES.** One of the best ways to familiarize yourself with the gardening specifics of where you live is to ask other local gardeners a lot of questions. After the weather, one thing everybody loves to talk about is their garden. Don't be bashful about approaching your neighbors, the farmer down the road, and old-timers in town with even simple questions. (The answers might turn out to be not so simple.)

There are also institutional resources at your

fingertips. Nurseries and greenhouses, Agricultural Extension Service offices, garden clubs, horticultural societies, arboretums, museums, college departments — these organizations are filled with people who have accumulated years of local gardening lore and knowledge. They are your fellow-travelers in the gardening journey, and spreading that knowledge and their own love of gardening is a big part of their mission.

Such people can give you great tips about things like timing, appropriate plant varieties that grow well in the area, and local weather patterns. They may know of mail-order companies that sell seed or plants grown under similar climatic conditions to your own. Gardening is always a win-win proposition, and gardeners are more than willing to share what they know.

# *Favorite Regional Books* continued

Gardening in the Lower Midwest: A Practical Guide for the New Zones 5 and 6 *by Diane Heilenman* (Indiana University Press, 1994).

Thoughtful, engaging garden philosophy and practice for "the Zombie Zones," this large area of weather transition where wild temperature swings are the norm. Very personal writing with a strong ecological ethic, on topics such as "the night garden," water gardens, and "the gone-wild garden," with good specifics and suggestions. Includes a planning calendar, and a helpful chapter on "Problems." 224 pages, paperback, $14.95.

Midwest Gardens *by Pamela Wolfe* (Chicago Review Press, 1991).

Profiles of 22 gardens in Iowa, Illinois, Indiana, Minnesota, Wisconsin, and Michigan, some of them thematic (such as hostas, or a prairie garden). Gorgeous, creative photographs. Good information on climate characteristics, plant selection, and cultural specifics, and good resource lists. 224 pages, hardcover, $39.95.

The Prairie Garden Planner: A Personal Journal *by Jan Mather* (Red Deer College Press, 1996).

For the Canadian prairies and the U.S. Upper Midwest. A weekly planner and journal with space for three years of notes and records. Full of helpful tips, with lots of nice color photographs. A good how-to guide, but not comprehensive or systematic, so it could be a bit difficult for absolute beginners to use without other references. 256 pages, paperback, $22.95.

## SOUTHERN CALIFORNIA AND THE SOUTHWEST

The Low-Water Flower Gardener *by Eric A. Johnson and Scott Millard* (Ironwood Press, 1993).

Excellent descriptions of 15 regional microclimate zones. Has a plant gallery nicely formatted with easy-to-read "fast facts" next to lengthier discussions that include recommended species, cultivation information, and very nice photos. Covers perennials, shrubs, ground covers, and grasses. 144 pages, paperback, $14.95.

Low Water-Use Plants for California and the Southwest *by Carol Shuler* (Fisher Books, 1993).

For landscaping, not vegetables. Has a good explanation of the dynamics of arid and semi-arid climates. Alphabetical list of 200 low-water-use plants, with basic descriptive and cultural information and beautiful photographs. Excellent, easy-to-use tables organized by type of plant (tree, shrub, vine, etc.). 144 pages, paperback, $17.95.

The Xeriscape Flower Gardener: A Water-Wise Guide for the Rocky Mountain Region *by Jim Knopf* (Johnson Books, 1991).

Oriented toward landscape design, with useful worksheets and site examples. Very good charts and resource lists, good but limited plant profiles. 190 pages, paperback, $16.95.

The Subtropical Garden *by Jacqueline Walker* (Timber Press, 1992).

For regions with warm summers and mild, frost-free winters, in either humid or dry conditions. Inspirational and imaginative, not a reference book. Emphasizing form and foliage, this book gives basic descriptive and cultural information on palms, bamboo, tree ferns, flowering trees, bromeliads, orchids, and bog plants, among others. Spectacular photos; good index, bibliography, and list of suppliers. 176 pages, paperback, $24.95.

Southwestern Landscaping with Native Plants *by Judith Phillips* (Museum of New Mexico Press, 1987).

A sampling (not comprehensive) with site design examples. Geared to low-maintenance landscaping. Excellent plant profiles, good botanical information. Nice illustrations. 160 pages, paperback, $24.95.

Tropicals *by Gordon Courtright* (Timber Press, 1988).

A "visual plant dictionary" of over 500 trees, shrubs, and vines appropriate for Hawaii, Southern California, Florida, and greenhouse growing. Nearly 400 photos, many in landscape settings. Entries are brief, pithy, and interesting, though lacking in cultural details. Good, easy-to-use botanical index. 156 pages, paperback, $24.95.

## PACIFIC NORTHWEST

Growing Vegetables West of the Cascades *by Steve Solomon* (Sasquatch, 1988).

A classic from a genuine garden philosopher, chronicling his journey from "a true-believing, capital-O Organic garden writer," to founding the Territorial Seed Company, to combining organic with "the best of an 'establishment' scientific outlook."

Everything you need to know, tailored to this region: botany, organic soil science, year-round vegetables, irrigation, appropriate varieties, plus a growing guide. Refer to Water-Wise Vegetables for the Maritime Northwest (next entry) to follow the evolution of Solomon's thinking. 352 pages, paperback, $14.95.

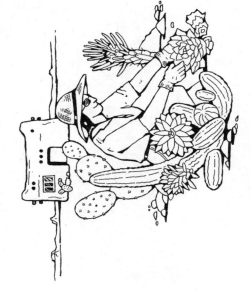

# Favorite Regional Books *continued*

## PACIFIC NORTHWEST

*continued*

The following five books published by Sasquatch Books in 1993 as the Cascadia Gardening Series are all concise and excellent. **Waterwise Vegetables for the Maritime Northwest Gardener** by *Steve Solomon* is a clear and passionate guide to dry-climate gardening. Note that Solomon's method — low plant density — contradicts the conventional wisdom of raised beds with dense inter-planting. 96 pages, paperback, $8.95.

**North Coast Roses for the Maritime Northwest Gardener** by *Rhonda Massingham Hart* is excellent on both the basics of rose growing and specific regional information. 96 pages, paperback, $8.95. **Winter Ornamentals for the Maritime Northwest Gardener** by *Daniel Hinkley* presents a nice visual and aesthetic perspective on taking advantage of the mild winter climate of the Pacific Northwest. 112 pages, paperback, $9.95.

**Seasonal Bulbs for the Maritime Northwest Gardener** by *Ann Lovejoy* (96 pages, paperback, $10.95) is reviewed in the "Bulbs" chapter; and **Growing Herbs for the Maritime Northwest Gardener** by *Mary Preus* (104 pages, paperback, $9.95) is reviewed in the "Herbs" chapter.

**Sunset Western Garden Book,** 6th edition (Sunset Publishing, 1995). A superb, comprehensive reference manual. Excellent on distinctive regional climate zones. Plant selection guide includes topics such as "plants that attract hum-mingbirds and butterflies," "plants that resist deer," and "plants for under oaks."

Huge, informative, easy-to-use encyclopedia. (Also suitable for Southern California and the Southwest.) 624 pages, paperback, $29.95.

**Sunset Western Garden Annual,** 1996 edition (Sunset Publishing, 1996). The "Western Garden Companion." Organized by month, the chapters include short feature items and tips, a garden checklist, and longer feature articles drawn from *Sunset Magazine.* Includes the indispensable Sunset climate zone discussion. Articles are short, to the point, and readable (Also suitable for southern California and the Southwest.) 336 pages, paperback, $17.95.

**The Year in Bloom: Gardening for All Seasons in the Pacific Northwest** by *Ann Lovejoy* (Sasquatch Books, 1987). Fifty-two short essays that offer a month-by-month personalized view of gardening in this region. Focus is on ornamentals, and the coverage of subject matter is more deep than broad. Very lively writing, for example a hilarious essay on "Slug Boots" and a gem about "Fleas and Killer Oranges." 278 pages, paperback, $11.95. See also Lovejoy's sequel, **The Border in Bloom: A Northwest Garden Through the Seasons** (Sasquatch Books, 1990). More wonderful short essays, this time focusing on the design aspects of ornamental horticulture appropriate to the Pacific Northwest. Contains a set of nicely illustrated planting diagrams; has good appendices. 264 pages, paperback, $14.95.

**Northwest Garden Style: Ideas, Designs, and Methods for the Creative Gardener** by *Jan Kowalczewski Whitner* (Sasquatch Books, 1996). A tour through 23 gardens chosen to illustrate effective solutions to common landscaping and gardening problems or circumstances; emphasis is on design. Vivid photos, good plant lists, and checklists of helpful hints, but not much how-to or cultural information. 308 pages, paperback, $19.95.

**Island Gardening: A Month-by-Month Guide for West Coast Gardeners** by *Ramona Sommer* (Orca Book Publishers, 1994). For Vancouver Island and the west coast of British Columbia. Pretty comprehensive, includes lawns and indoor plants as well as trees, shrubs, and vegetable and flower gardening. Suggestions for varieties, with cultural information. Good weather statistics and horticultural tables. Great list of Canadian garden catalogs. 192 pages, paperback, $14.95.

**Winter Gardening in the Maritime Northwest: Cool Season Crops for the Year-Round Gardener** by *Binda Colebrook* (Sasquatch Books, 1989). Very good how-to manual. Simple and folksy. Specific recommendations on varieties appropriate to each season. Helpful planting guides and source/supplier appendices. 176 pages, paperback, $10.95.

## SOUTH

**Warm-Climate Gardening: Tips, Techniques, Plans, Projects for Humid or Dry Conditions** by *Barbara Pleasant* (Garden Way Publishing, 1993). An excellent primer offering a clear view into a master warm-climate gardener's world. Very informative, easy to read, and personal. Chapters on 60 vegetables, fruits, flowers, grasses, and ground covers, and organic pest control. Chock full of good hints. 208 pages, paperback, $12.95.

**Gardening Southern Style** by *Felder Rushing* (University Press of Mississippi, 1987). A good introduction to gardening in the South; better on ornamentals than vegetables. Especially good chapters on trees, lawns and ground covers, fruits, and annuals and perennials. Has a useful month-by-month almanac, and lots of good Question and Answer boxes. However, his approach is not particularly organic. 256 pages, paperback, $17.95.

**The New Orleans Garden: Gardening in the Gulf South** by *Charlotte Seidenberg* (University Press of Mississippi, 1993). All ornamental, relevant for the Gulf Coast and Zone 9. Excellent historical information, very good on variety and plant selection, good resource list; fair on the horticultural basics. 528 pages, paperback, $18.95.

# Web Sites

### Gardening.com
http://www.Gardening.com/Directory
*A directory of gardening-related web sites sorted by region.*

### GardenWeb
http://www.gardenweb.com/vl/ces.html
*An index to the Cooperative Extension Service by state, with links to their web sites.*

### USDA Zonefinder
http://www.compassnet.com/hueppi/tropics/usdazon.htm
*Nice rendering of the hardiness zone map; figure out what zone you're in.*

### The Northern Gardener Home Page
http://www.geocities.com/RainForest/1329/
*A wonderful site hosted by Minnesota gardener and garden writer Terry L. Yockey. Includes many articles, fact sheets, photographs, and lots of links to other sites, including those relevant for regions other than the North.*

### Northwest Gardener's Resource Directory
http://www.cedarcroft-press.com/home.htm
*An introduction to, and taste of, the new 7th edition of the highly acclaimed Directory. Excerpts, links, and a great list (continually updated) of events, plants sales, shows, etc. in the region.*

### ICan Garden
http://www.ICanGarden.com
*Canadian resource with information on seed, plant, and tool suppliers, botanical gardens, organizations, and web sites of interest to northern gardeners.*

### Gardening in the Cabbage Patch
http://www.polarnet.fnsb.ak.us/Users/PBabcock/patch/
*A collection of articles written for the local newspaper by a gardener in Fairbanks, Alaska, on growing plants in sub-arctic regions. Lots of excellent, detailed information.*

### Stokes Tropicals
http://www.stokestropicals.com
*More than an on-line catalog. Detailed cultural information, discussion forums, book reviews, lots of great links.*

### Mojave Lawn and Gardens
http://www.intermind.net/mgarden/
*Created by the University of Nevada Cooperative Extension Service and Master Gardeners of Southern Nevada. Lots of FAQs (arranged by season), a publication index, climate information, and links to other sites for Greater Southwest gardening. Applicable to any desert or arid region.*

# Resources

To find the best regional resources, such as arboretums, plant societies, nurseries, etc., consult our recommended books and web sites. Here are a few of particular interest.

### National Council of State Garden Clubs, Inc.
401 Magnolia Ave.
St. Louis, MO 63110

### National Xeriscape Council
P.O. Box 163172
Austin, TX 78716

### Northwest Gardener's Resource Directory, 7th ed.
(for Oregon, Washington, and British Columbia gardeners)
Cedarcroft Press
59 Strawberry Point
Bellingham, WA 98226
360-733-3461
http://www.cedarcroft-press.com/home.htm
*$25.45 postpaid (plus 7.8% sales tax in Washington)*

### Stokes Tropicals
P.O. Box 9868
New Iberia, LA 70562-9868
800-624-9706
E-mail: gstoke@1stnet.com
http://www.stokestropicals.com
*Great catalog offering exotic tropical plants, books, art, and gear. Bananas, bromeliads, gingers, heliconias, plumerias.*

# general
# resources

PASSPORT TO GARDENING

GENERAL RESOURCES

V irtually everyone who gardens needs to find specific information at some time or another: from the casual "weekend warrior" who has a lawn to tend and maybe a few flowers in containers or beds, to the horticultural expert or professional grower. Whether you simply want to identify a plant that you find growing in the woods, or learn how to tackle some big job, like installing a waterfall or setting up a hydroponic growing system, it's important to know where to start looking for the information you require.

## Garden Reference Books

Libraries, of course, are the logical first stop for all kinds of reference information. If you live near a state land-grant university, or if your local public library has a strong gardening section, you have a wonderful resource at your disposal. Many smaller public libraries, on the other hand, don't have the budget to buy the most current gardening titles. Not that newer is invariably better; many older books are timeless and useful, and we have tried to recommend some of these classics in the preceding chapters. Yet, when it comes to reference books, newer works usually offer the most complete and up-to-date information available, building on what has been published before. What's more, new varieties of plants are being introduced all the time; gardening knowledge and techniques evolve and improve; and even the botanical names and classifications of plants can change over time. You might find lots of terrific and useful growing information in a book from the 1950s, but in this day and age, when environmental concerns are a priority, you wouldn't, for instance, want to follow outdated pest-control advice and spray your garden with DDT. Times change, and gardening practices change with them, usually for the better.

Bookstores are another place to look for new and relevant information, but the sheer number of new gardening titles introduced each year means that finding the best books for your purpose can be a daunting, time-consuming task. And we should know. In the course of researching the *Passport to Gardening*, the two of us spent many hours in bookstores, in search of the best new titles to include in our chapters. Not that we were unfamiliar with what was already out there: both of us have built extensive garden libraries at home. Yet even professional garden writers find it hard to keep abreast of all the latest books. When one big publisher puts out a book on, say, water gardening, a half-dozen other publishers suddenly feel the need to issue one on the same subject — often containing much of the same information. By recommending our favorite books for each chapter of the *Passport to Gardening*, we have tried to eliminate some of the sensory overload you probably feel at the bookstore, and to steer you in the direction of those books that we feel offer the best, most thorough, or most original take on any given subject.

In much the same way, the books we've listed below are some of the best general reference works that we've encountered over the years. Most of them we either have at home or consult on a regular basis. For answering your gardening questions, these books are the next best thing to having a master gardener as your next-door neighbor.

## Periodicals

Of course, books are not the only source for the facts you need about gardening. Subscribing to various garden magazines is an excellent way to keep up on the latest trends and current wisdom, and to find reviews of the newest books, plant varieties, tools, and techniques. Again, we've listed below the periodicals that we find most valuable. They range from expensive, glossy magazines like *Garden Design* and *Fine Gardening* to no-nonsense, just-the-facts-ma'am newsletters like *The Avant Gardener* and *HortIdeas*.

No one has the time to read all these magazines every month. Our advice is to look over each

of the periodicals at the newsstand (or request a sample issue), then select the one or two you like best and subscribe to those. Another strategy is to subscribe to the harder-to-find periodicals yourself, and read the more popular magazines at your local library. For instance, you're a lot more likely to find *Organic Gardening* than *Hort Ideas* on the newsstand or in the library's periodicals room. Maybe you can even cut a deal with your local librarian: offer to donate your personal issues of a magazine to the library, and ask if, in exchange, you can get first crack at any gardening magazines that the library is discarding.

## On-line Gardening

In today's Information Age society, more and more people are making use of the Internet for research and entertainment. Gardening is well represented on-line, with lots of terrific web sites devoted to both general and esoteric garden topics. Throughout this book, we have listed our favorite sites on each chapter topic — ones we've found to be the most informative, useful, or well-conceived. The web sites listed below include some of the better, more comprehensive general gardening pages available on-line at the time of this writing.

These sites are intended only as a starting-point for your own on-line explorations, and represent more of a snapshot than any sort of definitive listing. Internet sites are constantly being created, dropped, improved, and updated. Just in the year or so that it has taken to compile this book, we've seen a big change in the number and quality of gardening web pages. Clearly, this is an exciting new medium, one that already contains lots of great information for gardeners, and that only promises to become even better and easier to use in the future.

Whether you're looking for a very specific or rather general topic — say, information on purple coneflowers or water gardening — the Internet can be a good alternative to (if not exactly a substitute for) looking up the subject in a garden encyclopedia or other reference book. Using a good search engine, type in your key words, like "purple coneflower," and see what pops up. Until you get the hang of searching the Net, you will come up with

# The Reference Shelf

thousands of possible links, including some that seem truly bizarre. For people who are book-oriented, this kind of research can prove a bit frustrating at first. But after a few hours of playing around, and learning how to focus your search, you'll find that the Internet can indeed provide a lot of useful data on almost any imaginable topic.

Another benefit of going on-line is that you can communicate with other gardeners; ask questions, post responses, even carry on a running correspondence. As with any advice, you learn to take the gardening tips you get on-line with a grain of salt, but it's still exciting to hear from other people about their own garden problems or solutions, then put them to the test in your own backyard. Earlier we mentioned that it would be ideal to have a master gardener as your next-door neighbor. Well, at its best, that's what the Internet is all about: a way of connecting to gardeners all over the world, a vast network of people who collectively possess the knowledge and experience that can help us improve our own gardens.

## DICTIONARIES AND ENCYCLOPEDIAS

**Hortus Third: A Concise Dictionary of Plants Cultivated in the United States and Canada,** compiled and edited by the staff of the L. H. Bailey Hortorium, Cornell University (Macmillan, 1976).

The granddaddy of all garden reference books, this third edition of L. H. Bailey's classic work is old and needs to be updated and reissued. Still, it remains *the* definitive guide to North American plants. Organized alphabetically by botanical names, *Hortus Third* contains nearly 30,000 entries, with descriptions for plant families, genera, and species; the book also mentions subspecies, varieties, and cultivars. In addition, there are 187 general articles, and many notes on culture, use, and propagation. Because of its high cover price, *Hortus Third* can be extremely hard to find in bookstores. Fortunately, most good libraries have it in their reference stacks. If yours doesn't, recommend that they purchase it. Though some botanical names have changed since 1976, the breadth and scope of *Hortus* make it the go-to guide when you really need to find the right name for virtually any plant. 1,312 pages, hardcover, $150.00.

**Index of Garden Plants: The New Royal Horticultural Society Dictionary** by Mark Griffiths (Timber Press, 1994).

More compact and condensed than *Hortus Third*, this index is even more comprehensive, listing names for over 60,000 plants. Strictly a shelf reference, it's ideal for looking plants up by their botanical name, but the tiny print, cramped design, and numerous abbreviations aren't nearly as reader-friendly as *Hortus*. 1,234 pages, hardcover, $59.95.

**Wyman's Gardening Encyclopedia, 2nd Edition** by Donald Wyman (Macmillan, 1986). A well-written, useful reference, with around 10,000 alphabetical entries. Fully updated and expanded from the original 1971 edition. Features lots of good general articles, from growing and propagation advice to less-expected entries like a how-to on "Christmas Decorations from Evergreens." 1,248 pages, hardcover, $65.00.

**The National Gardening Association Dictionary of Horticulture** (Penguin, 1994). Around 15,000 brief entries describing ornamental plants, fruits, herbs, vegetables, botanical terms, insects, and garden chemicals. Includes hundreds of drawings and diagrams. Well done and very

**The Wise Garden Encyclopedia** (HarperCollins, 1990). Although many people swear by *Wyman's Gardening Encyclopedia*, *Wise* is an excellent alternative, especially for the home gardener. The design, the illustrations, and the color photo gallery of plants broken down by category are all excellent, as are the plant tables for vines, herbs, rock-garden plants, etc. With only around 5,000 entries, *Wise* is somewhat more selective than other garden encyclopedias, and there will be many times when you will not find a less-common genus or species listed. Best used in conjunction with *Hortus Third*, especially because the botanical names in *Wise* are more up-to-date than either *Hortus Third* or *Wyman's*. Much more reader-friendly than *Wyman's* and fun to browse through. 1,082 pages, hardcover, $45.00.

**The Gardener's Dictionary of Horticultural Terms** by Harold Bagust (Cassell, 1994).
Nearly 3,000 entries, most extremely brief, giving only the bare-bones definitions of horticultural terms. Includes around 1,200 simple line drawings. 384 pages, paperback, $17.95.

**Horticulture Gardener's Desk Reference** by Anne Halpin (Macmillan, 1996). Aside from a section on gardening techniques and selected tips, this book is largely a reference and resource guide. If you

**Dictionary of Plant Names** by Allen J. Coombes (Timber Press, 1985).
A fun little book that demystifies all those tongue-twisting, esoteric Latin names of plants. Gives the pronunciation, derivation, and English meaning of botanical names, and supplies their common-name equivalents. For instance, did you know that *Myosotis* (forget-me-nots) comes from the Greek for "mouse ears"? 208 pages, hardcover, $10.95.

affordable for the home library. 848 pages, paperback, $16.95.

# The Reference Shelf continued

want to find the names of the All-America Selections through the years, which trees and shrubs have colorful foliage, or the recommended planting distance for a particular vegetable, this book is handy to have on your shelf. *560 pages, hardcover, $35.00.*

**Manual of Woody Landscape Plants: Their Identification, Ornamental Characteristics, Culture, Propagation and Uses, 4th Edition** *by Michael A. Dirr* (Stipes Publishing, 1990).

Judging from the dog-eared, well-thumbed copies of Dirr's book we see hanging around at nurseries and landscape businesses, this is the professional's choice when it comes to identifying and selecting woody plants. Clear, easy-to-read, no-nonsense entries on everything from balsam fir (*Abies balsamea*) to Chinese date (*Ziziphus jujuba*). Especially recommended for Dirr's notes on landscape use and the extensive descriptions of cultivars. No color photos, just line drawings of leaves for ID purposes. *1,016 pages, paperback, $39.95.*

**Manual of Herbaceous Ornamental Plants, 4th Edition** *by Steven M. Still* (Stipes Publishing, 1994).

Similar to Michael Dirr's book (see previous listing), but with better illustrations and a color photo section. Perhaps not as definitive as Dirr, simply because so many other books feature information on perennials. However, Still is one of the experts in the field, and president of the Perennial Plant Association. Well worth consulting for its recommended landscape uses for plants and its extensive

lists of cultivars. *828 pages, paperback, $38.80.*

## BOOKS FOR BEGINNERS

**The Garden Primer** *by Barbara Damrosch* (Workman, 1988).

Not a mere how-to reference, this is one of our favorite general gardening books. The author's personal style of writing is delightful, and the information is very solid, with complete instructions for growing and tending 300 types of plants, both ornamental and edible. Terrific illustrations and the judicious use of charts and diagrams round out this garden classic. Highly recommended. *684 pages, paperback, $16.95.*

**Rodale's All-New Encyclopedia of Organic Gardening**, *eds. Fern Marshall Bradley and Barbara W. Ellis* (Rodale, 1992).

Probably the best basic A–Z guide to plants and organic growing techniques. Over 400 entries ranging from specific plants (abelia, okra) to topics like double digging and layering. Plant entries include descriptions, growing information, landscape uses, and best cultivars. Lots of tips, sidebars, and resource information. *704 pages, paperback, $19.95.*

**The Big Book of Gardening Skills** *by the editors of Garden Way Publishing* (Garden Way Publishing, 1993).

An excellent guidebook for beginners, with especially good sections on vegetables, fruits, and garden pests and diseases. Not as much on flower growing. *352 pages, paperback, $18.95.*

**Your Organic Garden with Jeff Cox** *by the editors of Rodale Garden Books* (Rodale, 1994).

Like the previous book, this one has much more to say on edible plants than ornamentals, though it does have chapters on flower gardens, trees and shrubs, and lawns and ground covers. Lots of material on pests and diseases, including nonchemical control solutions. Easy to read, with lots of boxes thrown into the mix. *352 pages, paperback, $16.95.*

**The Organic Garden Book** *by Geoff Hamilton* (Dorling Kindersley, 1993).

Definitely the best-looking design of all the general organic gardening guides, with full-color photos (including step-by-step sequences), illustrations, and charts. As with the previous books, there's more emphasis on edible plants, but this book also contains sections on container gardens, aquatic plants, etc. Originally published in England, but doesn't suffer from "transplant shock" like other British books. *288 pages, paperback, $14.95.*

**A Starter Garden: The Guide for the Horticulturally Hapless** *by Cheryl Merser* (HarperCollins, 1994).

An outstanding book; one of the very best for beginners, with more flair than a simple, chirpy how-to guide. Deals with all aspects of planning, planting, and tending the garden and includes sections on: turning a yard into a garden; a field trip to the nursery; the middle of the border; shrubs and grasses; and decorating the garden. Highly recom-

mended. *272 pages, paperback, $13.00.*

**Gardening for Dummies**, *ed. Michael MacCaskey and the editors of the National Gardening Association* (IDG Books, 1996).

We have to admit to a prejudice against books that belong to ongoing series and refer to potential readers as "dummies" and "idiots." Having said that, this book is a useful one for absolute beginners, with concise but worthwhile information that focuses mainly on ornamental plants and basic techniques. *368 pages, paperback, $16.99.*

**The Complete Idiot's Guide to Gardening** *by Jane O'Connor and Emma Sweeney* (alpha books, 1996).

Depending on your sensibilities, you'll either be delighted or insulted by the simplicity and brevity of the information presented in this book. The format features one-paragraph quick definitions of the basics. How-to sections include instructions on improving soil and lawn repair and renewal, as well as sample garden plans. The best and most complete information are the lists of the easiest shrubs, herbs, vines, annuals, perennials, and bulbs. *400 pages, paperback, $16.95.*

## BOOKS FOR EXPERIENCED GARDENERS

**Botany for Gardeners: An Introduction and Guide** *by Brian Capon* (Timber Press, 1990).

Definitely not for dabblers, the plant science is presented

in a clear, understandable manner, but is not "dumbed down" or oversimplified. Information on cells and seeds, roots and shoots, plant adaptations, growth and development, and genetics. Good, clear line drawings and close-up color photos. An excellent basic course in botany for the serious gardener who has a strong interest or background in biological science. 220 pages, paperback, $17.95.

**The American Horticultural Society Encyclopedia of Gardening**, *ed. Christopher Brickell, et al.* (Dorling Kindersley, 1993). The first half of this illustrated guide teaches you how to create a garden, with chapters on design, plant selection, cultivation, and care. The second half discusses how to maintain your garden, and includes chapters on tools, soils, propagation, and plant problems. Attractive design features over 3,000 color photographs, many of them illustrating techniques. Highly recommended. 648 pages, hardcover, $59.95.

**Principles of Gardening: The Practice of the Gardener's Art** *by Hugh Johnson* (Simon & Schuster, 1996). First published in 1979, this revised and updated edition by a prominent British gardener focuses on the foundations and essential premises of gardening. It succeeds admirably, providing readers with a deeper understanding of underlying principles, and giving them the big picture. Intriguing sections include "What Makes a Plant Gardenworthy?" and "How Plants Are Improved." Highly recommended. 272 pages, hardcover, $40.00.

**Burpee Complete Gardener** *by Maureen Heffernan, et al.* (Macmillan, 1995). The heart of this book is the plant portraits, which give descriptive and growing information for more than 420 plants, both edible and ornamental. Also includes chapters on garden planning and design, pests and diseases, and tools and equipment. Nice sharp color photos used for IDs with the plant portraits. 432 pages, hardcover, $29.95.

**The American Practical Gardening Encyclopedia** *by Peter McHoy* (Lorenz Books, 1997). A visually attractive book with a very strong step-by-step format illustrated with color photos. The text is quite concise and a bit superficial at times, but there's good information on garden design and features, such as how to install garden lighting. The book is produced in Britain and organized seasonally; gardeners in the northern U.S. and Canada may snicker at sections that show how to "Winter-Dig the Vegetable Plot," but the basic techniques are sound and adaptable to any climate. 256 pages, hardcover, $30.00.

**The Book of Outdoor Gardening** *by the editors of Smith & Hawken* (Workman, 1996). A meaty general garden book that benefits from the contributions of several fine garden experts. There's more focus on garden trends, traditions, and designs than in other similar books. Nicely produced, with solid information and interesting sidebars. The "Guide to Garden Plants" feature gives specific growing information for a wide range of plants. Mainly concerned with ornamentals. 544 pages, hardcover, $29.95.

**The Gardener's Home Companion** *by Betty Mackey, et al.* (Macmillan, 1991). The plant profiles are the best part of this book, with the main focus on flowers. The profiles feature concise descriptive and cultural information for each plant, followed by more detailed growing information, tips, and recommended cultivars. Very few illustrations and a hohum design, but lots of useful facts. 670 pages, hardcover, $31.00.

**The Concise Gardening Encyclopedia: The Complete Guide to Planning, Creating, and Maintaining Your Garden** *by David Squire* (Running Press, 1997). Crammed full of concise information on both recommended plants and different garden styles and settings, such as rock gardens, water gardens, window boxes, etc. Good material on pruning, propagating, and greenhouse growing. The two-color format, the small drawings, and the busy design can make specific information somewhat hard to find. 352 pages, hardcover, $17.98.

**The Essential Gardener** *by Derek Fell* (Crescent Books, 1993). This is a comprehensive encyclopedia that includes the fundamentals on design, selection, and growing, illustrated with 900 color photographs. Includes annual and perennial flowers, bulbs, roses, trees, shrubs, herbs,

## VISUAL ENCYCLOPEDIAS

**American Horticultural Society Encyclopedia of Garden Plants**, *ed. Christopher Brickell* (American Horticultural Society, 1989). This superb encyclopedia is a standard work of reference for your gardening bookshelf. Written by a team of 40 experts, it describes over 8,000 plants, 4,000 of which are shown in full-color photographs. Features guides to garden planning and plant usage, an index of over 2,500 common plant names, and a glossary. 608 pages, hardcover, $49.95.

**Taylor's Master Guide to Gardening** *eds. Rita Buchanan and Roger Holmes* (Houghton Mifflin, 1994). This one-volume compendium draws together experts from around the country to discuss everything you need to know, from planning and design to plant descriptions to how-to growing fundamentals. The "gallery" contains 1,000 color photos of outstanding plants, and the encyclopedia has descriptions of 3,000 plants. Good cultural information and variety and cultivar recommendations. Easy to use. 612 pages, hardcover, $60.00.

# The Reference Shelf continued

and vegetables. Good topical plant selection guides, such as "annuals with yellow and orange flowers," "perennials for woodland gardens," and "herbs for dyes." Also an extensive chapter with sample garden designs. 704 pages, hardcover, $34.99.

**Sunset National Gardening Book** *by the editors of Sunset Books and Sunset Magazine* (Sunset Books, 1997). Contains over 6,000 plant listings and 2,500 color photographs, and features a guide to plant selection for 45 climate zones. 656 pages, paperback, $34.95.

**America's Garden Book** *by Louise and James Bush-Brown* (Macmillan, 1996). Originally published in 1939, the fourth edition of this mammoth general reference has been updated and expanded, with new chapters on city gardens, gardening by the sea, and more. The writing is uneven; some sections are well wrought, while others are dull, with little personality; chapters on fruits and vegetables are especially well done and useful. Extensive plant lists offer lots of good recommendations. Contains over 1,000 color photographs. A comprehensive but very basic reference, mainly for beginners and novice gardeners. 1,056 pages, hardcover, $65.00.

**Ward Lock Encyclopedia of Practical Gardening** *by Anita Pereire* (Ward Lock, 1995). Three-quarters of this book consist of plant dictionaries, including 2,000 flowers and 2,000 trees and shrubs; information is in-depth but concise, and the photographs are

excellent. The rest of the book presents basic gardening techniques, and a very comprehensive quick-reference plant guide. 704 pages, hardcover; out-of-print.

## SOURCEBOOKS

**Gardening by Mail, A Source Book, 4th Edition** *by Barbara J. Barton* (Houghton Mifflin, 1994). A comprehensive and easy-to-use directory to mail-order plant and garden product suppliers in North America. Includes a huge section on seed companies and nurseries that sell by mail, plus listings of plant societies, periodicals, horticultural libraries, and geographical and company name indexes. Most listings have descriptions, so this sourcebook is more than just an address list. The author is currently working on an updated fifth edition. Highly recommended. 400 pages, paperback, $19.95.

**The Gardener's Sourcebook: A Guide to Horticultural Sources** *by Sheila Buff* (Lyons & Burford, 1996). This reference contains only the addresses of garden suppliers and sources, making it somewhat less useful and certainly less interesting than the Barton and Skolnick books. 272 pages, paperback, $18.95.

**The 1997 Gardener's Source Guide (GSG)**, *compiled and published by R. J. Armstrong*. An annual directory of 990 mail-order sources for the home gardener. Lists addresses and phone numbers only. Arranged alphabetically by plant, category, and subject type (e.g., "Hydroponic Supplies," "Plumeria," "Pumps," "Rare Plants," "Water Gardens," etc.). 44 pages; available for $5.95 postpaid from Gardener's Source Guide, P.O. Box 206, Gowanda, NY 14070-0206.

**The Home Gardener's Source: The Ultimate Guide to Shopping for Your Garden by Mail, Fax, or Phone** *by Solomon M. Skolnick* (Random House, 1997). A new and well-done sourcebook, organized by plant or product type ("Roses," "Kidstuff," "Furniture and Ornaments," etc.). The best feature of this book is the author's very good descriptive notes on suppliers and their catalogs. Contains both geographical and alphabetical indexes. 464 pages, paperback, $19.00.

## HINTS, TIPS, AND TECHNIQUES

**The Experts Book of Garden Hints: Over 1,500 Organic Tips and Techniques from 250 of America's Best Gardeners**, *ed. Fern Marshall Bradley* (Rodale, 1993). Step-by-step directions, tips, and projects from professional horticulturists, garden designers, and organic growers. First section focuses on garden skills like pruning, planting, propagation, and seed saving. Plant chapters cover edible and ornamental plants, as well as lawns and ground covers. Good text information, and lots of interesting sidebars. 352 pages, hardcover, $27.95.

**Step-by-Step Gardening Techniques Illustrated** *by Elayne Sears, et al.* (Garden Way Publishing, 1996). Compiled from the popular "Step-by-Step" feature in *Horticulture* magazine, Elayne Sears' clear illustrations show how to do a multitude of garden tasks: everything from restoring a grapevine to raising ferns from spores. Projects are organized by season. This terrific book contains 86 projects, with instructions from seven garden writers. Highly recommended; there's something for every gardener here. 224 pages, hardcover, $22.95.

**Rodale's Illustrated Encyclopedia of Gardening and Landscaping Techniques**, *ed. Barbara W. Ellis* (Rodale, 1990). One of the best books of this kind, with tons of useful material on both ornamental and edible plants. Organic, chemical-free focus. From forcing hardy bulbs to making apple cider, this book covers a lot of ground in a thorough, accessible way. Good plant lists and charts. Highly recommended. 432 pages, hardcover, $23.95.

**The Gardener's Complete Q&A** *by the editors of Garden Way Publishing* (Garden Way Publishing, 1995). Organized into seven main parts: Lawns, Landscapes, Annuals, Perennials, Herbs, Fruits, and Vegetables. The question-and-answer device seems a bit phony at first and takes some getting used to, but the information is solid, and the illustrations and color photos add a lot to the book. 736 pages, hardcover, $39.95.

# The Reference Shelf continued

**The Harrowsmith Country Life Book of Garden Secrets** by Dorothy H. Patent and Diane Bilderback (Camden House, 1991).

Perfect for readers who want to understand the "why" as well as the "how to." The book focuses on various crops and explores them in some depth, explaining things like how food is stored in root vegetables, the effects of daylength and temperature on leaf crops, and much more. Explanations are clear and nontechnical. Recommended for all serious vegetable gardeners. 352 pages, paperback, $17.95.

**The Best of Organic Gardening,** ed. Mike McGrath (Rodale, 1996).

Once you get past the cutesy, annoying tone of the book's introduction, this book contains a lot of useful organic growing information gleaned from over 50 years of the magazine. Experts abound, with pollination tips from Lewis Hill, composting basics from Jeff Cox, short-season corn-growing tips from Sam Ogden, and other classics. An eclectic assortment, but with something to interest almost any gardener. 320 pages, paperback, $12.95.

**Just the Facts!: Dozens of Garden Charts, Thousands of Gardening Answers** by the editors of Garden Way Publishing (Garden Way Publishing, 1993).

This book takes a unique approach: all the information is presented in charts that cover almost everything, from "Plants that Have Interesting Seed Heads or Seedpods" to "Natural Controls for Vegetable Pests." A nice mix, and fun to browse through. For gardeners who want basic, easy-to-access information without a lot of chit-chat. 224 pages, paperback, $16.95.

**Dirt Cheap Gardening: Hundreds of Ways to Save Money in Your Garden** by Rhonda Massingham Hart (Garden Way Publishing, 1995).

Lots of tips and advice, including the wise admonition to invest in high-quality plants or tools when you do spend money. Homemade solutions and tips for maximizing garden productivity abound. 176 pages, paperback, $9.95.

## RIGHT PLANT, RIGHT PLACE

**Right Plant, Right Place: The Indispensable Guide to the Successful Garden** by Nicola Ferguson (Fireside, 1992).

This is the most comprehensive plant encyclopedia of the three books considered in this section. Covers 27 topics, including some not found in other reference books, such as plants tolerant of atmospheric pollution; plants with green flowers; plants with red, purple, or bronze leaves; and plants suitable for paving crevices. Organized by growing conditions, purpose, and appearance. Each topic has a very good introduction, and each of the 1,500 entries is accompanied by a color photograph and full descriptive and cultural information. Highly recommended. 292 pages, paperback, $17.00.

**Plants for Problem Places** by Graham Rice (Timber Press, 1995).

Identifies thirteen garden site problems, including "New Gardens," "Windy Gardens," "North and East Facing Walls and Fences," and "Water-logged Soils." Describes the characteristics of the problem, explains how to alleviate the problem, and suggests plants that will grow well in that environment. Very useful for gardeners dealing with problematic conditions. 184 pages, paperback, $19.95.

**Ideal Home: The Plant Guide: Successful Plants for Every Garden** by David Joyce (Conran Octopus, 1995).

Describes a wide range of site and design situations, and the flowers, trees, and shrubs that are suitable for them. Charts containing the essential plant information are integral to each section. Topic coverage is broad but slightly eclectic: has sections on ivies, clematis, and container gardens as well as problem soils, formal beds, borders, and roses, among others. Over 135 wonderful color photos. 160 pages, hardcover, $27.50. (Available from Trafalgar Square, North Pomfret, Vermont, 05053; 802-457-1911.)

# Magazines

**The American Gardener**
American Horticultural Society
7931 East Blvd. Dr.
Alexandria, VA 22308-1300
Monthly; $45.00 annual membership includes the magazine.

The country's premier horticultural publication. Geared to intermediate and advanced gardeners.

**The Avant Gardener**
P.O. Box 489
New York, NY 10028-0489
Monthly; $20.00.

A horticultural news service presenting a monthly compilation of the newest and most interesting information gathered from over 400 gardening-related publications. No advertising. Just the facts. Now in its third successful decade.

**Fine Gardening**
P.O. Box 5506
Newtown, CT 06470
Bimonthly; $28.00.

An excellent publication for the intermediate to advanced gardener. Garden style, how-tos, noteworthy gardens, and in-depth features on particular plant species.

**Garden Design**
P.O. Box 5429
Harlan, IA 51593-2929
e-mail:
gardendesign@here.com
Bimonthly; $27.00.
Profiles of beautiful gardens,

**The American Cottage Gardener**
131 E. Michigan Street
Marquette, MI 49855
e-mail: randbear@nets.com
Quarterly; $35.00.

More like a literary quarterly, with beautiful paper and fine illustrations. For the intermediate to advanced gardener who loves to read.

# Magazines continued

articles on style, and a monthly literary excerpt of interest to gardeners. Featured gardens are more elaborate than what the average backyard gardener would attempt, but the articles are well executed and inspiring.

### Garden Gate
2200 Grand Avenue
P.O. Box 842
Des Moines, IA 50304
e-mail: 75330.2301@compuserve.com
*Bimonthly; $19.95.*
*Interesting articles written by avid gardeners from around the country. Beginning and intermediate gardeners will find lots of inspiration on these pages. No advertising.*

### Gardens Illustrated
P.O. Box 754
Manhasset, NY 11030
e-mail:
gardens@johnbrown.com.uk
*Bimonthly; $45.00.*
*A sumptuous magazine from England. All the latest trends from abroad, and windows into some of the most beautiful gardens in the world.*

### Green Prints
P.O. Box 1355
Fairview, NC 28730
*Quarterly; $17.95.*
*A literary magazine for gardeners. Essays, poetry,*

and more, often sprinkled with plenty of humor.

### The Green Scene
Pennsylvania Horticultural Society
325 Walnut Street
Philadelphia, PA 19106
*Bimonthly; $12.95.*
*A publication from one of the country's oldest and largest state horticultural organizations. East-coast orientation.*

### Horticulture
98 N. Washington
Boston, MA 02114
e-mail: hortmag@aol.com
*10 issues; $26.00.*
*Geared to intermediate and advanced gardeners, this well-respected publication is a dependable reference with feature articles on design, specific plant varieties, emerging trends, and more.*

Fourteen to sixteen pages of new and interesting excerpts gleaned from both popular and technical horticultural literature from around the world. Of interest to intermediate and advanced gardeners.

### National Gardening Magazine
180 Flynn Avenue
Burlington, VT 05401
*Bimonthly; $18.95.*
*A general interest magazine geared to beginning and intermediate gardeners. An emphasis on vegetable gardening.*

### Organic Gardening
33 E. Minor Street
Emmaus, PA 18098
*9 issues; $25.00.*
*Organic vegetable gardening is the central theme of this publication, though it has increased its coverage of flower gardening. Oriented to the beginning and intermediate backyard gardener.*

### HortIdeas
Rt. 1, Box 302
Gravel Switch, KY 40328
e-mail:
hortideas@mcimail.com
*Monthly; $20.00 (via e-mail is $15.00).*

### Plant & Garden News
Brooklyn Botanic Garden
1000 Washington Avenue
Brooklyn, NY 11225
*Newsletter plus quarterly publications, $35.00.*

### Sunset
P.O. Box 56653
Boulder, CO 80323-6653
http://www.pathfinder.com/vg/Magazine
Rack/Sunset
*Monthly; $26.00.*
*A venerable gardening and lifestyle magazine with special editions tailored to different regions of the West.*

For an extensive online directory of magazines of interest to gardeners, visit one of the following three web sites:

### GardenNet
http://trine.com/GardenNet/Magazine/
magguide.htm

### PrairieNet
http://www.prairienet.org/ag/garden/
magazine.txt

### Gardening by Mail
(at Virtual Garden)
http://pathfinder.com/vg

---

# Resources

## VIDEO RESOURCES

### National Video Source at Garden Net
http://trine.com/GardenNet/NVS/
*An on-line catalog of gardening videos.*

### A. C. Burke & Co.
2554 Lincoln Blvd.,
Suite 1058
Marina Del Ray, CA 90291
310-574-2770
http://www.acburke.com
*Free catalog of gardening videos, software, and books.*

## EDUCATIONAL RESOURCES

### National Gardening Association
180 Flynn Avenue
Burlington, VT 05401
802-863-1308
http://www.garden.org

### The Garden Conservancy
P.O. Box 219
Cold Spring, NY 10516

### American Horticultural Society
7931 E. Boulevard Drive
Alexandria, VA 22308

## BOOK CATALOGS

### Capability's Books
2379 Highway 46
Deer Park, WI 54007-7506
800-247-8154

### American Nurseryman Horticultural Books, Videos, and Software Catalog
77 W. Washington Street,
Suite 2100
Chicago, IL 60602-2904

### Wood Violet Books
3814 Sunhill Drive
Madison, WI 53704
608-837-7207

### The Garden
Royal Horticultural Society
Membership Department
80 Vincent Square
London, England SW1P2PE
011-44-171-821-3000
*The monthly journal of the world's premier horticultural organization. First-year membership is £32. To join, call or write with a credit card number. Second-year memberships are £25.*

# Resources continued

## CD ROMS

We have not reviewed the following CDs. Contact the numbers listed for more information.

**Better Homes and Gardens Complete Guide to Gardening**
800-850-7272
Windows or Mac; $20.00.
Covers gardening fundamentals, garden types, gardening index, and a gardener's almanac with tips and a place for entering notes.

**Garden Encyclopedia**
800-242-4546
http://www.sierra.com/titles/btw
Windows; $30.00.
Information on more than 1,500 annuals, perennials, vegetables, trees, shrubs, and ground covers. Each entry has a plant profile and a photo.

**Microsoft Complete Gardening**
800-426-9400
Windows; $35.00.

**Garden Problem Solver**
800-829-0113
Windows or Mac; $40.00.
An encyclopedia with color photos of bugs, plant diseases, and weeds, and recommended solutions for each.

Features regional sections with plant recommendations, a search for articles on different topics, a plant encyclopedia, and video clips on maintenance techniques.

# Web Sites for Gardeners

The web sites listed below were current at the time of printing. If you have trouble getting to a particular site, it may be because the address (URL) has changed. Please e-mail corrections to info@gardeners.com.

**The Gardening Launch Pad**
http://tpoint.net/neighbor/
An incredible 1,500 links in 58 categories. Virtual garden tours, and much more.

**Come Into My Garden**
http://www.hal-pc.org/~trobb/horticul.html
An amazingly complete set of gardening links maintained lots more.

**GardenEscape**
http://www.garden.com
Features software to design your garden, on-line shopping, a monthly magazine, chat room, search engine, and lots more.

**Plant World**
http://www.plantworld.com
A must-see site that is organized like a real town, with a library, a store, a travel agency, and more. Fun to use and well designed, with lots of great material and ideas.

## MAILING LISTS, NEWSGROUPS, AND CHAT FORUMS

**LISTSERVS or Mailing Lists**
These are programs designed to handle large mailing lists of subscribers interested in a specific topic. To subscribe, you send a message that says: "subscribe" followed by the name of the list and then your name (no punctuation). Messages sent are distributed to all subscribers. You will

by a Texas A&M booster, Tom Robb. Takes several minutes to load all the links.

**The Virtual Garden**
http://vg.com
Among many other things, there's an on-line version of Barbara Barton's book Gardening by Mail. You'll find virtual garden tours, links to botanical gardens around the world, a plant finder, and a bulletin board for questions or discussions.

**Better Homes and Gardens**
http://www.bhglive.com/gardening
Hardiness zones down to the county level, FAQs, chat sessions, feature articles, links.

**CompuServe forums**
If you are a CompuServe member, you can visit the Gardening Forum (type "Go Garden"). There are more

receive messages via e-mail into your mailbox. There is an extensive list of these mailing lists by category at The Garden Gate:
http://www.prairienet.org/garden-gate/mailist.htm.

**Newsgroups**
These are bulletin boards for posting and viewing messages from other users on specific topics. Rather than being sent to your e-mail address, like the LISTSERVS, responses are posted on a central bulletin board. You can click on the messages that interest you. Some newsgroups, including rec.gardens, became so large that there are now subgroups, including rec.gardens.orchids, rec.gardens.roses, rec.arts.bonsai, and rec.ponds.

then 65,000 members worldwide. Post a question on the bulletin board and you will get at least one response and usually several others. Special topic discussions, are held several times each month.

## HORTICULTURAL SOCIETIES

There are dozens of membership organizations devoted to special-interest gardening topics, such as the American Dianthus Society, the American Fern Society, the American Iris Society, and the American Rock Garden Society. For a directory of these organizations, consult Barbara Barton's book, Gardening by Mail (described on page 297). Her book is also available on the Internet via the Virtual Garden web site:
http://pathfinder.com/vg

**The Garden Gate**
http://www.prairienet.org/garden-gate
Links to sites around the world, garden tours, books, software reviews, and lots more.

**Sue's Gardenlink**
http://www.synapse.net/~ewl/home.htm
Maintained by an avid gardener in Canada. Comprehensive set of links and a search engine.

**GardenNet**
http://trine.com/GardenNet
Book and software reviews, dozens of links, access to on-line magazines. Descriptions of and addresses for dozens

# Web Sites for Gardeners continued

of gardening magazines. The site also features an on-line magazine.
(http://trine.com/GardenNet/Magazine/magguide.htm).

**Joe and Mindy's WebGarden**
http://www.nhn.ou.edu/~howard/garden.html
*A beautiful, informal site with gardening tips, articles, and links.*

**Gardener's Supply Company**
http://www.gardeners.com
*Thousands of innovative gardening products as well as on-line gardening bulletins and other information of interest to gardeners.*

**Internet Links**
http://www.gardeninginbc.com/links.html
*Links to many, many different gardening web sites.*

**American Gardening Societies**
http://www.altgarden.com/society.html
*Links to American gardening societies on-line.*

**Garden Mart**
http://www.gardenmart.com/glinks.html
*Links to clubs, experts, hydroponics, horticultural societies, and shopping. Includes a search engine from Books That Work.*

**The Trellis**
http://wormsway.com/trellis.html
*Lots of good links to other gardening-related sites*

**The World of Gardening On-Line**
http://www.digthenet.com
*On-line searches for everything related to gardening. From the Virtual Garden.*

**Garden Town**
http://www.gardentown.com
*A friendly, complete site for meeting other gardeners. Share pictures, information, and resources.*

**Master Gardener Data Base**
http://leviathan.tamu.edu/ls/mg
*Search for in-depth articles on hundreds of gardening topics. Lots of links.*

**The Garden Spider's Web**
http://mirror.wwa.com/mirror/garden/spidrsweb.htm
*A great set of links in a narrative format.*

**W. Atlee Burpee Co.**
http://garden.burpee.com
*Order from their catalog, link to other sites, or ask a horticultural question.*

**Cooperative Extension Services by State**
http://www.gardenweb.com/vl/ces.html
*From the WWW Virtual Library.*

**Gardening.com**
http://Gardening.com
*From Books That Work. Includes a directory and reviews of other gardening sites, the Ortho Problem Solver, a search engine, and gardening software. Also an index of gardening magazines*

on the web and a plant encyclopedia with information about more than 1,500 plants. There's even a Yellow Pages for locating plant materials and gardening supplies near your home.

**The Complete Guide to Garden Stuff**
http://www.btw.com/garden_archive/toc.html
*A well-organized site from Books That Work. Useful information on all aspects of gardening.*

**Horticulture and Crop Science in Virtual Perspective at the Ohio State University**
http://hortwww-2.ag.ohio-state.edu/
*A specialized, but important site with research-based information about the technical and economic efficiencies of producing, marketing, and managing plants.*

**The Horticultural Web**
http://www.horticulture.com
*Oriented to commercial plantsmen, but has links and useful information for all.*

**Cindi's Catalog of Gardening Catalogs**
http://www.cog.brown.edu:80/gardening/
*An exhaustive list of 2,628 gardening catalogs!*

**I Can Garden**
http://www.ICanGarden.com
*Links to all major Canadian gardening-related sites. From Alberta, Canada.*

**HortWorld**
http://www.hortworld.com
*Geared to the commercial horticulture industry, but information of interest to others as well.*

**Garden Web**
http://www.gardenweb.com
*Discussion groups, tips, links, and an on-line magazine.*

**Dig Magazine**
http://www.digmagazine.com
*An on-line magazine with readers' comments. Also chats and forums.*

**Royal Horticultural Society**
http://www.rhs.org.uk
*A guide to the venerable society's gardens, programs, and publications.*

**The Gardener's Companion**
http://www.almanac.com/garden/index.html
*A version of the Old Farmer's Almanac geared specially to gardens.*

**Garden Links**
http://www.geocities.com/West Hollywood/2445/links.html#top
*An incredibly comprehensive and well-organized list of gardening-related links. Nicely categorized for easy browsing.*

**Internet Gardening**
http://learning.lib.vt.edu/garden.html
*Good list of links maintained by a gardener at the Virginia Polytechnic Institute.*

# index

# acknowledgments

Permission to reprint copyright material is gratefully acknowledged to:

Ames Lawn and Garden Tool Company, Parkersburg, West Virginia, for use of a chart on cut flowers.

Ayer Company Publishers, Inc., Lower Mill Road, North Stratford, NH 03590, for excerpts from *Colour Schemes for the Flower Garden* by Gertrude Jekyll, 1983.

Barron's Educational Publishing, for an excerpt from *Water Gardens* by Peter Stadelmann © 1992. Reprinted by arrangement with Barron's Educational Series, Inc.

Brooklyn Botanic Garden, for the rose classification system excerpted from *Easy-Care Roses* © 1995 by The Brooklyn Botanic Garden.

Peter Burford, for use of an excerpt and an illustration from *The Garden Design Primer* by Barbara Ashmun, originally published by Lyons & Burford, 1993.

Chapters Publishing Ltd., for excerpts from *Orchids Simplified* by Henry Jaworski, Houghton Mifflin Co., 1992.

The Countryman Press, for an excerpt reprinted from *Living with Herbs* © 1996 by Jo Ann Gardner, with permission of the publisher, The Countryman Press, Woodstock, Vermont.

DK Publishing, for an excerpt and accompanying illustration reprinted from *The Indoor Garden Book* by John Brookes © DK Publishing, 1994.

Fulcrum Publishing, Inc., 350 Indiana St., Suite 350, Golden, CO 80401, 800-992-2908, for excerpts from

*Greenhouse Gardener's Companion* by Shane Smith © 1994; and *The Undaunted Gardener* by Lauren Springer © 1994.

David R. Godine, Publisher, Inc., for an excerpt from *Herbs and the Earth* by Henry Beston ©1935.

Good Earth Publications, for an excerpt from *Backyard Market Gardening: The Entrepreneur's Guide to Selling What You Grow* by Andrew W. Lee © 1993 by Good Earth Publications, P.O. Box 160, Columbus, North Carolina, 28722.

Grove/Atlantic, Inc. for an excerpt from *Second Nature* by Michael Pollan copyright © 1991. Used by permission of Grove/Atlantic, Inc.

Gulf Publishing Company, for excerpts from *Container Vegetables* by Sam Cotner. Copyright © 1987 by Gulf Publishing Company. Used with permission. All rights reserved.

Henry Holt & Company, for excerpts from *The Gardener's Eye* by Allen Lacy © 1992 Henry Holt & Co.; and *Elements of Garden Design* by Joe Eck, © 1996 by W. Joseph Eck. Reprinted by permission of Henry Holt and Company, Inc.

Houghton Mifflin Company, for an excerpt from *One Man's Garden* by Henry Mitchell Copyright © 1992; for an excerpt from *The Perennial Gardener* by Frederick McGourty © 1989. Reprinted by permission of Houghton Mifflin Company. All rights reserved.

Ironwood Press, for illustrations from *The Natural Rose Gardener* by Lance Walheim, illustrations © Don Fox. Published by Ironwood Press, 1994.

Johnny's Selected Seeds, photo courtesy of Johnny's Selected Seeds, Albion, ME.

Michael Joseph, Ltd. for an excerpt from *Vita Sackville-West's Garden Book*, copyright © 1979 by Atheneum.

The Lyons Press, for an excerpt from *Fruit Trees for the Home Gardener* © 1994 by Allen A. Swenson. Reprinted with permission of The Lyons Press, New York.

Metamorphic Press, PO Box 1841, Santa Rosa, CA 95402, for an illustration from *Drip Irrigation for Every Landscape and All Climates* by Robert Kourik, 1992.

Shepherd Ogden, for an excerpt from *Step by Step Organic Vegetable Gardening*, originally published by Harper Collins, 1992. Available in $16.00 paperback from The Cook's Garden, PO Box 535, Londonderry, VT 05148, 800-457-9703, http://www.cooksgarden.com; and for product images from the Cook's Garden catalog.

Pavilion Books, for excerpts from *Some Flowers* by Vita Sackville-West, including the introduction by Stephen Dobell.

Penguin Books USA for excerpts and an illustration from *Intensive Gardening Round the Year* by Paul Doscher, Timothy Fisher, and Kathleen Kolb. Copyright © 1981 by Stephen Greene Press, 1983. Used by permission of the The Stephen Greene Press, an imprint of Penguin Books USA Inc.

Permanent Publications, for concepts contained in illustrations by Trisha Cassel-Gerard from *How to Make a Forest Garden* by Patrick Whitefield, 1996.

Prairie Moon Nursery, Rte. 3, Box 163, Winona, MN 55987, for a chart on soil moisture categories.

Reader's Digest, for material reprinted from *Success with Houseplants*, copyright © 1979 The Reader's Digest Association, Inc. Used by permission of The Reader's Digest Association, Inc.

Peter Robinson, for permission to use an illustration from *Water Gardening* by Perry D. Slocum and Peter Robinson, published by Timber Press, Inc., 1996.

Rodale Press, for material reprinted from *The New Seed-Starter's Handbook* © 1988 by Nancy Bubel;

*The Rodale Book of Composting* © 1992 by Deborah Martin and Grace Gershuny; *Rodale's Illustrated Encyclopedia of Gardening and Landscaping Techniques* © 1995 ed. Barbara W. Ellis; *The Organic Gardener's Handbook of Natural Insect and Disease Control* © 1996 eds. Barbara W. Ellis and Fern M. Bradley; *The Chemical-Free Lawn* © 1989 by Warren Schultz; *Greenhouse Gardening* © 1985 by Miranda Smith; and *Rodale's Illustrated Encyclopedia of Perennials* © 1993 by Ellen Phillips and C. Colston Burrell. Permission granted by Rodale Press, Inc., Emmaus, PA 18098.

Rosewell Publishing, for an excerpt reprinted from *The Healthy Indoor Plant* by C.C. Powell and Rosemarie Rossetti, Rosewell Publishing Inc., 1992.

Seed Saver's Exchange, for use of an illustration from the 1996 Summer Edition catalog.

Sterling Publishing Company, for permission to reprint an illustration from *Orchid Growing Basics* by Dr. Gustav Schoser, originally published and © in Germany by Falken-Verlag Gmbh, English translation © by Sterling Publishing Co., Inc., 387 Park Ave. S., New York, NY 10016.

Storey Publishing, for permission to reprint material from *From Seed to Bloom* © 1995 by Eileen Powell; *Waterscaping* © 1994 by Judy Glattstein; *Extend Your Garden Season* © 1996 by Fred Stetson; *The Gardener's Bug Book* © 1994 by Barbara D. Pleasant; and *Water-Conserving Gardens and Landscapes* © 1992 by John M. O'Keefe.

Texas A&M University, for permission to use a chart prepared by Dr. Guy Fipps of the Department of Agricultural Engineering.

Wildseed Farms, for permission to use a hardiness zone map with recommended sowing dates, reprinted from *Wildflower Reference Guide & Seed Catalog*, Wildseed Farms, Fredericksburg and Eagle Lake, Texas.

Robin Wimbiscus, for the use of illustrations originally published in *Solar Gardening* by Leandre Poisson and Gretchen Vogel Poisson, Chelsea Green Publishing, 1994 © Robin Wimbiscus.

Researching and compiling the information for a book like the *Passport to Gardening* is a daunting task. We, the authors, have supplied you, the reader, with what we believe are some of the best and most interesting resources and ideas in the world of gardening.

Yet, as careful and as diligent as we have tried to be in compiling and writing this book, it's inevitable that we've left out some excellent names — seed companies, nurseries, suppliers, organizations, books, magazines, videos, web sites, and tools or products — that deserve to be mentioned in the *Passport*. What's more, we might have neglected some aspect of gardening that you feel deserves a chapter all to itself.

So, as a final request, we'd like to enlist your help to make future editions of this sourcebook even more inclusive, up-to-date, and relevant for all gardeners. Send us your ideas, your comments, your corrections, and your recommendations to the address listed below. Would you like to see a chapter devoted to Rock Gardening or Bonsai? Are there new or classic books that you think we should review? Have you visited any spectacular web sites that we should know about? Send us as much information as you can about the resource or product that interests you. We'll collect all of your comments and consider each and every one as we work on the next edition of the *Passport to Gardening*. The more suggestions we receive, the more useful and interactive this sourcebook will become.

**Passport to Gardening**
Gardener's Supply Company
128 Intervale Road
Burlington, Vermont 0540l
*phone:* 800-863-1700
*fax:* 800-551-6712
*e-mail:* info@gardeners.com
*web site:* http://www.gardeners.com

All submissions become the property of Gardener's Supply Company, and may be used in future editions of the *Passport to Gardening* or for promotional materials connected to the sale of this book.

Thanks in advance for your ideas. May the sun shine on your perennials, may all your bugs be beneficial ones, may all your tomatoes be red, and all your neighbors green (with envy) at the sight of your garden.

# GARDENER'S SUPPLY COMPANY

128 INTERVALE RD. BURLINGTON VT 05401

**FOR FASTEST SERVICE ON CREDIT CARD ORDERS:**

## 800-863-1700

Ask about our Phone Specials!

You can order 24 hours a day, 7 days a week. If we are not here to speak with you, our easy-to-use order answering system will take your call.

TDD Machine: 802-660-3530 M-F, 8AM-4PM

FAX ORDERS: **800-551-6712**

E-MAIL: **info@gardeners.com**

WEB SITE: **http://www.gardeners.com**

---

## A ORDERED BY: (full street address and PO Box)

Name _____

Address _____

City _____ State _____ Zip _____

Gift Message _____

Daytime Phone (____) _____

DEPT.CODE: Passport

## B SHIP TO or GIFT ADDRESS: (full street address and PO Box)

☐ Check if delivery is to a business address.

☐ Check if order is a gift for person listed at right.

Name _____

Address _____

City _____ State _____ Zip _____

Gift Message _____

*Quantity: When ordering sets, enter the number of sets, not the number of items in the set.

| PRODUCT # | QTY* | DESCRIPTION | CIRCLE ADDRESS | COLOR/SIZE | ITEM PRICE | TOTAL |
|---|---|---|---|---|---|---|
| | | | A  B | | | |
| | | | A  B | | | |
| | | | A  B | | | |
| | | | A  B | | | |
| | | | A  B | | | |
| | | | A  B | | | |
| | | | A  B | | | |
| | | | A  B | | | |

| | |
|---|---|
| Merchandise Total | |
| 5% Sales Tax (shipments within VT only) | |
| **SUBTOTAL** | |
| Shipping & Handling (see chart at left) ADD: | |
| **TOTAL in US Funds** (no stamps or cash) | |

*Thank you for your order!*

**SHIPPING AND HANDLING CHARGES**
*(Call for rates to AK, HI, PR and VI)*

| TOTAL ORDER: | ADD: |
|---|---|
| Under $15 | $3.95 |
| $15 – $24.99 | $5.75 |
| $25 – $34.99 | $6.90 |
| $35 – $49.99 | $8.50 |
| $50 – $74.99 | $9.50 |
| $75 – $99.99 | $11.50 |
| $100 – $124.99 | $13.00 |
| Over $125 | add 10% |

New England Mail Order Association

Mailorder Gardening Association

## METHOD OF PAYMENT: *(Please do not send cash)*

☐ Check or Money Order
☐ VISA
☐ Mastercard
☐ American Express
☐ Discover

CARD NUMBER ☐☐☐☐☐☐☐☐☐☐☐☐☐☐☐☐

EXP. DATE _____

NAME (Please PRINT exactly as it appears on card) _____

---

## Friendly and Knowledgeable Staff

We are a company of gardeners, and we're committed to providing the products, information, and services that will help you garden more successfully. We're happy to answer questions about the products we sell, and are also available to help you identify a pest or jump-start a sluggish compost pile.

## 100% Satisfaction Guarantee

Order with confidence. We guarantee your complete satisfaction. If for any reason you are not pleased with your purchase, you may return it for replacement or refund —whichever your prefer.

## Speedy Delivery Service

Most orders leave our warehouse within 48 hours after we receive them. We also offer overnight and two-day delivery for most items. Please call us for rates.

Oversized products may require an additional charge when shipping to Alaska, Hawaii, and U.S. Territories. Please call for rates. Sorry, we cannot ship to APO's, FPO's, Canada, Mexico, or overseas.

## Price and Availability

Products and prices in this book were accurate as of Fall 1997, but are subject to change. To ensure a product is still available and to check current pricing, please call us at 800-863-1700.

## Visit us in Vermont

We love meeting our customers! If you're in Vermont, please visit our store and gardens. You'll find most of our catalog products on display, as well as many other innovative gardening supplies. Call ahead for directions and seasonal hours: 802-660-3505.

# Chelsea Green Publishing Company

In the sustainable world all human activities are designed to co-exist and cooperate with natural processes, rather than dominate nature. Resources are recognized to be finite. Consumption and production are carefully and consciously balanced so that all of the planet's species can thrive in perpetuity.

Chelsea Green specializes in providing the information people need to create and prosper in such a world.

Sustainable Living has many facets. Chelsea Green's celebration of the sustainable arts has led us to publish trend-setting books about organic gardening, solar electricity and renewable energy, innovative building techniques, regenerative forestry, local and bioregional democracy, and whole foods. The company's published works, while intensely practical, are also entertaining and inspirational, demonstrating that an ecological approach to life is consistent with producing beautiful, lucid, and useful books, videos, and audio tapes.

For more information about Chelsea Green, or to request a free catalog, call (800) 639-4099, or write to us at P.O. Box 428, White River Junction, VT 05001.

## Chelsea Green's bestselling titles include:

| | |
|---|---|
| *The New Organic Grower* and *Four-Season Harvest* | Eliot Coleman |
| *Beyond the Limits* | Donella Meadows, Dennis Meadows, and Jørgen Randers |
| *Wind Power for Home and Business* | Paul Gipe |
| *Loving and Leaving the Good Life* | Helen Nearing |
| *The Independent Home* | Michael Potts |
| *The Contrary Farmer* and *The Contrary Farmer's Invitation to Gardening* | Gene Logsdon |
| *The Straw Bale House* | Athena Swentzell Steen, Bill Steen, and David Bainbridge |
| *The Rammed Earth House* | David Easton |
| *Forest Gardening* | Robert Hart |
| *Independent Builder* | Sam Clark |
| *The Flower Farmer* | Lynn Byczynski |

# There's More!

Chelsea Green publishes books on a variety of subjects related to sustainable living. Return this card for a complete catalog of our books. Please indicate the subject(s) that interest you the most:

_____ Renewable Energy _____ Shelter _____ Food _____ Gardening _____ Nature _____ Environment

Other topics that interest you: _____

In which book was this inserted? _____ Where purchased: _____

Which best describes your satisfaction with this book:

_____ Disappointed _____ Could be improved _____ Met expectations _____ Exceeded expectations

Comments for the author or publisher? _____

_____

Name: _____

Address: _____

*Thanks very much!*

Chelsea Green Publishing
PO Box 428
White River Junction, VT  05001

*Books for Sustainable Living*